Flights
of
Terror

Flights of Terror

Aerial hijack and sabotage since 1930

David Gero

Haynes Publishing

Second Edition

First published in 1997 by Patrick Stephens Ltd
Second edition published in November 2009 by Haynes Publishing

A catalogue record for this book is available from
the British Library.

ISBN 978 1 84425 644 0

Library of Congress catalog card number: 2009928028

Published by Haynes Publishing, Sparkford,
Yeovil, Somerset BA22 7JJ, UK
Tel: +44 (0)1963 442030   Fax: +44 (0)1963 440001
Email: sales@haynes.co.uk
Website: www.haynes.co.uk

Haynes North America, Inc., 861 Lawrence Drive,
Newbury Park, California 91320, USA

Printed and bound in the UK by JF Print, Sparkford.

Contents

Introduction

Aerial terrorism. Just the thought of a ticking bomb hidden in a suitcase, or a gun- or knife-wielding assailant commandeering a commercial flight, is enough to send chills down the back of even the most seasoned air traveller.

Terrorism, like mid-air collisions, adverse weather conditions and mechanical failure, is a real threat to aviation, and like other issues pertaining to air safety must be dealt with in a factual and responsible manner. This is what I have tried to do in *Flights of Terror*, which chronicles the various kinds of hostile actions committed against commercial aircraft from the earliest days of air travel. This latest edition of the book brings these events up to date, well into the 21st century.

I have employed a somewhat more casual format in this work than in *Aviation Disasters*, which used a straightforward chronological approach. Events have instead been broken down into several categories, such as all hijackings ending or intending to end in Cuba. All serious acts of terrorism are included if they targeted commercial aircraft. Military and general aviation operations, the latter including air taxi services utilising light aircraft, have been excluded, as these are technically not 'public' transportation. This latest edition includes a chapter on the horrific events of 11 September 2001, which occurred in the US but jolted commercial aviation throughout the world. Another section deals with the closely related subject of aircraft attacked or downed in quasi-combat situations, but, generally speaking, bomb-scares that do not involve direct action and frivolous threats that had no legal implications have been omitted unless they in some manner involved casualties. To keep sticklers for detail happy, I have included registration numbers in cases where aircraft were destroyed.

As with my previous work, *Flights of Terror* is the result of considerable research throughout the world, by both myself and others, and, as with *Aviation Disasters*, I have included events occurring in all parts of the globe. Though I hope that everyone will find something of interest here, it is particularly exciting for me to share my interest, as well as my tremendous wealth of information, with other aviation enthusiasts, wherever they may be.

David Gero
San Gabriel, California

ACKNOWLEDGEMENTS

The author would like to thank the following organisations and individuals for their help in the preparation of this book:

Airclaims Ltd; Air Incident Research; Aviation Safety Network (website); (UK) Civil Aviation Authority; Chris Kimura, author/researcher; (US) Federal Aviation Administration (FAA); Graham K. Salt, researcher; International Civil Aviation Organisation (ICAO); The Language Institute; Poly-Languages Institute; Terry Denham, author/researcher; and Patricia Michell-Vazquez, Rosana Volpert and Victoria Aranda, translators.

PUBLICATIONS CONSULTED

Accident to Itavia DC-9 paper by A. Frank Taylor, Cranfield University (IASI Forum, March 1995)
Aircraft Hijackings and Other Criminal Acts Against Commercial Aviation (US Department of Transportation)
Airliner Production Lists by John Roach and Tony Eastwood (The Aviation Hobby Shop)
Air Piracy, Airport Security and International Terrorism: Winning the War Against Hijackers by Peter St John (Quorum Books)
Aviation Week and Space Technology magazine
Aviation Terrorism, Historical Survey, Perspectives and Responses by Jin-Tai Choi (St Martin's Press)
Bloodletters and Badmen by Jay Robert Nash (M. Evans & Co.)
Flight International magazine
Great Mysteries of the Air by Ralph Barker (Macmillan)
Hostile Actions Against Civil Aviation by Michael Morris (Air Incident Research)
La Opinion newspaper
Lloyd's List newspaper
Los Angeles Times newspaper
New York Times newspaper

1
The early years (–1969)

Before it had become an everyday tool in global trade and commerce, the aeroplane saw service as a weapon of war. Commercial aviation started in earnest after the First World War, with the introduction of both passenger and mail services utilizing fixed-wing aircraft, and it was not long before the peacetime aviation industry began experiencing hostilities of its own as the phenomenon of aerial terrorism was born.

First came the forced diversion of aircraft, or hijackings (sometimes referred to today as skyjackings, so as not to be confused with piracy at sea), followed by the even more frightening prospect of aerial sabotage. The number of aerial hijackings increased greatly after the Second World War, though the early post-war diversions were mostly of a 'benevolent' variety, often involving aircraft being pirated out of countries

An Imperial Airways Armstrong Whitworth Argosy, one of which was believed to have been the first commercial airliner destroyed in an act of aerial sabotage. (British Aerospace)

behind the 'Iron Curtain'. Ironically, after the fall of Cuba to Communism hijackings again increased significantly, with aircraft going in the opposite direction (a subsequent chapter is devoted to this phenomenon). Para-military and guerrilla forces entered the hijacking scene in the late 1950s, while a decade later Middle Eastern politics became a motivating factor in many such actions.

With the exception of incidents falling into a designated category, such as terrorism related to Middle East affairs or the North American sabotage-for-insurance schemes, the following is a list of unspecified acts of aerial terrorism prior to 1970.

22 FEBRUARY 1931

COMMERCIAL aviation got its first taste of terrorism with the hijacking of a Pan American-Grace Airways trimotored Fokker F.VII in Peru. The US-registered mail aircraft was commandeered by a group of Peruvian revolutionaries with the intention of dropping propaganda leaflets. There were no casualties.

28 MARCH 1933

THOUGH never proven with certainty, the first airline disaster believed to have been an act of sabotage was the destruction of the Imperial Airways 'City of Liverpool'. The trimotored Armstrong Whitworth Argosy (G-AACI) met a fiery demise in the Belgian countryside, near the town of Dixmude, located some 60 miles (100km) west-north-west of Brussels, where it had stopped during a scheduled service originating at Cologne, Germany, with an ultimate destination of London.

The airliner had been cruising at an altitude of about 4,000ft (1,200m) and a speed of around 100mph (150kph) when fire was observed near its tail assembly. Continuing to descend, the pilot apparently trying for an emergency landing in an open field, the Argosy finally suffered catastrophic structural failure at around 14:30 local time, its fuselage splitting in two at an approximate height of 250ft (75m) above the ground.

It then plummeted to earth and burned. All 15 persons aboard, including three crew members, were killed.

The first proven case of aerial sabotage, occurring on 10 October 1933, involved a United Air Lines Boeing 247 such as this. (Boeing)

Investigation traced the origin of the fire to the rear of the passenger cabin, either in the lavatory or the luggage rack. Two explanations considered possible were the detonation of a timed incendiary device in a suitcase, or a fire being deliberately started in the lavatory. There was no evidence of a technical failure in the aircraft or its engines.

Found about a mile (1.5km) from the main wreckage was the body of a passenger named Albert Voss, who would become the centre of controversy in this case. The 69-year-old dentist had been returning home from a business trip to Brussels. With burns apparent only on his hands and face, it would seem that he had jumped or fallen from the Argosy before the fire had intensified. Seated alone towards the rear of the cabin, he had the opportunity to start the blaze without being noticed. There also appeared to be ample motive for such behaviour: he was known to have been deeply in debt; in his work, he had access to anaesthetics, which can be highly inflammable; his background was tainted with rumours of drug trafficking and addiction; and he had reportedly spoken of suicide. Sufficient evidence did not exist to directly tie Albert Voss in with the loss of the 'City of Liverpool', but could he have been responsible? The question remains unanswered.

10 OCTOBER 1933

IN the first proven case of sabotage in the history of commercial aviation, all seven persons aboard were killed, including a crew of three, when a United Air Lines Boeing 247 (NC-13304) was blown up during a scheduled US domestic flight. The twin-engine transport had been en route from Cleveland, Ohio, to Chicago, Illinois, one segment of a service originating at Newark, New Jersey, when it plummeted to earth and burned shortly after 21:00 local time near Chesterton, Indiana, located some 10 miles (15km) west of Gary.

Consolidation of the available evidence led to the conclusion by airline and federal officials that the aircraft had been destroyed by an explosive device that used nitro-glycerine and was probably attached to a timing device. The blast severed the empennage from the rest of the fuselage. The bomb was thought to have been put aboard at the Newark airport, possibly concealed in a brown package. However, no one was ever prosecuted in connection with this case.

3 MAY 1947

A TACA de Costa Rica twin-engine Lockheed Lodestar (TI-84) crashed and burned near Nicoya, Costa Rica, located some 100 miles (150km) west of San José and from where it had just taken off on a scheduled domestic service, killing all 12 persons aboard, including two pilots. The investigation found that, in what may have been an act of sabotage, sand had been poured into one of the aircraft's power plants.

6 APRIL 1948

THE first case of air piracy related to an escape from the 'Iron Curtain' involved a Ceskoslovenske Aerolinie (CSA) DC-3 on a scheduled domestic service from Prague to Bratislava, Czechoslovakia. The transport was seized by about three-quarters of the 26 persons aboard, including the pilot and two other members of the crew. It landed safely in a US zone of Germany, near Munich.

4 MAY 1948

A Ceskoslovenske Aerolinie (CSA) DC-3 on a scheduled domestic service within Czechoslovakia, from Brno to Ceske Budejovice, was commandeered at gunpoint by its five passengers, who forced it to land in Germany. The two crew members, who were the only other occupants of the transport, elected to return to Czechoslovakia.

4 JUNE 1948

A Jugoslovenske Sovjet Transport Aviacija (JUSTA) Lisunov Li-2 with 28 persons aboard was seized by the radio-operator and a passenger during a scheduled domestic flight within Yugoslavia, from Belgrade to Sarajevo. The twin-engine airliner, a Soviet version of the Douglas DC-3, landed safely in Italy, near Bari.

17 JUNE 1948

A Transporturi Aeriene Romana Sovietica (TARS) Ju.52 trimotored airliner was commandeered during a scheduled Romanian domestic service with 23 persons aboard, landing at Salzburg, Austria.

30 JUNE 1948

VIOLENCE marked this seizure, by half-a-dozen assailants, of a Bulgarske Vazdusne Sobsteine (BVS) trimotored Ju.52 that had been on a scheduled domestic flight from Varna to Sofia, Bulgaria, with 20 persons aboard. The pilot of the aircraft was killed and two other crew members were wounded before it made a safe landing at Istanbul, Turkey.

12 SEPTEMBER 1948

WHILE on a scheduled domestic service from Athens to Salonika with 23 persons aboard, a DC-3 flown by the Greek carrier Technical Aeronautical Exploitations (TAE) was commandeered by eight passengers, some of whom reportedly beat members of the crew. The transport landed safely at Tetovo, Yugoslavia.

4 JANUARY 1949

DURING a scheduled domestic service from Pecs to Budapest with 25 persons aboard, a twin-engine Lisunov Li-2 of the Hungarian airline Magyar-Szoviet Legiforgalmi Tarseaag (MASZOVLET) was diverted to Germany, landing at Munich. In a prearranged conspiracy, someone had taken over the controls from the pilot, who was also involved in the hijack.

30 JANUARY 1949

SIX persons hijacked a China National Aviation Corporation transport, believed to be either a DC-3 or a C-46, on a scheduled domestic flight from Shanghai to Tsingtso, forcing it to land at T'ainan, Taiwan. The other occupants were held for a month before being released; the aircraft was not returned.

29 APRIL 1949

A young man armed with a revolver hijacked a Transporturile Aeriene Romano-Sovietice (TARS) DC-3, which had been on a scheduled Romanian domestic service from Timisoara to Bucharest with 25 persons aboard, and forced it to land at an airfield near Salonika, Greece. The hijacker, another passenger and a security guard were granted political asylum.

7 MAY 1949

A Philippine Air Lines Douglas DC-3 (PI-C-98) crashed in the Sibuyan Sea off the Philippine island of Elalat while en route to Manila from Daet, Camarines, one segment of a scheduled domestic service originating at Tacloban, on Leyte. All 13 persons aboard (ten passengers and a crew of three) were killed. The last radio communication with the flight was shortly after 16:00 local time. The following week some wreckage and the body of the pilot were recovered, and examination of the former indicated a sudden explosion in the aircraft's tail assembly.

Two ex-convicts later confessed to planting a time bomb on the DC-3 in order to kill the husband of a woman who was involved with another man. Their payment for the mass murder: 185 pesos, or less than $100. Their penalty: death.

16 SEPTEMBER 1949

A Polskie Linje Lotnicze (LOT) (Polish Airlines) transport, believed to have been a twin-engine Lisunov Li-2, was commandeered by five assailants while on a scheduled domestic service from Gdansk to Lodz with 16 persons aboard, and was diverted to Sweden. Low on fuel, the aircraft landed safely at around 09:00 local time at a military airfield located some 65 miles (105km) south of Stockholm.

9 DECEMBER 1949

A Transporturi Aeriene Romano-Sovietice (TARS) airliner, either a DC-3 or its Soviet derivative, the Li-2, was hijacked by four passengers during a scheduled internal Romanian service from Sibiu to Bucharest, with 24 persons aboard. A security guard was shot dead before the transport landed at Belgrade, Yugoslavia.

16 DECEMBER 1949

A Polskie Linje Lotnicze (LOT) Li-2 airliner, on a scheduled domestic service from Warsaw to Gdynia, Poland, was flown to the West, landing near Roenne, on the Danish island of Bornholm. All but two of the 18 persons aboard were involved in the mass defection.

24 MARCH 1950

THREE DC-3 transports flown by Ceskoslovenske Aerolinie (CSA) and carrying a total of 83 persons were flown to Erding Airfield, near Munich, (West) Germany, by their passengers and crews. All three of the aircraft involved in the mass defection were on scheduled domestic services, which had originated at Brno, Ostrava and Bratislava respectively, and had an ultimate destination of Prague, Czechoslovakia.

13 APRIL 1950

OPERATING on a scheduled service to Paris from Northolt Airport, serving London, a British European Airways (BEA) Vickers Viking 1B was approximately halfway across the English Channel and flying at 3,500ft (1,100m) when it was extensively damaged by the detonation of an 'infernal' device in the lavatory, which probably had been placed in the used towel receptacle. Of the 32 persons aboard, a stewardess was seriously injured, but the airliner returned safely to its point of origin. No arrests were ever made for this act of sabotage.

17 APRIL 1950

THIS case of attempted sabotage was motivated by a combination of greed and passion. The saboteur, John Grant, had placed a bomb in a valise that was to be loaded aboard a United Air Lines DC-3 bound from Los Angeles to San Diego, California, with 16 persons aboard. Among the passengers were his wife and children, whom he had insured for $25,000. Reportedly, he was heavily in debt and infatuated with an airline stewardess. However, the device detonated as it was being loaded on to the aircraft; there were no injuries. John Grant was convicted and sentenced to up to 20 years' imprisonment.

11 AUGUST 1950

A Czech aeroplane, possibly a twin-engine Si 204 operated by Ceskoslovenske Aerolinie (CSA), which was on a commuter service with ten persons aboard, got hijacked by two of its passengers, landing in (West) Germany.

17 OCTOBER 1951

A Jugoslovenski Aerotransport (JAT) DC-3, on a scheduled Yugoslav domestic flight, was seized by the pilot and co-pilot,

A British European Airways Viking of the type that survived a sabotage attempt over the English Channel on 13 April 1950. (British Airways)

who were accompanied by their wives and two children, and flown to Zürich, Switzerland, where they asked for political asylum. The three other crew members and 22 passengers returned to Yugoslavia.

18 APRIL 1952

A Jugoslovenski Aerotransport (JAT) airliner on a scheduled Yugoslav domestic service from Zagreb to Ljubljana was commandeered by six passengers and forced to fly to Austria, where it landed safely.

26 JUNE 1952

THREE hijackers commandeered a Jugoslovenski Aerotransport (JAT) DC-3 that was on a scheduled domestic service from Zagreb to Pola, Yugoslavia, with 32 persons aboard. Two of them held the passengers at gunpoint as the third broke into the cockpit with an axe and took over the controls, landing the aircraft at an airstrip near Foligno, Italy, where they requested political asylum.

24 SEPTEMBER 1952

FIVE passengers were injured, two seriously, when a bomb placed in a suitcase exploded in the forward baggage compartment of a Compañia Mexicana de Aviación SA DC-3, which, operating as Flight 575, was on a domestic service from Mexico City to Oaxaca with 20 persons aboard, including a crew of three. The airliner managed a safe emergency landing at a military airbase despite sustaining substantial damage in the blast.

The act of sabotage had been an attempt to collect more than $200,000 in insurance taken out on six of the passengers. Two men were later convicted for their involvement in the crime, with one being sentenced to 30 years' imprisonment and the other to eight years.

30 DECEMBER 1952

THE pilot and purser of a Philippine Air Lines DC-3 were shot and killed in the attempted hijacking of the transport during a scheduled domestic service from Laoag to Aparri. Although the gunman demanded to be flown to China, the DC-3, with ten persons aboard, was damaged by machine-gun fire from Nationalist Chinese aircraft and landed on the Taiwanese island of Quemoy, where he was captured. He was later sentenced to a life prison term in the Philippines.

2 FEBRUARY 1953

ALL three of its crew members (and only occupants) were killed when a Douglas DC-3 (F-OAFR) operated by the French carrier Air Outre-Mer crashed shortly after its departure from Lai Chau, Indochina (Vietnam), located some 100 miles (150km) north-west of Hanoi, reportedly after an in-flight bomb explosion.

23 MARCH 1953

A Ceskoslovenske Aerolinie (CSA) DC-3 with 29 persons aboard was hijacked by four assailants while on a scheduled domestic flight from Prague to Brno, Czechoslovakia. Pilot Miroslav Slovak 'hedgehopped' the aircraft across the border into (West) Germany, where it had to circle for about half-an-hour as the defectors sought permission to land from the US authorities before setting down at Rhein-Main Airport, serving Frankfurt. Two other passengers joined the defectors seeking asylum.

6 JULY 1954

AN armed 15-year-old boy who stormed aboard and tried to commandeer an American Airlines DC-6B was shot dead by its armed captain at Hopkins Municipal Airport, serving Cleveland, Ohio, where the aircraft, designated as Flight 153, had stopped during an international service originating at New York City, with an ultimate destination of Mexico City.

11 APRIL 1955

POLITICAL terrorism was the apparent motive behind the sabotage of an Air-India International Lockheed 749A Constellation (VT-DEP). The airliner was on a non-scheduled service originating at Hong Kong, its passengers consisting of Chinese delegates and journalists on their way to a conference at Bandung, Indonesia. While cruising at 18,000ft (5,500m) over the South China Sea, a muffled explosion was heard, and almost immediately smoke started entering the cabin; soon thereafter, a localised fire was detected on the starboard wing.

The flight crew, who had already initiated an emergency descent, then put into effect fire-fighting procedures, during which time the No 3 power plant was feathered, but the aircraft experienced both hydraulic and electrical systems failure due to the effects of the blaze. Dense smoke in the cockpit reduced visibility to almost nil, and the Constellation ultimately crashed in the sea about 100 miles (150km) north of Kuching, Sarawak (Malaysia), at about 17:30 local time. Of the 19 persons aboard, only three members of the crew survived.

A Chinese aircraft cleaner had reportedly been bribed to place an incendiary device in the starboard wheel well of VT-DEP, with its subsequent detonation puncturing the No 3 fuel tank and leading to the uncontrollable fire. Reportedly, the suspect fled to Taiwan to escape the British authorities in Hong Kong.

4 MARCH 1956

AN explosive device detonated in the forward cargo compartment of a Skyways Ltd Handley Page Hermes 4 as the British-built and registered airliner was parked at the airport serving Nicosia, Cyprus, resulting in considerable damage. There were, however, no injuries.

13 JULY 1956

SEVEN hijackers commandeered a Magyar-Szoviet Legiforgalmi Tarseaag Li-2 carrying 20 persons on a scheduled domestic service from Gyor to Szombathely, Hungary. After a struggle with crew members and passengers, in which several were injured, one of the hijackers took over the controls and landed the airliner at an unused airbase near Ingolstadt, (West) Germany. The hijackers asked for political asylum; their hostages and the transport returned to Hungary.

15 OCTOBER 1956

AN Li-2 operated by the Hungarian airline Magyar Legiskozlekedesi Vallalat (MALEV) and bound for Hungary on a scheduled international service originating at Belgrade, Yugoslavia, was targeted for hijack by three assailants who wanted to be taken to Munich, (West) Germany. However, two security guards opened fire on the hijackers, killing one of them and wounding the other two.

A large hole in the fuselage was created by the bomb blast aboard the Mexicana DC-3 on 24 September 1952. (Photo © Irma Carranza)

19 DECEMBER 1957

A Sud-Est Armagnac of the French carrier Société Auxiliare de Gerance et de Transports Aériens (SAGETA) was on a scheduled Air France flight to Paris from Oran, Algeria, when a bomb detonated in a lavatory, tearing a hole of approximately 3ft (1m) in the fuselage. There were no injuries among the 95 persons aboard, and the four-engined airliner landed safely at Lyon, France, at around 19:00 local time, or about an hour and a half after the explosion.

16 FEBRUARY 1958

A Korean National Airlines DC-3, operating as Flight 302 on a domestic service from Pusan to Seoul, South Korea, with 34 persons aboard, was commandeered by what were reported as North Korean agents. The aircraft landed at Pyongyang, North Korea, and along with eight of its occupants was not returned to the South, though most of the passengers and crew were released some three weeks after the hijacking. South Korea subsequently enacted tighter security measures throughout its air carrier operations.

9 APRIL 1958

IN the first of a series of hijackings involving pre-Castro Cuba, a Compañia Cubana de Aviación SA DC-3, on a domestic service from Havana to Santa Clara with 16 persons aboard, was flown by its crew to Mérida, Mexico. The aircraft and passengers were returned to Cuba.

13 APRIL 1958

A Cubana DC-3 airliner carrying 15 persons on a scheduled domestic run from Havana to Santa Clara was flown to Miami, Florida, US, by its crew, who complained that the Cuban government was requiring them to fly over areas in Cuba where guerrilla fighting was taking place.

21 OCTOBER 1958

A Cubana DC-3 airliner was commandeered by anti-government rebels during a scheduled domestic flight from Cayo Mambi to Moa Bay, with 14 persons aboard. It was forced to land in rebel-controlled territory, and, although its pilot was shot and wounded, the hostages were subsequently released.

6 NOVEMBER 1958

HIJACKED during a scheduled Cuban domestic service from Manzanillo to Holguin, a Cubana DC-3 with 25 persons aboard was held at a rebel airstrip before the hostages were released. As a result of this latest incident, the airline cancelled most domestic flights.

9 APRIL 1959

Half-a-dozen revolutionaries commandeered a DC-3 of the Haitian airline COHATA on a scheduled domestic service from Auxcayes to Port-au-Prince, with 34 persons aboard. Killing its pilot, they forced the co-pilot to land at Santiago de Cuba.

16 APRIL 1959

Three hijackers took over an Aerovías 'Q' SA C-46 as the Cuban airliner was on a scheduled domestic service from Havana to the Isla de Pinos (Isla de la Juventud) with 22 persons aboard. It subsequently landed at Miami, Florida, US.

25 APRIL 1959

A Cubana Viscount turboprop airliner carrying 16 persons was commandeered shortly after it had taken off from Varadero, Cuba, on a scheduled domestic service to Havana. The four hijackers, who included a military general who had served under former Cuban President Fulgencio Batista and two women who had reportedly hidden pistols under their skirts, asked to be taken to Miami, but as the aircraft was low on fuel they settled for Key West, Florida, US.

8 JULY 1959

WHILE on a scheduled domestic flight from Cattaro to Belgrade, Yugoslavia, with 27 persons aboard, a Jugoslovenski Aerotransport (JAT) DC-3 airliner was hijacked by a lone gunman who fired a warning shot and then ordered the pilot to land at the nearest Italian airport, which happened to be Bari.

8 SEPTEMBER 1959

A passenger aboard a Compañia Mexicana de Aviación SA Douglas DC-3, who was suspected of carrying a bomb hidden in his suitcase, was blasted out of an access door and killed when the device detonated as the airliner was flying at 11,000ft (3,400m) over the Bay of Campeche, on a scheduled domestic service originating at Mexico City, with an ultimate destination of Mérida, in Yucatan. Among the other 15 persons aboard, who included three crew members, six passengers and the co-pilot suffered injuries.

Following the explosion, which occurred around 12:30 local time, the transport successfully force-landed at Poza Rica, Vera Cruz, despite a fire that was successfully extinguished by the crew.

2 OCTOBER 1959

THREE passengers armed with pistols and a hand grenade commandeered a Cubana Viscount turboprop that was on a scheduled domestic flight from Havana to Santiago de Cuba with 40 persons aboard. The airliner landed safely at Miami, Florida.

2 DECEMBER 1959

A Panair do Brasil SA Constellation on a scheduled Brazilian domestic service from Rio de Janeiro to Belém was commandeered by a group of hijackers engaged in a revolt against the Brazilian Government. The airliner was flown to Buenos Aires, Argentina.

12 APRIL 1960

THE pilot, two other crew members and one passenger seized Cubana Flight 800 as the Viscount turboprop was on a scheduled domestic service from Havana to Santiago de Cuba. After landing at Miami, Florida, the hijackers disabled the airliner by setting fire to its four engines.

5 JULY 1960

A Cubana Britannia turboprop airliner was hijacked by two members of its flight crew and diverted to Miami, Florida, while on a scheduled transatlantic service to Havana from

Madrid, Spain, with 42 persons aboard. The two pilots would subsequently seek political asylum in Spain.

17 JULY 1960

THE pilot of a Cubana Viscount carrying 56 persons commandeered the turboprop airliner during a scheduled service to Miami, Florida, from Havana, Cuba, landing it in Jamaica.

19 JULY 1960

AN attempt was made to hijack to Singapore a Trans-Australia Airlines four-engined turboprop Electra, operating as Flight 408, on a domestic service from Sydney to Brisbane with 49 persons aboard. However, what would have been the first act of aerial piracy in the history of the island nation failed when the lone assailant, armed with a rifle and an explosive device, was overpowered by the first officer and an off-duty pilot near its destination. The would-be hijacker would later serve ten years in prison.

28 JULY 1960

A Cubana DC-3 on a scheduled domestic service to Havana from Cuba's Oriente province was commandeered by the pilot, with the help of two passengers. The trio were then joined by two women and two children when the aircraft landed at Miami, Florida.

21 AUGUST 1960

THE attempted take-over of an Aeroflot aircraft by a couple, which occurred during a scheduled domestic service in the USSR, was thwarted when members of the crew, though wounded, overpowered the hijackers.

29 OCTOBER 1960

NINE men commandeered a Cubana DC-3, operating as Flight 905, on a domestic service from Havana to the Isla de Pinos (Isla de la Juventud) with 38 persons aboard. A security guard was shot dead during the hijacking, and the pilot, co-pilot and one passenger, a 13-year-old boy, were wounded, though the airliner landed safely at Key West, Florida. The hijackers sought asylum in the US.

8 DECEMBER 1960

THE attempted hijacking by five passengers of a Cubana airliner that was on a scheduled domestic service erupted into a gun battle that left one person dead and four wounded. Subsequently, the transport crash-landed at the airport serving Cienfuegos, Cuba, the act of air piracy ending in failure. Four of the assailants were executed two days later.

10 MAY 1961

AN Air France Lockheed 1649A Starliner (F-BHBM) crashed and burned in the Sahara Desert of eastern Algeria, about 30 miles (50km) south-west of Ghadamis, Libya. All 78 persons aboard (69 passengers and nine crew members) perished.

Operating as Flight 406, the airliner had been en route from Fort Lamy (N'Djamena), Chad, to Marseilles, France, one segment of a service originating at Brazzaville, Congo, with an ultimate destination of Paris. It broke up in early morning darkness, around 02:30 local time, and clear meteorological conditions while cruising at an approximate height of 20,000ft

(6,000m). The airline concluded that the most probable cause of the catastrophe was sabotage with a nitro-cellulose explosive.

3 JULY 1961

A group of 11 men and three women commandeered a Cubana DC-3 that was on a scheduled domestic service from Havana to Varadero. A security guard assigned to the aircraft was shot and wounded during the hijacking, which ended in Miami, Florida.

31 JULY 1961

WHILE a Pacific Air Lines DC-3 was at the airport in Chico, California, US, preparing for an intrastate service to San Francisco, as Flight 327, its pilot and a ticket agent were shot and wounded, the former being blinded. The assailant was later convicted of three counts of assault with intent to commit murder and sentenced to three terms of up to 14 years in prison each, to run consecutively.

9 AUGUST 1961

IN the seizure of an Aerovías 'Q' SA C-46 airliner, which had been on a Cuban domestic service from Havana to the Isla de Pinos (Isla de la Juventud) with 53 persons aboard, the pilot and two other persons were killed and six more wounded. The co-pilot crash-landed the aircraft near the capital. Two assailants were executed the following month and more than 30 other persons reportedly received prison sentences for their involvement in the attempted hijacking.

10 NOVEMBER 1961

WITH the intention of dropping leaflets over the Portuguese capital, six men commandeered a Transportes Aéreos Portugueses (TAP) Super Constellation that was on a scheduled service to Lisbon from Casablanca, Morocco. The aircraft landed at Tangier, Morocco, and the hijackers were then expelled to Senegal, and subsequently granted political asylum in Brazil.

27 NOVEMBER 1961

AN AVENSA DC-6B got hijacked by a group of armed students during a scheduled Venezuelan domestic service from Caracas to Maracaibo with 43 persons aboard. After being used to drop anti-government leaflets over Caracas, the airliner landed at Curaçao, Netherlands Antilles, from where the five assailants were extradited back to Venezuela, and there served prison sentences of more than four years each.

17 MARCH 1962

ONE of 32 prisoners being transported aboard a chartered twin-engine aircraft on a French internal flight from Paris to Saint Martin de l'Ardoise was shot by a guard and wounded during an attempted hijacking. There were no other casualties, and the aircraft landed safely.

16 APRIL 1962

A lone assailant armed with a starter's pistol who wanted to go to (East) Berlin commandeered a KLM Royal Dutch Airlines DC-7C carrying 53 persons en route from Amsterdam to Lisbon, Portugal, the first segment of a scheduled international flight ultimately bound for Santiago, Chile, but he was captured by police after it returned to Schiphol Airport, from where it had taken off earlier.

26 APRIL 1962

AN explosive device apparently planted by a terrorist group destroyed an Air Algérie Lockheed 749A Constellation airliner (F-BAZE) that was parked at the airport serving Algiers, Algeria. There were no casualties.

28 NOVEMBER 1963

SIX hijackers commandeered an AVENSA twin-engine Convair 440 as it was on a scheduled domestic service from Ciudad Bolívar to Caracas, Venezuela, with 11 persons aboard. The aircraft landed in Trinidad, from where the assailants were extradited back to Venezuela for prosecution.

AUTUMN 1964

BOTH pilots were wounded in the attempted hijacking of an Aeroflot An-2 biplane by two men during a scheduled domestic service in the USSR, from Shadur-Lungu to Izmail, Ukraine. The two assailants were captured after the aircraft landed at Kishinev.

8 DECEMBER 1964

ALL 17 persons aboard (13 passengers and a crew of four) were killed in the crash of an Aerolíneas Abaroa DC-3 (CP-639) near Tripuani, La Paz, Bolivia. The airliner was on a scheduled domestic service from Caranavi to the city of La Paz when it exploded in flight shortly after 10:00 local time, falling in the Andes Mountains, where the terrain was about 14,000ft (4,300m) above sea level. The cause of the tragedy was determined to have been a violent explosion of a 'criminal origin' in the rear of the transport, which tore off its empennage.

A suicide-for-insurance swindle was suspected in the destruction of CP-639.

An Ilyushin Il-18, shown in the old livery of the Soviet airline Aeroflot, which was the type flown by Cubana involved in an unsuccessful hijacking in March 1966. (Aviation Photo News)

REPORTED 15 JUNE 1965

AN Aeroflot airliner that was flying over the Baltic region of the USSR, on a scheduled domestic service bound for Leningrad, was targeted for hijack by a man and a woman who shot to death the flight engineer before they were overpowered by other members of the crew. This event was believed to have occurred some months before it was reported.

31 AUGUST 1965

A Hawaiian Airlines DC-3, designated as Flight 358 on an inter-island service to Kauai from Honolulu, Oahu, US, was commandeered by a 16-year-old boy armed with a knife and a broken bottle, who wanted the aircraft to return to its point of origin. He was captured after the transport landed at the Honolulu international airport. Convicted of interference with an aircraft crew, he was sentenced to a juvenile correctional facility, and paroled in November 1967.

11 OCTOBER 1965

AN attempt to hijack Aloha Airlines Flight 755, a twin-engine turboprop F-27, occurred as it was boarding passengers on the Hawaiian island of Molokai in preparation for an inter-island service to Honolulu, Oahu. The assailants were two US Navy sailors armed with knives, who were overpowered by the crew. Court-martialled by the Navy, both were sentenced to four years' imprisonment and dishonourably discharged from the service.

27 MARCH 1966

TWO crew members were shot to death in the unsuccessful attempt to commandeer an Empresa Consolidada Cubana de Aviación four-engine turboprop Ilyushin Il-18B during a scheduled domestic service from Santiago de Cuba to Havana with 91 persons aboard. The hijacker was the flight engineer, who first killed a guard and then the pilot, who had duped

him into believing he had landed at Miami, Florida, but had actually set down at Havana's José Martí Airport under cover of darkness. He also wounded the co-pilot when he learned of the trick, causing the aircraft to swerve off the runway and strike a fence. The assailant escaped, only to be captured about two weeks later. Convicted of the crime, he was later executed.

7 JULY 1966

THIS successful hijacking of an Empresa Consolidada Cubana de Aviación Il-18 turboprop was carried out by nine persons, including the pilot, during a scheduled domestic service from Santiago de Cuba to Havana. The co-pilot was wounded, but the aircraft landed safely in Jamaica.

AUGUST 1966

ONE passenger was wounded and the three hijackers were captured during an attempt to commandeer an Aeroflot aircraft that was on a Soviet domestic service, and which landed at Batumi, Georgian SSR.

28 SEPTEMBER 1966

AN Aerolíneas Argentinas DC-4 was hijacked by a group of 18 nationalists defending their country's claim to the Falkland Islands while on a scheduled domestic flight from Buenos Aires to Rio Gallegos with 49 persons aboard. The airliner was diverted to the island region located near the southern tip of Argentina, landing safely in a flat area used as a racetrack. After being extradited back to Argentina, the five leaders of the group were sentenced to five years' imprisonment and the others to three years.

23 APRIL 1967

FIVE men commandeered a Nigeria Airways Fokker F.27 Friendship Mark 200 (5N-AAV) that was carrying 29 persons on a scheduled domestic service from Benin City to Lagos, diverting it to Enugu. Never returned to the operator and seized by the Biafran Air Force, 5N-AAV was conducting a

'bombing raid' near Lagos, Nigeria, on 7 October 1967 when it either got shot down or crashed when a home-made explosive device it was carrying exploded, with all eight persons aboard the twin-engined turboprop being killed.

A few days after the original hijacking, new security procedures, consisting of guards aboard aircraft and hand-searches of luggage, were introduced by the airline.

29 MAY 1967

A DC-4 operated by the Colombian airline Aerocóndor, on a scheduled service from Barranquilla to Bogotá, was sabotaged with a time bomb, which blew a hole in its rear fuselage. There were no injuries among the 22 persons aboard the transport, which landed safely.

12 OCTOBER 1967

ALL 66 persons aboard (59 passengers and a crew of seven) were killed when a British European Airways (BEA) de Havilland Comet 4B jetliner (G-ARCO) was blown up with an explosive device over the Mediterranean Sea off the south-western coast of Turkey.

Designated as Flight 284, which originated at London, the aircraft had stopped at Athens, Greece, before proceeding on towards Nicosia, Cyprus. The second half of the service was being conducted by BEA on behalf of Cyprus Airways. The last radio contact with the Comet was heard around 07:20 local time; about three hours later, its wreckage was spotted floating some 100 miles (150km) east-south-east of the island of Rhodes. The bodies of 51 victims were found, but most of the aircraft's wreckage sank in water that was more than 6,000ft (1,800m) deep and could not be recovered.

The indications of a high-explosive device were discovered in one of the seat cushions plucked from the sea, which

A British European Airways Comet 4B, the type blown up over the Mediterranean. (BAe Systems)

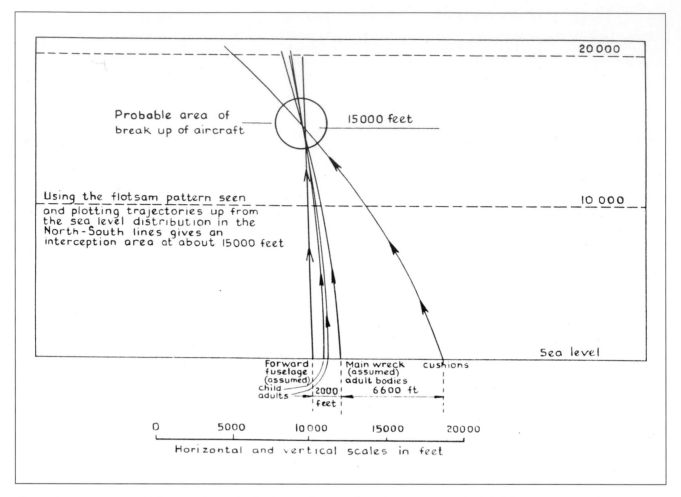

Probable area of
break up of aircraft

15000 feet

20000

Using the flotsam pattern seen
and plotting trajectories up from
the sea level distribution in the
North-South lines gives an
interception area at about 15000 feet

10000

Sea level

Forward
fuselage
(assumed)
child
adults   2000
                feet

Main wreck   cushions
(assumed)
adult bodies
6600 ft

0   5000   10000   15000   20000

Horizontal and vertical scales in feet

Chart indicates trajectory of falling wreckage after bombing of the BEA Comet. (Accidents Investigation Branch)

contained many small particles of metal and fibres as well as about 20 perforations. The bomb had detonated in the cabin, probably on or above the floor and near to the side support of a seat that was believed to have been occupied by a passenger. Never determined was the type of explosive used in the device. An analysis of how the debris was distributed indicated that the structural break-up of the Comet did not occur at the cruising altitude of 29,000ft (8,900m). The blast must have caused severe damage and sent the aircraft out of control, with the fuselage snapping into at least two major sections at an approximate height of 15,000ft (5,000m).

Although at first thought to have been an assassination attempt on the leader of Greek forces in Cyprus, who had been incorrectly identified as being among the passengers, this was possibly some kind of insurance scam. Two of the passengers were found to be carrying abnormally high coverage, with one of the policies having been taken out shortly before the departure from Athens, but neither suspects nor motive were ever positively established.

12 NOVEMBER 1967

A crude home-made explosive device detonated in the rear baggage compartment of an American Airlines Boeing 727-23 as

the jetliner was on a scheduled domestic service from Chicago, Illinois, to San Diego, California, with 78 persons aboard. The blast occurred around 12:00 local time as the aircraft was cruising near Alamosa, Colorado, but caused only minor damage and no injuries, and the 727 reached its intended destination safely. A minor executive had planted the bomb in a suitcase belonging to his wife, who was a passenger; he was convicted and sentenced to prison.

9 FEBRUARY 1968

AN American serviceman armed with a pistol forced his way aboard a Pan American World Airways DC-6B that was on the ground at Da Nang, (South) Vietnam, preparing for a US military charter service to Hong Kong. He was captured and later court-martialled, but was subsequently diagnosed as a schizophrenic and given a medical discharge.

4 JULY 1968

AN attempt to hijack to Mexico a Trans World Airlines Boeing 727 jet, which was designated as Flight 329 and on a service from Kansas City, Kansas, to Las Vegas, Nevada, with 71 persons aboard, ended with the capture of the lone assailant, who claimed to be carrying a gun and dynamite but was actually unarmed. He was sentenced to prison and subsequently received additional time for an escape attempt.

30 OCTOBER 1968

A Servicios Aéreos Especiales SA (SAESA) C-46 airliner, on a scheduled Mexican domestic service from Tampico to Reynosa with 32 persons aboard, was hijacked to the US, landing at Brownsville, Texas. The lone assailant was extradited back to Mexico for prosecution.

2 NOVEMBER 1968

DEMANDING to be taken to (South) Vietnam, a 17-year-old boy armed with a shotgun boarded Eastern Airlines Flight 224 at the airport serving Birmingham, Alabama, as the DC-9 jet was preparing for a domestic service to Chicago with 54 persons aboard. He was disarmed by the pilot while the aircraft was still on the ground. Because of his youth, he was placed on probation, and given psychiatric treatment.

5 NOVEMBER 1968

FOUR men armed with guns and hand grenades seized a Philippine Air Lines F.27 Friendship on a scheduled domestic service to Manila from the island of Mactan with 43 persons aboard, and shooting broke out between them and a security guard at around 21:00 local time. One passenger was killed and two others wounded. Also injured were the guard and one of the gunmen, whose mutilated body was found three days later; he and the other three fled when the twin-engine turboprop landed at Manila's international airport.

It was reported that one of the assailants was later captured and sentenced to death.

8 NOVEMBER 1968

AN Olympic Airways Boeing 707 jetliner with 130 persons aboard was commandeered by two Italians, who passed out handbills and ordered the Greek aircraft to return to Paris, France, from where it had taken off earlier on a scheduled service to Athens, Greece. The hijackers were sentenced to six months' and eight months' imprisonment, respectively.

19 NOVEMBER 1968

A fire occurred in the right aft lavatory of a Continental Air Lines Boeing 707-324C jet, designated as Flight 18, as it was descending from an altitude of 24,000ft (7,300m) in the vicinity of Gunnison, Colorado, preparing to land at nearby Denver while on a domestic service from Los Angeles, California. The blaze occurred shortly before 11:00 local time, but was extinguished by the crew, and the 707 landed safely with no injuries among the 81 persons aboard. A passenger who was seen leaving the lavatory before the fire was arrested by the FBI and charged with the attempted destruction of the aircraft.

2 JANUARY 1969

A lone assailant hijacked Olympic Airways Flight 944, a DC-6B carrying 102 persons on a domestic service to Athens from the Greek island of Crete, and diverted it to Cairo, Egypt. The hijacker spent eight months in an Egyptian jail before being sent to Sweden, where he was imprisoned for another one year and 10 months. Extradition to Greece for further prosecution was denied.

11 MARCH 1969

IN an apparent act of sabotage, two explosions in the passenger cabin severely damaged an Ethiopian Airlines Boeing 707 jet that had landed at Frankfurt, (West) Germany, and was parked and unoccupied. There were no casualties.

3 JUNE 1969

TWO men and a woman armed with a machine gun, a rifle and a hunting knife tried to hijack to Finland an Aeroflot Il-14, operating as Flight 3794 on a Soviet domestic service from Leningrad, RSFSR, to Tallinn, Estonia. Although shots were fired at the cockpit, the crew managed to land the aircraft. One of the men was killed and the other two hijackers were captured, the second man being sentenced to 11 years' imprisonment and three years in exile, while the woman, who was married to the dead assailant and sister of the other man, was sentenced to 13 years' imprisonment and five years in exile.

4 JUNE 1969

A DC-3 operated by DTA-Linhas Aéreas de Angola, on a scheduled domestic service from Ambrizete to San Antonio with 11 persons aboard, was commandeered by three hijackers, landing at Pointe-Noire, Congo.

11 AUGUST 1969

SEVEN students hijacked an Ethiopian Airlines DC-3 that was carrying 19 persons on a scheduled domestic service from Bahir Dar to Addis Ababa, with the transport landing at Khartoum, Sudan.

16 AUGUST 1969

A Greek doctor who was accompanied by his wife and their two children hijacked an Olympic Airways DC-3 during a scheduled domestic service from Athens to Agrinion, Greece, with 28 persons aboard. Disarmed by soldiers after the airliner had landed in Albania, the air pirate was sentenced to 3½ years' imprisonment in Sweden in 1971.

6 SEPTEMBER 1969

A Philippine Air Lines twin-engine turboprop Hawker Siddeley 748 Series 2 on a scheduled domestic service from the island of Mactan to Zamboanga City, on Mindanao, via Dipolog City, was the target of this act of sabotage. At around 15:30 local time, or some 15 minutes before the planned arrival of the flight, an explosion occurred in the aircraft's lavatory, on its right side, at an approximate height of 2,000ft (600m). The suspected saboteur, who had entered the lavatory about five minutes earlier, was apparently killed in the blast and blown out of the fuselage; his body was later found in a rice field some five miles (8km) north of the aircraft's destination.

Among the other 30 persons aboard, including a crew of three, five were injured, none seriously. The transport managed a safe landing at Zamboanga airport.

13 SEPTEMBER 1969

AN Ethiopian Airlines DC-6B carrying 66 persons on a scheduled flight from Addis Ababa, Ethiopia, to Djibouti, French Somaliland, was commandeered by three men who wanted to be taken to Mogadishu, Somali Republic. Due to insufficient fuel, the transport landed at Aden, South Yemen, and during this time one of the assailants was shot and wounded by a security guard, who himself was injured in an apparently accidental confrontation with ground security personnel. The other two hijackers were taken into custody.

13 SEPTEMBER 1969

A lone hijacker commandeered a Servicio Aéreo de Honduras SA (SAHSA) DC-3 that was on a scheduled domestic service from La Ceiba to the Honduran capital of Tegucigalpa with 36 persons aboard. He was taken into custody when the airliner landed in El Salvador.

16 SEPTEMBER 1969

A Turkish Airlines (THY) Viscount turboprop, designated as Flight 124 and on a domestic service from Istanbul to Ankara with 63 persons aboard, was diverted to Sofia, Bulgaria, where the lone hijacker, who was reportedly protesting Turkish travel restrictions, was taken into custody. He would later be committed to a psychiatric facility.

19 OCTOBER 1969

A Polish Airlines (LOT) Il-18 turboprop carrying 74 persons to (East) Berlin from Warsaw, Poland, was hijacked by two armed defectors, landing in (West) Berlin. Both assailants spent two years in a German prison.

31 OCTOBER 1969

A hijacking that set a record for straight distance travelled involved Trans World Airlines Flight 85, a Boeing 707-131 jetliner en route from Los Angeles to San Francisco, California, one segment of a US domestic service that had originated at Baltimore, Maryland. The aircraft first landed at Denver, Colorado, where the 40 passengers and all but one of the four cabin attendants disembarked. It also landed for refuelling at New York City; Bangor, Maine; and in Ireland, before reaching Rome, Italy, a total distance of 6,800 miles (almost 11,000km).

Responsible for the diversion was Raffaele Minichiello, one day short of his 20th birthday. A member of the US Marine Corps, he was absent-without-leave from Camp Pendleton, California, and also faced a court-martial on charges of breaking and entering a post exchange. He was armed with an M-1 carbine, with which he fired one shot in anger as the aircraft was on the ground at New York's John F. Kennedy International Airport. (The captain of the 707 blamed his behaviour largely on the actions of FBI agents, who gathered around the aircraft as it was being refuelled.) After forcing an Italian policeman to drive him away at gunpoint, he was captured south of Rome. He served 18 months in prison in his native Italy, but remained a fugitive from US charges.

10 NOVEMBER 1969

A knife-wielding 14-year-old boy took a girl hostage and then forced his way aboard Delta Air Lines Flight 670 at Greater Cincinnati Airport, located near Hebron, Kentucky, where the twin-jet DC-9 was preparing for a domestic service to Chicago with 75 persons aboard. He later surrendered. Declared as mentally incompetent, the youth was held in juvenile detention for about 1½ years.

20 NOVEMBER 1969

TWO hijackers 'armed' with toy pistols and a fake bomb took over a Polish Airlines (LOT) twin-engine turboprop An-24 that was carrying 20 persons on a scheduled service from Wroclaw, Poland, to Bratislava, Czechoslovakia. The aircraft landed in Austria, where the two assailants were sentenced to prison for two years and 27 months, respectively.

11 DECEMBER 1969

The hostilities between North and South Korea, which had flared up into outright conflict nearly two decades earlier, were still evident in this hijacking of a Korean Air Lines YS-11 Series 100 turboprop, which had been on a scheduled South Korean domestic service from Kangnung to Seoul with 51 persons aboard. Reportedly commandeered by a North Korean 'spy', the aircraft may have been damaged on landing near Wonsan, North Korea. Despite protests, North Korean authorities did not release any of the hostages for more than two months, and 11 of the occupants, including the crew, remained behind, either intentionally or, most likely, against their will. Nor was the aircraft (HL5208) ever returned to its owner.

After the hijacking, the airline subsequently began placing personnel trained in security matters aboard its aircraft.

12 DECEMBER 1969

ETHIOPIA's hard-line policy of dealing with air piracy was illustrated in this attempted hijacking of an Ethiopian Airlines Boeing 707. The jetliner was bound for the capital, Addis Ababa, from Asmara, one segment of a scheduled international service originating at Madrid, Spain, when two members of the Eritrean Liberation Front guerrilla organisation, reportedly carrying explosives, ordered the crew to fly to Aden.

The aircraft diverted instead to Athens, Greece, with both young male assailants dead. Security guards, placed aboard Ethiopian aircraft after two earlier hijackings, had overpowered and tied them up, and then slit their throats. There were no other casualties.

22 DECEMBER 1969

AN Air Vietnam Douglas DC-6B (B-2005) on a scheduled domestic flight over (South) Vietnam, from Saigon to Da Nang, sustained substantial damage when an explosive device detonated in its cabin as it was descending to land at Nha Trang, an en-route stop located some 200 miles (320km) north-east of the capital. The blast created a hole about 5ft (1.5m) in diameter in the fuselage and knocked out most of the aircraft's systems, including its hydraulics.

After the undercarriage had been lowered by gravity, a nose-high flapless landing was made at Nha Trang airport, with the DC-6B becoming airborne briefly before touching down again. The throttles were closed, but its pneumatic brakes could not be applied, and the airliner overran the runway, ploughed into houses and a school and caught fire. Most of the 34 persons killed were on the ground; of the 77 aboard the aircraft, including a crew of seven, all but 10 passengers survived. About 35 others suffered injuries in the crash, which occurred around 14:30 local time. The bomb had exploded in the vicinity of the front left lavatory, slightly ahead of the engines.

2
Destination Cuba

Cuba's fall to Fidel Castro in 1959 was a blow to the Western World, especially to the United States, which, for the first time in a century, found itself facing a hostile nation on its very doorstep.

As had been the case with Eastern Europe, the first few years of Communism in Cuba saw a number of defections by air. Subsequently, however, the island would become a haven for dropouts, misfits and political dissidents at odds with Western culture. Following several incidents in the early 1960s – few of which were successful – the hijacking-to-Cuba craze got into full swing late in the decade, reaching its peak in the period 1968–70. They continue to occur periodically, despite the implementation of preventative policies and procedures.

While most of the aircraft taken were American, such

What was to become a common sight in the late 1960s: US air travellers returning home after an unplanned diversion to Cuba. (Wide World Photos/AP/Press Association Images)

diversions could begin at almost any point in the world. The following is a list of every known hijacking of a commercial airliner to Cuba.

1 MAY 1961

THE first successful hijacking of a commercial transport on a US domestic service involved National Airlines Flight 337, as the twin-engine Convair 440 was en route from Miami to Key West, Florida, with ten persons aboard. Armed with a revolver and a knife, the lone assailant forced the aircraft to Cuba. He was arrested in Miami 14 years later, and subsequently sentenced to 20 years' imprisonment for kidnapping (there was no Federal law for aerial piracy in the US at the time of the hijacking).

24 JULY 1961

OPERATING as Flight 202, an Eastern Air Lines Electra turboprop was hijacked to Cuba by a single gunman during a domestic intrastate service from Miami to Tampa, Florida, with 38 persons aboard.

3 AUGUST 1961

THE first hijacking targeting a commercial jet transport involved a Continental Air Lines Boeing 707-124, designated as Flight 54 and carrying 73 persons on a US domestic service from Phoenix, Arizona, to El Paso, Texas, which was commandeered by a man and his 16-year-old son, who were armed with pistols. The attempted diversion to Cuba ended on the ground at El Paso airport when law enforcement personnel shot out the aircraft's tyres and captured both suspects.

As there was no US air piracy law in effect at the time, the father was convicted of 'obstruction of commerce by extortion' and 'intrastate transportation of a stolen aircraft', and sentenced to 20 years in prison. Facing juvenile charges on the same two counts, his son spent three years in a correctional facility.

9 AUGUST 1961

FLIGHT 501, a Pan American World Airways DC-8 jetliner carrying 79 persons on a service between Mexico City and Guatemala, got hijacked to Cuba by a single man armed with a pistol. The assailant was subsequently deported to Mexico and convicted there of robbery and illegal possession of firearms, receiving a prison sentence of eight years and nine months. He was reported to have later returned to the US by ship from France. After this incident, plans were made to place armed guards on US airliners flying Latin American routes.

26 OCTOBER 1965

A lone assailant armed with an air pistol tried to commandeer to Cuba a National Airlines Electra turboprop, designated as Flight 209, which was on an intrastate service from Miami to Key West, Florida. Overpowered by the crew, he was captured, but was subsequently acquitted of aircraft piracy and assault charges on grounds of mental incompetence.

17 NOVEMBER 1965

GUNSHOTS were fired during an attempt to commandeer to Cuba a National Airlines DC-8 jet, operating as Flight 30 on a US domestic service from Houston, Texas, to Melbourne, Florida, with 91 persons aboard. Subdued by another passenger, the 16-year-old assailant was convicted of assault and incarcerated for 18 months in a juvenile facility.

6 AUGUST 1967

CARRYING 78 persons, a DC-4 flown by the Colombian carrier Aerovías Cóndor de Colombia Ltda (Aerocóndor) was commandeered by five men during a scheduled domestic service from Barranquilla to the island of San Andrés, and forced to fly to Havana.

9 SEPTEMBER 1967

FLYING on a scheduled Colombian domestic service from Barranquilla to Magangue, an AVIANCA DC-3 airliner with 19 persons aboard was hijacked to Cuba by three men.

21 FEBRUARY 1968

THE modern hijacking-to-Cuba craze began in earnest with the case of Delta Air Lines Flight 843, a DC-8 jetliner commandeered shortly after take-off from West Palm Beach, Florida, bound for Miami, the final, intrastate segment of a service that had originated at Chicago, Illinois. The aircraft landed safely around 17:00 at José Martí Airport, serving Havana, Cuba, which would be seeing a lot of American commercial transports over the next few years. The DC-8 had been carrying 109 persons, including a crew of seven, and all were returned safely, with the single exception of the pistol-wielding hijacker.

The air pirate surrendered in Spain two years later, and after his extradition to the United States he was committed to a psychiatric facility.

5 MARCH 1968

A four-engine DC-4 operated by the Colombian airline AVIANCA was hijacked during a scheduled domestic flight from Riohacha to Barranquilla with 32 persons aboard. The air pirates were identified as three young men, two of whom were reportedly taking their guerrilla leader to Cuba for medical attention. The transport landed safely at Santiago de Cuba, its fuel supply nearly exhausted due to the strong head winds it had encountered.

12 MARCH 1968

OPERATING as Flight 28, a National Airlines DC-8 jetliner was hijacked over Florida while on the Tampa to Miami intrastate segment of a service originating at San Francisco, California. The aircraft, with 58 persons aboard, had been commandeered by three armed men, one of whom disembarked weeping at Havana, apparently having 'lost his nerve' about committing the hijacking shortly before the landing. Unconfirmed reports indicated that two members of the trio later died in Cuba.

21 MARCH 1968

AN AVENSA twin-engine turboprop Convair 580 became the first Venezuelan airliner hijacked to Cuba. Commandeered by three assailants, the aircraft, carrying 50 persons on a domestic service from Caracas to Maracaibo, landed safely – but precariously low on fuel – at Santiago de Cuba.

19 JUNE 1968

VENEZOLANA Internacional de Aviación SA (VIASA) Flight 797 was commandeered while en route from Santo Domingo, Dominican Republic, to Curaçao, Netherlands Antilles, one segment of a service originating at Miami, Florida, with an ultimate destination of Caracas, Venezuela. The twin-jet DC-9 Series 10, with 78 persons aboard, landed safely at Santiago de Cuba.

After leaving Cuba, the hijacker was sentenced to 20 years' imprisonment by a Dominican court in August 1970.

29 JUNE 1968

A Southeast Airlines DC-3, operating as Flight 101 and bound for Miami from Key West, Florida, was forced to Havana by a passenger, one of its 17 occupants. Staying behind after the release of the aircraft was both the hijacker and the pilot, Captain George Prellezo, who, having flown from Cuba aboard an airliner he had commandeered eight years earlier, found himself jailed as a defector. He was released by the Cuban authorities and returned to the US after being held for more than three weeks.

1 JULY 1968

ORIGINATING at Minneapolis, Minnesota, Northwest Airlines Flight 714 was commandeered while en route from Chicago, Illinois, to Miami, Florida, with 92 persons aboard, and flown to Havana. The Boeing 727 jet returned to the US mainland sans passengers, who were flown back on a piston-engine Douglas DC-7B. This marked the beginning of a policy by Cuban officials of not allowing fully-loaded Western jets to take off from an airfield not suited to them.

12 JULY 1968

THIS unsuccessful hijacking, which ended with the air pirate surrendering to the first officer, involved Delta Air Lines Flight 977, a Convair 880 jetliner on a US domestic service from Baltimore, Maryland, to Houston, Texas, with 55 persons aboard. Charges against the pistol-wielding hijacker, who wanted to be taken to Cuba, were dismissed, and he was committed to a mental hospital.

17 JULY 1968

FLIGHT 1064, a National Airlines DC-8 jet carrying 64 persons on a transcontinental US domestic service from Los Angeles to Miami, was hijacked shortly after taking off from Houston, Texas, an en-route stop. The pilot managed to talk the armed hijacker – a Cuban who was heard to say 'Fidel ordered me back' – into landing at New Orleans, Louisiana, for refuelling before proceeding on to Havana.

The passengers were driven to Varadero and then flown back to the US aboard a chartered aircraft, the Cuban authorities again being unwilling to risk a take-off from José Martí Airport by a heavily-loaded jet transport.

11 SEPTEMBER 1968

A US citizen commandeered an Air Canada Viscount 700 turboprop airliner that was on a scheduled domestic service from Moncton, New Brunswick, to Toronto, Ontario. He surrendered in Montreal, Quebec, and asked for asylum in Canada. Instead, he was sentenced to prison there, and after being deported to the US in 1971 was jailed again, this time for a bank robbery and a related offence committed in Texas a month before the hijacking.

20 SEPTEMBER 1968

WHILE en route from San Juan, Puerto Rico, to Miami, Florida, with 53 persons aboard, Eastern Airlines Flight 950 was hijacked over the Bahamas by an armed passenger who identified himself as a Cuban. The Boeing 720 jetliner returned from Cuba without its passengers, these coming back on a Lockheed Electra turboprop.

22 SEPTEMBER 1968

TWO aircraft flown by the Colombian carrier AVIANCA were hijacked to Cuba after their departure from Barranquilla, Colombia, both on scheduled domestic flights. The first was a Boeing 727-59 jetliner carrying 78 persons, which landed at Camaguey. Some three hours later, the second, a piston-engine DC-4 with 61 aboard, touched down safely at Santiago de Cuba.

6 OCTOBER 1968

AN Aeromaya SA twin-engine turboprop Hawker Siddeley 748 with a total of 17 persons aboard was hijacked while flying from the Island of Cozumel to Mérida, Mexico. Commandeered by an armed woman accompanied by two children, the Mexican airliner landed safely at Havana, where a fourth passenger also defected.

4 NOVEMBER 1968

DESIGNATED as Flight 186 and carrying 65 persons, a National Airlines Boeing 727-235 jetliner was hijacked by a self-styled 'black nationalist freedom fighter' shortly after take-off from New Orleans, Louisiana, an intermediate stop during a domestic service originating at Houston, Texas, with an ultimate destination of Miami, Florida. Before landing at Havana, the gunman robbed the passengers, ordering a stewardess to collect the loot in a sack. The money was subsequently returned to the victims by the Cuban authorities; the hijacker was not. Nearly two decades later, he would be sentenced to 25 years in prison by a US court for the crime of kidnapping, related to his seizure of Flight 186.

18 NOVEMBER 1968

A Compañia Mexicana de Aviación SA DC-6 airliner, on a scheduled domestic flight from Mérida to Mexico City with 23 persons aboard, was hijacked to Cuba by two armed men, landing safely at Havana.

23 NOVEMBER 1968

A band of five men, a woman and three children, who complained of 'juvenile delinquency and corruption existing in the United States', commandeered Eastern Airlines Flight 73, which was on a service to Miami from Chicago, Illinois. A total of 90 persons were aboard the Boeing 727-25 jet, which landed at José Martí Airport, serving Havana.

Eastern Airlines would experience more of its aircraft being hijacked to Cuba than any other carrier, including a Boeing 727-25 like this one in November 1968. (Eastern Airlines)

A man who reportedly purchased the tickets for the passengers but did not directly participate in the hijacking was later arrested.

24 NOVEMBER 1968

ONLY hours after the Eastern Airlines hijacking, Pan American World Airways Flight 281, a Boeing 707 jetliner with 103 persons aboard en route from New York City to San Juan, Puerto Rico, was commandeered by three armed men who told a stewardess that this was the 'easiest way' to get to Cuba. Two of them were apprehended separately in Puerto Rico in the mid-1970s and sentenced to 15 and 12 years' imprisonment respectively, for endangering the lives of an aircraft crew with a gun and knife; the third returned to the US in October 2009.

30 NOVEMBER 1968

FLIGHT 532, an Eastern Airlines Boeing 720 jet, was commandeered by a lone assailant during a US domestic service from Miami, Florida, to Dallas, Texas. The transport, with 45 persons aboard, reached Cuba safely.

3 DECEMBER 1968

A National Airlines Boeing 727 jetliner, operating as Flight 1439 and carrying 35 persons, was commandeered by a hijacker armed with a pistol and a hand grenade after taking off from Tampa, Florida, an en-route stop during a US domestic service from New York City to Miami, Florida.

11 DECEMBER 1968

OPERATING as Flight 496, a Trans World Airlines Boeing 727-31 jet that was carrying 39 persons while inaugurating a new US domestic route to Miami, Florida, from St Louis, Missouri, was hijacked by a married couple after it had taken off from Nashville, Tennessee, an intermediate stop. The aircraft reached Havana without further incident.

19 DECEMBER 1968

AN Eastern Airlines McDonnell Douglas DC-8 Super 61 jetliner with 151 persons aboard, on a US domestic service to Miami from Philadelphia, Pennsylvania, as Flight 47, was commandeered to Havana by a man accompanied by his four-year-old daughter. Cuban radio later described the 'weapons' he had used as a toy pistol and a fake container of nitro-glycerine. The hijacker returned to the US via Canada about a year later and served 16 months in prison for interfering with an aircraft crew member.

2 JANUARY 1969

AN Eastern Airlines McDonnell Douglas DC-8 Super 61 jetliner, designated as Flight 401, on a New York City to Miami domestic service with 146 persons aboard, was commandeered by a couple accompanied by their infant daughter and diverted to Cuba. The man was killed in a bank hold-up in New York two years later; his widow would, nearly 20 years after the hijacking, plead guilty in a US court to the lesser charge of interfering with an aircraft crew for her involvement in the seizure of Flight 401.

7 JANUARY 1969

A piston-engine DC-4, flown by Colombian airline AVIANCA on a scheduled domestic service from Riohacha to Maicao, was forced to Cuba by a lone hijacker.

9 JANUARY 1969

FLIGHT 831, an Eastern Airlines Boeing 727 jet operating on a international service to the Bahamas from Miami with 79 persons aboard, was commandeered to Cuba by a knife-wielding assailant, who returned to the US via Canada later in the year and received a 20-year prison sentence for air piracy in 1972.

11 JANUARY 1969

AEROLÍNEAS Peruanas SA (APSA) Flight 60, a Convair 990A Coronado jet airliner en route from Buenos Aires, Argentina, carrying 118 persons, was hijacked while preparing to land at Miami, Florida, landing instead at Havana. The air pirate was sent to Mexico four years later, where he received a 25-year prison sentence. He was later returned to Cuba with 29 other prisoners released by Mexico.

11 JANUARY 1969

UNITED Air Lines joined the ranks of carriers experiencing hijackings when its Flight 459 was commandeered over Florida while on an intrastate service from Jacksonville to Miami with 20 persons aboard. The tri-jet Boeing 727 reached Havana without further incident. The hijacker returned to the US via Canada four months later, and was subsequently acquitted of all charges on grounds of temporary insanity.

13 JANUARY 1969

AN unsuccessful attempt to hijack Delta Air Lines Flight 297 ended with the capture of the shotgun-armed assailant, who subsequently received a 15-year sentence for interference with a flight crew member. The Convair 880 jet, carrying 77 persons, had been on a US domestic service to Miami from Detroit, Michigan.

19 JANUARY 1969

AN Eastern Airlines McDonnell Douglas DC-8 Super 61 jetliner, designated as Flight 9, was en route from New York City to Miami with 171 persons aboard when it was commandeered by a man holding an apparently live hand grenade. The suspect was later captured and sentenced to five years' imprisonment in the Dominican Republic.

19 JANUARY 1969

TEN persons were captured after the attempted hijacking of a Compañia Ecuatoriana de Aviación SA Lockheed Electra turboprop, which had been on a scheduled Ecuadorean domestic service from Guayaquil to Quito, with 88 persons aboard. All ten were later successfully prosecuted.

24 JANUARY 1969

FLIGHT 424, a National Airlines Boeing 727 jet with 47 persons aboard, was hijacked by a 19-year-old deserter from the US Navy who said he didn't want to go to Vietnam. Holding a knife at the throat of a stewardess, he commandeered the aircraft to Havana during an intrastate service to Miami from Key West, Florida.

28 JANUARY 1969

OPERATING as Flight 64, a National Airlines McDonnell Douglas DC-8 Super 61 jet on a transcontinental service from Los Angeles to Miami with 32 persons aboard, was commandeered by two men armed with a revolver and dynamite. They were escapees from the California Institute for Men, where they had been serving time for robbery. The aircraft landed safely at Havana.

Nearly 32 years to the day after the diversion, one of the assailants, who had been captured in Nigeria, was returned to the US to face prosecution for the hijacking, and would later be sentenced to a prison term of 12 years. The other hijacker was widely thought to have been killed in Algeria years earlier.

28 JANUARY 1969

ONLY hours after the National Airlines hijacking, Eastern Airlines Flight 121 was diverted to Cuba by three armed men during a US domestic service to Miami that had originated at Philadelphia, Pennsylvania. There were 113 persons aboard the DC-8 Super 61 jetliner. One hijacker was caught in Cleveland, Ohio, in 1975, and received a five-year suspended sentence; his cohorts returned to the US in 1978, both later being sentenced to seven years' imprisonment for interference with a flight crew.

31 JANUARY 1969

A National Airlines DC-8 jetliner, designated as Flight 44, got diverted to Cuba during a US domestic service from San Francisco, California, to Tampa, Florida, with 63 persons aboard. The lone hijacker, who had used a pistol

to commandeer the aircraft, was extradited to the US from Yugoslavia in 1976, and the following year received a 15-year prison sentence for interfering with a flight crew.

3 FEBRUARY 1969

A couple armed with a knife and an aerosol can filled with insecticide attempted to hijack a National Airlines Boeing 727 jet, operating as Flight 11 and carrying 70 persons on a US domestic service from New York City to Miami, but were convinced by the pilot that they should land at the intended destination and were then captured. Both served 19 months in prison for the lesser charge of interfering with an aircraft crew.

3 FEBRUARY 1969

EASTERN Airlines Flight 7, a Boeing 727-25 jetliner with 94 persons aboard, on a US domestic service to Miami from Newark, New Jersey, was commandeered by a trio of hijackers armed with a knife and an alleged bomb, reaching Havana without further incident.

5 FEBRUARY 1969

A DC-4 flown by the Colombian carrier Sociedad Aeronáutica de Medellín Consolidada SA (SAM), on a scheduled domestic service from Barranquilla to Medellín, was taken to Cuba by a lone hijacker. He later fled to Czechoslovakia, and then to Sweden, where he was arrested and sentenced to 20 months' imprisonment in 1972.

8 FEBRUARY 1969

THE attempted hijacking of a Compañia Mexicana de Aviación SA DC-6, which was on a scheduled domestic service from Mexico City to Villahermosa, Tabasco, ended when the air pirate was overpowered by other passengers and captured.

10 FEBRUARY 1969

FLIGHT 950, an Eastern Airlines DC-8 Super 61 jetliner carrying 119 persons on an international service from San Juan, Puerto Rico, to Miami, Florida, was commandeered by a lone gunman and diverted to Havana.

11 FEBRUARY 1969

A twin-jet DC-9 of Línea Aeropostal Venezolana was hijacked to Cuba by three men during a scheduled Venezuelan domestic service from Maracaibo to Caracas, with 73 persons aboard.

25 FEBRUARY 1969

AN Eastern Airlines DC-8 jetliner, operating as Flight 955 and carrying 67 persons, was commandeered during a US domestic service to Miami from Atlanta, Georgia. In September 1969 the hijacker, who had used a revolver, surrendered to US authorities in Prague, Czechoslovakia, and the following July he was sentenced to life imprisonment for air piracy and kidnapping.

5 MARCH 1969

A National Airlines Boeing 727 jet on a New York City to Miami run with 26 persons aboard, and designated as Flight 97, was hijacked by what witnesses described as a 'grubby-looking character' armed with a revolver, who also robbed some of the passengers in the process of forcing the aircraft to Havana.

11 March 1969: a crew member from a Colombian DC-4 runs from the aircraft moments before he was mistakenly killed; the real hijacker lies wounded beside the aircraft. (UPI/Corbis-Bettmann)

After spending 11 years in prison in Cuba, the air pirate returned to the US, and in 1981 was sentenced to five years' probation for air piracy.

11 MARCH 1969

THE first 'Destination Cuba' hijacking to result in a fatality involved a Sociedad Aeronáutica de Medellín Consolidada SA (SAM) DC-4 carrying 40 persons on a scheduled Colombian domestic service from Medellín to Cartagena.

In what could be described as a case of bad timing, a 17-year-old boy holding a stick of dynamite demanded to be taken to Cuba shortly before the planned arrival of the airliner at Crespo Airport, serving Cartagena, only to learn that it had to land due to its low fuel supply. He gave the pilot ten minutes

A Delta Air Lines DC-9 identical to this found itself winging its way to Cuba on 17 March 1969, one of two aircraft hijacked in a single day. (McDonnell Douglas)

to refuel, but the police and military authorities had other plans, moving in closer when the engines were shut down. Before they could take any action, however, some occupants of the DC-4 took the situation into their own hands.

A passenger struck the hijacker, causing him to drop the dynamite. During a struggle, the assailant, another passenger and an airline mechanic all tumbled out of a door and on to the tarmac, whereupon airport guards, believing all three to be hijackers, opened fire. The mechanic was killed and the air pirate seriously injured. The drama ended around 12:40 local time, some 105 minutes after it had begun.

15 MARCH 1969

A piston-engine DC-6 of the carrier Aerovías Cóndor de Colombia Ltda (Aerocóndor) was hijacked to Cuba by a lone hijacker during a domestic service from Barranquilla to San Andrés Island with 47 persons aboard.

17 MARCH 1969

DURING a US domestic service originating at Dallas, Texas, with an ultimate destination of Charleston, South Carolina, a Delta Air Lines twin-jet DC-9 Series 30, designated as Flight 518, was

commandeered between Atlanta and Augusta, Georgia, by a man who claimed to be carrying a shoebox filled with dynamite. The bomb proved to be a fake, but it got him a trip to Havana, along with the other 63 persons aboard the aircraft.

Later that year, the hijacker returned to the US via Canada, and was subsequently confined to a mental health facility for three years.

17 MARCH 1969

LESS than two hours after the hijacked Delta DC-9 had landed at Havana, a Boeing 727 jetliner of Peru's Compañía de Aviación Faucett SA touched down at José Martí Airport, having been seized while on a scheduled domestic service from Lima to Arequipa. During a refuelling stop at Guayaquil, Ecuador, the four hijackers, who were carrying explosives, allowed the other 69 passengers to disembark before the aircraft proceeded on to Cuba.

19 MARCH 1969

DELTA Air Lines Flight 918, a Convair 880 jet with 97 persons aboard, was the target of an attempted hijacking between Dallas, Texas, and New Orleans, Louisiana, by a man armed with a revolver. Charges against him would later be dismissed on the basis of insanity, and he was then transferred to a mental health facility in Arizona.

25 MARCH 1969

A Delta Air Lines Douglas DC-8 jetliner on a transcontinental service to Los Angeles from Newark, New Jersey, as Flight 821, was commandeered shortly after taking off from Dallas, Texas, one of two en-route stops. Among the 114 persons aboard the aircraft were some two dozen Marine recruits on their way to San Diego, California. The hijacker was reported to have died in Cuba in 1975.

11 APRIL 1969

A group of hijackers composed of three men accompanied by three women and four children commandeered a Compañía Ecuatoriana de Aviación SA DC-6 flying on a scheduled domestic route between Guayaquil and Quito, Ecuador, carrying 60 persons, and ordered it to Cuba.

13 APRIL 1969

FOUR men took over Pan American World Airways Flight 460 between San Juan, Puerto Rico, and Miami, forcing the Boeing 727 jetliner, with 91 persons aboard, to fly to Havana.

14 APRIL 1969

A Sociedad Aeronáutica de Medellín Consolidada SA (SAM) DC-4 got hijacked to Cuba by three assailants during a scheduled Colombian domestic service from Medellín to Barranquilla, with 29 persons aboard.

5 MAY 1969

TWO hijackers commandeered a National Airlines Boeing 727 jet, operating as Flight 91 and carrying 75 persons, during a US domestic service from New York City to Miami. Both men returned to Canada a decade later, where one received a six-month prison term for bombings in that country; extradition to the US was later denied for both of them.

20 MAY 1969

AN AVIANCA Boeing 737 jet airliner was hijacked to Cuba by three assailants during a scheduled Colombian domestic service from Bogotá to Pereira, with 59 persons aboard.

26 MAY 1969

DESIGNATED as Flight 6, a Northeast Airlines Boeing 727 jet was commandeered by three armed men while en route from Miami to New York City. The aircraft and its 20 passengers and crew members reached Havana without further incident.

30 MAY 1969

A man who claimed to be carrying a hand grenade but was in fact unarmed unsuccessfully tried to commandeer Texas International Airlines Flight 669, a twin-engine turboprop Convair 600 with 44 persons aboard on an intrastate service to New Orleans from Alexandria, Louisiana. Criminal charges against him were later dropped on grounds of insanity and he was committed to a psychiatric facility for two years.

17 JUNE 1969

A Trans World Airlines Boeing 707 jetliner, operating as Flight 154, was hijacked to Cuba by a lone gunman after it had taken off from Oakland, California, on a transcontinental US domestic service to New York City, carrying 89 persons.

20 JUNE 1969

A vintage DC-3 flown by the Colombian airline Líneas Aéreas La Urraca, on a scheduled domestic service from Villavicencio to Monterrey, was hijacked to Cuba by three men and a woman.

22 JUNE 1969

WHILE on a US domestic service to Miami from Newark, New Jersey, Eastern Airlines Flight 7, a DC-8 Super 61 jet with 89 persons aboard, was commandeered by an assailant armed with a knife and a jar marked 'poison'. The hijacker was accompanied by his daughter and ailing wife, the latter of whom reportedly wanted to visit other members of her family in Cuba.

25 JUNE 1969

ABOUT a quarter of an hour after its take-off from Los Angeles, on a transcontinental service to New York City, United Air Lines Flight 14, a DC-8 Super 61 jetliner with 58 persons aboard, was commandeered by a single gunman while still over California, landing late in the evening at Havana.

28 JUNE 1969

EASTERN Airlines Flight 173, a Boeing 727 jetliner with 104 persons aboard, was hijacked off the east coast of Florida while on a service to Miami from Baltimore, Maryland, and diverted to Cuba. The knife-wielding air pirate returned to the US via Canada five months later, and was sentenced to 15 years' imprisonment in 1970 for interference with an aircraft crew.

3 JULY 1969

A couple that was accompanied by their two children commandeered a Sociedad Anónima Ecuatoriana de Transportes Aéreos (SAFTA) DC-3 during a scheduled Ecuadorian domestic service from Tulcan to Quito. All but eight of the 21 persons who had been aboard the airliner reportedly remained in Cuba.

10 JULY 1969

AN attempt to commandeer an AVIANCA DC-4 after it had left Barranquilla, Colombia, on a scheduled domestic flight to Santa Maria, ended when the hijacker was overpowered. The aircraft returned safely to its point of departure.

10 JULY 1969

FOR the second time in a single day, a Colombian DC-4 airliner was targeted for hijack during a scheduled domestic service, this one, flown by the carrier Sociedad Aeronáutica de Medellín Consolidada SA (SAM), being en route from Cali to Bogotá. As with the attempt described above, this one also ended with the lone air pirate being overpowered and the transport landing safely in Colombia.

26 JULY 1969

IN one of Mexico's comparatively rare hijackings to Cuba, a Compañia Mexicana de Aviación SA DC-6 was commandeered by two assailants while on a scheduled domestic service from Minatitlan, Veracruz, to Villahermosa, Tabasco, with 32 persons aboard.

26 JULY 1969

FLIGHT 156, a Continental Air Lines DC-9 jet with 57 persons aboard, was commandeered by a knife-wielding man after it had taken off from El Paso, Texas. The aircraft stopped for refuelling at Midland, Texas, where it was scheduled to land, and proceeded on to Havana after its passengers had been allowed to disembark. The hijacker returned to the US later the same year, and in 1970 he was sentenced to 50 years' imprisonment for air piracy.

29 JULY 1969

A MALE rebel fighter dressed as a female tried to take over a C-46 airliner flown by Líneas Aéreas de Nicaragua (LANICA) on a scheduled domestic service from Managua to Bluefields with 35 persons aboard, but the assailant was 'distracted' and then captured by the pilot.

31 JULY 1969

THIS daring hijack was committed by a man who had been arrested in connection with a bank robbery that had occurred four years earlier. The prisoner was being accompanied by two guards on Trans World Airlines Flight 79, a Boeing 727-231 jetliner on a US domestic service from Pittsburgh, Pennsylvania, to Los Angeles, California, when he asked to go to the lavatory. Here he apparently found a razor blade, which, after hiding it until the right moment, he suddenly put to the throat of a stewardess and ordered the aircraft to Cuba.

The hijacker was arrested in the state of Indiana 12 years later, and was sentenced that year to 25 years in prison for air piracy and kidnapping.

4 AUGUST 1969

AN AVIANCA DC-4 on a scheduled Colombian domestic service from Santa Marta to Riohacha was hijacked to Cuba by a trio of men.

5 AUGUST 1969

THE unsuccessful hijacking of an Eastern Airlines DC-9 jet on a US domestic service from Philadelphia, Pennsylvania, to Tampa, Florida, designated as Flight 379 and carrying 70 persons, resulted in the capture of the 73-year-old suspect, who had been armed with a knife and a straight razor. Criminal charges against him were dropped the following year, and he was later committed to a mental health facility.

14 AUGUST 1969

A Northeast Airlines Boeing 727 jetliner, operating as Flight 43 on a US domestic service to Miami from Boston, Massachusetts, with 52 persons aboard, was hijacked in the vicinity of Jacksonville, Florida, by two men armed with a revolver and a knife, and proceeded on to Cuba.

23 AUGUST 1969

TWO men commandeered an AVIANCA Avro 748 twin-engine turboprop airliner to Cuba. It had been on a scheduled Colombian domestic service from Bucaramanga to Bogotá with 30 persons aboard.

29 AUGUST 1969

NATIONAL Airlines Flight 183, a Boeing 727 jet carrying 55 persons on a US domestic service from Miami to New Orleans, Louisiana, was diverted to Cuba by a lone armed assailant.

6 SEPTEMBER 1969

TWO DC-3 airliners operated by the carrier Transportes Aéreos Militares Ecuatorianos (TAME) were commandeered in an apparently co-ordinated effort by a band of 13 terrorists, divided almost evenly between them, shortly after they had taken off from Quito, Ecuador, at around dawn, on scheduled domestic flights to Esmeraldas. A total of more than 50 persons were aboard the two aircraft, whose hijackers demanded to be flown to Cuba because they wanted 'freedom'.

Both aircraft landed for refuelling at Tumaco, Colombia, where the co-pilot of one was killed when he resisted and another flight crewman was wounded. The transport on which the shooting had taken place was left behind, the hijackers herding some of their hostages on to the second DC-3, which reached its intended destination late that evening.

7 SEPTEMBER 1969

AN Eastern Airlines DC-8 Super 61 jetliner, designated as Flight 925 and carrying 96 persons, was hijacked to Cuba by a single gunman during an international service from New York City to San Juan, Puerto Rico. After remaining a fugitive from American justice for nearly three decades, the alleged hijacker was arrested in the US during a routine trip across the border from Canada, where he had been living for seven years. He was later sentenced to a relatively short prison sentence – 6½ years – for the lesser crime of endangering the passengers and crew of the Eastern flight.

10 SEPTEMBER 1969

THE unsuccessful attempt to commandeer Eastern Airlines Flight 929 as the DC-8 Super 61 jet was en route from New York City to San Juan, Puerto Rico, with 202 persons aboard, ended with the unarmed assailant being subdued by other passengers and members of the crew. He was committed to a mental health facility in January 1970.

24 SEPTEMBER 1969

A National Airlines Boeing 727 jetliner got hijacked to Cuba while operating as Flight 411 on a US domestic service to Miami from Charleston, South Carolina, with 84 persons aboard. The air pirate, who had used a pistol and an alleged bomb in the take-over, returned to the US with Cuban refugees in 1980, and the following year was sentenced to five years' imprisonment for interfering with an aircraft flight crew.

8 OCTOBER 1969

A Serviços Aéreos Cruzeiro do Sul SA Caravelle jet airliner with 67 persons aboard was hijacked to Cuba by four men during a scheduled Brazilian domestic service from Belém to Manaus.

8 OCTOBER 1969

AN Aerolíneas Argentinas Boeing 707 jetliner, carrying 50 persons, was commandeered to Cuba by a single hijacker during a scheduled international service to Miami from Buenos Aires, Argentina.

9 OCTOBER 1969

DESIGNATED as Flight 42, a National Airlines DC-8 jetliner was hijacked during a transcontinental US domestic service from Los Angeles to Miami with 70 persons aboard. The aircraft landed safely at Havana's José Martí Airport. The lone gunman had reportedly told the pilot that he was 'homesick'.

21 OCTOBER 1969

A Pan American World Airways Boeing 720B jetliner, operating as Flight 551 and carrying 37 persons on an internal Mexican service from Mexico City to Mérida, was hijacked by a 17-year-old armed with a revolver, landing safely in Havana.

28 OCTOBER 1969

A Colombian-registered twin-engine Beechcraft Queen Air A80, operated by Aerotaxi SA, on a domestic service from Buenaventura to Bogotá with eight persons aboard, was hijacked to Cuba by two men.

4 NOVEMBER 1969

THE first hijacking of the day involved a Boeing 707 jet operated by the Brazilian airline SA Empresa de Viação Aérea Rio Grandense (VARIG), and designated as Flight 863, which was commandeered to Cuba during a service from Rio de Janeiro, Brazil, to Santiago, Chile, with 101 persons aboard, six of them hijackers.

4 NOVEMBER 1969

THE second hijacking of the day almost failed when the commandeered Líneas Aéreas de Nicaragua SA (LANICA) BAC One-Eleven jetliner, which had been on a scheduled service from Managua, Nicaragua, to San Salvador, El Salvador, carrying 32 persons, landed on Grand Cayman Island, in an attempt to trick the two air pirates into believing that it was Cuba. One of the hijackers was in fact captured after getting off, but

was released when the other one, still aboard, threatened a stewardess with a gun. The aircraft then proceeded to Cuba with both assailants aboard.

8 NOVEMBER 1969

THIS potentially tragic hijacking of an Argentine jet airliner had a peaceful conclusion. The Austral Líneas Aéreas SA BAC One-Eleven was seized on a scheduled domestic flight from Córdoba to Buenos Aires by a man who threatened to shoot a child unless the pilot headed for Cuba. However, after the aircraft had landed for refuelling at Montevideo, Uruguay, the gunman was persuaded to release all the passengers, and some 80 minutes later he gave himself up to the authorities.

12 NOVEMBER 1969

TWO juveniles who attempted to hijack a LAN-Chile Caravelle jet airliner, which had been on a scheduled domestic service from Santiago to Puerto Montt, were overpowered by the two members of the flight crew after taking off from Antofagasta, Chile.

12 NOVEMBER 1969

ON a scheduled domestic service from Manaus to Belém with 12 persons aboard, a twin-engine turboprop NAMC YS-11, operated by the Brazilian carrier Serviços Aéreos Cruzeiro do Sul SA, was hijacked to Cuba by a single assailant.

13 NOVEMBER 1969

AN AVIANCA DC-4, carrying 61 persons on a scheduled Colombian domestic service between Cúcuta and Bogotá, was hijacked to Cuba by six men. During a refuelling stop at Barranquilla, a pregnant woman and one other passenger were allowed to disembark.

28–29 NOVEMBER 1969

THIS was the first case of a hijacking to Cuba from Europe. Flight 827 of the Brazilian carrier SA Empresa de Viação Aérea Rio Grandense (VARIG), a Boeing 707 jet carrying 95 persons on a transatlantic service originating at London and destined for Rio de Janeiro, Brazil, was commandeered over Portugal by an assailant armed with a revolver and a knife, reaching Cuba early on the second day of the hijacking.

2 DECEMBER 1969

FLIGHT 54, a Trans World Airlines Boeing 707 jet on a US domestic service from San Francisco, California, to Philadelphia, Pennsylvania, with 28 persons aboard, was forced to Cuba by a passenger who held a knife to the throat of a stewardess and forced his way into the cockpit. Though the 707 reached Havana safely, a US Air National Guard F-102 jet fighter that was to have provided an escort for the airliner crashed near Jacksonville, Florida, the pilot parachuting to safety.

The air pirate returned to the US a decade later and was then sentenced to ten years in prison for interfering with an aircraft crew.

19 DECEMBER 1969

A Línea Aérea Nacional de Chile (LAN-Chile) Boeing 727 jetliner, on a scheduled domestic service from Santiago to Arica with 99 persons aboard, was hijacked to Cuba by a single assailant.

23 DECEMBER 1969

A twin-engine C-46 flown by Líneas Aéreas Costarricenses SA (LASCA) got commandeered by a single hijacker while on a scheduled domestic flight from Puerto Limón to San José, Costa Rica. During a stop, 30 passengers were allowed to disembark before the airliner proceeded on to Cuba.

26 DECEMBER 1969

OPERATING as Flight 929 en route from New York City to Chicago, Illinois, a United Air Lines Boeing 727 jet with 32 persons aboard was commandeered by a lone gunman shortly after its departure from La Guardia Airport, landing at Havana. In 1983 the hijacker turned himself in to the authorities in San Juan, Puerto Rico, and the following year was sentenced to life imprisonment for air piracy.

1–3 JANUARY 1970

THIS prolonged hijacking involved a Serviços Aéreos Cruzeiro do Sul SA Sud-Aviation Caravelle, the Brazilian twin-jet airliner having been commandeered by four assailants while en route to Rio de Janeiro, Brazil, from Montevideo, Uruguay. Due to a technical problem, the aircraft had to land at Lima, Peru, where police helplessly looked on as a new generator was flown in from Santiago, Chile, and then installed. The trouble didn't end at that point, as the Caravelle had to land in Panama because of more generator troubles. After electricians had wired up 22 automobile batteries in order to start the engines, the aircraft finally took off for Havana, landing 46 hours after the start of the hijacking.

9 JANUARY 1970

A twin-engine DC-3 operated by the carrier Rutas Aéreas Panameñas SA (RAPSA) was commandeered by a lone assailant demanding to be taken to Cuba during a scheduled Panamanian domestic flight from David to Bocas del Toro, but

An Eastern Airlines Boeing 727-225 was diverted to Cuba in February 1970, as US hijackings continued into the new decade. (Eastern Airlines)

after returning to its point of origin for refuelling, National Guard personnel refused to let it take off. One guardsman then entered the airliner through a cockpit window and shot dead the hijacker. Another passenger, whom the assailant had been holding hostage, was wounded.

24 JANUARY 1970

TWO men and two women hijacked an ALM Dutch Antillean Airlines Fokker F.27 Friendship, the twin-engine turboprop being forced to Cuba during a scheduled service from Santo Domingo, Dominican Republic, to Curaçao, Netherlands Antilles.

6 FEBRUARY 1970

ONE air pirate was killed and four other persons were wounded, a stewardess seriously, in an unsuccessful attempt to hijack to Cuba a Línea Aérea Nacional de Chile (LAN-Chile) Caravelle VI-R. Two students commandeered the twin-jet airliner, which was on a scheduled domestic service from Puerto Montt to Santiago, and it then landed at the capital for refuelling. The hijackers released 29 of the passengers, all women and children, before a police detective went aboard, disguised as a catering employee. Shooting then broke out in the aircraft's cabin, apparently after another passenger had tried to disarm one of the hijackers. Among those wounded was the second air pirate, who was captured.

16 FEBRUARY 1970

WHILE on a service to Miami from Newark, New Jersey, an Eastern Airlines Boeing 727-225 jetliner, designated as Flight 1, was hijacked by a Spanish-speaking man accompanied by his wife and two children. At one point the man held a flaming Molotov cocktail and exclaimed 'Viva Cuba!' However, the aircraft, carrying a total of 104 persons, landed safely at Havana despite the fiery threat.

11 MARCH 1970

OPERATING as Flight 361, a United Air Lines Boeing 727-222 jetliner carrying 106 persons on a US domestic service from Cleveland, Ohio, to Atlanta, Georgia, was hijacked by an armed

assailant who was accompanied by his wife and four children. Imprisoned in Cuba, he was shot and killed during an escape attempt in 1973, his family returning to the US the following year.

11 MARCH 1970

A Boeing 727 jet, operated by the Colombian airline AVIANCA and on a scheduled domestic service from Bogotá to Barranquilla with 78 persons aboard, was hijacked to Cuba by four men.

12 MARCH 1970

A Boeing 707 jet of the Brazilian airline VARIG, operating as Flight 866 on a transatlantic service to London from Santiago, Chile, was hijacked to Cuba with 41 persons aboard.

24–25 MARCH 1970

AN Aerolíneas Argentinas Comet 4 jet airliner, carrying 68 persons on a scheduled domestic flight from Córdoba to Tucumán, was commandeered by a couple. Stopping at Lima, Peru, for repairs, it reached Cuba the following day.

25 APRIL 1970

A single hijacker commandeered a Viação Aérea São Paulo SA (VASP) Boeing 737 jet flying on a scheduled Brazilian domestic service from Brasilia to Manaus. All but one of the other passengers, who stayed aboard voluntarily, were released when the aircraft landed for refuelling in Guyana before proceeding on to Cuba.

1 MAY 1970

TWO hijackers took over a British West Indian Airways Boeing 727 jetliner on a scheduled service from Kingston, Jamaica, to Grand Cayman Island, in the Bahamas, with 68 persons aboard. After it had landed in Cuba, the authorities there managed to convince the assailants that a proposed flight on to Algeria would be beyond the aircraft's range.

12 MAY 1970

A group of eight Dutch revolutionaries armed with automatic weapons and hand grenades pirated an ALM Dutch Antillean Airlines Fokker F.27 Friendship twin-engine turboprop, which was carrying 33 persons on a scheduled flight from Santo Domingo, Dominican Republic, to Curaçao, Netherlands Antilles, and forced it to fly to Cuba.

14 MAY 1970

A Boeing 737 jet of the Brazilian carrier Viação Aérea São Paulo SA (VASP), carrying 48 persons, was commandeered by a single assailant armed with a pistol and explosives during a scheduled domestic service from Brasilia to Manaus. The aircraft made two refuelling stops before proceeding on to Cuba.

21 MAY 1970

AN AVIANCA DC-3 on a scheduled Colombian domestic service from Yopal to Sogamoso, Boyacá, with 26 persons aboard was commandeered by four hijackers, landing at Barrancabermeja and Barranquilla, Colombia, before proceeding on to Cuba.

24 MAY 1970

MEXICO, which had established routes to and from Cuba, had been understandably victimised far less by hijackers than the US. But on this occasion revenge for the killing by Mexican authorities of a Guatemalan guerrilla leader two years earlier was the apparent motive behind the piracy by four men of a Compañia Mexicana de Aviación SA Boeing 727 jetliner, which was on a service to Mexico City from Mérida with 79 persons aboard.

25 MAY 1970

THE first of two US airline hijackings in a single day involved American Airlines Flight 206, a Boeing 727 jet on a domestic service from Chicago to New York City with 74 persons aboard. It was taken over by a lone assailant armed with a pistol.

25 MAY 1970

DELTA Air Lines Flight 199, a Convair 880 jetliner, was commandeered after it had taken off from Atlanta, Georgia, while carrying 102 persons on a US domestic service from

Delta Air Lines, with an extensive route structure in the American South-east, was the victim of numerous hijackings, one in May 1970 involving a Corvair 880 jet. (Delta Air Lines)

Chicago to Miami. The armed hijacker was a Spanish-speaking woman, whose 12-year-old son served as translator. She returned to the US a decade later with Cuban refugees, and was subsequently sentenced to 20 years in prison for air piracy.

31 MAY 1970

A couple accompanied by five children took over a Hawker Siddeley 748 twin-engine turboprop airliner being flown by the Colombian carrier AVIANCA on a scheduled domestic service from Bogotá to Bucaramanga, forcing it to Cuba.

26 JUNE 1970

AN AVIANCA Boeing 727 jet airliner with 99 persons aboard was hijacked to Cuba by two assailants during a scheduled Colombian domestic service from Cúcuta to Bogotá.

1 JULY 1970

OPERATING as Flight 28, a National Airlines DC-8 jet with 39 persons aboard was diverted to Cuba while en route from New Orleans, Louisiana, to Tampa, Florida, one segment of a US domestic service originating at San Francisco, California, with an ultimate destination of Miami. Four passengers, all US service personnel, were reportedly 'roughed up' by the Cuban authorities on the ground at Havana.

1 JULY 1970

DURING a plot to hold its passengers as hostages in exchange for jailed terrorists, this attempted hijacking to Cuba of a Serviços Aéreos Cruzeiro do Sul SA Caravelle 6R jetliner ended with the capture of the four assailants on the ground at Rio de Janeiro, Brazil, where the flight – a scheduled domestic service

Cuba would see its first wide-bodied Boeing 747 when a Pan American aircraft was hijacked there in August 1970. (Pan American World Airways)

to São Paulo with 31 persons aboard – had originated. The pilot of the aircraft and a police officer were wounded in the hijacking.

4 JULY 1970

A YS-11 twin-engine turboprop, operated by Serviços Aéreos Cruzeiro do Sul SA and on a scheduled Brazilian internal flight from Belém to Macapá with 63 persons aboard, was commandeered by a single hijacker carrying a bottle of what he said was nitro-glycerine. All of the passengers were allowed to disembark during two of the five stops made on the way to Cuba.

25 JULY 1970

AFTER being hijacked, Aeronaves de México SA Flight 600, a DC-9 jet airliner carrying 31 persons on a scheduled domestic service from Acapulco to Mexico City, landed at the capital for refuelling before proceeding on to Cuba. Three of the four assailants were Dominican prisoners who had been released and sent to Mexico in exchange for a US diplomat kidnapped earlier in the year.

28 JULY 1970

AN Aerolíneas Argentinas Boeing 737 jetliner carrying 32 persons was taken over during a scheduled domestic service from Salta to Buenos Aires. About half of the passengers disembarked at Córdoba, but while on the way to Cuba the aircraft encountered a snowstorm over the Andes and had to turn back. The hijacker, who was armed with two pistols, surrendered to police after the aircraft had returned to Córdoba.

2 AUGUST 1970

CUBA got its first glimpse of a wide-bodied jetliner with the hijacking of Pan American World Airways Flight 299, a Boeing 747-121 on a service from New York City to San Juan, Puerto Rico, with 379 persons aboard. The lone air pirate,

who had carried out the hijack by means of a pistol and an alleged nitro-glycerine explosive, returned to the US in 1978, and was convicted of kidnapping. He was sentenced to life imprisonment later that year.

19 AUGUST 1970

A Trans-Caribbean Airways DC-8 jetliner, operating as Flight 401, got hijacked to Cuba by three assailants during a service from Newark, New Jersey, to San Juan, Puerto Rico, with 154 persons aboard.

20 AUGUST 1970

A Delta Air Lines twin-jet DC-9, designated as Flight 435 and carrying 82 persons on an intrastate service from Atlanta to Savannah, Georgia, was hijacked to Cuba by a single assailant allegedly carrying a bomb. He was arrested five years later in San Juan, Puerto Rico, and after being returned to the US received a 20-year prison term for air piracy.

24 AUGUST 1970

A man who said he had a bomb (which turned out to be a fake) commandeered Trans World Airlines Flight 134, a Boeing 727 jet on a US domestic service from Las Vegas, Nevada, to Philadelphia, Pennsylvania, with 86 persons aboard. The hijacker was deported back to the US from Cuba the following month, but found mentally incompetent to stand trial, and was committed to a psychiatric facility for three years.

19 SEPTEMBER 1970

FLIGHT 730, an Allegheny Airlines Boeing 727 jetliner on a US domestic intrastate service from Pittsburgh to Philadelphia, Pennsylvania, carrying 98 persons, got hijacked to Cuba by a lone assailant armed with a pistol and, according to him, explosives. He returned to the US in 1978 and was sentenced to 15 years' imprisonment for air piracy the same year.

22 SEPTEMBER 1970

A single assailant threatened to start a fire during the attempted hijacking of Eastern Airlines Flight 945, a DC-8 jetliner on a service from Boston, Massachusetts, to San Juan, Puerto Rico, but the aircraft nevertheless landed at its intended destination. The suspect surrendered there. Rather than air piracy, he was convicted on outstanding state charges of murder and robbery and was sentenced to life imprisonment.

21 OCTOBER 1970

A twin-engine C-46 operated by Líneas Aéreas Costaricenses SA (LASCA), on a scheduled domestic service from Limón to San José with 44 persons aboard, was commandeered by a group of five men and two women. The flight landed on San Andrés Island for refuelling, whereupon the hijackers boarded a second aircraft for the trip to Cuba.

30 OCTOBER 1970

OPERATING as Flight 43, a National Airlines DC-8 jetliner with 58 persons aboard was hijacked to Cuba by an armed man accompanied by his wife and five children during an intrastate service from Miami to Tampa, Florida.

1 NOVEMBER 1970

UNITED Air Lines Flight 598, a Boeing 727 jet with 74 persons aboard on an intrastate service from San Diego to Los Angeles, California, was hijacked by a gunman accompanied by his two children. The aircraft landed for refuelling at Tijuana, Mexico, before proceeding on to Cuba.

13 NOVEMBER 1970

DESIGNATED as Flight 257, an Eastern Airlines twin-jet DC-9 was hijacked to Cuba by an armed man during a US domestic service from Raleigh, North Carolina, to Atlanta, Georgia, with 78 persons aboard.

19 DECEMBER 1970

AN unsuccessful attempt to detour a Continental Air Lines DC-9 jet, which was operating as Flight 144 on a US domestic service from Albuquerque, New Mexico, to Tulsa, Oklahoma, with 30 persons aboard, ended with the capture of the unarmed hijacker. He was later sentenced to five years in prison for 'conveying false information to commit air piracy'.

3 JANUARY 1971

TWO pistol-wielding couples, one of them accompanied by their four children, commandeered a National Airlines DC-8 jetliner, operating as Flight 36 on a US domestic service from Los Angeles, California, to Miami, Florida, with 96 persons aboard. The married couple and their family were apprehended in San Juan, Puerto Rico, in 1975, the husband receiving a sentence of 20 years for air piracy, while charges against the wife were dropped. The other couple were arrested in Chicago the same year, the man likewise receiving a 20-year sentence and the woman getting five years on a lesser charge.

22 JANUARY 1971

ARMED with a hatchet and an alleged bomb, a single assailant hijacked Northwest Airlines Flight 433, a Boeing 727 jet on an interstate US domestic service from Milwaukee, Wisconsin, to Detroit, Michigan, with 60 persons aboard. He first asked to go to Algeria but settled for Cuba instead. Returning to the US in 1978, he received a 15-year prison sentence for air piracy and kidnapping.

26 JANUARY 1971

THE attempted hijacking of a Dominican Republic-registered Constellation, flown by Aerovías Quisqueyanas C por A and on a scheduled service from Santo Domingo, Dominican Republic, to San Juan, Puerto Rico, with 74 persons aboard, ended with the transport landing in the nation of registry and the crew overpowering the single assailant.

4 FEBRUARY 1971

DESIGNATED as Flight 379, a Delta Air Lines DC-9 jet was commandeered to Cuba during a US domestic service from Chicago to Nashville, Tennessee, with 27 persons aboard. The hijacker, who had allegedly been carrying nitro-glycerine, was captured four years later and subsequently sentenced to 20 years' imprisonment for air piracy.

25 FEBRUARY 1971

WESTERN Air Lines Flight 328, a Boeing 737 jetliner carrying 98 persons on a US domestic service originating at San Francisco, California, with an ultimate destination of Seattle, Washington, was diverted to Vancouver, British Columbia, by a 19-year-old military draftee who had first asked to be taken to Cuba. He was deported to the US the following month and later sentenced to ten years' imprisonment for interfering with an aircraft crew.

31 MARCH 1971

A 14-year-old boy tried to hijack a Delta Air Lines twin-jet DC-9, designated as Flight 400 and carrying 22 persons, while it was on the ground at Birmingham, Alabama, US. He was later sentenced to three years' probation on the lesser charge of carrying a weapon aboard an aircraft.

31 MARCH 1971

FLIGHT 939, an Eastern Airlines stretched DC-8 jetliner with 82 persons aboard, on a service from New York City to San Juan, Puerto Rico, was commandeered to Cuba by a single assailant allegedly carrying a pistol and a bomb. He returned to the US via Bermuda in 1974, and was released on probation the following year.

5 APRIL 1971

An American Air Taxi Inc Cessna 402A with four persons aboard, on a domestic intrastate commuter service from Key West to Miami, Florida, diverted to a new destination after a passenger, who was accompanied by a young woman and armed with a pistol, got up from his seat and said out loud 'Cuba!'

25 APRIL 1971

THE attempted hijacking of an AVIANCA DC-4, which took place during a scheduled Colombian domestic service from Barranquilla to Medellín, ended with other passengers and the crew overpowering the lone assailant.

29 APRIL 1971

A Boeing 707 jet airliner operated by the Colombian carrier AVIANCA was commandeered while on a scheduled service from Los Angeles, California, to Bogotá, Colombia, but the lone hijacker was captured when it landed in Panama.

29 MAY 1971

A hijacker armed with two knives diverted Pan American World Airways Flight 442, a Boeing 707 jetliner en route from Caracas, Venezuela, to Miami, Florida, with 69 persons aboard.

18 JUNE 1971

THE attempted hijacking of Piedmont Airlines Flight 25, a Boeing 737 jet that was on the ground at the airport serving Winston-Salem, North Carolina, US, ended with the capture of the lone assailant, who said he had a bomb and a container of acid but was, in fact, unarmed. He was sentenced to five years in prison for the lesser crime of conveying false information in an attempt to commit air piracy.

21 JUNE 1971

THE lone hijacker who attempted to commandeer a DC-4 of Colombia's airline AVIANCA during a scheduled domestic service from Montería to Medellín was overpowered and disarmed by the crew.

24 JULY 1971

DESIGNATED as Flight 183, a National Airlines DC-8 jet, carrying 83 persons on an intrastate service from Miami to Jacksonville, Florida, was hijacked to Cuba by a man armed with a pistol and a stick of dynamite. One passenger and a stewardess were shot and slightly wounded.

3 SEPTEMBER 1971

OFF-DUTY crew members and other passengers overpowered a hijacker who, armed with an ice pick, tried to take over an Eastern Airlines twin-jet DC-9, operating as Flight 993 on a US domestic service from Chicago to Miami with 86 persons aboard. In 1972 he was sentenced to 20 years in prison for interfering with the crew of an aircraft.

9 OCTOBER 1971

EASTERN Airlines Flight 953, a Boeing 727 jet en route from Detroit, Michigan, to Miami, Florida, carrying 46 persons, was commandeered by an armed assailant. He was apprehended in Michigan in 1976 and subsequently sentenced to 40 years' imprisonment.

12 OCTOBER 1971

AN AVENSA twin-engine turboprop Convair 580, operating as Flight 564, got hijacked to Cuba by two assailants during a scheduled Venezuelan domestic service from Barcelona to Caracas with 41 persons aboard.

18 OCTOBER 1971

AN attempt to hijack to Cuba a Wien Consolidated Airlines Boeing 737 jet, designated as Flight 15 and carrying 35 persons on an intrastate Alaskan service from Anchorage to Bethel, ended with the lone gunman surrendering to the Canadian authorities at Vancouver, British Columbia. He was deported to the US and subsequently sentenced to 20 years in prison for air piracy.

20 OCTOBER 1971

SIX hijackers, two of them women, took over a Sociedad Anónima Ecuatoriana de Transportes Aéreos (SAETA) Viscount 700 as the turboprop airliner was on an Ecuadorean domestic service from Quito to Cuenca, and ordered it to Cuba.

25 OCTOBER 1971

WHILE on a service from New York City to San Juan, Puerto Rico, an American Airlines Boeing 747 wide-bodied jetliner, designated as Flight 98 and carrying 236 persons, was commandeered by a single assailant armed with a pistol that was actually a fake. The hijacker returned to the US in 1978 and was later sentenced to three years in prison for interference with the crew of an aircraft.

17 NOVEMBER 1971

AN Arawak Airlines twin-engine Convair 440 with 21 persons aboard, including a crew of three, was taken over during a scheduled domestic inter-island service from Trinidad to Tobago. Hijacked by an assailant who wanted to be flown to Cuba, the aircraft returned to its departure point after the pilot claimed that it had insufficient fuel to reach the island nation. After the Convair had landed at Piarco International Airport, serving Port of Spain, the hijacker released the other occupants but held hostage the stewardess for some three hours before surrendering.

27 NOVEMBER 1971

OPERATING as Flight 106 and carrying 49 persons, a Trans World Airlines Boeing 727 jet was hijacked by three men armed with pistols and a knife while on the ground at Albuquerque, New Mexico, preparing to depart for Chicago, Illinois. One of the three assailants reportedly died of accidental drowning in Cuba 16 months later.

12 DECEMBER 1971

COSTA Rican President José Figueres Ferrer personally oversaw an attack on a pirated Líneas Aéreas de Nicaragua (LANICA) BAC One-Eleven Series 400 at El Coco Airport, San José, Costa Rica. The twin-jet airliner, operating as Flight 419 and carrying 54 persons, had been commandeered by three men during a service from Miami, Florida, to Managua, Nicaragua, demanding to be taken to Cuba.

After it had landed for refuelling, Costa Rican authorities refused to allow the One-Eleven to depart. During a siege lasting more than two hours, the aircraft's tyres were shot out and one power plant erupted into flames after being hit, although the fire was extinguished. In a subsequent assault by members of the civil guard, one hijacker was killed. The other two were captured and sent back to Nicaragua, but both escaped from custody in the Nicaraguan earthquake of 23 December 1972.

26 DECEMBER 1971

IN one of the few Canadian airline hijackings, an Air Canada twin-jet DC-9, designated as Flight 932 and carrying 89 persons, was commandeered to Cuba during a domestic service from Thunder Bay to Toronto. The assailant was

An Air Canada DC-9 similar to this was involved in one of Canada's few hijackings, on 26 December 1971. (Air Canada)

armed with a gun and a hand grenade, the airport at Thunder Bay, Ontario, having no weapon detection system at the time. Three decades later, the hijacker was located in the US and, extradited back to Canada, sentenced to a prison term of three years.

7 JANUARY 1972

OPERATING as Flight 902, a Pacific Southwest Airlines Boeing 727-214 jetliner on an intrastate service from San Francisco to Los Angeles, California, with 151 persons aboard, got hijacked by a couple armed with a pistol and a shotgun and accompanied by a child. They initially asked to be taken to Africa, but subsequently settled for Cuba. The male assailant returned to the US in 1978 and was later sentenced to 50 years' imprisonment for air piracy. His accomplice was later also found in the US and, more than 15 years after the hijacking, was convicted for her role in the crime.

26 JANUARY 1972

A pistol-wielding suspect held hostage an employee at a helipad used by San Francisco & Oakland Helicopter Airlines at Berkeley, California. He first demanded a helicopter and a jet to take him to Cuba, but subsequently surrendered, and was later committed to a psychiatric facility.

7 MARCH 1972

WHILE it was on the ground at Miami, Florida, two armed men commandeered a Grumman 73 Mallard amphibian operated by the US air-taxi company Chalk's International Airline, on a scheduled service to the Bahamas with nine persons aboard. While the aircraft was on the ground the pilot and a mechanic were wounded, after which the co-pilot completed the flight to Cuba. One of the assailants was himself shot and killed three years later in Jamaica; the second was sentenced in the US to ten years' imprisonment in 1985.

8 APRIL 1972

TWO hijackers who attempted to take over a Compañia de Aviación Faucett SA Boeing 727 jetliner during a scheduled Peruvian domestic service from Piura to Chiclayo were overpowered and disarmed by the crew.

5 MAY 1972

FLIGHT 407, a Western Air Lines Boeing 737 jet on a US domestic service from Salt Lake City, Utah, to Los Angeles, California, with 81 persons aboard, was hijacked by a lone gunman who first wanted to be taken to North Vietnam but settled for Cuba, owing to the limited range of the aircraft. He returned to the US in 1975 and was later sentenced to ten years in prison.

15 AUGUST 1972

AN Austral Líneas Aéreas SA BAC One-Eleven twin-jet airliner, operating as Flight 811 on a domestic service from Trelew to Buenos Aires, Argentina, with 96 persons aboard, was commandeered by a group of ten terrorists and convicts who had broken out of a prison in southern Argentina. The aircraft subsequently landed at Santiago, Chile, where the hijackers were granted political asylum before eventually going on to Cuba via a regular flight.

25 AUGUST 1972

FOUR men commandeered to Cuba an Aerolíneas TAO Viscount 785D turboprop airliner that was on a scheduled Colombian domestic service from Neiva to Bogotá with 30 persons aboard.

29 OCTOBER 1972

FOUR gunmen, including a father and his two adult sons wanted for murdering a bank manager and a policemen during an attempted robbery the previous week, shot their way aboard an Eastern Airlines Boeing 727 jetliner at the Houston,

Law enforcement personnel use a fuel truck to deliver ransom and food to a hijacked Southern Airways DC-9 in November 1972. (UPI/Corbis-Bettmann)

Texas, Intercontinental Airport. A ticket agent was killed and a second employee wounded before the assailants forcibly boarded the aircraft, which, designated as Flight 496, was preparing for departure on a US domestic service to Atlanta, Georgia, with 47 persons aboard. They then ordered the crew to fly to Cuba. Subsequently returning to the US, the father and sons were apprehended in July 1975 and later sentenced to 50 years' imprisonment each for kidnapping and air piracy. The fourth suspect remained a fugitive.

6 NOVEMBER 1972

A hijacker who took over a Japan Air Lines Boeing 727 jetliner on a scheduled domestic service from Tokyo to Fukuoka with 126 persons aboard demanded $2 million and a flight to Cuba, but while boarding a longer-range DC-8 at Tokyo he was captured by police. He was later sentenced to 20 years' imprisonment.

8 NOVEMBER 1972

A Compañia Mexicana de Aviación SA Boeing 727 jet airliner, operating as Flight 705 on a domestic service from Monterey to Mexico City with 110 persons aboard, was hijacked by four terrorists. These demanded the release of six colleagues being held in prison, as well as four million pesos, automatic weapons, and a doctor to accompany a wounded prisoner. All their demands were met, and the ten flew on to Cuba, which returned the ransom money and automatic weapons to Mexico.

10–12 NOVEMBER 1972

THE longest and perhaps most gruelling of the Cuban hijackings involved Southern Airways Flight 49. Commandeered by three fugitives shortly after its departure from Birmingham, Alabama, on an intrastate service to Montgomery, the 30-hour odyssey would see the DC-9 jet

hopping about all over the American south-east and midwest, landing at Jackson, Mississippi; Lexington, Kentucky; Key West, Florida; Cleveland, Ohio; and even Toronto, Canada; before eventually arriving at Havana, Cuba.

At one point it circled the country retreat of the American President, Richard Nixon, and at another the hijackers threatened to crash the aircraft into the atomic power plant located at Oak Ridge, Tennessee. In its last stop in the US, the DC-9 landed at McCoy Air Force Base, near Orlando, Florida, where the FBI decided to take action, shooting out the aircraft's two port tyres. This enraged the hijackers, who shot and wounded the first officer while the aircraft was still on the ground. Miraculously, the captain managed to get the aircraft into the air despite the flat tyres.

The aircraft and its 31 passengers and crew members finally returned to Havana, where it had already landed once, skidding to a stop. The Cuban authorities would later return the $2 million US received by the hijackers – a portion of the $10 million they had demanded – and imprisoned all three men. They were returned to the US in 1980, and sentenced to further prison terms there, one receiving a 25-year sentence and the others 20 years each.

18 MAY 1973

THREE men and a woman commandeered an AVENSA twin-engine turboprop Convair 580, which was on a scheduled Venezuelan domestic service from Valera to Barquisime with 37 persons aboard, with the intention of freeing 79 prisoners held in Venezuela. When their demand was refused, the aircraft instead proceeded to Cuba.

4 JULY 1973

AN Aerolíneas Argentinas Boeing 737 jetliner, on a scheduled domestic service from Buenos Aires to Tucumán, was hijacked by a single assailant with a strange demand. He asked the government of Argentina to provide $200,000 to medical agencies in the country. Passengers were released at stops in Argentina, Chile, Peru and Panama before the aircraft proceeded on to Cuba.

20–22 OCTOBER 1973

FOUR hijackers commandeered an Aerolíneas Argentinas twin-jet Boeing 737, carrying 49 persons on a scheduled domestic flight from Buenos Aires to Salta. They released most of the other occupants after landing at Yacuiba, Bolivia, and after two days freed the rest and surrendered when promised safe passage to Cuba.

31 OCTOBER 1973

THE hijacker of an AVENSA DC-9 jetliner, who threatened a stewardess with a pistol during a scheduled Venezuelan domestic service from Barquisimeto to Caracas, shot and seriously wounded himself when told by the pilot that the aircraft was low on fuel and had to land.

21 JANUARY 1974

AN Aeropesca Colombia Viscount 700 turboprop airliner on a scheduled domestic service from Pasto to Popayán was hijacked to Cuba, landing for refuelling at Cali, Colombia, where the 22 other passengers were allowed to disembark.

10–11 MAY 1974

AN Aerovías Nacionales de Colombia SA (AVIANCA) Boeing 727-59 jet airliner, with 92 persons aboard, was commandeered

Passengers escape from an AVIANCA Boeing 727 at Bogata, 11 May 1974, where one gunman was killed by police and two others captured. (UPI/Corbis-Bettmann)

shortly before it was to have landed at El Dorado Airport, serving Bogotá, during a scheduled domestic service from Pereira. The three assailants, armed with pistols and what they said was a bomb, originally wanted to be taken to Cuba, but then changed their demand to eight million pesos in return for the rest of the passengers after releasing 25 women and children on the ground at Bogotá.

The aircraft then took off, landing at Perua and Cali before returning to the capital, where, on the second day of the hijacking, the 727 was stormed by police. One of the assailants was killed and the other two, one of whom had been wounded, were captured. In the emergency evacuation of the aircraft, 14 passengers and a stewardess suffered injuries.

25 APRIL 1975

AN unarmed passenger who said he was carrying a pistol and a bomb attempted to hijack a United Airlines Boeing 727 jetliner, designated as Flight 344 and carrying 68 persons on a US domestic service from Raleigh, North Carolina, to Newark, New Jersey, but later surrendered. He was convicted of the lesser charge of conveying false information regarding the destruction of an aircraft, and sentenced to five years' imprisonment.

9 SEPTEMBER 1975

THREE hijackers tried to commandeer a Haiti Air Inter Twin Otter turboprop to Cuba during a scheduled domestic service from Port-au-Prince to Cap-Haitien, but when the aircraft landed at Gonaives for refuelling they were overpowered by two passengers.

25 DECEMBER 1977

DURING the attempted hijacking of Eastern Airlines Flight 668, a twin-jet DC-9 carrying 36 persons from Jacksonville, Florida, to Atlanta, Georgia, the lone assailant – who was carrying a toy pistol and a fake explosive device – was overpowered by police and FBI agents. He was later sentenced to 25 years in prison for air piracy.

18 JANUARY 1978

DURING an Ecuadorean domestic flight from Quito to Guayaquil with 66 persons aboard, a man and a woman commandeered a Sociedad Anónima Ecuatoriana de Transportes Aéreos (SAETA) Caravelle jet airliner, forcing it to fly to Cuba.

28 JANUARY 1978

AN unarmed man who claimed to have a gun commandeered Piedmont Airlines Flight 964 as the twin-engine turboprop YS-11, with 14 persons aboard, was on the ground at Kinston, North Carolina, an en-route stop during a US domestic service from Washington, DC, to Wilmington, North Carolina. He was overpowered by other passengers and members of the crew, and later sentenced to 35 years in prison for air piracy.

13 MARCH 1978

A lone assailant who claimed to have a bomb hijacked United Airlines Flight 696, a Boeing 727 jet carrying 75 persons on a US domestic service from San Francisco, California, to

Seattle, Washington, demanding to be taken to Cuba. After the aircraft had landed at Denver, Colorado, he surrendered to the authorities. No explosives were found. The hijacker was declared legally insane and committed to a psychiatric hospital.

14 DECEMBER 1978

REPORTEDLY intoxicated, a man who motioned as though he had a gun in his pocket tried to hijack National Airlines Flight 97, a Boeing 727 jetliner on a US domestic service from New York City to Miami, Florida, with 54 persons aboard. He was persuaded to return to his seat and later taken into custody. His punishment was five years' probation for interference with an aircraft crew.

16 MARCH 1979

A man who said he had a 'cutter' in his pocket, but was in reality unarmed, took over Continental Air Lines Flight 62 shortly after the Los Angeles-bound Boeing 727 jet had taken off from Phoenix, Arizona, with 98 persons aboard. He demanded $200,000 and a trip to Cuba, but after the aircraft had landed at Tucson, Arizona, the passengers and all but one of the cabin attendants were released. Subsequently, the three-member flight crew escaped through a cockpit window and the remaining stewardess locked herself in a restroom, allowing FBI agents to move in and arrest the suspect. He was found mentally incompetent and committed to a psychiatric facility.

11 JUNE 1979

THE first successful hijacking of a US airliner to Cuba in 6½ years involved Delta Air Lines Flight 1061, an L-1011 TriStar wide-bodied jet on a service from New York City to Fort Lauderdale, Florida, with 207 persons aboard. Armed with a pocket knife, the lone assailant also claimed to have a gun and a bomb planted in the aircraft, but neither were found after the L-1011 had landed at Havana.

30 JUNE 1979

SHOUTING pro-Castro remarks and wielding a bottle of rum, a single assailant tried to commandeer an Eastern Airlines L-1011 TriStar to Cuba as the wide-bodied jetliner, operating as Flight 932, was en route from San Juan, Puerto Rico, to Miami, Florida, carrying 306 persons. He was overpowered by other passengers and members of the crew, but criminal charges against him were later dropped on grounds of mental incompetence.

20 JULY 1979

DESIGNATED as Flight 320, a United Airlines Boeing 727 jetliner with 126 persons aboard, on a US domestic service from Denver, Colorado, to Omaha, Nebraska, was commandeered by a lone assailant who knocked on the cockpit door and asked to be taken to Cuba, saying that he had plastic explosives in his pocket. After landing at Omaha, he released the other passengers and the cabin attendants. While the aircraft was on the ground, the hijacker allowed the cockpit door to remain open, and once he had taken both his hands out of his pockets, FBI agents, on receiving a signal from the flight engineer, rushed aboard and overpowered him. No explosives were found, and the suspect would later be found not guilty by reason of insanity.

16 AUGUST 1979

A passenger who said he was carrying a bomb, and threatened a flight attendant with a penknife, tried to hijack to Cuba an Eastern Airlines Boeing 727 jet, operating as Flight 980, during a service to Miami from Guatemala City, Guatemala, with 91 persons aboard. As the aircraft was approaching to land at Varadero, Cuba, the hijacker was convinced to go to Key West, Florida, where he was subsequently overpowered. He was found mentally incompetent and was later admitted to a psychiatric hospital.

25 JANUARY 1980

DELTA Air Lines Flight 1116, an L-1011 TriStar wide-bodied jetliner carrying 63 persons, was diverted to Cuba during a US domestic service to New York City from Atlanta, Georgia. While on the ground at Havana, the armed hijacker, who was accompanied by his wife and two young daughters, refused either to let anyone get off or any Cuban authorities to board the aircraft, and at one point he demanded to be flown to Iran.

After several hours, with the assailant remaining in the cockpit, the cabin attendants and most of the passengers escaped through a floor hatch. Upon discovering this, the hijacker demanded that the aircraft take off, but this was prevented by a truck blocking its path. A short while later he disembarked and surrendered to the Cuban authorities. He subsequently returned to the US, was arrested in New York later in the year and was sentenced to 40 years' imprisonment.

9 APRIL 1980

A lone assailant armed with a pistol scaled a fence at the airport in Ontario, California, then boarded an American Airlines Boeing 727 jetliner which, as Flight 348, was being readied for a US domestic service to Chicago, Illinois; no passengers were aboard. The gunman forced the crew to take off and proceed to Cuba, stopping for refuelling at Dallas, Texas. Late the next year he was arrested after returning to Southern California, and was subsequently sentenced to 50 years' imprisonment for air piracy.

22 JULY 1980

A Delta Air Lines L-1011 TriStar wide-bodied jet, operating as Flight 1135 and carrying 158 persons, was commandeered to Cuba during a service from Miami, Florida, to San Juan, Puerto Rico. Bad weather prevented the aircraft from landing at Havana, and it proceeded on to Camaguey, where the hijacker surrendered. He reportedly received a three-year prison term in Cuba.

10 AUGUST 1980

DESIGNATED as Flight 4, an Air Florida Boeing 737 jet airliner with 35 persons aboard, on an intrastate service from Miami to Key West, Florida, was hijacked by a Spanish-speaking passenger holding what resembled a bomb and shouting

several times 'Cuba!' The aircraft reached Havana safely, where the assailant surrendered; his package was found to contain only soap.

13 AUGUST 1980

SHORTLY after it had taken off, an Air Florida twin-jet Boeing 737 on a service to Miami from Key West, Florida, as Flight 707, was commandeered by seven hijackers who poured gasoline in the aisle and in other parts of the aircraft, then raised lit matches and cigarette-lighters while shouting 'Cuba!' The aircraft, with 74 persons aboard, reached Havana safely, where the assailants surrendered. Reportedly all seven wound up serving prison sentences in Cuba.

14 AUGUST 1980

EN route from Miami to San Juan, Puerto Rico, National Airlines Flight 872, a DC-10 wide-bodied jet carrying 224 persons, was commandeered by two men, one of whom held up a quart-sized bottle of liquid and the other a cigarette-lighter. After the aircraft landed in Havana, the hijackers were taken into custody, the Cuban authorities subsequently sentencing both to prison, for four and five years respectively.

16 AUGUST 1980

THIS day saw three American jetliners hijacked to Cuba, and in every case the weapon used was a flammable liquid. Eastern Airlines Flight 90, a Boeing 727 with 53 persons aboard, was commandeered by a half-dozen assailants during an intrastate service from Miami to Orlando, Florida; Republic Airlines Flight 228, a DC-9 carrying 116 persons on the same route, was taken over by four hijackers; and a Delta Air Lines wide-bodied L-1011, designated as Flight 1065, on a service from Miami to San Juan, Puerto Rico, with 165 persons aboard, was hijacked by a lone assailant. Except for the Republic Airlines' hijackers, who would be freed by judicial order, the air pirates involved in these hijackings would reportedly receive prison sentences in Cuba of from two to four years.

18 AUGUST 1980

JUST before Eastern Airlines Flight 348 was due to land at Atlanta, Georgia, on a service from Melbourne, Florida, a cabin attendant received a two-page note written by a hijacker, claiming that he had a bomb in the baggage compartment and a means of detonating it by remote control. He was demanding $3.4 million, the release of two prisoners, and a trip to Cuba. As the twin-jet DC-9, with 59 persons aboard, was already on final approach, the crew elected to land at Atlanta airport, where the assailant was taken into custody by the local police. His baggage contained a handgun, but no bomb. Charges against him were later dropped due to his mental incompetence.

26 AUGUST 1980

FLIGHT 401, an Eastern Airlines L-1011 wide-bodied jet carrying 242 persons on a US domestic service from New York City to Miami, was hijacked by three assailants who, speaking through a translator, threatened to start a fire unless taken to

An Eastern Airlines L-1011, one of the aircraft involved in the rash of US hijackings in the summer of 1980. (Eastern Airlines)

Cuba, having already poured a liquid throughout the interior of the aircraft. All three ended up in prison in Cuba, sentenced to terms of from two to three years.

8 SEPTEMBER 1980

A man holding what appeared to be an unlit Molotov cocktail commandeered Eastern Airlines Flight 161, a Boeing 727 jet on a US domestic service from New York City to Tampa, Florida, with 90 persons aboard. Landing for refuelling at Tampa, the aircraft proceeded on to Cuba, where the hijacker was reportedly sentenced to two years in prison.

12 SEPTEMBER 1980

A lone assailant, holding a cigarette-lighter and two red sticks that had 'TNT' marked on them, tried to hijack to Cuba an Eastern Airlines Boeing 727 jet, designated as Flight 5, which was carrying 85 persons on a US domestic service to Miami from Newark, New Jersey. Correctly judging that the red sticks were not explosives, a flight attendant hit him on the wrist, and he was then overpowered by two passengers. Convicted of air piracy, he was sentenced to 20 years' imprisonment.

13 SEPTEMBER 1980

USING what was by now a proven hijacking technique, two men commandeered a Delta Air Lines Boeing 727 jet, which was operating as Flight 334 on a US domestic service from New Orleans, Louisiana, to Atlanta, Georgia, with 88 persons aboard. The pair, who threatened to set fire to what was believed to have been rubbing alcohol that had been splashed about in the interior of the aircraft, were taken to Cuba as demanded, but there were sentenced to three and four years' imprisonment, respectively.

14 SEPTEMBER 1980

BY threatening to set off a bomb somewhere in the city of Tampa, Florida, where Flight 115 had originated, a lone assailant tried to hijack the Eastern Airlines Boeing 727 jet to Cuba. The aircraft, with 102 persons aboard, instead landed at Miami, its intended destination, where the man was arrested.

His bomb threat proved to be a hoax; the 15-year prison sentence he received for interfering with an airline crew member was not.

17 SEPTEMBER 1980

WHEN nearing the end of a US domestic service from Atlanta, Georgia, to Columbia, South Carolina, Delta Air Lines Flight 470, a Boeing 727 jet with 111 persons aboard, was commandeered to Cuba by two assailants holding cigarette-lighters and bottles of what was apparently gasoline. In a surprise change of policy, the Cuban authorities turned the two hijackers over to US Marshals in Havana. Both were later sentenced to 40 years' imprisonment in the US for air piracy.

25 OCTOBER 1980

A passenger on Continental Air Lines Flight 67, a Boeing 727 jet en route to Houston, Texas, with 132 persons aboard, threatened a cabin attendant in Spanish that he would start a fire unless taken to Cuba. The captain, second officer, and a flight attendant then attacked and overpowered him, and the aircraft returned safely to Miami, Florida, its point of origin. The would-be hijacker was later sentenced to 30 years in prison for air piracy.

6 NOVEMBER 1980

AN AVENSA DC-9 jet airliner was seized during a scheduled Venezuelan domestic service from Caracas to Puerto Ordaz with 62 persons aboard. The two hijackers, who claimed to have a bomb wrapped in a gasoline-soaked cloth, were taken into custody after landing in Havana.

12 NOVEMBER 1980

A twin-engine turboprop Convair 600 operated by the Uruguayan airline Argo was hijacked during a scheduled service from Colonia, Uruguay, to Buenos Aires, Argentina, with 37 persons aboard. The assailant, armed with a pistol and a small can that he said contained explosives, first demanded to be taken to Cuba, but was told that this was not possible. The aircraft then landed in Buenos Aires, where he released most of his hostages. One of three women who tried to disarm him was shot and wounded. The assailant was subsequently talked into surrendering by his uncle, who had been allowed on board, and he later received an 11-year prison sentence.

15 DECEMBER 1980

SEVEN armed men, members of the Colombian guerrilla group M-19, commandeered an AVIANCA Boeing 727 jet airliner during a scheduled Colombian domestic service from Bogotá to Pereira with 137 persons aboard. Before proceeding on to Havana, the aircraft landed twice in Colombia, once in Panama, and at Mexico City, with a number of passengers being released at every stop.

5 FEBRUARY 1981

A passenger on Eastern Airlines Flight 929 told a cabin attendant that he had a bomb, and demanded to be taken to Cuba. The L-1011 TriStar jet, on a service from New York City with 242 persons aboard, proceeded on to San Juan, Puerto Rico, its intended destination, the crew having convinced the hijacker that it was going to Cuba. In an altercation after the aircraft landed, the assailant was knocked out of a door and tumbled down a stairway. He was later found not competent to stand trial and was committed to a psychiatric facility.

10 APRIL 1981

IN this attempted hijacking to Cuba, a passenger armed with a flammable liquid grabbed a stewardess aboard an Eastern Airlines A300B wide-bodied jet, which was operating as Flight 17 on a US domestic service from New York City to Miami, Florida, with 148 persons aboard. He died of asphyxiation while being overpowered and captured by a passenger and a member of the crew.

10 JULY 1981

TWO men, who were accompanied by two women and four children, hijacked Eastern Airlines Flight 71, an L-1011 TriStar wide-bodied jetliner with 192 persons aboard, during a US domestic service to Miami from Chicago, Illinois. Bursting into the cockpit holding three small bottles with burning wicks, they demanded to be taken to Havana. The Cuban authorities were not as affable as the hijackers might have believed, reportedly sentencing both men to ten years in prison.

7 DECEMBER 1981

ON this day, three Venezuelan jetliners carrying a total of 262 persons were hijacked while on scheduled domestic operations, all having taken off earlier from Caracas. Two DC-9s flown by Línea Aeropostal Venezolana were commandeered by three and four men respectively, one aircraft while en route to Puerto Ordaz and the other to Barcelona; and seven men took over an AVENSA Boeing 727 during a service to San Antonio. The hijackers were asking for $10 million in ransom, the release of a number of prisoners, and the publication of a manifesto citing their political complaints and demands.

The three aircraft hopped about over South and Central America, landing at various locations where a number of passengers were released in exchange for fuel and supplies. At one point, both DC-9s landed at Tegucigalpa, Honduras, and the 727 at Guatemala City, where the hijackers demanded to speak to the respective Venezuelan ambassadors. All were then flown to Panama, where the same demands were made. Eventually the three aircraft reached Havana, where the 14 air

pirates surrendered to the Cuban authorities. Under the terms of an agreement with Venezuela, Cuba would be responsible for prosecuting the hijackers.

27–29 JANUARY 1982

NINE members of the M-19 guerrilla organisation commandeered an Aerotal Colombia Boeing 727-114 jetliner that was on a scheduled domestic flight from Bogotá to Pereira with 128 persons aboard. Returning first to the capital city, the aircraft then proceeded on to Cali, where about a third of the passengers were released. After shots were fired outside the aircraft, the pilot inadvertently advanced the power levers and the jetliner struck two military vehicles blocking the runway, resulting in damage to the 727. This was followed by an exchange of gunfire between the hijackers and military personnel. After the terrorists agreed to free the rest of their hostages, a corporate jet was made available with a crew, which flew them on to Cuba.

Tightened security measures were recommended in the wake of the hijacking.

2 FEBRUARY 1982

A lone assailant, reportedly a 'homesick' Cuban carrying a cigarette-lighter and a plastic bottle allegedly filled with a flammable liquid, commandeered an Air Florida Boeing 737 jet, designated as Flight 710, which was on an intrastate service from Miami to Key West, Florida, with 77 persons aboard. The aircraft proceeded on to Havana, where the Cuban authorities reportedly sentenced the hijacker to 12 years' imprisonment.

1 MARCH 1982

A passenger carrying a bottle of liquid and a cigarette-lighter, and claiming that he had a bomb, tried to hijack United Airlines Flight 674, a Boeing 727 jetliner carrying 97 persons, during a US domestic service from Chicago to Miami. When he found that the crew had tricked him and landed in Miami instead of Cuba he became very agitated, but was subsequently overpowered by the pilot and other passengers. Charges against him were dismissed on grounds of mental incompetence.

5 APRIL 1982

THREE men commandeered Delta Air Lines Flight 591, a Boeing 727 jet carrying 103 persons en route from Chicago to Miami. Pouring gasoline throughout the cabin, they demanded to be taken to Cuba; one of them splashed some gasoline on a stewardess when she asked him to stop, resulting in injuries to both her eyes. Arriving in Cuba they received stiff penalties, all three reportedly being sentenced to 20 years' imprisonment.

28 APRIL–1 MAY 1982

FOUR men armed with pistols and explosives commandeered an Aerovías Nacionales de Honduras SA (ANHSA) Dash 7 turboprop airliner that was on a scheduled domestic service from La Ceiba to San Pedro Sula with 48 persons aboard. Claiming to be a group opposed to the Honduran Government, the terrorists demanded the release of 86 prisoners, a ransom of one million lempiras, publication of a political statement, and fuel for the aircraft. The other passengers were eventually released or

A de Havilland Dash-7 flown by the Honduran airline ANHSA was successfully diverted to Cuba in April 1982. (de Havilland Canada)

escaped from the aircraft, with two of them suffering injuries. Three days after the start of the siege, the hijackers were transferred to another aircraft and flown to Cuba.

18 MAY 1982

THIS attempted hijacking to Cuba involved a Taxi Aéreo del Guaviare DC-3 on a scheduled Colombian domestic air-taxi service to Villavicencio, Meta, from Miraflores, Guaviare, with the knife-wielding assailant stating that he had also planted explosives in the aircraft. The pilot was wounded in the incident, but other passengers and members of the crew overpowered the hijacker, who was subsequently remanded for psychiatric tests.

22 JULY 1982

TWO hijackers, who poured gasoline on the floor and seats and shouted that they wanted to be taken to Cuba, successfully commandeered a US-registered Marco Island Airways Martin 404, operating as Flight 39 on an intrastate service from Miami to Key West, Florida, with 12 persons aboard. Both men were reportedly sentenced to 15 years' imprisonment in Cuba.

16 AUGUST 1982

A passenger aboard a Dolphin Airways EMBRAER Bandeirante, which was designated as Flight 296, told the pilot that he had a bomb in the bag he was carrying and demanded to be flown to Cuba after the twin-engine turboprop had landed during an intrastate service from Tampa to West Palm Beach, Florida. The bomb threat proved to be a hoax. Later captured by law enforcement officers, he was sentenced to five years' imprisonment for air piracy, with the stipulation

that he would be released upon completion of an alcohol rehabilitation programme.

15 FEBRUARY 1983

A Rio Airways de Havilland Dash 7, operating as Flight 252 on an intrastate service from Killeen to Dallas/Fort Worth, Texas, was commandeered by a lone assailant armed with a military-type rifle and a bag in which he claimed to have explosives. He demanded to be taken first to Mexico, and then to Cuba. The four-engine turboprop, with 20 persons aboard, landed in Nuevo Laredo, Nuevo León, Mexico, where negotiations went on for several hours.

In exchange for the release of his hostages, the gunman was taken to Mexico City, and during this flight he surrendered. He was subsequently sentenced to eight years' imprisonment for air piracy.

1 MAY 1983

DURING a service to Miami from San Juan, Puerto Rico, a passenger aboard a Capitol Air DC-8 Super 63 jet airliner, designated as Flight 236 and carrying 212 persons, scattered notes in the cabin citing his unemployment, misery and grief, and threatened to blow the US-registered aircraft up with a bomb if not taken to Cuba. On landing at Havana, the hijacker was found not to be carrying any weapons or explosives. Reportedly, he was hospitalised in a psychiatric facility in Cuba.

12 MAY 1983

A woman armed with a flare pistol hijacked Capital Air Flight 236, a DC-8 Super 63 jet, shortly before it was to have landed at Miami while on a service from San Juan, Puerto Rico, with 231 persons aboard. She was taken into custody by the Cuban authorities after landing at Havana.

19 MAY 1983

OPERATING as Flight 24, an Eastern Airlines Boeing 727 jet with 132 persons aboard was hijacked to Cuba during a US domestic service to New York City from Miami. The lone assailant shouted 'Cuba!' several times and held up what appeared to be a stick of dynamite. He was taken into custody after the aircraft landed at Havana.

14 JUNE 1983

AN Eastern Airlines Airbus A300 wide-bodied twin-jet transport, designated as Flight 414, en route from Miami to New York City with 95 persons aboard, was hijacked to Cuba by a lone assailant allegedly carrying a bottle of flammable liquid.

24 JUNE 1983

A lone assailant who held a razor to the neck of a cabin attendant tried to commandeer an Aeroméxico DC-9 jetliner to Cuba shortly before it was to have landed at Mérida, Mexico, an en-route stop during a scheduled flight from Mexico City to Miami, Florida. As it was low on fuel the aircraft still landed at Mérida, where a police officer disguised as a mechanic went aboard and captured the hijacker.

2 JULY 1983

FLIGHT 378, a Pan American World Airways Boeing 727 jet carrying 61 persons on an intrastate service from Miami to Orlando, Florida, was hijacked to Cuba by two men, one carrying a plastic bottle containing what smelled like gasoline and the other displaying a pear-shaped object wrapped in cloth that had a protruding wick.

7 JULY 1983

OPERATING as Flight 8, an Air Florida Boeing 737 jet carrying 47 persons on an intrastate service from Fort Lauderdale to Tampa, Florida, got hijacked to Cuba by a passenger who said he had an explosive device, taking the alleged bomb out of an athletics bag. He would later be returned to the US to face a charge of air piracy.

17 JULY 1983

STANDING up and shouting 'Cuba!' several times, three men armed with knives and an aerosol can seized a Delta Air Lines Boeing 727 jet, designated as Flight 722, on an intrastate service from Miami to Tampa, Florida, with 107 persons aboard. The pilot got the message and diverted to Havana, where Cuban authorities boarded the aircraft and took the hijackers into custody.

19 JULY 1983

HAVING nearly completed a service from New York City to Miami, Eastern Airlines Flight 1, an L-1011 wide-bodied jetliner carrying 232 persons, was commandeered by a passenger who distributed several copies of typewritten notes in broken English claiming to have a bomb and demanding to be taken to Cuba; he also held a briefcase as if it contained such a device. The aircraft proceeded to Havana without further incident.

21 JULY 1983

THIS bungled hijack involved Northwest Airlines Flight 714, a Boeing 727 jet on an intrastate service to Miami from Tampa, Florida, with 97 persons aboard. The lone assailant threatened a cabin attendant with a knife and instructed the pilot to take him to Cuba. When he set the weapon down to accept a drink, two other passengers attacked and subdued him. He was later sentenced to ten years in prison for air piracy.

2 AUGUST 1983

SHORTLY after it had taken off from Miami, bound for Houston, Texas, an attempt was made to hijack a Pan American World

Three stretched DC-8 jets flown by the US carrier Capitol Air were involved in hijackings to Cuba during a four-month period in 1983. (McDonnell Douglas)

Airways Boeing 727 jet, operating as Flight 925 and carrying 130 persons. Speaking in Spanish, the assailant made a statement to the effect that he intended to take command of the aircraft and force it to fly to Cuba. Three other passengers then grabbed him and tied him to a seat. He would later receive a 12-year prison sentence for interference with an aircrew.

4 AUGUST 1983

FOR the third time in approximately three months, a Capitol Air DC-8 Super 63 jet that was designated as Flight 236 got hijacked to Cuba during a service to Miami from San Juan, Puerto Rico. This time a lone assailant carrying a very real-looking toy pistol, a bottle of a clear liquid, and what resembled sticks of explosives, took over an aircraft with 264 persons aboard. He was taken into custody by the Cuban authorities after the aircraft had landed at Havana.

18 AUGUST 1983

DELTA Air Lines Flight 784, a Boeing 727 jet with 79 persons aboard on an intrastate service from Miami to Tampa, Florida, was successfully commandeered by a passenger who, after take-off, stood up and shouted 'Take this national to Cuba!' He had also displayed a plastic bottle containing a fluid that smelled like kerosene or gasoline, pouring it on himself and the seat he occupied and then lighting a candle to validate his demand.

On 27 March 1984 a Piedmont Airlines Boeing 737 identical to this was diverted to Cuba by a lone assailant who turned out to be unarmed. (Boeing)

22 SEPTEMBER 1983

EN route from New York City to St Thomas, Virgin Islands, an American Airlines Boeing 727 jet, designated as Flight 625 and carrying 112 persons, was hijacked to Cuba by a passenger who, in a note, threatened to blow up the aircraft. His purported bomb appeared to be a small box with a battery taped to its side and several wires emerging.

3 FEBRUARY 1984

AN A300 wide-bodied jetliner, operating as Flight 302 of the Brazilian airline Cruzeiro, on a domestic service from Rio de Janeiro to Manaus with 176 persons aboard, was hijacked by a man and a woman, who had a small child with them. The aircraft landed in Suriname, where the passengers were released, before proceeding on to Camaguey, Cuba.

27 MARCH 1984

A lone assailant, claiming to have explosives and two accomplices, commandeered Piedmont Airlines Flight 451, a twin-jet Boeing 737 on a US domestic service to Miami, Florida, from Charleston, South Carolina, with 59 persons aboard. Among his demands were a $5 million ransom and the release of his brother from prison in South Africa. Even though the captain advised him that the aircraft was low on fuel, the hijacker threatened that passengers would be killed if not taken to Cuba. The aircraft managed to reach Havana, where the assailant, who was found to have not been carrying any explosives, was reportedly sentenced to 15 years in a Cuban prison.

28 MARCH 1984

FLIGHT 357, a Delta Air Lines Flight Boeing 727 jet carrying 26 persons on a US domestic service from New Orleans, Louisiana, to Dallas, Texas, got hijacked to Cuba by a passenger holding a bottle of liquid, threatening to set fire to a cabin attendant if his demand was not met.

2 OCTOBER 1984

A Líneas Aéreas del Caribe (LAC Colombia) DC-8 cargo jet was commandeered by a gunman accompanied by four members of his family, including two children, while on the ground at Cartagena, Colombia, an en-route stop during a domestic service from Barranquilla to Bogotá. The aircraft, which was also carrying five other passengers and a crew of three, proceeded on to Havana.

31 DECEMBER 1984

AN American Airlines DC-10 wide-bodied jet, designated as Flight 626 and bound for New York City from St Croix in the Virgin Islands with 198 persons aboard, was diverted to Cuba by a convicted mass-murderer who had been under escort by three armed law enforcement officers but suddenly emerged from a lavatory carrying a pistol. The weapon he used had apparently been planted aboard by someone else as part of a well-executed escape plan.

18 JANUARY 1985

THE attempted hijacking of an Eastern Airlines A300 was foiled by trickery on the part of the crew. Operating as Flight 403 and carrying 132 persons, the wide-bodied jet was en route to Miami from Newark, New Jersey, when the assailant emerged from a lavatory shouting in Spanish that he wanted to go to Cuba. He was holding a cigarette-lighter in one hand and what appeared to be explosives in the other, and also stated that he had poured gasoline on himself.

The hijacker was informed that the aircraft had arrived in Cuba when in fact it landed at Orlando, Florida, and after dropping the bag and lighter he was overpowered by crew members. His 'bomb' turned out to be a fake, but he was nevertheless charged with air piracy.

7 MARCH 1987

A man whose only words that English-speaking passengers could understand were 'Cuba! Cuba!' tried to commandeer Alaska Airlines Flight 93, a Boeing 727 jet carrying 109 persons on a US domestic service from Seattle, Washington, to Anchorage, Alaska, but he was subdued by members of the crew and other passengers. He was found not guilty of air piracy by reason of insanity.

5–6 JUNE 1987

ARMED with an explosive device, a passenger on a Virgin Islands Seaplane Shuttle Grumman 73 Mallard demanded to be taken to Cuba during a scheduled inter-island service from St Thomas, in the Virgin Islands, to San Juan, Puerto Rico. The twin-engine amphibian, with 17 persons aboard, instead landed at its intended destination, where, early on the second day of the seizure, the hijacker surrendered.

23 MAY 1988

AN AVIANCA Boeing 727 jetliner, carrying 136 persons on a scheduled Colombian domestic service from Medellín to Bogotá, got hijacked by a lone assailant who said he was terminally ill and wanted to die in another country. He ordered the aircraft to Cuba, but due to insufficient fuel it had to land in Panama. It then stopped at Aruba before flying to Cartagena, Colombia, where the hijacker escaped. He was captured the following day.

11 DECEMBER 1988

FLIGHT 469, a Trans World Airlines Boeing 727 jet en route to Miami from San Juan, Puerto Rico, with 128 persons aboard, was hijacked by a lone assailant who claimed to have a bomb and wanted to go to Cuba. He was tricked and captured when the aircraft landed instead on Grand Turk Island.

27 MAY 1989

A man who had escaped from a psychiatric facility and wanted to return to his native Cuba tried to take over American Airlines Flight 1098, a Boeing 727 jetliner that was on a US domestic service to Miami from Dallas, Texas, but he surrendered after it had landed at its intended destination.

16 JANUARY 1990

A lone assailant who claimed to have an explosive device tried to hijack to Cuba an America West Airlines twin-jet Boeing 737, designated as Flight 727, on a US domestic service from Houston, Texas, to Las Vegas, Nevada. When it landed for refuelling at Austin, Texas, he was overpowered by a police officer who had entered the aircraft through an escape hatch. Found guilty of air piracy and assault, the would-be hijacker was sentenced to a prison term of 24 years.

10 FEBRUARY 1991

SMOKING is prohibited on US domestic flights, but that didn't deter one passenger from wanting to light up aboard a Southwest Airlines Boeing 737 jetliner, operating as Flight 335 on an intrastate service from Oakland to San Diego, California. He first began arguing with the crew over the issue and was so perturbed by the rule that, in anger, he shortly afterwards passed them a note saying he was carrying explosives and demanding $13 million and a flight to Cuba. He later said the threat was just a joke!

FBI agents weren't amused, however, and arrested him on charges of air piracy after the aircraft landed at its intended destination. A federal judge did not get the joke either when he sentenced him in 1992 to 30 years in prison.

15 AUGUST 1995

Claiming to have an incendiary device that was actually an empty bottle, a lone assailant commandeered Phoenix Airways Flight 506, a Boeing 727 jetliner carrying 104 persons on a South African domestic service from Cape Town to Johannesburg, demanding to be taken to Cuba. Owing to insufficient fuel and the lack of proper navigational charts the aircraft returned to Cape Town, and shortly after landing the hijacker was overpowered by members of the crew.

3

Hijacking disasters

Every airline hijacking is in a way a small disaster. At the very least, the diversion of a commercial flight involves the disruption of dozens or perhaps hundreds of travellers and those awaiting their arrival, the sheer terror of some of those involved, and increased costs to the airlines in terms of additional fuel and misused crew time. Occasionally a hijacking can have tragic consequences, resulting in injury or death. But in a few cases an airline hijacking has proven to be catastrophic, involving the crashing or destruction of the aircraft and heavy loss of life.

An Aeroflot Tu-104 of the type that crashed in a hijacking attempt while on a Soviet domestic service in May 1973.
(Aircraft Photographic)

Although the intentional crashing of commandeered aircraft have been rare events, hijackings can sometimes lead to accidental crashes, often when the air pirates interfere with or in some way incapacitate the flight crew. The first actual crash of a hijacked airliner took place in the early days of aerial terrorism, in 1948, when aircraft were generally smaller and the loss of life in single crashes was generally much lower than in the modern era. Unfortunately, and perhaps not unsurprisingly, considering how commercial aviation is often slow to react to different kinds of threats, it was not until the era of jet transports that much was done to help protect flight crews and otherwise prevent the possibility of a hijacking disaster. As a result several such crashes have involved commercial jets, and some have resulted in triple-digit fatalities.

This chapter deals with hijackings that have ended in the crash or destruction of the aircraft involved and in fatalities among its occupants, excluding those incidents relating to Middle East affairs and the intentional crashing of airliners during the 9/11 attacks in the US. Nor does it cover cases of aircraft sabotage, which technically fall into a different category.

16 JULY 1948

THE first crash to occur during an airline hijacking involved a Consolidated Catalina amphibian (VR-HDT) of the Hong Kong-based carrier Cathay Pacific Airways, which had been on a scheduled flight to Hong Kong from Macao, China. Shortly after 18:00 local time, or about ten minutes after it had taken off, the twin-engine aircraft plunged into the Pearl River estuary, located in the Canton River delta approximately ten miles (16km) north-east of Macao. All but one passenger among the 26 persons aboard were killed, including the crew of three.

The sole survivor of the crash later admitted being a member of a gang of robbers who had commandeered the aircraft, which had gone out of control after the pilot and co-pilot were shot.

1 NOVEMBER 1958

COMPAÑIA Cubana de Aviación SA Flight 495, a four-engine turboprop Vickers Viscount 755D (CU-T603), had departed from Miami, Florida, the previous evening, bound for Varadero, Cuba, a trip of about 200 miles (320km). But it never reached its destination. Hijacked by five Cuban rebels, the airliner was observed circling in the vicinity of Antilla, Oriente province, before finally making a wide turn and, after passing over the town, crashing in Nipe Bay. All but three passengers among the 20 persons aboard were killed, including the crew of four.

The crash occurred in darkness shortly after 02:00 local time, as the Viscount attempted to land at the Preston airport. During the final approach, its fuel supply was effectively exhausted, with only eight gallons (about 36 litres) left in the tanks. Following a loss of control, it plunged into water about 10ft (3m) deep some 1,300ft (400m) off shore and approximately 1.2 miles (2km) from the airport, its tail initially striking the surface of the water and separating from the rest of the fuselage.

Most of its wreckage and nearly all of the victims' bodies were later recovered.

28 APRIL 1960

A Douglas DC-3 (YV-C-AFE), flown by the airline Línea Aeropostal Venezolana and on a scheduled Venezuelan domestic service originating at Caracas, with an ultimate destination of Puerto Ayacucho, was rocked by a midair explosion and then crashed in flames about ten miles (16km) from Calabozo, in the state of Guarico, an en-route stop. All 13 persons aboard were killed, including the crew of four.

Two victims were found alive in the wreckage, and before succumbing to their injuries they confirmed that the aircraft's destruction had been caused by the detonation in the cabin of a hand grenade brought aboard by another passenger, a Russian immigrant. The blast had occurred around 08:20 local time, when the captain tried to disarm the assailant after what may have been an attempt to commandeer the flight.

23 JANUARY 1971

A Korean Air Lines Fokker F.27 Friendship Mark 500 (HL-5212), carrying 60 persons, was commandeered by a lone assailant after its departure from Sokch'o, South Korea, which was an en-route stop during a scheduled domestic service originating at Kangnung, with an ultimate destination of Seoul. Ordered to fly to North Korea, the twin-engine turboprop apparently turned in that direction, but when an attempt was made to overpower the hijacker he detonated two hand grenades, killing himself and one of the aircraft's five crew members. The damaged F.27 subsequently landed on the shore near the village of Chodo-ri, Hyon nae-myon, some 30 miles (50km) north of Kansong, around 14:20 local time, but ran into the sea and was destroyed. Besides the two fatalities in the air, 13 other persons were injured in the incident, which, considering the circumstances, could have been much worse.

24 APRIL 1973

UNLESS he was taken to Sweden, a lone assailant who was reportedly a 'registered psychopath' threatened to set off an explosive device aboard an Aeroflot Tupolev Tu-104B jetliner (SSSR-42505), which had been on a scheduled Soviet domestic service from Leningrad to Moscow with an estimated 80 persons aboard. He did just that when the crew elected to land at another Leningrad airport, the explosion killing him and the flight engineer. The aircraft was approximately 500ft (150m) above the ground at the time, but nevertheless got down safely, though with a hole blasted in the right side of its fuselage the Tu-104 was beyond repair.

18 MAY 1973

THE incident that had occurred less than a month earlier served as a harbinger of this catastrophe, the first major hijacking disaster involving a commercial jet. In this case, an Aeroflot Tupolev Tu-104B (SSSR-42411) crashed in Siberia after an attempt was made to divert the Soviet aircraft to China. All 82 persons aboard (74 passengers and a crew of eight) perished. The Tu-104 had been on a scheduled domestic service from Irkutsk to Chita when the crash occurred some 60 miles (100km) west of its destination, reportedly after an explosive device carried by the assailant detonated aboard the twin-engine jet at an altitude of about 30,000ft (10,000m).

15 SEPTEMBER 1974

AN Air Vietnam Boeing 727-121C jet airliner (XV-NJC), operating as Flight 706, was hijacked, reportedly by three assailants, during a domestic service from Da Nang to Saigon (now Ho Chi Minh City). The aircraft subsequently crashed near the airport serving Phan Rang, located some 150 miles (250km) north-east of the South Vietnamese capital, and all 75 persons aboard (67 passengers and a crew of eight) perished.

It was believed that one of the hijackers had detonated two hand grenades after the pilot refused an order to fly to Hanoi, North Vietnam, and instead attempted to land. The aircraft flew past the centreline of Runway 22 in an apparent go-around manoeuvre, and after entering a left turn appeared to go out of control and plummeted to earth from a height of around 1,000ft (300m), exploding on impact. The crash occurred around 12:00 local time.

An Aeroflot Tu-134 similar to this was involved in a violent hijacking in November 1983 that claimed several lives. (Aviation Photo News)

Subsequent to the incident, security measures were tightened by the South Vietnamese authorities, especially at 'high risk' airports in the country.

21–23 MAY 1976

THIS hijacking and subsequent stand-off between a group of terrorists and military forces, lasting some 45 hours, ended in death and the destruction of a jet transport. The Philippine Airlines BAC One-Eleven Series 527FK (RP-C-1161), designated as Flight 116, was commandeered about 15 minutes after its departure from Davao, on a domestic service to Manila. Including a crew of five, there were 93 persons aboard the aircraft, which diverted to the airport at Zamboanga, located on Mindanao.

The hijackers were demanding a ransom of $375,000, semi-automatic rifles and a longer-range DC-8 to take them to Libya. Through negotiations, 14 women and children were initially released, followed by two more passengers and a cabin attendant.

To help persuade them to give up peacefully, relatives of the hijackers, bringing food with them, were allowed aboard. But when they began to leave and some of the other occupants tried to slip out with them, shots were fired and one of the assailants loosed a hand grenade. Troops then rushed the aircraft, marking the beginning of the violent end of the hijacking, shortly after 12:30 local time on 23 May. In the blast, ensuing fire and indiscriminate shooting, 13 persons lost their lives, including three hijackers. Another 22 persons were injured and the jetliner was gutted by fire.

The three surviving terrorists, one of whom was seriously wounded, were captured and subsequently sentenced to death.

28–29 AUGUST 1976

AN Air France Sud-Aviation Caravelle III jet airliner (F-BSGZ), preparing to take off on a scheduled service to Bangkok, Thailand, was commandeered by a lone assailant who produced two hand grenades during a security check on the ground at Tan Son Nhut Airport, serving Ho Chi Minh City, Vietnam. The following day, after the other passengers and the crew had been released, he detonated the grenades when security forces rushed the aircraft, killing himself. There were no other casualties, but the Caravelle was damaged beyond repair.

4 DECEMBER 1977

THIS hijacking with a disastrous conclusion, the first such incident to result in triple-digit fatalities, involved a Malaysian Airline System Boeing Advanced 737-2H6 jetliner (9M-MBD), designated as Flight 653. The aircraft was commandeered by at least one assailant during a domestic service from Penang to Kuala Lumpur. As it was proceeding towards Singapore, the 737 entered a descent from a height of 21,000ft (6,400m), but the exact sequence of events thereafter differs in the various reports.

Initially, 9M-MBD was observed in the darkness to pitch up from level flight before plunging into a swamp some 30 miles (50km) south-west of Johor Baharu, Malaysia, exploding and disintegrating in flames around 20:15 local time. All 100 persons aboard (93 passengers and seven crew members) perished.

It was believed that both pilots had been shot, but the reason for this remains unclear. The hijacker in the flight deck may also have shot himself. There may have been an immediate loss of control, or the assailant or others may have attempted to manipulate the controls, leading to the uncontrolled descent. Following this disaster security measures were implemented in Malaysian airline operations.

18 NOVEMBER 1983

AN Aeroflot Tupolev Tu-134A jet, operating as Flight 6833 and en route from Tbilisi to Batumi, Georgian SSR, one segment of a Soviet domestic service with an ultimate destination of Leningrad, got hijacked by seven assailants, three of them women. Armed with guns and training grenades, they demanded to be taken to Istanbul, Turkey. However, they were forced out of the flight deck when the co-pilot initiated a series of violent in-flight manoeuvres, after which the aircraft, with 59 persons aboard, returned to Tbilisi airport, where it was stormed by security personnel around 16:20 local time. The flight engineer, a stewardess and two passengers were shot dead. In turn, members of the crew killed two of the hijackers, while a third committed suicide. The aircraft (SSSR-65807) was damaged beyond repair by excessive gravitational forces, and also suffered dozens of bullet holes.

Subsequently, the four captured male hijackers were executed. An Aeroflot lounge attendant was also prosecuted for aiding in the smuggling of weapons aboard the flight.

8 MARCH 1988

ELEVEN members of one family attempted to divert to London an Aeroflot Tupolev Tu-154B-2 jetliner, designated as Flight 3739, on a Soviet domestic service from Irkutsk to Leningrad, via Kugan, with 77 persons aboard. Landing to refuel, the aircraft set down at a military airfield near Vyborg, RSFSR, where, seeing Soviet troops, the hijackers opened fire. An assault team then stormed aboard, and nine persons were killed, including five of the family members and a cabin attendant, while 35 others were wounded. The aircraft (SSSR-85413) was gutted by fire. The surviving hijackers were sentenced to prison.

2 OCTOBER 1990

THOUGH China had not previously been the victim of many airline hijackings – or at least, not many such incidents had been reported – it was nevertheless the scene of this particularly disastrous event.

Operating as Flight 8301, a Xiamen Airlines twin-jet Boeing Advanced 737-247 (B-2501) was commandeered during a domestic service to Canton from Xiamen, Fujian, by a lone assailant who claimed to have explosives strapped to his body. He demanded to be taken to Taiwan, reportedly refusing an offer by the captain to fly to Hong Kong. The dispute continued until the aircraft's fuel supply became critically low, necessitating a landing at Baiyan Airport, serving Canton.

The pilot and hijacker were alone in the flight deck when shouts and the sounds of a struggle were heard just before the aircraft landed hard, then veered off the runway. After striking a parked China Southwest Airlines Boeing Advanced 707-3J6B jet (B-2402), the out-of-control Xiamen aircraft slammed into a China Southern Airlines Boeing 757-21B (B-2812) that had been waiting to take off on a scheduled domestic flight to Shanghai, the crash occurring around 09:15 local time. A total of 132 persons were killed, comprising all but 18 of the 102 aboard the 737, including the hijacker and seven members of its crew of nine; 47 of the 122 aboard the 757, all of them passengers; and the driver of an airport service vehicle. Some 50 others suffered injuries, including the pilot (and sole occupant) of the 707, which was damaged beyond repair. The other two jetliners were destroyed by impact forces and post-crash fire.

In the wake of this disaster, the Chinese authorities are said to have ordered managerial restructuring, and admitted procedural deficiencies that had allowed B-2812 to taxi during a hijacking.

28 AUGUST 1993

LOADED with nearly three times its designed passenger capacity, a Tajik Air Yakovlev Yak-40 (SSSR-87995) crashed during a coerced take-off at Khorugh, Tajikistan, Commonwealth of Independent States. All but four passengers among the 86 persons aboard were killed, including the crew of five.

The tri-jet transport, which had been on a scheduled domestic service to Dushanbe, located some 180 miles (290km) to the north-west, was commandeered by armed men who demanded that it take off. As disobeying them could

have meant being shot, the crew chose the option that they undoubtedly felt offered better odds for survival. But with an airfield elevation of about 7,000ft (2,000m) and SSSR-87995 approximately 6,600lb (3,000kg) overweight, their action proved fatal. The aircraft never got airborne during its take-off roll, overran the airport runway, and after striking with its main undercarriage an embankment and then a concrete pill-box it careened down a riverbank, the crash occurring around 10:45 local time. There was no post-impact fire.

25–27 OCTOBER 1994

THE only casualties in this incident were the hijacker and the aircraft, a Yak-40 (RA-88254) flown by the Russian carrier Donavia. Designated as Flight D9-156 on an international service originating at Ashkahadbad, Turkmenistan, with an ultimate destination of Rostov-na-Donu, the jet airliner was forced by a lone assailant to return to Makhachkala, also in Russia, which was an en-route stop. He was demanding a $2 million ransom and a flight to Iran. Negotiations went on for two more days, with most of the 26 hostages being released before, early on the third day (27 October), the remaining two crew members escaped after the hijacker apparently fell asleep. Then, shortly before 07:00, as security forces prepared to board the aircraft, the assailant detonated a home-made bomb he was carrying and was killed. The Yak-40 was damaged beyond repair.

23 NOVEMBER 1996

ETHIOPIAN Airlines had demonstrated a stern response to aerial terrorism in the past (see pages 18 and 135), and several would-be hijackers had been killed in the act. However, this time – perhaps due to simple complacency – the carrier suffered the world's worst hijacking incident to date, in terms of fatalities aboard a single aircraft.

Operating as Flight 961, a Boeing 767-260ER (ET-AIZ) wide-bodied jetliner had taken off from Bole International Airport,

Shown in Aeroflot livery, this Yak-40 is otherwise the same as the aircraft that crashed during hijacking in August 1993. (Philip Jarrett)

The initial impact is captured on videotape as the hijacked Ethiopian Airlines Boeing 767 crashes into the Indian Ocean. (Paris Match)

serving Addis Ababa, Ethiopia, bound for Nairobi, Kenya, the first segment of a service with an ultimate destination of Abidjan, Ivory Coast. Some 20 minutes after departure, three Ethiopian passengers got up from their seats and stormed into the cockpit. Although the security measures in effect at Addis Ababa had been successful in preventing them from smuggling weapons on to the aircraft, the assailants 'improvised' their assault tactics, first claiming – falsely – to have a bomb, then grabbing an axe and a fire extinguisher from their respective stowage areas in the cockpit. They also beat the first officer and forced him out of the flight deck, before ordering the pilot, Captain Leul Abate, to fly them to Australia, and not allowing him to send any radio transmissions after informing the Addis Ababa control centre of the seizure of the aircraft. The hijackers also rejected Captain Abate's request to land for refuelling, based on their understanding of the range capability of the 767. In reality, ET-AIZ did not have sufficient fuel on board to make the trip non-stop, and this misunderstanding would set the stage for catastrophe.

An opportunity to prevent the subsequent disaster may have been lost at one point, while all three assailants were in the cabin, when the captain appealed over the public address system for the other passengers to 'react to the hijackers'. His message was given only in English, however, and as a result the other passengers did not understand his plea for help and took no action, despite the fact – especially considering their number – the passengers and cabin personnel could probably have overpowered the assailants, who were not heavily armed.

The assailants subsequently rejected another request from the pilot to refuel, with the lead hijacker showing his nonchalance as he reportedly fiddled with the controls from the first officer's seat while drinking whiskey. Even after the low fuel caution light had illuminated, the hijackers warned Captain Abate not to descend below the cruising altitude of 39,000ft (12,000m), and when the starboard engine failed due to fuel exhaustion they began manipulating the controls, which caused the flight path of the 767 to become erratic. The aircraft

completed three irregular circles before it assumed a near-northerly course, and during this time the port power plant flamed out. As the aircraft descended in unpowered flight, the first officer was able to force his way back into the cockpit to help the captain and, finally, the hijackers stopped harassing the pilots. Meanwhile, the cabin crew members began preparing the passengers for an inevitable ditching at sea.

As it glided over the Indian Ocean in the region of the Comores island group, with only the RAM air turbine available to power the standby instruments, the flight crew tried to turn the 767 in order to land parallel to the waves, but at that moment it struck the surface of the water while in a left wing-low attitude, its undercarriage and flaps still retracted, and the jetliner then slammed into the ocean some 1,500ft (500m) offshore near Galawa Beach, located on the northern end of Grande Comore, breaking into four main sections. Paying with their lives for their arrogance and stubbornness, the three hijackers were among the 125 persons killed in the disaster. The crash occurred in good weather conditions on a Saturday afternoon, around 15:20 local time, in full view of beach-goers and rescue personnel, who rushed to the scene, and it was probably thanks to their action that 50 others aboard ET-AIZ survived, including its three flight crew members and three of the nine cabin staff. Many of the survivors were seriously hurt, however, with only four passengers reporting no physical injury. All of the victims' bodies were subsequently recovered, and although no post-mortem examinations were performed, most of the fatalities were believed to have resulted from impact trauma, with some of the deaths apparently attributed to drowning.

It was noted in the report of the investigative committee that the use of on-board security personnel, which in the past had thwarted hijackings targeting Ethiopian Airlines aircraft, might have been beneficial in this case. Additionally, the carrier's security training procedures dealing with terrorism and other unusual situations were found not to have been conducted in a formal or well-structured manner. One of the recommendations made in the report was that the aircraft's fire axe be stored so as to be inaccessible to anyone other than the members of the flight crew.

4

Terror from the Middle East

Terrorism is almost synonymous with Middle Eastern affairs, the political and religious strife in that part of the world having been associated with many acts of terror over a long period of time. Aerial terrorism, however, is a relatively new phenomenon in the region, the first hijackings not occurring here until the late-1960s. Such incidents were soon joined by ground attacks on civil aircraft and, shortly afterwards, by aerial sabotage.

Some of the world's bloodiest hijackings and deadliest cases of sabotage have involved groups or individuals based in or related to the Middle East. The worst of the latter was

the destruction of Pan Am Flight 103 over Scotland a few days before Christmas 1988, an act of terrorism which proved that even flights not originating from Middle Eastern countries were not immune. Indeed, attacks spawned in the Middle East have taken place in many different parts of the world.

Except for the attacks in the US of 11 September 2001,

A BOAC Super VC-10 disappears in a cloud of dust and debris as it is blown up with two other jets in September 1970, just one of numerous terrorist attacks occurring in the Middle East. (UPI/Corbis-Bettmann)

which are dealt with separately, the following is a list of acts of terrorism – including hijackings, bombings and ground attacks on airliners – either suspected or proved to be related to Middle Eastern affairs, or which involved carriers from or flights that originated at or ended up in this part of the world.

22 NOVEMBER 1966

AN Aden Airways Douglas DC-3 (VR-AAN) was destroyed in an act of sabotage during a scheduled domestic service from Meifah to Aden. Flying at 6,000ft (1,800m), the airliner plunged into the desert some 130 miles (210km) east of its destination at around 12:20 local time, or approximately 20 minutes after take-off, following an in-flight blast. All 30 persons aboard (27 passengers and a crew of three) lost their lives.

The crash was linked to the detonation of an explosive charge in hand luggage being carried in the aircraft's cabin, which occurred on the port side just above the wing.

7 FEBRUARY 1967

A United Arab Airlines An-24 turboprop carrying 45 persons on a scheduled Egyptian domestic service from Cairo to Hurghana was hijacked to Jordan, reportedly by an Egyptian intelligence officer. Though the assailant managed to escape from the Jordanian authorities and fled to Sweden, he was arrested and imprisoned there for other crimes.

30 JUNE 1967

AN Aden Airways four-engine turboprop Vickers Viscount 760D (VR-AAV) was destroyed by a bomb while parked unattended on the apron at Khormaksar Airport, serving Aden, Yemen. There were no injuries in the blast, which occurred at around 15:30 local time after the airliner had been placed in 'quarantine' due to concerns that an explosive device had been planted aboard.

23 JULY 1968

THE first case of the hijacking of a commercial flight in or out of the Middle East involved what today would be considered a most unlikely target: the national airline of Israel, El Al. Following a delay for an apparently unrelated bomb threat, Flight 426 departed from Rome, Italy, bound for Tel Aviv, Israel, the second leg of a service originating at London. Aboard the Boeing 707-458 jet were 38 passengers and a crew of ten. Less than an hour later, El Al Captain Oded Abarbanell radioed an ominous message: 'I am being forced to head for Algiers'.

Three passengers, brandishing pistols and hand grenades and identified as members of the Popular Front for the Liberation of Palestine, had commandeered the aircraft over the Italian island of Capri. During this time the aircraft's co-pilot was wounded, though not seriously. It appeared that the intention of the air pirates was not so much to get from point A to point B, but rather to humiliate the government of Israel. Their destination was wisely chosen, as Algeria had been on hostile terms with Israel since the war in the Middle East the previous year.

Algerian complicity was suspected simply by the way the hijacking appeared to be planned – a television news crew was already on hand when the 707 arrived in the early hours of the following day at Algiers' Dar el Baida Airport. Immediately afterwards, the authorities took into custody 22 Israeli nationals who had been on the flight, as either passengers or crew members. The other 26 were not only freed but were treated royally, some even being given a tour of the city! Among those released were three Jews who concealed their religion.

Five days later, ten Israeli women and children, the former including three stewardesses, were released. The other hostages were freed some five weeks after the hijacking, despite Israel's refusal to release any of the Arab prisoners it held. The aircraft itself was later flown back by an Air France crew.

Never again would El Al be a victim of a successful hijacking, the company subsequently implementing the most rigid security measures of any carrier in the Western World. These would include the placement of plain-clothes security personnel aboard aircraft, and hand searches of all luggage. The government of Israel also adopted a policy of retaliation in response to aggressive acts against its citizens.

26 DECEMBER 1968

EL Al Israel Airlines was victimised again in this ground attack on one of its aircraft at Athens. Operating as Flight 253, which had stopped at Athens airport during a service from Tel Aviv to Paris, with an ultimate destination of New York City, the Boeing 707-358B jet had been taxiing to take off when it was attacked by two terrorists armed with automatic weapons and hand grenades. One passenger among the 47 persons aboard was killed and another wounded. Damage to the aircraft was considerable, with fire erupting in one engine, which was quickly extinguished.

Both terrorists were captured and imprisoned, although they were released as ransom following the hijacking of a Greek airliner in 1970. Two days after the El Al 707 incident at Athens, helicopter-borne Israeli commandos raided the international airport at Beirut, Lebanon, blowing up a dozen Lebanese-registered aircraft in retaliation for the attack.

18 FEBRUARY 1969

OFFICIALS at Zürich-Kloten Airport had initially enacted strict security measures following the attack on the Israeli jetliner two months earlier. That these precautions were subsequently relaxed proved unfortunate for El Al Flight 432, which had stopped in Switzerland during a service to Tel Aviv from Amsterdam.

As the Boeing 720B was taxiing to its take-off position, four members of the Popular Front for the Liberation of Palestine suddenly appeared and sprayed the jet with machine-gun fire. At least one hand grenade was also thrown but caused no damage. A trainee pilot seriously wounded in the attack later died. One of the attackers was also killed when an armed passenger opened an emergency door and returned fire. Hit some 40 times, the aircraft sustained substantial damage.

The guerrillas had driven to the centre of the airport and then hid behind a snowbank, carrying out the attack in twilight conditions. The three survivors were all captured, and later sentenced to 12 years' imprisonment each, but were released as ransom after the hijacking of a Swissair jetliner to Jordan in September 1970.

18 AUGUST 1969

TWO brothers, one of whom was accompanied by his wife and three children, commandeered a United Arab Airlines An-24 turboprop airliner on a scheduled Egyptian domestic service from Cairo to Luxor with 30 persons aboard, diverting the flight

to El Wagah, Saudi Arabia. There the assailants were arrested, then returned to Egypt for prosecution, with one of the men, a doctor, receiving a life prison sentence. His brother was sentenced to seven years' imprisonment.

29 AUGUST 1969

TRANS World Airlines Flight 840 was carrying 127 persons, including a crew of 12, and had been en route from Rome to Athens, with an ultimate destination of Tel Aviv, Israel, when it was hijacked over the Adriatic. Upon reaching Tel Aviv, a female hijacker used the aircraft's radio to broadcast propaganda messages. The Boeing Advanced 707-331B jetliner was then diverted to Damascus, Syria, landing at the city's international airport. Minutes after escape chutes had been deployed and an emergency evacuation accomplished, one of the hijackers tossed in a package of explosives given to him by someone on the ground; the resulting blast blew the cockpit section away from the rest of the aircraft. One passenger was slightly injured in the emergency evacuation, which occurred around 17:15 local time. The aircraft would later be rebuilt.

The occupants were released almost immediately, except for six Israelis. Of these, four women were freed on 1 September, and the remaining two men were released in exchange for 13 Syrian military prisoners held by Israel, but only after more than three months in captivity. The Popular Front for the Liberation of Palestine claimed responsibility for the hijack.

8 JANUARY 1970

A Trans World Airlines Boeing 707 jetliner, operating as Flight 802 on a service from Paris to Rome, and carrying 20 persons, was hijacked to Beirut, Lebanon. After it landed, the assailant, a young Frenchman, fired about a dozen shots into the aircraft's instrument panel; he then surrendered, and was subsequently sentenced to nine months' imprisonment in Lebanon and eight months' imprisonment in France, the sentences running consecutively.

21 FEBRUARY 1970

MIDDLE East-spawned terrorism took a deadly new turn with this case of aerial sabotage, involving Swissair AG Flight 330, a Convair 990A Coronado (HB-ICD), which had taken off from Zürich, Switzerland, on a service to Tel Aviv, Israel. In command

August 1969: it's nose shattered by an explosion, a TWA Boeing 707 rests on the ground at Damascus, Syria, after its passengers and crew escaped safely. (UPI/Corbis-Bettmann)

was Captain Karl Berlinger; his co-pilot was First Officer Armand Etienne. Seven minutes after its departure from Zürich-Kloten Airport, the flight crew reported that they were having trouble with the aircraft's cabin pressure and were returning to land. In a radio transmission shortly afterwards, the crew said they suspected an explosion in the 'aft compartment', and asked for immediate descent clearance. Also requested was fire-fighting equipment and a police investigation.

As the Coronado was returning to the airport, the crew announced 'Fire on board'; then, having noted that their navigational instruments were not functioning properly, they asked for a ground-controlled approach (GCA). An electrical power failure was then reported. Despite navigational assistance from the approach radar controller, the aircraft deviated to the west. In the final desperate moments of the flight, one of the pilots mentioned 'smoke on board', and exclaimed 'I can't see anything!'

Out of control, the jetliner made a left turn of about 180° before it slammed into a forest some 15 miles (25km) north-west of the airport and disintegrated in a fiery explosion at 13:34 local time. All 47 persons aboard (38 passengers and a crew of nine) perished. At the moment of impact, the Coronado was headed towards the east, descending at an angle of approximately 12° and banked to the left. Just before that, its indicated air speed was around 485mph (780kph). The meteorological conditions at the time and location of the crash consisted of rain, a low ceiling, with 3/8 cloud coverage at about 1,000ft (300m) and a solid overcast at approximately 2,000ft (600m), and visibility of no more than three miles (5km). The winds were out of the south at 15 to 20 knots.

An investigation of the disaster confirmed the crew's early suspicion of foul play. The remains of an explosive device, which used an altimeter mechanism, were found in the wreckage of the aircraft. The bomb had detonated in the rear cargo hold as the jet was at an estimated height of 14,000ft (4,300m). The resulting fire, which must have been sustained by such combustible material as the lining of the compartment, spread into the passenger cabin. Smoke from the blaze would have reduced

ABOVE: *A Swissair Convair 990A Coronado, identical to the aircraft destroyed in a suspected Arab terrorist bombing on 21 February 1970.* (Swissair)

BELOW: *Fallen trees and bits of debris mark the crash site of the Swissair jetliner in a forest near Zurich.* (Swiss Federal Aircraft Accident Investigation Bereau)

visibility to almost zero in both the cabin and the cockpit, and there was evidence that the flight crew and passengers alike had donned emergency oxygen masks before the crash.

There was no evidence that the mechanical controllability of the aircraft had been reduced by the blaze. It was positively determined that there had been no electrical failure prior to impact. The report of such from the crew must have resulted from a short-circuit and, in turn, a loss of synchronisation of the generators, after the flames spread to a bundle of wires in the cargo hold. The navigational difficulties mentioned by the crew must have been due to the effects of the blaze on the aircraft's antenna equipment, the receiving wire of which was routed near the compartment.

No arrests were ever made in connection with this terrorist act, but sabotage by Palestinian extremists was considered likely, possibly to avenge the conviction of three terrorists in a Swiss court two months earlier.

On the same day as the Swissair tragedy, and just two hours earlier, an Austrian Airlines twin-jet Caravelle 6R suffered an in-flight explosion while it was at an approximate height of 10,000ft (3,000m) after its departure from Frankfurt, (West) Germany, but the aircraft landed safely with no injuries among the 39 persons aboard. This blast was also caused by a bomb using an altimeter trigger, which had been placed in a package being mailed to Israel.

The Swiss government reacted to the terrorist attack by requiring visas for all Arabs coming into the country. Some airlines in Europe temporarily suspended mail and freight services to Israel, while at some major airports stronger security measures were adopted, even to the point of opening luggage and frisking passengers.

A British Overseas Airways Corporation Super VC-10 like the one hijacked to the Middle East with four other aircraft in September 1970. (British Aerospace)

14 MARCH 1970

AN explosive device detonated in the left power plant of a United Arab Airlines An-24B (SU-AOC) that was on a scheduled Egyptian domestic service from Alexandria to Cairo. Two passengers among the 15 persons aboard were injured in the blast when shrapnel entered the cabin, and the twin-engine turboprop was damaged beyond repair in a subsequent wheels-up landing carried out on the sand beside Runway 05 at Cairo airport.

21 JUNE 1970

AN Iran National Airlines Boeing 727 jet was commandeered by three hijackers, one of them a young boy, during a scheduled domestic service from Tehran to Abadan, and diverted to Baghdad, Iraq.

22 JUNE 1970

FLIGHT 119, a Pan American World Airways Boeing 707 jet carrying 143 persons en route from Beirut to Rome, was hijacked to Cairo by a lone gunman. The hijacker was arrested in Los Angeles, California, in 1973, and later sentenced to 15 years' imprisonment for interference with an aircraft crew.

12 JULY 1970

A Saudi Arabian Airlines Boeing 707 jet with about 140 persons aboard was commandeered during a scheduled service from Riyadh, Saudi Arabia, to Beirut, Lebanon. After landing at Damascus, Syria, the assailant fired a number of shots into the air before being detained by airport security personnel.

22 JULY 1970

A Boeing 727 jetliner flown by Olympic Airways of Greece and operating as Flight 255, on a service to Athens from Beirut with 61 persons aboard, was commandeered by six Arab guerrillas who demanded the release by the Greek government of seven other terrorists. Upon their release, the passengers were freed and the aircraft flew from Athens to Cairo.

6–12 SEPTEMBER 1970

PALESTINIAN guerrillas, who had already proven their ability to use air piracy as a tool of extortion, stunned the aviation community with this multiple hijacking and mass seizure of hostages. Five jet airliners, all but one of them on transatlantic routes with an ultimate destination of New York City, were targeted.

The first aircraft victimised was Pan American World Airways Flight 93, which had stopped at Amsterdam, The Netherlands, during a service originating at Brussels, Belgium. The wide-bodied Boeing 747-121 (N752PA) carried 153 passengers and 17 crew members. The three hijackers, who had been denied passage on El Al Israel Airlines for their suspicious appearance, were searched by the Pan American captain and service director for the same reason; unfortunately the men merely hid their pistols by their seats before being frisked.

Meanwhile, another US jet, operating as Trans World Airlines (TWA) Flight 741, was commandeered by two men less than 15

The hijacked Pan Am Boeing 747 was blown up almost immediately after its landing at Cairo, Egypt. (UPI/Corbis-Bettmann)

minutes after its departure from Frankfurt, (West) Germany. Aboard the Boeing Advanced 707-331B (N8715T) were 141 passengers and a crew of ten.

The third aircraft hijacked was Swissair Flight 100, a McDonnell Douglas DC-8 Series 53 (HB-IDD) carrying 143 passengers and 12 crew members, commandeered by two men after taking off from Zürich. Stopping briefly at Beirut, Lebanon, where several more guerrillas carrying explosives boarded, the 747 proceeded on to Cairo, where it landed before dawn on 7 September. It was then that the explosives were put to use; following a short landing and emergency evacuation, the aircraft was blown up, apparently a gesture aimed at humiliating the Egyptian government for its participation in peace talks with Israel. This was the first operational loss of a 747. Fortunately, however, there were no casualties.

The 707 and DC-8 landed at Dawson Field, located in Jordan, where, three days later, they were joined by another jetliner – British Overseas Airways Corporation (BOAC) Flight 775, a BAC Super VC-10 (G-ASGN) with 114 persons aboard, which had been hijacked by three assailants shortly after leaving Bahrain during a service to London from Bombay. (All of the aircraft were to have been landed at the desert airstrip, but the Pan American pilot had convinced his hijackers that the terrain could not support the massive 747.) A few days later, the American, British and Swiss jets were destroyed by explosives after all the hostages had been taken away. These were later released.

But the air pirates failed to capture their most prized target, an El Al Israel Airlines jet. Designated as Flight 219 on a service originating at Tel Aviv, the Boeing 707 had taken off on 6 September from Amsterdam with 158 persons aboard. As it flew over the county of Essex in England, the two hijackers, a man and a woman, made their move; but the pilot, Captain Uri Bar-Lev, immediately threw the aircraft into a left bank, knocking both off balance. The male hijacker was then attacked by a steward, and in the ensuing struggle both men were shot, the hijacker fatally.

The woman, Leila Khaled, who had hijacked a TWA jet in August 1969, was meanwhile attacked by a young American. With the help of other passengers, he managed to wrestle her to the floor and then tied her with string and a necktie. During the struggle, a hand grenade she had been holding dropped to the floor, its pin pulled, and the aircraft's occupants probably owe their lives to a faulty spring that prevented it from exploding. Subsequently, the 707 landed safely at London's Heathrow Airport. Leila Khaled was subsequently released in return for the release of hostages from the BOAC aircraft.

10 SEPTEMBER 1970

AN attempt to hijack an Egyptian airliner on a scheduled service to Cairo from Beirut ended in failure when security officers subdued the three assailants. The aircraft was believed to have been operated by United Arab Airlines.

12 SEPTEMBER 1970

AIRLINE security personnel subdued and arrested a lone hijacker after his attempt to commandeer an Egyptian airliner, believed to have been flown by United Arab Airlines, on a scheduled service to Cairo from Tripoli, Libya.

16 SEPTEMBER 1970

A United Arab Airlines An-24 turboprop, on a scheduled Egyptian domestic service from Luxor to Cairo with 46 persons aboard, was targeted for hijack, but the lone assailant was disarmed by a security guard aboard the airliner.

10 OCTOBER 1970

A steward was wounded in the hijacking of an Iran National Airlines Boeing 727 jet during a scheduled domestic service from Tehran to Abadan with 44 persons aboard. The aircraft landed at Baghdad, Iraq, where the three air pirates were taken into custody.

9 NOVEMBER 1970

NINE men, six of whom were identified as petty criminals being extradited for trial, commandeered an Iran National Airlines DC-3 on a scheduled service from Dubai to Bandar Abbas, Iran, with 22 persons aboard. After a refuelling stop, the airliner proceeded on without further incident to Baghdad.

10 NOVEMBER 1970

A Saudi Arabian Airlines DC-3 was commandeered by a lone hijacker while on a scheduled service to Riyadh from Amman, Jordan. It landed at Damascus, Syria.

22 AUGUST 1971

AN attempt to hijack to Israel a United Arab Airlines Il-18 turboprop that was on a scheduled service from Cairo, Egypt, to Amman, Jordan, ended when the lone assailant was overpowered by a security guard.

24 AUGUST 1971

AN Alia Royal Jordanian Airlines Boeing 707 jetliner was extensively damaged by a bomb that detonated in an aft lavatory as the aircraft was parked on the ground at Madrid, Spain. There were no injuries.

8 SEPTEMBER 1971

A lone assailant commandeered an Alia Royal Jordanian Airlines twin-jet Caravelle that was on a scheduled service from Beirut to Amman with 56 persons aboard. The hijacker was taken into custody after it landed at Banghazi, Libya.

16 SEPTEMBER 1971

SECURITY personnel thwarted an attempt to hijack to Iraq an Alia Royal Jordanian Airlines Caravelle jetliner that had been on a scheduled service from Beirut to Amman, and the lone assailant was later sentenced to death.

4 OCTOBER 1971

GUARDS overpowered the two would-be hijackers of an Alia Royal Jordanian Airlines twin-jet Caravelle, which was on the ground at Amman, Jordan.

16 OCTOBER 1971

AN Olympic Airways twin-engine turboprop YS-11A, carrying 64 persons on a scheduled Greek domestic service from Kalamata to Athens, was hijacked to Beirut by a passenger who claimed to have a bomb. He was arrested and later sentenced to prison for eight years and two months.

19 FEBRUARY 1972

AN attempt to hijack an Alia Royal Jordanian Airlines Caravelle jet during a scheduled service from Cairo to Amman failed when security personnel overpowered the lone assailant.

22 FEBRUARY 1972

A Lufthansa German Airlines Boeing 747 wide-bodied jetliner, designated as Flight 649 and carrying 189 persons on a service from New Delhi to Athens, was commandeered by five air pirates who demanded, and were paid, a ransom of $5 million. The assailants were taken into custody after the aircraft had landed at Aden, but they were later released by the South Yemen authorities.

8–9 MAY 1972

THE 'Black September' faction of the Palestine Liberation Organisation, which would gain notoriety with a brazen attack

A blood-splattered female terrorist is taken off a SABENA 707 at Lod Airport following the Israeli commando attack on 9 May 1972. (UPI/ Corbis-Bettmann)

on the 1972 Summer Olympic Games in Munich, achieved considerably less success in this hijacking of a Belgian jetliner that was tied to an extortion plot.

Among the passengers who boarded SABENA Flight 517 at Brussels airport were two Palestinian women whose responsibility it was to smuggle aboard the weapons to be used in the subsequent take-over. They hid firearms and explosives in cosmetic cases they carried and in special girdles that they wore. During a scheduled stop at Vienna, the second half of the guerrilla team, consisting of two men, went aboard. Shortly after the Boeing 707-329 had taken off on the next leg of its service to Tel Aviv with a total of 101 persons aboard, the hijackers made their move.

Though well-planned and executed so far, the scheme contained one serious flaw: the decision to proceed on to, and land at, the flight's planned destination, Tel Aviv's Lod Airport. It was there that the terrorists announced their demands to the Israeli government, threatening to blow up the 707 unless more than 300 imprisoned Arab guerrillas were released. Israel offered to free a smaller number of prisoners, the Israeli cabinet having meanwhile already planned a military response.

Commandos, disguised as mechanics who were to prepare the aircraft for its flight out of Israel, suddenly burst into the cabin, ordering the hostages to lie down as they opened fire on the hijackers.

Both men were killed, and an Israeli passenger who stood up in panic was mortally wounded; she succumbed later in hospital. The two female hijackers were captured, one of them, along with two other passengers, having been wounded. Both were sentenced to life imprisonment, although they would later be released as part of a prisoner exchange with Lebanon.

Later that month, in retaliation for the action taken by Israeli forces, three Japanese Red Army terrorists opened fire after disembarking from a flight at Lod Airport; 26 persons were killed and 70 wounded in the attack. The sole survivor among the terrorists was also given a life prison sentence.

16 AUGUST 1972

AN explosive device hidden in a record player detonated in the aft baggage compartment of a Tel Aviv-bound El Al Israel Airlines Boeing 707 jetliner shortly after it had taken off from Rome. There were no serious injuries among the 148 persons aboard the aircraft, which landed safely.

Two young English women had unwittingly brought aboard the record player, which had been given to them by two suspected terrorists.

22 AUGUST 1972

TWO men and a woman commandeered an Alyemda Democratic Yemen Airlines DC-6B that was carrying 61 persons and had been on a scheduled service from Beirut to Aden, diverting it to Banghazi, Libya.

29 OCTOBER 1972

LUFTHANSA German Airlines Flight 615, a Boeing 727 jet carrying 20 persons on a scheduled service from Beirut, Lebanon, to Ankara, Turkey, was hijacked by two assailants with the intention of freeing three Arabs imprisoned for their involvement in the murder of Israeli athletes at the

Olympic Games in Munich. The released prisoners boarded the aircraft at Zagreb, Yugoslavia, and it then flew on to Banghazi, Libya.

9 APRIL 1973

ARAB guerrillas in two jeeps opened fire on an Arkia Israel Inland Airlines Viscount 800 turboprop at the airport serving Nicosia, Cyprus, after the passengers had disembarked. A security guard then stepped out of the aircraft and fired back with a sub-machine gun, hitting one vehicle and killing one of its occupants. Sent out of control, the jeep then smashed into one of the Viscount's four engines, resulting in substantial damage to the aircraft. The surviving assailants were captured.

20–24 JULY 1973

IN the 87 hours between the take-over of a Japan Air Lines Boeing 747-246B (JA8109) and its fiery demise, the motive of its hijackers never became exactly clear. The five terrorists, who included both Palestinians and members of the leftist Japanese Red Army, had commandeered the wide-bodied jetliner, operating as Flight 404, shortly after its departure from Amsterdam bound for the US. There were a total of 145 persons aboard, including 22 crew members. Just before the hijacking, a female member of the guerrilla team was killed when a grenade went off in her hand. The chief purser was wounded, and the blast also cracked a window in the aircraft, necessitating flight at a lower altitude throughout the rest of the ordeal.

The air pirates first demanded the release by Israel of Kozo Okamoto, the sole survivor of the three-man team responsible for the massacre at Tel Aviv's Lod Airport 15 months earlier. They then demanded a ransom of $5 million. However, some of the passengers were told by one terrorist that the hijacking was a protest against Israeli, German, Japanese and American 'imperialism'. Whatever their reasoning, the surviving guerrillas and their hostages finally set down at Dubai, in the United Arab Emirates, the aircraft having been denied permission to land at Beirut and Damascus (the Lebanese and Syrian authorities perhaps fearful of Israeli retaliation). After 79 hours on the ground there, and following the release of two passengers, the 747 took off again. Libyan officials at first denied its entry into that country too, but after the terrorists had threatened to blow it up in the air the aircraft was cleared to land at Banghazi. Shortly after a successful evacuation, the 747 was set afire and ultimately destroyed.

A possible opportunity to stop the hijacking from ever taking place was thwarted when, despite receiving a tip-off from the Israeli secret service regarding possible terrorist activity, Amsterdam airport authorities failed to take any precautions.

Libya's leader, Colonel Muammar al-Qaddafi, later stated that the hijackers would face 'death, amputation of a foot or hand or prison' for their crime.

16 AUGUST 1973

A lone hijacker took over a Middle East Airlines Boeing 720B jetliner that was carrying 119 persons on a scheduled service from Banghazi to Beirut. After it had landed at Tel Aviv, security personnel boarded the Lebanese-registered aircraft and

Smoke rising from a Japan Air Lines 747 on 24 July 1973 marks the beginning of the blaze that ultimately destroyed the wide-bodied transport. (AP/Press Association Images)

captured the hijacker; he was subsequently committed to a psychiatric facility.

25 AUGUST 1973

AN Alyemda Democratic Yemen Airlines DC-6B was commandeered as it was on a scheduled flight from Taiz, Yemen, to Asmara, Ethiopia, with 16 persons aboard. The sole hijacker surrendered after the airliner landed in Kuwait and his security had been guaranteed.

25 NOVEMBER 1973

THREE terrorists hijacked KLM Royal Dutch Airlines Flight 861, a Boeing 747 wide-bodied jet carrying 288 persons on a service from Beirut to New Delhi, diverting it to Nicosia, Cyprus. The air pirates demanded the release of other terrorists jailed in Cyprus and also guarantees that the Dutch would not assist Israeli war efforts; they subsequently released their hostages when promised safe passage to an undisclosed country.

17–18 DECEMBER 1973

THIS hijacking to the Middle East began with a ghastly attack on the ground at Leonardo da Vinci Airport, serving Rome. One band of terrorists, who would later identify themselves as Palestinians, took automatic weapons out of their overnight bags while still in the terminal building and opened fire around 13:00 local time. They then ran out on to the flight field, where several commercial aircraft were parked, among them a Pan American World Airways Boeing Advanced 707-321B (N407PA), designated as Flight 110, which was preparing for departure on a service to Beirut with an ultimate destination of Tehran.

The open front cabin door was an invitation to attack for the terrorists, who tossed incendiary bombs into the jetliner, turning its fuselage into a fiery death chamber. Of the 69 persons aboard the 707, including ten crew members, 30 lost their lives in the holocaust, among them a stewardess and the wife of the pilot, Captain Andrew Erbeck, who was travelling as a passenger. Another 18 persons suffered injuries and the aircraft itself was destroyed.

Following the assault on the American transport the terrorists ran across the tarmac to a Lufthansa German Airlines Boeing 737 that had already been commandeered by a second band of guerrillas. They took with them ten hostages who had been rounded up inside or outside the terminal building. In resisting, an Italian customs agent was fatally shot in the back. The jet, carrying the guerrillas, their hostages and its crew, then took off on an odyssey that would not end until the following day.

During its 16 hours on the ground after landing at Athens airport, the hijackers demanded the release by the Greek government of two Palestinians being held in connection with a previous act of terrorism that had left four persons dead. When their demands were not met, the gunmen killed a hostage and threatened to crash the 737 into the centre of Athens. Greek officials rebuffed the extortion attempt, and the aircraft finally departed.

Refused landing clearance in both Lebanon and Cyprus, the jet finally set down in Damascus, where it was refuelled

The gutted hulk of a Pan American 707 after the terrorist attack at Rome airport in December 1973. (AP/Press Association Images)

before taking off again. Although Kuwait airport also denied a request to land, Lufthansa Captain Jo Kroese put the 737 down safely on a secondary runway. It was there that the terrorists surrendered, though they were released as ransom following the hijacking of a British Airways jet the following November.

3 MARCH 1974

A British Airways Super VC-10 (G-ASGO) was commandeered during a scheduled service to London from Beirut with 104 persons aboard. The jetliner landed at Schiphol Airport, serving Amsterdam, where the assailants started a fire using liquor and other flammable fluids that ultimately gutted the aircraft. The passengers and crew escaped safely. The two hijackers were sentenced by a Dutch court to five-year prison terms.

A Trans World Airlines Boeing 707, similar to the two aircraft targeted for destruction, one successfully, in a two-week period in 1974. (Trans World Airlines)

26 AUGUST 1974

TRANS World Airlines (TWA) Flight 841, a Boeing 707, had a close brush with disaster when a bomb set to destroy it malfunctioned. A fire apparently caused by the device was discovered in the aft baggage compartment after the jetliner had landed at Rome, on an international service from Athens. There were no injuries this time, but just two weeks later TWA Flight 841 would again be targeted by terrorists.

8 SEPTEMBER 1974

OPERATING as Flight 841, a Trans World Airlines Boeing Advanced 707-331B jetliner (N8734) was apparently blown up by a bomb over the Ionian Sea some 50 miles (80km) west of the Greek island of Kefallinia and approximately 200 miles (320km) west-north-west of Athens, where it had last stopped during a service originating at Tel Aviv, with an ultimate destination of New York City. All 88 persons aboard (79 passengers and nine crew members) were killed in the disaster, which occurred at around 09:40 local time.

The occupants of another aircraft saw the 707 pitch up, roll

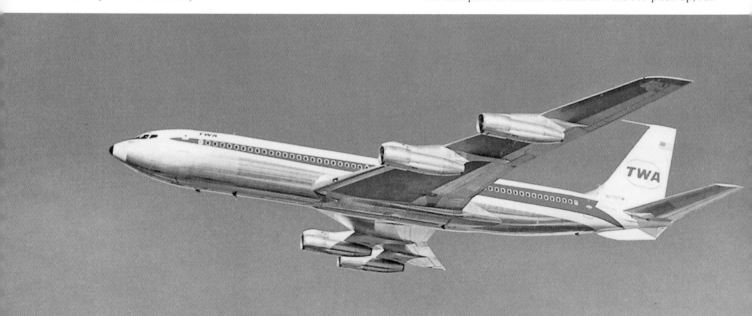

to the left and spiral down into the water, the depth of which was about 10,000ft (3,000m). Searchers recovered the bodies of 24 victims and a small amount of debris, and examination of the latter revealed indications of an in-flight explosion. It was later concluded that a high-explosive device had detonated in the aft cargo compartment of the aircraft at its cruising altitude of 28,000ft (8,500m). The blast probably buckled and damaged the cabin floor in such a manner that one or more of the elevator and rudder system cables were stretched and perhaps broken, which would have resulted in the violent pitch-up and yaw and led to a loss of control.

A Palestinian organisation claimed responsibility for the mass murder, with the device apparently having been put aboard at Athens (which was notorious for its lax security). Trans World Airlines subsequently instituted a policy of ensuring the inspection of all luggage going aboard its aircraft.

6 NOVEMBER 1974

THREE assailants commandeered an Alia Royal Jordanian Airlines twin-jet Caravelle that had been on a scheduled domestic service from Amman to Aqaba with 21 persons aboard. They requested political asylum when it landed at Banghazi, Libya.

22–28 NOVEMBER 1974

FOUR Palestinians commandeered British Airways (BA) Flight 870, a Super VC-10 carrying 93 persons, on the ground at Dubai airport, where the jetliner had landed during a service from London to Brunei, Borneo. The aircraft was diverted first to Tripoli, Libya, then on to Tunis, Tunisia. It was there, on the second day of the ensuing stand-off, that a German man was slain. There were threats to kill other passengers unless the demands of the hijackers were met. The authorities finally gave in, releasing 13 prisoners jailed in Egypt, and two others held in The Netherlands for hijacking another BA VC-10 the previous March; all 15 were flown to Tunis to join the others. They all surrendered on the seventh day of the siege, after their protection was assured by Tunisian officials.

13 JANUARY 1975

IN what was believed to been have a Middle East-spawned attack, a missile fired at an El Al Israel Airlines Boeing 707 jet struck a parked Jugoslovenski Aerotransport (JAT) twin-jet DC-9 at Orly Airport, serving Paris, leaving a hole in its fuselage. Three persons suffered minor injuries, including a steward. There were no casualties among the 148 persons aboard the 707, which was preparing to take off on a scheduled transatlantic service to New York City.

23 FEBRUARY 1975

A lone assailant hijacked a Yemen Airways DC-3 that was on a scheduled domestic service from Hodeida (Al Hudaydah) to San'a. He was captured when the transport landed at Qizon, Saudi Arabia. His subsequent sentence of death was later commuted to life imprisonment.

1 MARCH 1975

AN attempt to hijack an Iraqi Airways Boeing 737 jetliner, which had been on a scheduled domestic service from Mosul to Baghdad, ended in a gun-battle between the three air pirates and security guards on the ground at Tehran, Iran. One hijacker was killed in the shoot-out and the other two were captured. On 7 April these were executed by an Iranian firing squad.

1 JANUARY 1976

ALL 81 persons aboard (66 passengers and a crew of 15) perished when a Middle East Airlines Boeing 720B jetliner (OD-AFT) was sabotaged over north-eastern Saudi Arabia. Operating as Flight 438, the Lebanese aircraft crashed in the desert shortly before dawn, around 05:30 local time, some 25 miles (40km) north-west of Al Qaysumah during a service from Beirut, Lebanon, to Muscat, Oman, with an en-route stop at Dubai, United Arab Emirates. It was concluded that a high-explosive device must have detonated in its forward cargo compartment as the 720B was cruising at 37,000ft (11,300m), causing the disintegration of the aircraft.

27 JUNE–3 JULY 1976

ONE of the most daring rescue operations in modern times began with the hijack of Air France Flight 139, an A300B4 wide-bodied jet airliner, which was carrying 268 persons and had last stopped at Athens during a scheduled service from Tel Aviv to Paris.

After refuelling at Banghazi, Libya, the commandeered aircraft proceeded on to Entebbe, Uganda. About half of the hostages were released, but the hijackers held the French crew and all passengers with Israeli passports, demanding the release of more than 50 pro-Palestinian prisoners held captive in several countries.

Just before midnight on 3 July, Israeli commandos arrived by air and rescued the remaining hostages. In the assault at Entebbe airport, two passengers, one Israeli soldier, all four of the air pirates and at least 20 Ugandan soldiers were killed. In addition, an elderly woman who had earlier been taken to a hospital, and was thus left behind, was reportedly murdered. A number of Ugandan MiG jet fighters were destroyed, but the A300 was later retrieved.

6 JULY 1976

A Libyan Arab Airlines Boeing 727 jetliner, carrying 98 persons on a scheduled domestic service from Tripoli to Banghazi, was hijacked by a man armed with two knives and two replica pistols. He ordered it to Tunis, Tunisia, where it was denied entry, and then surrendered after it landed at Palma de Mallorca, Spain.

23 AUGUST 1976

THREE assailants commandeered an Egyptair twin-jet Boeing 737 that had been on a scheduled domestic flight from Cairo to Luxor with 102 persons aboard. The hijackers were overpowered by security forces after the aircraft had landed at its intended destination, and were subsequently sentenced to life imprisonment.

4 SEPTEMBER 1976

KLM Royal Dutch Airlines Flight 366, a DC-9 jet carrying 82 persons, was hijacked during a service to Amsterdam from Nice, France, and finally landed in Cyprus. There the three Arabic-speaking air pirates surrendered, and they were subsequently turned over to the Libyan embassy.

19 MARCH 1977

TWO assailants hijacked a Turkish Airlines (THY) Boeing 727 jet that had been on a scheduled domestic service from Diyarbakir to Ankara with 181 persons aboard. They surrendered when it landed at Beirut, Lebanon.

5 JUNE 1977

A Middle East Airlines Boeing 707 jet carrying 112 persons on a scheduled service from Beirut to Baghdad got hijacked by a lone assailant who demanded a ransom. He was overpowered after the Lebanese aircraft landed in Kuwait, and subsequently deported to Lebanon.

29 JUNE 1977

CARRYING 68 persons, a VC-10 jetliner operated by the Bahrain-based airline Gulf Air was hijacked during a scheduled flight from London to the United Arab Emirates and Oman. It was diverted to Oman, where the lone assailant was taken into custody.

8 JULY 1977

SIX men hijacked a Kuwait Airways Boeing 707 jet that had been on a scheduled service to Kuwait from Beirut, demanding the release of some 300 prisoners held in various Arab countries. The assailants surrendered after landing at Damascus, Syria.

A negotiator raises his arms to show hijackers aboard Lufthansa Flight 181 that he is unarmed, October 1977.
(AP/Press Association Images)

12 AUGUST 1977

A 19-year-old student hijacked an Air France A300 wide-bodied jet that had been on a scheduled service from Paris to Cairo with 242 persons aboard. He ordered it to Banghazi, Libya, which refused it permission to land, as did Athens. Low on fuel, the aircraft finally landed at Brindisi, Italy, where the hijacker was captured.

13–18 OCTOBER 1977

LUFTHANSA German Airlines Flight 181, a twin-jet Boeing 737-230QC with 91 persons aboard on a service to Frankfurt was commandeered shortly after it had taken off from Palma de Mallorca, Spain, ultimately landing at Mogadishu, Somalia. The hijackers were demanding the release of 11 terrorists held in Germany and two Palestinians held in Turkey. After two deadlines passed, they killed the pilot and tossed his body out of the aircraft.

Early on the morning of 18 October, in a raid reminiscent of the one by Israeli forces at Entebbe a year earlier, German commandos stormed the aircraft, killing three of the four air pirates and freeing the hostages; a stewardess, one of the soldiers, and the surviving terrorist were wounded. Upon hearing of the assault, three of the imprisoned terrorists whose release had been demanded committed suicide.

The alleged lone surviving hijacker, a Palestinian woman, moved to Norway in 1991, where she was arrested when her identity became known. She was subsequently extradited to Germany for prosecution, and would later be sentenced to 12 years' imprisonment.

18–19 FEBRUARY 1978

EGYPTIAN commandos sent to free hostages aboard a hijacked Cyprus Airways DC-8 Series 52 jetliner were themselves attacked by Cypriot troops at Larnaca Airport, serving Nicosia, the fighting erupting in darkness at around 20:30 local time. The botched raid saw 15 commandos killed, 17 wounded and an Egyptian Air Force C-130H turboprop transport destroyed. The DC-8 had been seized earlier by two Palestinian terrorists suspected in the killing of an Egyptian newspaper editor, and had been forced to take off carrying them, a dozen hostages taken earlier and four crew members. Denied permission to land in five Middle Eastern and African nations, the aircraft finally set down in Djibouti before returning to Cyprus. The hijackers surrendered to the Cypriot authorities at about the same time as the fighting broke out.

12 JANUARY 1979

A Tunis Air Boeing 727 jetliner carrying 75 persons on a scheduled domestic service from Tunis to Djerba Island was commandeered by three hijackers using two starter pistols, a non-functional shotgun and batteries strapped together to resemble explosives. Their demands were for the release of a Tunisian union leader and a former Tunisian foreign minister, but they surrendered and requested political asylum when the aircraft landed a second time at Tripoli, Libya.

16 JANUARY 1979

SIX men armed with pistols commandeered a Middle East Airlines Boeing 707 jet that was on a scheduled flight from Beirut, Lebanon, to Amman, Jordan, with 73 persons aboard. They demanded the release of a Muslim spiritual leader and wanted to hold a press conference; the latter was granted after the Lebanese aircraft had been denied entry by Cyprus and Turkey and returned to Beirut. The hijackers then surrendered.

24 AUGUST 1979

A lone gunman commandeered a Libyan Arab Airlines Boeing 727 jet carrying 59 persons on a scheduled domestic service from Banghazi to Tripoli, and, low on fuel, it landed at Larnaca, Cyprus. Although the hijacker requested political asylum there, he was turned over to a Libyan delegation and returned to his own country, where reportedly he was executed.

7 SEPTEMBER 1979

AN Alitalia DC-8 Super 62 jetliner on a scheduled service to Rome from Beirut, with 183 persons aboard, was hijacked by three assailants who intended to fly to Havana, Cuba, and there appeal to the Non-aligned Movement Summit Conference to help secure the release of their religious leader, last seen in Libya the previous year. The Italian aircraft landed in Rome, where the passengers were released, and ultimately reached Tehran, Iran, where the hijackers surrendered after explaining their objectives on national radio and television.

16–17 OCTOBER 1979

THREE Syrian men seized a Libyan Arab Airlines Fokker F.27 Friendship turboprop that had been on a scheduled Libyan domestic flight from Hon to Tripoli. They demanded to be flown to Switzerland, but then agreed to land on Malta, where they surrendered after giving a press conference on the second day of the hijacking.

14 JANUARY 1980

A twin-jet DC-9 of Italy's airline Alitalia, flying from Rome to Tunis and carrying 90 persons, was taken over by a lone assailant, who demanded the release of 25 prisoners by the Tunisian Government. Bad weather prevented it from landing at Tripoli, Libya, the hijacker's intended destination, and he later surrendered after it set down at Palermo, Sicily. Viewing the circumstances of the case, the Italian authorities elected not to prosecute him.

18 JANUARY 1980

AGAIN trying to locate the whereabouts of the spiritual leader who disappeared in Libya in 1978, a pistol-wielding assailant hijacked a Middle East Airlines Boeing 720B jet that was on a scheduled service to Cyprus from Beirut with 81 persons aboard. The Lebanese-registered aircraft returned to its point of origin, where the gunman gave a press conference as part of his agreement to surrender.

28 JANUARY 1980

FOR the third time in less than five months, a hijacking was committed with the objective of locating a religious leader missing in Libya. Another Middle East Airlines Boeing 720B jetliner, on a scheduled flight to Beirut from Baghdad, was commandeered by a knife-armed man who was accompanied by his wife and four children. He was allowed to read a speech after the aircraft landed at its intended destination, then taken into custody.

10 MARCH 1980

STILL another attempt to bring to the attention of the world the fate of a Muslim leader missing in Libya was this hijacking of a Middle East Airlines Boeing 707 jet, which had been on a scheduled service to Beirut from Amman. After he gave a press conference at Beirut, the assailant was taken into custody by the Lebanese authorities, who released him the following month.

24 JULY 1980

DURING a scheduled service to Kuwait from Beirut, a Kuwait Airways Boeing 737 jetliner was hijacked by two assailants armed with pistols, hand grenades and dynamite, who were demanding payment of a large debt they claimed was owed to them by a Kuwaiti businessman. Landing in Kuwait, Bahrain and Iran, the aircraft finally returned to its intended destination, where the two pilots escaped; the air pirates subsequently surrendered.

2–14 MARCH 1981

A Pakistan International Airlines Boeing 720B jetliner designated as Flight 32, on a domestic service from Karachi to Peshawar with 148 persons aboard, was hijacked to Kabul, Afghanistan. The air pirates demanded the release by Pakistan of 'political prisoners' and mortally wounded one passenger, who was still alive when tossed out of the aircraft. Pakistan gave in to their demands, and on the twelfth day of the siege, after flying to Damascus, the three hijackers surrendered; they subsequently went back to Afghanistan.

5 JULY 1981

AN explosive device detonated beneath a Trans Mediterranean Airways Boeing 707-327C jetliner (OD-AGW) that was parked overnight at the international airport serving Beirut. Several persons were injured and the Lebanese-registered transport was destroyed in the bombing, the responsibility for which was claimed by an anti-Iranian organisation.

31 AUGUST 1981

A bomb damaged beyond repair an unoccupied and unattended Middle East Airlines Boeing 720B (OD-AFR) on the ground at the international airport serving Beirut, where the Lebanese-registered jetliner had landed following a scheduled service from Tripoli, Libya. There were no casualties in the blast, which occurred in pre-dawn darkness.

13 OCTOBER 1981

TWO baggage-handlers were killed and eight persons wounded when two explosive devices hidden in luggage detonated while being off-loaded from an Air Malta twin-jet Boeing Advanced 737-2K2C, which had just landed at Cairo at the end of a scheduled service from Tripoli, Libya. The blast occurred shortly after 14:00 local time, after the 90 passengers had disembarked. The aircraft sustained substantial damage.

7–10 DECEMBER 1981

DURING a scheduled service from Zürich, Switzerland, to Tripoli, Libya, a Libyan Arab Airlines Boeing 727 jet was hijacked by three men, who forced it to Beirut. There they demanded the release of their spiritual leader, missing in Libya for three years. This odyssey took the aircraft from Beirut to Athens and Rome, then back to Beirut, where a mob forced the airport authorities to allow its landing.

One passenger was shot and wounded, and after flying to Tehran the 727 returned to Beirut, where the three assailants were taken into custody. Four others who had joined the original hijackers during two stops were not detained.

24 FEBRUARY 1982

FLIGHT 538, a Kuwait Airways Boeing 707 jetliner on a service to Kuwait from Tripoli, Libya, with 105 persons aboard, had landed at Beirut as scheduled, when two vehicles drove up to the aircraft. From these dashed a dozen assailants, who boarded the 707 and took it over. Once again, their actions were largely to publicise and bring about the repatriation of their spiritual leader who had vanished in Libya four years earlier. They surrendered after being told that an international delegation would press for a United Nations' inquiry into the disappearance.

27 MAY 1982

A lone gunman commandeered a Royal Air Maroc Boeing 737 jet airliner with 100 persons aboard after its departure from Athens, an en-route stop during a scheduled service originating at Damascus with an ultimate destination of Casablanca, Morocco. He made various demands for improved morality and the observance of strict Islamic faith in Morocco, and ordered the aircraft to be flown to Tunis, where he surrendered.

11 AUGUST 1982

AN explosive device detonated under a seat in the rear cabin of a Pan American World Airways Boeing 747-121 wide-bodied jetliner flying over the Pacific Ocean with 285 persons aboard, including a crew of 15. One passenger, a 16-year-old boy, was killed in the blast and 15 other persons suffered injuries.

Designated as Flight 830 and on a service from Tokyo to Honolulu, the aircraft was at an approximate height of 25,000ft (7,500m), and some 150 miles (250km) west of its destination, when the explosion occurred at around 09:00 local time. Despite a hole in its cabin floor and a rapid decompression the aircraft arrived safely. Captured and prosecuted in Greece, the Palestinian responsible for the act of sabotage was released from prison in 1996, but was subsequently returned to the US, where he was sentenced to an additional seven years in 2006.

20 JANUARY 1983

AN Alyemda Democratic Yemen Airlines Boeing 707 jet with 50 persons aboard was commandeered by three men during a scheduled service to Kuwait from Aden. During the hijacking, two passengers were wounded. After forcing the aircraft to land in Djibouti the hijackers surrendered, and subsequently received suspended prison sentences.

20–23 FEBRUARY 1983

TWO men hijacked a Libyan Arab Airlines Boeing 727 jet carrying 160 persons on a scheduled domestic service from Sabhah to Tripoli, forcing it to land at Valletta, Malta. They then demanded to be taken to Morocco, but the government of that country refused the aircraft entry. Negotiations went on for three days at Valletta, until the hijackers surrendered. Within months they would be allowed to return to Libya.

22 JUNE 1983

LEASED from the Romanian carrier TAROM, a Libyan Arab Airlines Boeing 707 jetliner was commandeered by two men during a scheduled flight to Tripoli from Athens. Low on fuel, the aircraft finally landed at Larnaca, Cyprus, where the hijackers were later sentenced to seven years' imprisonment for hijacking and possession of explosives.

6 JULY 1983

SIX men armed with pistols, sub-machine guns and explosives hijacked an Iran Air Boeing 747 wide-bodied jet that had been on a scheduled domestic service from Shiraz to Tehran with nearly 400 persons aboard. The aircraft landed in Kuwait, where about half of the passengers were released. Though the air pirates wanted to be flown to Iraq, they agreed to go instead to Paris, where they subsequently surrendered. They were sentenced to prison terms, which were suspended, and were then granted political asylum by the French government.

19 AUGUST 1983

SHORTLY before it was scheduled to depart for Damascus, a Syrian Arab Airlines Boeing 727-294 jet was severely damaged when a fire erupted in its cabin during the boarding process at Rome. All of the occupants were evacuated safely, and there were no injuries. A glass bottle that probably contained a flammable liquid was later found near the ignition point, indicating that this had been an act of arson.

27–31 AUGUST 1983

AN Air France Boeing 727 jet with 119 persons aboard was commandeered during a scheduled service to Paris from Vienna. After three stops, the aircraft landed safely at Tehran, Iran, where the four assailants surrendered after three days of negotiations.

23 SEPTEMBER 1983

DESIGNATED as Flight 771, a Boeing Advanced 737-2P6 jet transport (A40-BK) operated by Gulf Air, the joint airline of Bahrain, Oman, Qatar and the United Arab Emirates, crashed and burned in the desert about 30 miles (50km) north-east of Abu Dhabi as it was preparing to land at the city's airport, an en-route stop during a service from Karachi, Pakistan, to Manama, Bahrain. All 112 persons aboard (107 passengers and a crew of five) perished.

The disaster took place at about 15:30 local time. There were indications of an in-flight explosion having occurred in a cargo hold that resulted in a fire, which in turn must have produced toxic fumes that overcame the flight crew and led to a loss of control, and evidence pointed to an act of sabotage rather than an electrical or fuel blaze. Some articles of luggage assigned to the flight had been checked in by a ticket-holder who did not board the aircraft.

5 APRIL 1984

A Syrian national being returned to his country hijacked a Saudi Arabian Airlines L-1011 wide-bodied jet, operating as Flight 287 on a service to Damascus from Jiddah, Saudi Arabia. He was overpowered by the flight crew after the aircraft had landed for refuelling at Istanbul, and was taken into custody.

26–27 JUNE 1984

TWO men commandeered an Iran Air Boeing 727 jet airliner that was carrying 147 persons on a scheduled domestic service from Tehran to Bushehr, forcing it first to Qatar, where the passengers were released. It then landed at Cairo, where the hijackers surrendered and requested political asylum. They were instead sent to Iraq, and one of them later returned to Iran, where he was arrested and subsequently executed.

21 JULY 1984

A lone assailant carrying a Molotov cocktail tried to hijack a Middle East Airlines Boeing 707 jet with 148 persons aboard, demanding that it return to Abu Dhabi, from where it had taken off earlier on a scheduled service to Beirut. Because it was low on fuel, the Lebanese-registered aircraft proceeded on to its intended destination, where, after giving a press conference, the hijacker was taken into custody.

31 JULY–2 AUGUST 1984

THREE men armed with pistols, sub-machine guns and explosives hijacked Air France Flight 747, a Boeing Advanced 737-228 jet that was on a service to Paris from Frankfurt with 64 persons aboard. Stopping along the way in Switzerland, Lebanon and Cyprus, the aircraft landed at Tehran, where the air pirates allowed the passengers and crew to disembark before setting off explosives in the cockpit and surrendering.

7 AUGUST 1984

AN Iran Air A300 wide-bodied jetliner that had taken off earlier from Tehran, carrying 315 persons on a scheduled service to Jiddah, Saudi Arabia, got hijacked by two assailants using a knife and a fake bomb. Refused entry into French airspace, the aircraft landed at Rome, where the hijackers surrendered. One of them was sentenced to 7½ years' imprisonment for air piracy; the other was released.

28 AUGUST 1984

A man and a woman commandeered an Iran Air A300 wide-bodied jetliner that had been on a scheduled domestic service from Shiraz to Tehran with 206 persons aboard, diverting it to Baghdad, Iraq, where they requested and were granted political asylum. The aircraft would not be returned to the nation of registry until 1990.

An Airbus A300, three of which, operated by Iran Air, were targeted for hijack during a five-week period in 1984. (Airbus Industrie)

1 SEPTEMBER 1984

DOZENS were injured in the emergency evacuation of a Kuwait Airways Boeing 747 wide-bodied jetliner at Dubai, in the United Arab Emirates, after the detonation of an explosive device aboard the aircraft, which occurred while it was on the ground.

8 SEPTEMBER 1984

AN Iranian policeman and a family of four commandeered an Iran Air Boeing 727 jet that was carrying 123 persons on a scheduled domestic flight from Bandar Abbas to Tehran. They were promised asylum after it landed at an undisclosed military airfield in Iraq.

12 SEPTEMBER 1984

FOUR men failed in an attempt to hijack an Iran Air A300 wide-bodied jet that was on a scheduled domestic service from Tehran to Shiraz, two of them being wounded by security guards. The airliner landed safely at Isfahan, Iran.

15 SEPTEMBER 1984

AN Iraqi Airways Boeing 737 jetliner with 110 persons aboard on a scheduled flight to Baghdad from Larnaca, Cyprus, was targeted over Syria for an attempted hijacking by Iranian terrorists, but all three men were killed by security guards.

An American hostage, in white shirt, is removed from the hijacked Kuwaiti Airbus moments before being shot by terrorists, 7 December 1984. The man on the stairs with his arms raised is an Iranian negotiator. (AP/Press Association Images)

5 OCTOBER 1984

THE attempted hijacking of an Iran Air Boeing 727 jet, which had been on a scheduled domestic service from Meshed to Tehran, ended with the lone armed assailant being overpowered and captured by security personnel.

5 NOVEMBER 1984

A Saudi Arabian Airlines L-1011 wide-bodied jetliner was diverted to Tehran by two assailants during a scheduled service from London to Riyadh, Saudi Arabia, with 131 persons aboard. Their demands included improved treatment of North Yemenis in Saudi Arabia and aid to the government of North Yemen. However, they were overpowered by other passengers and captured by Iranian troops. One of the hijackers was later sentenced to 12 years' imprisonment in Iran, while the second was freed.

4–9 DECEMBER 1984

A Kuwait Airways Airbus A310, operating as Flight 221 and carrying 166 persons, was commandeered after it took off from Dubai, an en-route stop during a service from Kuwait to Karachi, Pakistan. The wide-bodied jetliner was forced to land at Tehran, where about one-third of the hostages were released. On the same day, however, an American passenger was killed in a scuffle and his body was tossed out on to the runway.

The four hijackers were demanding the release of 21 prisoners held in Kuwait, three of whom were under sentence of death. On the second day of the siege, they reported planting explosives in the A310 and said they would detonate

them if their demands were not met. About 30 more hostages were freed before another American passenger was slain, his body also being thrown out of the aircraft.

Over the next couple of days, more hostages were released. Then, shortly before midnight local time on 9 December, the hijackers asked that a generator be attached to the aircraft and also requested a doctor and two cleaning men. Disguised as the latter, Iranian security men entered the jetliner and subsequently overpowered the assailants, freeing the remaining seven hostages.

It was reported that the hijackers were never prosecuted by Iran, and apparently fled to another country. The damaged aircraft was returned to Kuwait nearly a year-and-a-half after the incident.

5 JANUARY 1985

AN attempt to hijack an Iran Aseman Airlines F.27 Friendship turboprop was made during a scheduled domestic service from Khorrambad to Tehran, but the three assailants were overpowered by security guards.

11 JANUARY 1985

SECURITY personnel foiled the attempted hijacking of an Iran Air twin-jet Boeing 737 that had been on a scheduled domestic flight from Tehran to Kerman, with the lone assailant being captured.

7 FEBRUARY 1985

FOUR men drove up to and forcefully boarded a Cyprus Airways Boeing 707 jet at the international airport serving Beirut, beginning a five-hour siege aboard the aircraft. They surrendered on being told that their demand for the release of two Lebanese being held in Cyprus would be considered.

23 FEBRUARY 1985

A Middle East hijacking not related to either politics or religion was the commandeering of a Lebanese jetliner on the ground at Beirut international airport by an apparently disgruntled security guard. Designated as Flight 203, the Middle East Airlines Boeing 707-320C had been on a service to Paris and London.

After shots were fired by the hijacker, the 104 passengers and crew members began to evacuate via the emergency chutes, but the aircraft started to move. One passenger, a 65-year-old man, was killed as he tried to exit and was slammed to the ground by engine exhaust. Another 13 persons suffered injuries.

Following the fatality, which occurred at about 11:30 local time, the 707 took off and proceeded to Larnaca, Cyprus, where it landed twice before returning to Beirut. As negotiators waited, the hijacker was apparently spirited away.

9 MARCH 1985

A bomb exploded in the baggage compartment of an Alia Royal Jordanian Airlines L-1011 TriStar wide-bodied jetliner on the ground at Dubai, United Arab Emirates, where it had landed during a scheduled international service from Karachi to Amman. There were no casualties or significant damage to the aircraft, and although no organisation claimed responsibility, an 18-year-old Arab was arrested in connection with the bombing.

17 MARCH 1985

A lone assailant commandeered a Saudi Arabian Airlines Boeing 737 jet that had been on a scheduled domestic service from Jiddah to Riyadh with 97 persons aboard. The aircraft landed for refuelling at Dhahran, where the hijacker released all his hostages except the captain and first officer. Security forces subsequently boarded, and killed him when he tossed a hand grenade. There were no other casualties, and the blast caused only minor damage.

1 APRIL 1985

A lone assailant who claimed to have a gun and a bomb commandeered a Middle East Airlines Boeing 707 jetliner that was on a scheduled service from Beirut, Lebanon, to Jiddah, Saudi Arabia, carrying 76 persons. He first demanded financial aid for the anti-Israel resistance movement in southern Lebanon, but was persuaded to give himself up and was taken into custody after the Lebanese aircraft had landed at its intended destination.

4 APRIL 1985

THERE were no injuries when a rocket was fired into an Alia Royal Jordanian Airlines Boeing 727 jet that was taxiing to take off at Athens on a scheduled service to Amman, Jordan. The device failed to explode, and the aircraft sustained only minor damage.

11–12 JUNE 1985

ALIA Royal Jordanian Airlines Flight 402, a Boeing Advanced 727-2D3 (JY-AFW), was seized by five assailants shortly before it was to have taken off from Beirut, bound for Amman, Jordan, with 74 persons aboard. The jetliner flew to Cyprus, but was denied entry into either Tunisia or Syria and eventually returned to Beirut, where the hijackers released their hostages and then blew up the aircraft. Prosecuted in the US due to the fact that some of the passengers on Flight 402 had been American, the leader of the hijackers would later be sentenced to 30 years' imprisonment.

12 JUNE 1985

IN response to the Alia hijacking a day earlier, a lone assailant armed with a hand grenade commandeered a Middle East Airlines Boeing 707 before the Lebanese jetliner, on a scheduled service from Beirut, landed at Larnaca, Cyprus. He soon gave himself up and was returned to Amman, Jordan.

14–30 JUNE 1985

THE United States found itself bogged down in a major Middle East crisis with the hijacking of Trans World Airlines (TWA) Flight 847. Operating on a service from Athens to Rome and carrying 153 persons, the Boeing Advanced 727-231 jetliner was commandeered by two terrorists while in Italian airspace.

Landing at Beirut, the hijackers demanded the release by Israel of some 800 prisoners, mostly Lebanese (31 were ultimately freed). After 19 hostages, consisting of 17 women and two children, had been released, the 727 proceeded on to Algiers, Algeria, where it was first refused, then granted, permission to land. Here another 22 passengers were freed.

Early the next morning the aircraft returned to Beirut, the crew pleading that the airport lights be turned on in the darkness. It was here that US Navy diver Robert Stethem, a passenger, was murdered. More hijackers then boarded the 727 and additional food was brought aboard before the jetliner departed again, returning to Algiers, where the terrorists threatened to kill Greek passengers unless the authorities released a 21-year-old Lebanese arrested in Athens, who was accused of planning this hijacking. Facing more killings and the destruction of the aircraft, the Greek government complied, and the suspected terrorist was flown to Algiers.

Two days into the hijacking, more hostages were let go, and the jetliner returned a final time to Beirut. The remaining 39 hostages were taken into Beirut city, where 29 of them signed a letter to President Ronald Reagan asking him to negotiate their release and refrain from direct military action. All were freed 17 days later, and the aircraft was subsequently retrieved.

A US Navy ship commissioned ten years after the TWA incident was named in honour of Petty Officer Stethem. The terrorist convicted of his murder served nearly 20 years for the crime, and was released from a German prison in 2005.

5 AUGUST 1985

AN attempt by two men to hijack an Iran Air Boeing 727 jet during a scheduled domestic service from Tehran to Bandar Abbas ended with one being killed by security guards and the other arrested.

2 NOVEMBER 1985

A lone assailant was overpowered by security guards after trying to hijack an Iran Air Boeing 707 jet that had been on a scheduled domestic service from Bandar Abbas to Tehran.

Some of the passengers are released from a hijacked TWA jetliner following its landing at Beirut, Lebanon in June 1985. (Reuters/Corbis-Bettmann)

23–24 NOVEMBER 1985

THIS hijacking was believed to have been carried out by a pro-Libyan Palestinian splinter group hostile to Egyptian President Hosni Mubarak and Palestine Liberation Organisation (PLO) Chairman Yasser Arafat. An EgyptAir Boeing Advanced 737-266 (SU-AYH) jet airliner, operating as Flight 648 and carrying 98 persons, including a crew of six and four security guards, was commandeered while en route to Cairo from Athens. The aircraft was diverted to Malta, landing at Luqa International Airport, serving Valletta.

Under the cover of darkness on 24 November, and prompted by the shooting of passengers after a siege lasting more than 20 hours, Egyptian commandos who had arrived earlier on a C-130 transport stormed the aircraft at around 21:00 local time, blasting their way in through a cargo door. The hijackers immediately lobbed hand grenades into the cabin, touching off a fire that gutted the interior of the aircraft. Among the 62 persons killed were a guard shot in an exchange of gunfire while the 737 was still airborne, two female passengers slain after it had landed, and two of the three hijackers. Nearly all the survivors suffered injuries, although 11 women who had been released before the assault escaped unscathed. A Maltese court of inquiry would later blame virtually all of the fatalities on the commandos.

Despite being sentenced to 25 years in prison on Malta, the surviving terrorist was released in February 1993. But five months later he was arrested by FBI agents in Lagos, Nigeria, and following a trial in the US was sentenced to life imprisonment for the killing of two of the passengers who lost their lives on Flight 648.

25 NOVEMBER 1985

APPARENTLY trying to flee their country, two passengers hijacked an Iran Aseman Airlines Rockwell Commander 500S that had been on a domestic commuter service with

an ultimate destination of Bandar Abbas. The twin-engine aeroplane landed in Dubai, United Arab Emirates, and both assailants were returned to Iran the following day.

23 DECEMBER 1985

ONE hijacker was killed by security personnel during an attempt to take over an Iran Air jetliner that was on a scheduled domestic service from Sirri Island to Shiraz.

27 DECEMBER 1985

A reportedly 'mentally unbalanced' man armed with a razor blade tried to hijack a Saudi Arabian Airlines Boeing 747 wide-bodied jet that was on a scheduled service to Riyadh from Karachi, Pakistan, with 213 persons aboard. He was subdued and arrested by a security guard.

2 APRIL 1986

IN apparent retaliation for the sinking of two Libyan gunboats in a skirmish with US Navy forces in the Gulf of Sidra the previous week, a Trans World Airlines Boeing Advanced 727-231 jetliner, designated as Flight 840, was bombed over southern Greece, in the vicinity of Corinth. Four passengers among the 121 persons aboard, including a mother, daughter and baby granddaughter, lost their lives when the explosive device detonated on the cabin floor between the tenth and eleventh rows. Nine other passengers suffered injuries. The blast occurred at around 14:30 local time, as the aircraft was at an approximate height of 15,000ft (4,500m) and descending for a landing at Athens airport, an en-route stop during a service that had originated (as a Boeing 747) in Los Angeles, California, with an ultimate destination of Cairo. The 727 got down safely despite a hole measuring about 4ft by 5ft by (1.2m by 1.5m) in the right side of its fuselage, just forward of the wing. Those killed had been ejected from the aircraft by the blast, and all but one died in their fall to earth.

The primary suspect in this act of sabotage was a Lebanese woman who was thought to have planted the bomb the previous day during a flight from Cairo to Athens, but further investigation revealed the charge to be unfounded.

17 APRIL 1986

A vigilant security guard probably made the difference in this attempt to sabotage an El Al Israel Airlines Boeing 747 wide-bodied jetliner, designated as Flight 16, which was to have departed from London's Heathrow Airport, bound for Tel Aviv, with 375 persons aboard. A plastic explosive had been placed in a suitcase being carried by an Irish woman, believed to have been an innocent dupe. A man who planned to take another airline was subsequently arrested; he was later sentenced to 45 years' imprisonment.

The bomb had passed through the airport's security X-ray but was caught by the guard, who thought the bag seemed unusually heavy. The British government said it had evidence that the Syrian ambassador had been involved in the plot and as a result broke off diplomatic relations with Syria.

26 JUNE 1986

A bomb hidden in a suitcase exploded on the conveyor belt before it was to have been loaded on to a Tel Aviv-bound El Al Israel Airlines Boeing 747 wide-bodied jet at Barajas Airport,

ABOVE: *The intact but gutted hulk of an Egyptair Boeing 737 at Malta is examined following the disastrous commando attack of 24 November 1985.* (UPI/Corbis-Bettmann)

BELOW: *The large hole in the fuselage of a TWA Boeing 727 through which four victims were ejected in a terrorist bombing over Greece on 2 April 1986.* (AP/Press Association Images)

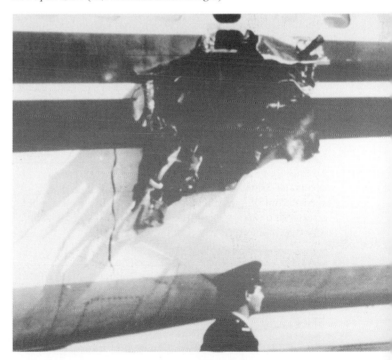

serving Madrid, and 13 persons were injured, three seriously. The perpetrator of the mass-injury attack, which could have been a mass-fatality catastrophe had it succeeded, was later sentenced to nearly 50 years' imprisonment in Spain.

5 JULY 1986

A lone assailant who wanted to go to Israel attempted to hijack a Sudan Airways Boeing 707 jetliner that had been on a scheduled international service from Khartoum, Sudan, to Baghdad, Iraq, but he was overpowered and captured.

5 SEPTEMBER 1986

NO aerial hijacking, this seizure of Pan American World Airways Flight 73 occurred after the Boeing 747-121 had landed at Karachi, Pakistan. Dressed as security guards and armed with automatic weapons, the four terrorists responsible, who were identified as Palestinians, boarded the wide-bodied jetliner via stairs after it had arrived from Bombay, one segment of a service originating at Frankfurt, (West) Germany, with an ultimate destination of New York City. They were demanding the release of detainees held by Cyprus.

The three-member flight crew escaped after hearing shots; the other 386 persons aboard, including the cabin crew, were held hostage as negotiations continued all day. They finally broke off in the evening, around 21:00 local time, when a power generator ran out of fuel oil, causing the failure of the aircraft's lights, air conditioning and radio. About an hour later, after they had herded their hostages into the centre part of the cabin, the terrorists opened fire and detonated hand grenades.

Among the 21 persons killed were a stewardess and an American passenger who had been shot and thrown out on the tarmac earlier. More than 100 others were wounded or otherwise injured. The hijackers were captured alive following the 17-hour ordeal and, along with a fifth assailant who had not actually been aboard the aircraft, were subsequently condemned to death, though the sentences would later be commuted. One of them was brought to the US in 2001 after serving 14 years' imprisonment in Pakistan, and three years later was sentenced to a prison term of 160 years. According to press reports, the other four were freed in 2008. Although the 747 sustained some damage in the attack, it remained structurally intact.

Despite earlier suspicions, Libyan involvement was suspected in the hijacking of Flight 73.

10 NOVEMBER 1986

AN attempt to commandeer an Iran Air Airbus A300 wide-bodied jet airliner that had been on a scheduled domestic service from Tehran to Tabriz ended when security personnel arrested the two assailants, identified as a man and a woman, reportedly 'before carrying out their plot'.

25 DECEMBER 1986

THIS hijacking that had a catastrophic ending involved an Iraqi Airways twin-jet Boeing Advanced 737-270C (YI-AGJ), designated as Flight 163 and en route from Baghdad to Amman, Jordan, with 107 persons aboard, including 15 crew members and a security guard.

After the aircraft had entered Saudi Arabian airspace,

cruising at a height of 28,000ft (8,500m), one of the two hijackers took out a hand grenade and forced his way into the cockpit. Shooting between the terrorists and the guard then erupted as the 737 was at an altitude of about 15,000ft (4,500m), and at least two hand grenades exploded, one near the cockpit, which injured the flight crew.

The jetliner diverted and attempted an emergency landing at Arar, Saudi Arabia, located some 250 miles (400km) south-west of Baghdad, under partial control and engine thrust; however, at about 12:30 local time it slammed into the desert and burst into flames, about half-a-mile (0.8km) from the airstrip. The final death-toll was 67, including three members of the crew, the fatalities resulting from the explosions, gunfire or the crash; all of the survivors were injured, 31 seriously.

Four underground groups claimed responsibility for the attempted hijacking, but none said they had planned to destroy the aircraft.

5 MAY 1987

AN Iran Air A300 wide-bodied jet airliner that had been on a scheduled domestic service from Shiraz to Tehran was targeted for hijack by a 'mentally-disturbed' assailant, but he was overpowered by security personnel.

24 JULY 1987

IN an apparent attempt to compel the release by (West) Germany of the Lebanese convicted of killing US Navy Petty Officer Robert Stethem in a TWA hijacking two years earlier, a lone assailant commandeered Air Afrique Flight 56, a DC-10 wide-bodied jet airliner en route from Rome to Paris, one segment of a service originating at Brazzaville, Congo, with 163 persons aboard.

After the aircraft had landed for refuelling at Cointrin Airport, serving Geneva, the hijacker shot dead a male passenger; immediately thereafter security personnel stormed the aircraft and captured the gunman. About 30 persons were injured in the emergency evacuation of the DC-10, and the hijacker was later sentenced to a life prison term.

28 DECEMBER 1987

AN attempt was made by 'counter-revolutionary' members of the outlawed Mujahedin Khala Organisation (MKO) to hijack an Iran Air A300 wide-bodied jet that had been on a scheduled domestic flight from Tehran to Mashhad, but the plot was foiled by Islamic Revolutionary Guard Corps (IRGC) personnel.

5–20 APRIL 1988

A Kuwait Airways Boeing 747 wide-bodied jetliner, designated as Flight 422 and carrying 112 persons, was commandeered by a group of as many as nine Lebanon-based, pro-Iranian hijackers during a service to Kuwait from Bangkok, Thailand. The aircraft first landed at Mashhad, Iran, where more terrorists boarded with additional weapons, and then proceeded to Beirut, Lebanon, where it was denied entry. It was there that a merciless ground controller engaged in a tense radio conversation with the Kuwait Airways pilot and one of the hijackers. In a plea for assistance, the pilot stated, 'They are forcing me to land ... we request to land ... if we don't they will shoot us ... I have a gun pointed at me ... please help me

... I don't have fuel ... please give permission to land'; but the controller only responded, 'It is not our problem ... the fuel in Lebanon is polluted ... go away.'

The aircraft finally diverted to Larnaca, on Cyprus, where it was allowed to land after permission was initially refused. Only after two Kuwaiti passengers were murdered over a period of three days was a request to refuel granted. The 747 then flew on to Algiers, landing at Houari Boumedienne Airport. The hijackers, who were demanding the release by Kuwait of 17 prisoners convicted of bombings there five years earlier, now reported that they had rigged the aircraft with explosives.

Over the next 15 days, the hijackers freed a number of other hostages, releasing the last few after Kuwait commuted the death sentences on three of the prisoners they held. The assailants themselves were ushered out of Algiers, and were believed to have returned to Lebanon through Syria.

21 DECEMBER 1988

THE worst case of aerial sabotage believed spawned in the Middle East was the destruction of Pan American World Airways Flight 103 over Scotland. A little more than two weeks earlier, an anonymous telephone message had been received at the American Embassy in Helsinki, Finland, warning that a sabotage attempt would be made against a Pan Am aircraft flying between Frankfurt, (West) Germany, and the US. This threat was made known to various American embassies, but not to the general public. The rationale behind this policy was simple: why give the perpetrators the publicity they were seeking and in the process do financial harm to the airline industry? Besides, some authorities had dismissed the threat as a hoax.

Flight 103 did originate at Frankfurt, stopping at London, where the continuing passengers were joined by nearly 200 others and transferred from a Boeing 727 to a wide-bodied 747-121 (N739PA). Baggage, already theoretically security-checked at Frankfurt, was also transferred, without further screening.

Having taken off almost half-an-hour late from Heathrow Airport, the jetliner was cruising in darkness at flight level 310 on its way to New York City when it was ripped apart by an explosion shortly after 19:00 local time. A high-explosive substance, believed to have been Semtex that was probably hidden in the shell of a radio-cassette player, had detonated in a suitcase placed in the left side of the forward cargo hold. The blast had caused catastrophic structural failure almost immediately, with the cockpit and forward fuselage section separating from the rest of the aircraft. As the main portion fell to earth, all four engines broke away, and the rear fuselage disintegrated.

Wreckage and victims were scattered over a wide area, but the greatest damage was done in the Sherwood Crescent residential district of Lockerbie, where the wings and centre fuselage section ploughed a huge crater and exploded in flames. All 259 persons aboard perished, including 16 crew members. Eleven more lost their lives on the ground, five others were injured, and more than 20 houses destroyed outright or damaged beyond repair.

Initially the bombing was believed to have been carried out with financial assistance from the government of Iran, this in retaliation for the accidental downing of an Iran Air Airbus A300 by a US warship the previous July. In late 1991, however,

The body of a second hostage killed at Cyprus airport is dropped from Kuwait Airways Flight 422, April 1988. (AP/Press Association Images)

the US Justice Department announced its indictment of two alleged Libyan intelligence agents in connection with the Pan Am tragedy. They were suspected of planting the bomb in a suitcase that was carried from Malta to Germany on an Air Malta flight, then interlined on to Flight 103. The mass murder was probably intended to avenge the US bombing of Tripoli, Libya, which, in the 'eye-for-an-eye' world of Middle East hostilities, had itself been in retaliation for a terrorist attack.

A major break in the case occurred in April 1999, when Libya turned over two of its agents suspected in the Pan Am bombing to Scottish authorities for trial in The Netherlands. One of the men, Abdul Basset Mohmed Ali al-Megrahi, was convicted in January 2001 and sentenced to prison, which, for the families of the victims, must have represented at least a sense of justice for their tremendous loss. (Terminally ill with cancer, he was granted a 'compassionate' release in August 2009 and returned to Libya.) This was accompanied by an agreement in which Libya would

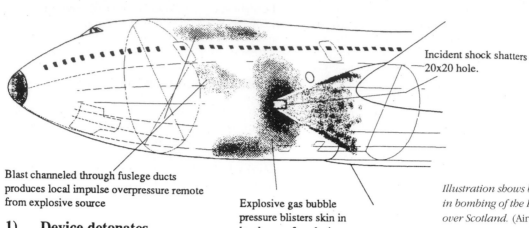

Blast channeled through fuslege ducts
produces local impulse overpressure remote
from explosive source

1)   Device detonates

Explosive gas bubble
pressure blisters skin in
local area of explosion

Incident shock shatters
20x20 hole.

*Illustration shows blast sequence
in bombing of the Pan Am 747
over Scotland.* (Air Accidents
Investigation Board)

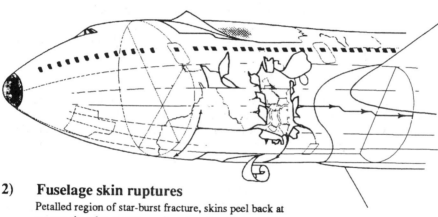

2)   Fuselage skin ruptures
Petalled region of star-burst fracture, skins peel back at
remote sites due to pressure impulses, long fractures propa-
gate away from petalled region driven by cabin pressurisation
loading.

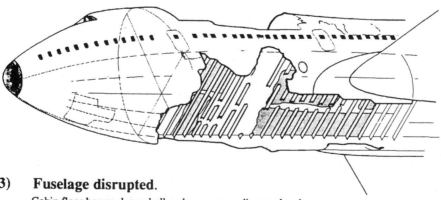

3)   Fuselage disrupted.
Cabin floor beams, lower hull and crown area disrupted and
structure separated; nose section retained by window belts only.

financially compensate the survivors to the amount of nearly $3 billion US. Continued negotiations with Libya would ultimately result in the restoration of diplomatic and economic relations with the Western World, and the repudiation of weapons of mass destruction by a country that was once considered a sponsor of terrorism – a bright spot in the tragic legacy of Flight 103.

23 AUGUST 1989

IN an attempted hijacking apparently intended to draw attention to the Palestinian situation, an Air France A300 wide-bodied jet with 115 persons aboard was targeted by a lone assailant during a scheduled service from Paris to Algiers. Denied clearance to land at three cities, the aircraft finally set down at its intended destination, where the hijacker, who had been carrying a fake explosive device, surrendered.

19 SEPTEMBER 1989

FRANCE'S backing of elements opposed to the government of Libya and/or its support of anti-Syrian forces in Lebanon were thought to have been the motivating factors behind this, the worst case of sabotage involving a European airline. Operating as Flight 772, the Union de Transports Aériens (UTA) McDonnell Douglas DC-10 Series 30 (N54629) had taken off from N'Djamena, Chad, bound for Paris, the second segment of a service originating at Brazzaville, Congo. About an hour later, or around 14:00 local time, the wide-bodied jet was shattered by an explosion while cruising at 35,000ft (10,500m) over Niger, in the vicinity of Bilma. Wreckage was scattered over an area of nearly 50 square miles (80km²) in the Ténéré Desert, a region of the Sahara. All 170 persons aboard, including a crew of 14, perished.

Traces of the explosive pentharite were identified, confirming that the aircraft had been destroyed by a bomb. The device was apparently hidden in a suitcase and detonated in the forward baggage compartment, resulting in the in-flight disintegration of the DC-10. The Libyan/Syrian connection was revealed by a subsequent French investigation. The bomb may have been carried aboard by a Congolese man who boarded the flight at Brazzaville and then disembarked at N'Djamena, or, perhaps, by an unsuspecting passenger who thought he was transporting 'secret' documents.

A review of security practices in effect at Brazzaville at the time revealed that they had not been in accordance with the standards of the International Civil Aviation Organisation (ICAO), such measures later being tightened. With specific regard to the UTA bombing, six Libyans were convicted of the crime in absentia by a French court in 1999; and as part of its improvement in relations with the Western World at this time, Libya agreed to financially compensate the families of those killed on Flight 772, paying $1 million US for each victim. The Libyan government also accepted responsibility for the actions of 'its officials', without acknowledging any direct involvement in the bombing.

23 NOVEMBER 1989

A loose wire probably prevented the detonation of a bomb in the luggage compartment of a Saudi Arabian Airlines Boeing 747 wide-bodied jet, operating as Flight 367, which had been over the Arabian Sea on a service from Islamabad, Pakistan, to Riyadh, Saudi Arabia, with 339 persons aboard. Ten passengers were subsequently arrested for their part in what appears to have been a suicide mission.

31 DECEMBER 1989

SECURITY personnel foiled an attempt to hijack Saudi Arabian Airlines Flight 450, a Boeing 747 wide-bodied jetliner on a domestic service from Jiddah to Riyadh. It began when a 'mentally unstable' assailant handed a letter to a stewardess demanding to be taken to Cyprus, and ended with his capture.

A French UTA DC-10 Series 30, identical to the transport blown up over the Sahara in September 1989. (Douglas Green)

25 JANUARY 1990

FOUR men armed with pistols and hand grenades attempted to hijack Iran Air Flight 133, a Boeing 727 jet airliner that had been on a domestic service from Shiraz to Bandar Abbas, but all were killed in a shoot-out with security guards.

2 AUGUST 1990

A British Airways Boeing 747-136 wide-bodied jetliner (G-AWND), operating as Flight 149 on a service from London to Kuala Lumpur, Malaysia, was caught up in the Iraqi invasion after landing in Kuwait, an en-route stop.

During the attack on Kuwait airport an emergency evacuation of the aircraft was carried out by the 385 persons aboard. All of the passengers and crew members were held hostage by Iraq, only being eventually released in December. The 747 was blown up by retreating Iraqi forces the following February.

15–16 AUGUST 1993

A KLM Royal Dutch Airlines Boeing 737-400 jet, designated as Flight 110 and carrying 135 persons, was commandeered during an international service to Amsterdam from Tunis, Tunisia, and landed at Dusseldorf, Germany. Early in the morning of the second day, police entered the aircraft and arrested the lone hijacker, who had demanded the release of the prime suspect being held in connection with the bombing of the World Trade Center in New York City earlier in the year, a terrorist attack related to Middle East issues.

27 AUGUST 1993

AN Alyemda-Air Yemen Boeing 737 jetliner on a scheduled domestic service from Ar Riyan to Al Ghaydah was commandeered by a lone assailant armed with a pistol and a hand grenade, and who wanted to be flown to Kuwait or Oman. The pilot convinced him that the aircraft had to land at its intended destination for refuelling, and on its arrival police stormed the 737 and arrested the hijacker.

22 OCTOBER 1993

A passenger believed to be psychologically disturbed hijacked an EgyptAir jetliner that was on a scheduled international service from Cairo to San'a, Yemen, but he was overpowered by security personnel. He was prosecuted in Yemen.

29 NOVEMBER 1993

AN Iran Air twin-engine turboprop Fokker F.27 with 38 persons aboard, on a scheduled domestic flight from Gachsaran to Ahvaz, was reportedly commandeered by a couple who were accompanied by their five children. They asked for political asylum when the airliner landed at Basra, Iraq.

7–8 MARCH 1994

A Saudi Arabian Airlines Airbus A300 wide-bodied jetliner with 139 persons aboard on a scheduled flight from Jiddah, Saudi Arabia, to Addis Ababa, Ethiopia, was diverted to Nairobi, Kenya, where the principal assailant, who had been carrying a toy gun, was wounded and captured on the second day of the hijacking. Two female accomplices were also arrested.

6 APRIL 1994

A lone gunman hijacked a Sudan Airways Boeing 737 jetliner that had been on a scheduled domestic flight from Khartoum to Dongola with 99 persons aboard. The aircraft subsequently landed at Luxor, Egypt, where the young Sudanese hijacker, speaking of the deteriorating political and economic conditions in his country, asked for political asylum.

25 APRIL 1994

AN Ethiopian Airlines Boeing 757 jetliner, carrying 148 persons on a scheduled international service from Jiddah to Addis Ababa, was commandeered by a lone assailant just before a planned stop in Djibouti. The authorities there refused to allow it to land, and the 757 proceeded to San'a, Yemen. After a hostage situation involving the aircraft's two pilots, the hijacker – an Ethiopian Army officer who originally wanted to be taken to London – surrendered to the Yemeni authorities.

19 JULY 1994

IN what was suspected to be a Middle East-spawned act of terrorism, a Compañia Alas Chiricanas SA EMBRAER EMB-110P1 Bandeirante (HP-1202AC) plummeted into a wooded area about five miles (8km) from Colón, Panama, from where it had taken off shortly before, on a scheduled domestic service to Panama City, as Flight 901. Including a crew of three, all 21 persons aboard were killed in the crash, which occurred at about 18:30 local time.

Metal fragments that were believed to have come from an explosive device were found in the wreckage and in some of the victims' bodies. A number of passengers on the flight were reported to have been Jewish businessmen, and a Lebanese group was said to have 'hinted' that they were responsible for the attack.

14 SEPTEMBER 1994

AN Alyemda–Yemen Airlines Boeing 737 jetliner with 80 persons aboard was targeted for hijack during a scheduled domestic service from Aden to San'a, but security personnel overpowered and captured the lone assailant.

11 DECEMBER 1994

WHILE at a height of 30,000ft (9,000m) over the Pacific Ocean, a bomb exploded under a seat in the cabin of a Philippine Airlines Boeing 747-283B Combi wide-bodied jet, which was operating as Flight 434 on a service from Manila, in the Philippines, to Tokyo. The passenger occupying that seat was killed and ten of the other 292 persons aboard suffered injuries in the blast, which occurred at around 11:30 local time some 185 miles (300km) east of Okinawa, where the aircraft landed safely. Hidden in a life-jacket beneath the seat, the bomb had apparently been planted during the segment of the trip that originated at Cebu, the Philippines.

This was reportedly the 'trial run' for a planned attempt to blow up a dozen US airliners on transpacific flights, designed to punish the United States for its continued support of Israel. The principal saboteur in the plot and a co-conspirator were later convicted in an American court, with both receiving life prison sentences.

24–26 DECEMBER 1994

FLIGHT 8969, an Air France Airbus A300B2 wide-bodied jet bound for Paris and carrying 289 persons, was seized by four Muslim extremists dressed as members of the cleaning staff as it prepared to take off at Houari Boumedienne Airport, serving Algiers, Algeria. Three passengers were killed there and 63 hostages released before the aircraft proceeded on to Marignane Airport, located near Marseille, France. Here, on the third day of the ordeal, shortly after 17:00 local time, or around dusk, an elite unit of French commandos stormed the aircraft, killing all four hijackers. Injured in the raid were ten other passengers, three members of the crew and nine commandos.

19 SEPTEMBER 1995

A Kish Air Boeing 707 jet airliner carrying 174 persons on an Iranian domestic charter service from Tehran to the island of Kish was commandeered by a steward, landing safely at a military base in southern Israel. Although Iran requested extradition of the assailant, Israel refused to hand him over, but also declined to grant him political asylum. He was indicted the following month on the charge of air piracy, and would serve approximately half of an eight-year prison sentence.

26 DECEMBER 1995

AN Ethiopian who was being returned to his country against his will tried to hijack a Saudi Arabian Airlines jetliner, probably a wide-bodied Airbus A300, which had been on a scheduled international service from Jiddah, Saudi Arabia, to Addis Ababa, Ethiopia, with 185 persons aboard. The aircraft landed at Asmara, Eritrea, where the assailant was arrested without incident.

27 MARCH 1996

AN EgyptAir Airbus A320 jetliner, designated as Flight 104 and on a domestic service from Luxor to Cairo with 152 persons aboard, got hijacked by a man and his son and nephew, who demanded to meet with world leaders. The aircraft landed at a military airbase at Martubah, Libya, where the three assailants surrendered, later to be returned to Egypt for prosecution.

26 JULY 1996

A Lebanese man, who would testify at his subsequent trial that he was fleeing his Palestinian homeland because of the poverty there, commandeered Flight 6621 of the Spanish carrier Iberia, a DC-10 wide-bodied jet airliner en route from Madrid to Havana, Cuba, with 232 persons aboard. After the aircraft had landed at Miami, Florida, the assailant, who had claimed to have a bomb that was actually a fake, surrendered to the American authorities.

A few days later, two Palestinians were arrested in Germany and admitted helping to plot the hijacking, but said they backed out of the plan after arriving in Madrid from Beirut. The one who actually committed the crime would the following year be sentenced by a US Federal Court to 20 years' imprisonment for air piracy.

Bullet holes in the windscreen of an Air France Airbus illustrate the violent end of a hijacking at Marseille airport on 26 December 1994. (AP/Press Association Images)

26–27 AUGUST 1996

SIX Iraqi men, who said they feared for their lives under their nation's brutal government, commandeered a Sudan Airways Airbus A310 wide-bodied jetliner, operating as Flight 150 on a service from Khartoum to Amman, Jordan. Following a refuelling stop on Cyprus, the aircraft, carrying 203 persons, landed safely at Stansted Airport near London about an hour before dawn on the second day of the hijacking, where the assailants – armed with knives and imitation explosives – surrendered to British security forces.

Their reasons for committing the crime apparently factored in the relatively light prison terms given them in England for air piracy, with sentences ranging from five to nine years, the latter being given to the leader of the group. However, the sentences were overturned in 1998 and all six men were freed.

3 SEPTEMBER 1996

A Tu-154 jet airliner operated by the Bulgarian carrier Hemus Air and carrying 158 persons was commandeered by a Palestinian during an international charter service from Beirut to Varna, Bulgaria. Claiming to have a bomb, the hijacker demanded to be taken to Norway, and released the passengers in exchange for fuel after the aircraft had landed at its intended destination. After setting down at the airport serving the Norwegian town of Gardermoen, located near Oslo, the assailant, whose bomb was a fake, surrendered and requested political asylum.

6 OCTOBER 1997

AN Iran Air jetliner, designated as Flight 257 and on a domestic service from Tehran to Bandar Abbas, was targeted for hijack by a lone gunman demanding to be taken to Iraq, and who reportedly shot at the aircraft's cockpit area and wounded a security guard. The assailant himself was wounded by another guard, then taken into custody after the aircraft reached its intended destination.

24–25 FEBRUARY 1998

A lone hijacker who said he was protesting the oppression of Muslims in Algeria commandeered a Turkish Airlines (THY) Avro RJ100 jet that was on a scheduled domestic service from Adana to Ankara with 68 persons aboard, demanding to be taken to Iran. After he was persuaded by the pilot to allow the aircraft to land at the Turkish city of Diyarbakir, the assailant was overpowered by other passengers on the second day of the hijacking and captured. He would later be sentenced to a prison term of eight years and four months.

19 OCTOBER 1999

OPERATING as Flight 838 and bound for Cairo, an EgyptAir Boeing 737 jetliner was commandeered shortly after its departure from Istanbul, Turkey, by a lone assailant who was being deported back to Egypt, and who threatened the crew with a 'knife' which turned out to be a ballpoint pen. The aircraft subsequently landed at Hamburg, Germany, where police apprehended the hijacker.

26 OCTOBER 1999

A lone assailant described as a 'lunatic', who claimed to have a bomb and 'pretended' to be a member of the opposition terrorist group MEK/MKO, tried to hijack to France an Iran Air jetliner that had been on a scheduled domestic service from Tehran to Orumyeh, Azarbayjan-e Ghari. He was overpowered and arrested by security personnel, and no explosives were found.

31 OCTOBER 1999

THE destination of this flight of terror accounts for its placement in this particular chapter. However, the crash of EgyptAir Flight 990 was not related to Middle East politics, religious strife or any other civil conflict. The circumstances of the catastrophe should be unsettling to air travellers anywhere, as it seemed to confirm the frightening prospect – suspected in two previous airline crashes – of a pilot intentionally crashing an aircraft loaded with passengers.

Having arrived the previous evening from Los Angeles, California, the Boeing 767-366ER wide-bodied jet airliner (SU-GAP) was on the ground at New York's John F. Kennedy International Airport for about 90 minutes before taking off on the second leg of its trip, to Cairo. During the stop-over there was a change in the flight crew, one member of whom was 59-year-old Relief First Officer Gameel el-Batouty. Less than half an hour after its departure, the 767 entered a descent from its cruising altitude of 33,000ft (10,000m) and plunged into the North Atlantic some 60 miles (100km) south-south-east of Nantucket Island, Massachusetts. All 217 persons aboard (203 passengers and 14 crew members) perished. The crash occurred in early morning darkness, around 01:50 local time, and in visual meteorological conditions.

Located in two debris fields some 1,200ft (350m) apart and at an approximate depth of 230ft (70m), about 70 per cent of the wreckage that comprised SU-GAP was recovered, as was a sufficient amount of human remains to allow for the identification of more than two-thirds of the victims. The recovery of the aircraft's flight data (FDR) and cockpit voice (CVR) recorders proved useful in reconstructing the final minutes of Flight 990 in an investigation conducted by the by the US National Transportation Safety Board (NTSB). The decision by the nation of registry to have the inquiry carried out by the American agency might be regarded as regrettable, however, as the findings of the report did not have the blessing of the Egyptian authorities.

It was determined that while the 767 was climbing to its cruising height, Relief First Officer el-Batouty suggested that he relieve the command co-pilot, indicating that he wanted to fly this portion of the trip, even though this changeover would normally have taken place three to four hours into the flight. After some initial resistance, the regular co-pilot agreed to relinquish his seat, and would subsequently leave the flight deck. Minutes later, after the jet had levelled off, Captain Ahmed al-Habashy also left the cockpit, in his case to use the lavatory. The next sequence of events would be revealed by the CVR tape. While alone in the flight deck, First Officer el-Batouty was heard to say to himself 'I rely on God.' This phase would be repeated another ten times. During this period, as indicated by FDR data, the autopilot was disconnected, and seconds later the thrust levers were retarded from cruise power to idle setting.

Almost simultaneous with the reduction of thrust, the jet pitched down and began to descend. Shortly thereafter, Captain al-Habashy returned to the flight deck, asking several times 'What's happening?' His queries elicited no response from the co-pilot, who continued to repeat 'I rely on God.' At an approximate height of 30,000ft (9,000m), the 767 exceeded its maximum operating velocity of nearly 90 per cent the speed of sound, as indicated by the activation of the master warning alarm in the cockpit.

With the aircraft descending in a nose-down angle of around 40°, the elevator surfaces began moving to reduced nose-down deflections, and subsequently the FDR recorded a 'split' elevator condition, with the left control surface in a nose-up position and the right one nose-down. In a rapid sequence of events, the engine start lever switches were moved to the cut-off position and the thrust levers from the idle position to full power, and the aircraft's speed brakes were then deployed. The switching off of the power plants prompted the captain to ask 'What is this? What is this?' In the final seconds of the recording, the captain said 'Get away in the engines', followed by 'Shut the engines.' This order evoked the only response from the co-pilot during the entire sequence: 'It's shut.' Until the recording ended, the captain was repeatedly heard to say to the first officer 'Pull with me!'

Based on wreckage distribution and primary data from ground radar, the initial descent had been arrested at around 15,000ft (4,500m), after which the 767 climbed to about 25,000ft (7,500m) and its heading changed from 80° to 140° before the final plunge into the ocean.

The NTSB found no evidence of any major technical failure that could have led to the descent, ruling that the behaviour of the aircraft must have resulted from the intentional actions of the first officer. And the absence of a disconnect warning tone on the CVR was consistent with the autopilot being manually disconnected through activation of the switch mounted on the control yoke. It was similarly concluded that the thrust lever movements from the cruise power setting to idle also resulted from deliberate manipulation by the co-pilot. It was noted in the investigative report that the redundant elevator system of the 767 had been designed so that pilots could overcome dual failures by allowing the operable surface to respond to any nose-up control input. The Board noted that the behaviour of the first officer was not consistent with a pilot encountering an unexpected or uncommanded flight condition, nor a first officer trying to assist the captain in trying to save the aircraft. Instead, the 'split' elevator condition noted during the descent must have resulted from the two men applying opposing control inputs, with the first officer holding his control wheel in the forward position and the captain pulling back on his. It was further observed that under the circumstances Captain al-Habashy would probably not have suspected that the actions of the co-pilot were directly responsible for the descent. The efforts of the former could have been complicated by a loss of electrically-powered displays after the engines were shut down. The intention and motivation of First Officer el-Batouty could not be explained by the Board. However, an alleged act of 'sexual misconduct' on his part in the US had reportedly led to disciplinary action by the airline, and the executive responsible for the reprimand was a passenger on Flight 990 at the time of the crash.

In a rebuttal of the NTSB report, and in defence of one of its pilots, EgyptAir asserted that recovered wreckage pointed

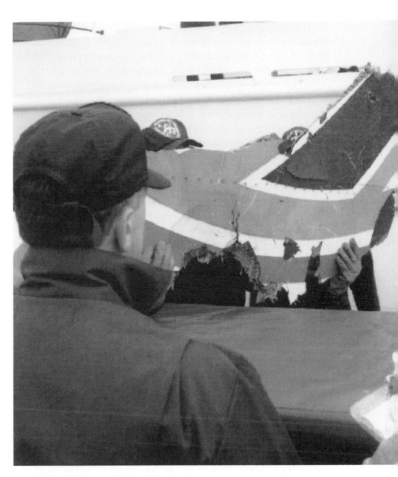

One of the fragments of the EgyptAir Boeing 767 is brought ashore after the suspected intentional crash of the jet (US Coast Guard)

to a sheared pin and an improperly positioned bias spring in one of the three power control actuator (PCA) units on the right elevator. According to the airline, malfunctions of two PCA units on the starboard elevator may have precipitated the dive, and the 'split' observed in the FDR data could have been a manifestation of the loss of the starboard elevator. Such a mechanical failure proved to be inconsistent with simulator tests conducted by Boeing, although the carrier complained that the technical analysis submitted by the manufacturer contained 'many inaccuracies, omissions and selective use of evidence'.

Coming less than three weeks after the intentional crash by of an aircraft by an Air Botswana pilot (see page 186), the EgyptAir disaster would, for once, force the aviation industry to face up to and develop methods to deal with this disturbing threat to aircraft safety.

24–31 DECEMBER 1999

IN the closing days of the 1990s, commercial aviation would experience one of the longest, in terms of duration, and most arduous aircraft hijackings of the 20th century, which involved Indian Airlines Flight 814. The A300 wide-bodied jetliner, carrying 189 persons and bound for New Delhi, was commandeered about half an hour after its departure from Kathmandu, Nepal, by five Islamic militants who may have been supported by others in Pakistan.

The aircraft was not allowed to land at Lahore, Pakistan, and, low on fuel, instead set down at Amritsar, India. It was around this time that one passenger was killed, apparently after failing to follow the instructions of the air pirates. Subsequently the A300 did proceed to Lahore, where the hijackers demanded, and were given, food, water and fuel. Proceeding on to Afghanistan, it was unable to land at the airport serving Kabul due to the absence of night-time facilities. After being denied permission to land in both Oman and Dubai, in the United Arab Emirates, it finally set down at an airbase in the latter country, where 27 passengers were released in exchange for more food and fuel. Two days into the hijacking, it flew on to Afghanistan, landing at Kandahar. Initially the assailants demanded the release by India of the imprisoned Pakistani leader of a Kashmiri separatist group, 35 other Islamic guerrillas, the body of a slain separatist and $200 million.

Eventually India agreed to a scaled-down demand, releasing three guerrillas in exchange for the aircraft and its other occupants. The five hijackers were allowed free passage out of Afghanistan by the ruling Taliban government, escaping prosecution for their crime. One of them was reportedly killed carrying out another terrorist attack in 2002.

6–10 FEBRUARY 2000

THE odyssey of Ariana Afghan Airlines Flight 805 began with the disappearance of the Boeing 727-200 jetliner and its 166 passengers and crew members during a domestic service within Afghanistan, from Kabul to Mazar-e-Sharif. But the aircraft had in fact been hijacked by a dozen men, and while a search for it was under way the 727 landed at Tashkent, Uzbekistan. It would subsequently land at Aktyubinsk, Kazakhstan, and at Moscow, with a small number of its occupants being released at each location, before finally setting down early on the morning of the second day at Stansted Airport near London.

Negotiations continued for the next three days, with nine more hostages being released. The hijackers became violent on the third day, after the escape of the flight crew, reportedly beating some of the remaining occupants. The next day, however, the remaining passengers and crew members were released, and the assailants surrendered. More than half of those who had been aboard the aircraft requested asylum, leading to the arrest of 19 of them on suspicion that they too had been involved in the seizure of the 727. The convictions of the nine found guilty were subsequently overturned, and after being released from prison in 2003 they were allowed to stay in the United Kingdom. Of those who returned to Afghanistan, three crew members were charged with complicity in the hijacking but escaped to Pakistan.

11 MAY 2000

AN EgyptAir A321 jet airliner, designated as Flight 233 and on a domestic service from Cairo to Aswan, was targeted for hijack by a lone assailant who claimed to have a bomb (which turned out to be a jar of hair gel) and wanted to be taken to Afghanistan. The aircraft landed at its intended destination after crew members overpowered the would-be hijacker, who would later be charged with air piracy.

5 JULY 2000

ARMED with a pistol and a grenade, a Syrian passenger who did not want to return home but instead to be taken to Germany or another European country tried to hijack a Royal Jordanian Airlines A320 jetliner, operating as Flight 435 on an international service to Damascus from Amman, Jordan, with 96 persons aboard. After firing two shots and pulling out the pin of the grenade he was shot and killed by an air marshal. The grenade then rolled down the aisle of the aircraft and detonated under a seat, injuring 15 other persons. Only slightly damaged, the A320 returned safely to its point of departure.

The weapons used were apparently hidden in a cassette recorder that was carried aboard by the assailants' two children, although none of his family members were believed to have been directly involved in the attempted hijacking.

14 SEPTEMBER 2000

A lone assailant armed with a 'large' knife commandeered a Qatar Airways A300 wide-bodied jetliner, designated as Flight 404 and on a service from Doha, Qatar, to Amman, Jordan, with 142 persons aboard, demanding that the aircraft land in Saudi Arabia. The hijacker got his way in that regard, in that the aircraft carried out a landing at the airport serving Ha'il, where he surrendered. Though he would later be sentenced to five years' imprisonment in Qatar, in a sense he got his way again, in that his original intention was probably to avoid being returned to his own country, Iraq, and, having previously been denied political asylum by the Qatari authorities, lacked the documentation to remain in Jordan.

24 SEPTEMBER 2000

AN Iran Air Fokker 100 jet airliner on a scheduled domestic service from Shiraz to Tehran was targeted for hijack by a lone assailant who demanded to be taken to France. He was overpowered by security personnel after trying to start a fire aboard the aircraft, which landed safely at the city of Esfahan.

28 SEPTEMBER 2000

HAVING nearly completed a scheduled international service from San'a, Yemen, a Royal Jordanian Airlines A310 wide-bodied jetliner with 199 persons aboard was preparing to land at Amman when the pilot received a note in which a passenger announced his intention to hijack the aircraft. After it had landed at its intended destination, the would-be hijacker, an Iraqi, surrendered. His attempted disruption of the flight was believed to have been motivated by a desire to seek asylum in Jordan.

14 OCTOBER 2000

OPERATING as Flight 115, a Saudi Arabian Airlines Boeing 777 wide-bodied jetliner carrying 117 persons and en route to London from Jiddah, Saudi Arabia, was commandeered over the Mediterranean by two armed assailants. The hijackers, who were identified as security personnel employed at Jiddah airport, demanded that the aircraft proceed to Syria, where it was refused permission to land. Late in the evening it finally landed at Baghdad, where the two would remain in custody after the release of the aircraft and its other occupants.

11–12 NOVEMBER 2000

FLIGHT 838 of Russia's Vnukovo Airlines, a Tu-154 jetliner with 59 persons aboard on a domestic service to Moscow from Makhachkala, in the breakaway republic of Dagestan, was hijacked to Israel by a lone assailant who was described as a 'deranged loner' and expressed scorn for individuals of Asian descent. The aircraft landed in Azerbaijan for refuelling, but was denied permission to land at Tel Aviv by the Israeli authorities over concerns that it might be blown up over the city. Around dawn on the second day of the seizure, it landed at Uvda Air Base, located in Israel's Negev Desert, near Elat, where the hijacker surrendered.

13 NOVEMBER 2000

A group of hijackers who were believed to have been members of four families and were demanding transport to the US tried to seize an Ariatour Yak-40 jet airliner, designated as Flight 1492 and on a domestic Iranian service from Ahvaz, Khuzestan, to Bandar-e 'Abbas, Hormozgan. The hijacking was disrupted by Iranian Revolutionary Guard Corps (IRGC) personnel, and ended after the aircraft landed at its intended destination and its two pilots escaped from the cockpit. Two IRGC personnel, a cabin attendant and five of the assailants were injured in the incident, which also led to the arrest of 23 persons. The death sentences of at least two of the assailants were suspended in 2005.

17 DECEMBER 2000

AFTER it was determined that he was carrying a false passport and therefore could travel no farther, an Egyptian passenger grabbed a butter knife and an oxygen bottle and commandeered a Pakistan International Airlines Boeing 747 wide-bodied jetliner, designated as Flight 787 and on a service originating at Karachi, during a stop-over at Dubai, United Arab Emirates. He demanded to be flown to London, which was the planned destination of the aircraft, but was overpowered and captured by a security official. Authorities in the UAE declined to press charges, and the man, his wife and two children were sent back to Pakistan.

23 JANUARY 2001

AN Iraqi citizen who claimed to be carrying explosives commandeered Yemen Airways (Yemenia) Flight 448, a Boeing 727 jetliner with 91 persons aboard on a domestic service within Yemen, from San'a to Al Hudaydah, and demanded to be taken to Baghdad. The flight crew persuaded him to allow the aircraft to land for refuelling at Djibouti, where he was overpowered after a scuffle in which the flight engineer was shot and slightly wounded. Extradited back to Yemen, the hijacker was later sentenced to 15 years in prison.

27 JANUARY 2001

A knife-wielding passenger, who later said he wanted to go to Australia, tried to hijack Flight 153 of the Middle East consortium Gulf Air, an Airbus A340 wide-bodied jet airliner carrying 213 persons on an international service from Bangkok to Abu Dhabi. The assailant, an Iraqi, was overpowered by two other passengers and a crew member, and was taken into custody after the aircraft had landed at its intended destination.

15–16 MARCH 2001

THIS hijacking was not directly related to the Middle East, but the commandeered aircraft ended up there anyway. Three ethnic Chechens protesting about the war in their country and demanding the release of a relative held in a Russian prison

A Saudi Arabian Airlines Boeing 777 of the type hijacked to Iraq during an international flight. (Douglas Green)

seized a Tu-154 jetliner operated by Russia's Vnukovo Airlines and on a non-scheduled international service to Moscow from Istanbul, with 174 persons aboard. During the take-over the aircraft momentarily plunged out of control, and one man was wounded.

Having been denied permission to land in either Egypt or Syria, the Tu-154 finally set down at Al Madinah (Medina), in Saudi Arabia. A number of occupants were released or escaped before Saudi special forces stormed the aircraft around noon on the second day of the hijacking. One of the assailants, another passenger and a cabin attendant were killed and several others suffered injuries. A request by Russia for the return of the two surviving hijackers was refused by Saudi Arabia.

22 DECEMBER 2001

THIS bungled act of Middle East-spawned terrorism that had potentially disastrous consequences involved American Airlines Flight 63, a Boeing 767 wide-bodied jetliner en route from Paris to Miami, Florida, with 197 persons aboard. One of the passengers was a would-be suicide bomber who had hidden an explosive substance in his shoes.

As the aircraft was cruising over the North Atlantic Ocean at 30,000ft (9,000m), a crew member observed the assailant trying to ignite the explosive and he was immediately overpowered by the crew and other passengers. Two cabin attendants were slightly injured in the altercation. The 767 diverted safely to Boston, Massachusetts, landing around 13:00 local time, and the assailant was taken into custody. It was theorised that moisture, possibly from perspiration, had hampered his ability to light the detonating fuses that were also in the shoes. Had they exploded, the shoes reportedly contained enough explosive to blow a hole in the fuselage of the jetliner. Significantly, the passenger was sitting near the aircraft's fuel tank area.

Richard Reid, a 28-year-old British citizen suspected of having ties to the al-Qaeda terrorist organisation, would admit to being an 'enemy' of the United States when, the following October, he pleaded guilty in a US Federal Court to trying to destroy the airliner. He was later sentenced to life imprisonment. This attempted act of terror led to the policy in the US airline industry of having passengers remove their shoes for inspection before boarding a flight.

15 OCTOBER 2002

AN armed passenger tried to seize Saudi Arabian Airlines Flight 450, an A300 wide-bodied jetliner carrying 204 persons on an international service to Jiddah, Saudi Arabia, from Khartoum, Sudan. However, the assailant was overpowered by security personnel and the aircraft returned safely to its point of departure.

17 NOVEMBER 2002

A passenger who reportedly had a dispute with a cabin attendant and was wielding a pocket knife rushed the cockpit of an El Al Israel Airlines Boeing 757 jetliner, operating as Flight 581 on an international service from Tel Aviv to Istanbul with 168 persons aboard. He was quickly taken down by security personnel. The assailant, who later denied any intention to hijack the aircraft, would later be prosecuted in Turkey.

13 SEPTEMBER 2003

A drunken Lebanese passenger threatened to hijack a Royal Jordanian Airlines jetliner, probably an Airbus, designated as Flight 184 and on an international service from Amman, Jordan, to Kuala Lumpur, Malaysia. He was detained after the aircraft landed at Bangkok, Thailand, and was subsequently returned to Lebanon for prosecution.

17 APRIL 2004

DEMANDING to be taken to Geneva, Switzerland, a Kuwaiti passenger tried to enter the cockpit of a Qatar Airways Airbus jetliner, operating as Flight 553 and en route from Casablanca, Morocco, to Doha, Qatar, with 92 persons aboard. The aircraft diverted to Cairo, where the assailant was taken into custody. He was later diagnosed as suffering from 'some form' of mental disturbance.

8 SEPTEMBER 2005

THIS bomb hoax that had fatal consequences involved a Saudi Arabian Airlines Boeing 747 wide-bodied jetliner, which had been on a scheduled international service from Sri Lanka to Jiddah, Saudi Arabia, with 420 persons aboard. In response to the threat the pilot returned to Bandaranaike International Airport, serving Colombo, and in a stampede occurring during the evacuation of the aircraft a woman passenger was killed and 62 other persons suffered injuries.

10 AUGUST 2006

A lone assailant who apparently wanted to be taken to Israel was overpowered by other passengers and a member of the flight crew after trying to enter the cockpit of a Qatar Airways Airbus wide-bodied jetliner that had taken off shortly before from Amman, Jordan, on a scheduled international service to Doha, Qatar, with 279 persons aboard. He was extradited to Qatar for prosecution, and would subsequently be sentenced to a prison term of five years.

18 AUGUST 2007

TWO men who claimed to be members of the al-Qaeda terrorist organisation and demanded to be taken to Iran hijacked Atlasjet Airlines Flight 1011, an MD-83 jetliner carrying 145 persons on a Turkish domestic service from Ercan to Istanbul.

After the MD-83 had landed shortly after 08:00 local time at Antalya, Turkey, for the purpose of refuelling, women and children on the flight were released, and most of the other passengers escaped through the aircraft's rear door while the pilots jumped out from the cockpit windows. Subsequently the assailants surrendered; the explosive they were reportedly carrying turned out to be made of modelling clay.

26–27 AUGUST 2008

A Sun Air Boeing 737 jet airliner was commandeered during a scheduled domestic service within Sudan, from Nyala to Khartoum, with 97 persons aboard. Denied permission to land at Cairo, the 737 set down at an airfield located in the Kufra Oasis region of eastern Libya, and after a stand-off there lasting some 22 hours the two hijackers surrendered and asked for asylum.

5
Aviation's day of infamy

Occurring nearly 60 years after America's official 'Day of Infamy' (the surprise attack on US military forces by the Empire of Japan in 1941), the events of 11 September 2001 were in many ways more damaging to the nation's psyche. Not only were there more casualties, but most of the victims were civilians. And for the first time, modern warfare touched the US mainland. This would also stand as the most disastrous day in the history of world commercial aviation.

The weather throughout the American East Coast on this Tuesday morning was nearly cloudless, ideal for flying, and on

this day would only serve to assist a brazen and unprecedented terrorist attack which would employ commandeered commercial jet transports as weapons of mass destruction against the United States' capital and its largest city.

Four aircraft would be hijacked as part of this operation by 'suicide' squads, members of the Islamic fundamentalist

United Flight 175 approaches Tower No 2 as north tower continues to burn after being struck earlier by another 767 in the 'nine-eleven' attack. (AP/Press Association Images)

al-Qaeda terrorist organisation, based primarily in Afghanistan. Two of the jets had departed from Logan International Airport, serving Boston, Massachusetts, both on domestic transcontinental trips to Los Angeles, California. The first to take off was American Airlines Flight 11, a wide-bodied Boeing 767-223ER (N334AA), which departed shortly before 08:00 local time. Aboard were a total of 92 persons, including nine cabin attendants and two pilots. It was followed 15 minutes later by United Airlines Flight 175, a 767-222 (N612UA). The second jetliner carried 65 persons, who included seven cabin attendants and two pilots. Among the passengers on these flights were a total of ten terrorists, evenly divided into two groups, with one member of each cell having received pilot training.

Flight 11 was apparently seized approximately 15 minutes after its departure. It was around this time that normal radio communications with the aircraft were broken off. Some ten minutes later a suspicious transmission from the 767 was heard at the Boston air traffic control (ATC) centre, which was later determined to have been a message sent by the hijacker-pilot, Mohamed Atta. It was intended for the occupants of the cabin but inadvertently broadcast over the air due to his incorrect use the aircraft's communications equipment. The crew of Flight 175 also must have heard this transmission, which they reported to the New York ATC centre. Minutes later contact with the United crew was also lost. In both cases the transponders of the aircraft were turned off or otherwise changed, although the primary targets representing the two transports remained visible on radar as they proceeded towards New York City.

As the cockpit voice recorder (CVR) of neither aircraft was subsequently available for analysis, the manner in which the flights were commandeered could not be ascertained. The rules of the US Federal Aviation Administration (FAA) require that cockpit doors be closed and locked in air carrier operations, although in at least one case the pilots could have been lured out of the flight deck by attacks on occupants in the cabin. Based on telephone conversations sent by them, passengers and crew members had reported such attacks, and according to a stewardess, two fellow cabin attendants on the American Airlines 767 had been stabbed. There were also indications that both flight crews had been physically harmed or killed. Also on both aircraft, the hijackers reportedly used knives or some kind of cutting tools and Mace pepper spray or some other aerosol irritant, and also claimed to have a bomb.

The hijackers of the two 767s were targeting what could be described as the best symbol of American economic power, the World Trade Center, located on lower Manhattan Island, New York. This complex of buildings included two towers rising to more than 1,000ft (300m), which would have been visible from a great distance on this particular day, considering their size and the prevailing meteorological conditions, with high clouds and good visibility being reported at La Guardia Airport, located some ten miles (16km) to the north-east. At 08:46 local time, N334AA was deliberately flown into the north or No 1 tower. Approaching from the north at a speed estimated at approximately 430mph (690kph), the jetliner struck near the top and on the north side of the building. Less than 20 minutes later, at 09:03, N612UA was crashed by its hijacker-pilot into the south or No 2 tower.

The final desperate moments aboard the United 767 were provided in stark terms by a passenger speaking to his father via telephone. 'I think we are going down,' he said. 'I think they intend to go to Chicago or some place and fly into a building. Don't worry, Dad, if it happens, it'll be very fast. My God, my God!' After going into a rapid descent as it proceeded in a northerly direction, opposite to that of the American 767, the jetliner slammed into the building at around the 80th floor and at a velocity estimated to have been in excess of 500mph (800kph). As in the case of the first strike, the crash touched off a huge explosion and raging fire. The intensity of the blaze was illustrated by the fact that a number of victims trapped on upper floors actually jumped from the North tower, plunging to their deaths.

But worse was yet to come. Shortly before 10:00, the South Tower, damaged by the crash and kerosene-fuelled fire, completely collapsed, its floors 'pancaking' on top of one another in a mass of smoke and dust. About half an hour later the North Tower fell in the same manner. Later the same day a 47-storey building that was part of the complex and had been ravaged by fire also collapsed.

The death toll was the highest ever recorded in a terrorist attack, and if this were classified as a single disaster would be nearly five times that of the worst commercial aviation accident. Among the 2,761 persons killed at the World Trade Center on 11 September were all 157 aboard the two aircraft and 343 members of the New York City fire department who had rushed to the scene in a futile attempt to extinguish the fires in both buildings. One of the victims died more than a year later and another in late 2008, both from the effects of inhaling toxic substances. Due to the nature of the catastrophe, approximately 1,100 of the victims were never identified, even using the most advanced scientific methods. More than 6,000 others suffered injuries.

Simultaneous with the aforementioned events was the hijacking of American Airlines Flight 77, a twin-jet Boeing 757-223 (N644AA) also bound for Los Angeles, California, which had taken off from Dulles International Airport, near Washington DC, at 08:20 local time. It was carrying 64 persons, including a crew comprised of four cabin attendants and two pilots. Five of its passengers were later identified as al-Qaeda terrorists, one of whom was capable of flying the aircraft. In some ways, the events that must have taken place aboard this aircraft were even less understood than those involving the flights out of Boston. Presumably the aircraft had been commandeered in the same manner, i.e. through the incapacitation or murder of the flight crew. There was no mention of stabbings in telephone conversations between passengers and relatives on the ground, although the former did report being moved to the rear of the cabin.

The hijacking was believed to have commenced between 30 and 35 minutes after departure, and after the 757 had reached its assigned cruising height. It then turned southwards and initiated a descent. With the aircraft's transponder having been turned off, the blip representing N644AA would have been difficult to discern on radar, and for a period of nearly ten minutes even its primary target was lost. The objective of the hijackers of Flight 77 was the Pentagon building, the huge US military complex located in Virginia, just across the Potomac

An American Airlines Boeing 757-200, the type that was crashed into the Pentagon building near Washington, DC. (Author)

River from the District of Columbia, which could have been easily located by the hijacker-pilot at the controls of the jet, especially considering the clear weather conditions in the area. After completing a 330° right turn, he increased power and descended towards the mammoth five-storey structure, hitting its north-west side at an approximate speed of 530mph (850kph) at 09:37 local time. The impact and consequent explosion resulted in the collapse of a portion of the building. Including all of those aboard the aircraft, a total of 189 persons perished in the attack. Service personnel and civilians alike lost their lives on the ground, while more than 100 others suffered injuries.

A fourth aircraft was also hijacked, a United Airlines Boeing 757-222 (N591UA) operating as Flight 93 on a transcontinental service to San Francisco, California. In addition to its five cabin attendants and two pilots, its occupants included four members of al-Qaeda. (The operative who, it was suspected, would have become the fifth hijacker had been refused entry into the US.)

To many, Flight 93 would become a symbol of American resistance on what was otherwise a day of humiliation. It had taken off around 08:40 local time from the international airport serving Newark, New Jersey. But its departure was nearly half an hour later than expected, a fact that would help to ensure that the hijackers would fail in their mission. The events taking place in the flight deck of Flight 93 would be recorded for history by the aircraft's CVR, which was later recovered for examination, but due to capacity limitations in the unit, transcript of the initial phase of the hijacking was erased. The jetliner was apparently commandeered shortly before 09:30 local time, while cruising over north-eastern Ohio. It was around this time that the Cleveland ATC centre heard

'unintelligible sounds of possible screaming or a struggle from an unknown origin' from the flight. One of the pilots also declared a 'Mayday' distress message. The CVR indicated that a woman who may have been a cabin attendant also struggled with at least one of the hijackers, who then killed or otherwise silenced her. Both pilots had probably met the same fate, based on telephone messages from passengers. The centre also twice heard a message that referred to a bomb being aboard the aircraft, apparently transmitted accidentally by the hijacker-pilot through incorrect use of the communications equipment. (A subsequent examination would reveal no evidence of either explosives or firearms having been on the 757.) Before its transponder was apparently switched off, N591UA was tracked on radar as it climbed above 40,000ft (12,000m), and its primary target was then observed as it assumed a south-easterly heading in the direction of Washington DC.

The occupants of Flight 93 learned of the other attacks in conversations with family members or others on the ground, giving them a preview of the intentions of the hijackers. This undoubtedly led them to develop a course of action in an attempt to save their own lives, and in the process might have saved countless others on the ground. The hijackers' target could not be ascertained, but available evidence pointed to either the Capitol building or the Presidential White House, both in Washington. However, before the aircraft reached the capital the passengers put their plan into action, assaulting the hijackers, one of whom may have remained in the cabin. Just beforehand, passenger Todd Beamer, who had been speaking with a telephone company supervisor on the ground, uttered the words that would become immortal in American vernacular: 'Let's roll!'

In response to the passengers trying to break into the flight deck, the hijacker-pilot, Ziad Jarrah, rolled the aircraft to the right and left, and pitched it up and down to try and disrupt them. One of the assailants was heard to say 'Allah is the greatest!' Then one asked 'Shall we put it down?' A second hijacker responded 'Put it in it, and pull it down!' Rolling over on to its back while descending, the 757 slammed to earth at 580mph (930kph) near Somerset, Pennsylvania, at 10:03 local time, and all 44 persons aboard perished. A smouldering crater in an open field marked the site of the tragedy, some 125 miles (200km) north-west of Washington.

As of early 2009, the death toll in the 11 September attack stood at 2,994, including the 19 identified hijackers who, technically, would have been considered passenger fatalities and thus among the 265 persons killed aboard the four aircraft.

The origin of what became known worldwide as 'nine-eleven' can be traced back some two decades, to the rise of al-Qaeda and its leader, Osama Bin Laden. There should have been ample warnings. The World Trade Center was targeted in an al-Qaeda truck bombing in 1993, in which six persons were killed. Bombings of US embassies in Kenya and Tanzania claimed more than 200 lives in 1998. The continuing threat

A crater marks the site where United Flight 93 was crashed by its hijackers in south-eastern Pennsylvania after passenger revolt. (AP/Press Association Images)

posed by al-Qaeda had led to US military action in the late 1990s, with only limited success. Considerable criticism was directed at certain US agencies and the administrations of American Presidents Bill Clinton and George W. Bush in a report issued by a commission formed to investigate the 11 September attacks. According to the report, the situation was reportedly 'blinking red' in the summer of 2001, and only five weeks before the attack President Bush had been advised of such a threat, with the possibility both of hijackings, presumably involving aircraft, and terrorist strikes in New York and Washington. There was no evidence of any significant action being taken by the American government in response to these warnings.

As for the men directly involved in the attack, their identities, backgrounds and roles were established in a lengthy inquiry conducted by the American Federal Bureau of Investigation. Most of the hijackers, all but four of whom were born in Saudi Arabia, were able to come to the US legally on tourist visas. Four of them were able to take flying lessons and also obtain simulator training to enable them to fly the large jets used as weapons, and three of the trained pilots had taken surveillance flights early in the summer of 2001 as part of their planning for the attacks. Two of the hijackers had actually been under surveillance by intelligence authorities as they travelled from the Middle East to South-East Asia, and ultimately to the US. But this information was not forwarded to the FBI in time. Meanwhile, another al-Qaeda operative, Zacarias Moussaoui, had been arrested on an immigration violation charge after beginning flight lessons in the US and participating in activities

similar to those of the 11 September hijackers. Though he was apparently not directly involved in the attack, the sharing of this information within the proper circles might have led to the disruption of the hijacking plot.

The security procedures then in effect at US airports were also deemed, in the report, to have been 'seriously flawed'. The most important and obvious part of the layered system of security used at the time in US commercial aviation was checkpoint screening at airports, which in this case was being handled for American and United Airlines by private contractors. Before boarding the aircraft, the hijackers were screened at Boston, along with other passengers, by a walk-through metal detector calibrated to detect at least the metal content of a .22 calibre handgun. But the hijackers did not use firearms to commandeer the aircraft. An X-ray machine would be used to screen their carry-on luggage. However, knives or other cutting objects were not prohibited items aboard commercial US flights at the time, and many potentially dangerous items, such as those used by the 11 September hijackers, might not have even set off metal detectors.

Some of the assailants were selected by a computerised security system to have their luggage held for screening, which meant the bags could not be loaded until it could be confirmed that the men were aboard the aircraft. But since the attack did not involve the use of bombs, this additional screening did not hinder the intentions of the terrorists. As a result, all of them cleared the airport checkpoints. Three of the hijackers boarding Flight 77 at Dulles International Airport were also subjected to computerised screening, with the same results. Two others were even selected for extra scrutiny because they seemed 'suspicious' to a customer agent, and one of them set off alarms when he placed his carry-on luggage on the belt of the X-ray and had to be directed through a second metal detector; setting it off, he was 'hand-wanded' by a screener, but this time passed the inspection. A subsequent review of a videotape of the screening process was reviewed by the FAA security office, and one expert labelled the work of the aforementioned screener as 'marginal at best', adding that whatever had set off the alarms should have been dealt with more diligently. And although one of the hijackers assigned to Flight 93 had been selected by computer for screening, none of the four had any difficulty passing through the checkpoint at the Newark airport.

Although the US airline industry had been dealing with hijackings for more than 40 years, a non-confrontational approach had been adopted over that period of time, one that was not compatible with the prospect of suicidal assailants. Even the arming of pilots, which was enacted on a limited basis after the attacks, may not have been useful here, as the flight crews would not have realised the intentions of the air pirates, and a slight change in their tactics could have led to a situation in which the assailants had both control of the aircraft and a weapon. The use of armed air marshals aboard aircraft could have been useful, but at the time the ranks of such 'aerial police officers' consisted of only about three dozen personnel within the entire US airline industry.

Poor planning and disorganisation also marked the response by the FAA and US military, including the North American Aerospace Command (NORAD), the latter of which was created in the late 1950s to deal primarily with the bomber and missile threat from the former Soviet Union. Multiple airline hijackers, on the other hand, had not been experienced anywhere in more than three decades, and never in American airspace. On the day of the attack, and after both the FAA and airline officials had begun to sense the severity of the situation, there had been no serious effort to get messages to other airline crews on a nationwide basis with the intention of heightening security until a single United Airlines dispatcher transmitted warnings to a number of transcontinental flights under his jurisdiction. One warning reached Flight 93 only about five minutes before its likely take-over. Discussing this issue with the commission, controllers stated that such advising was the responsibility of the airlines themselves.

With regard to intervention by the military, the Boston centre contacted the Northeast Air Defence Sector (NEADS) at around 08:40 local time, and two US Air Force F-15 fighters were airborne from Otis Air Force Base, Massachusetts, about 15 minutes later. But lacking a target, the jets were vectored to an area off Long Island and instructed to 'hold as needed'. They finally arrived over Manhattan shortly before 09:30, only after both World Trade towers were already ablaze. At about that same time, three F-16 jet fighters took off from Langley Air Force Base, Virginia, also under the directive of NEADS. In an apparent attempt to confront American Flight 11, which had already crashed, they got sent to the area around Baltimore, Maryland, and were some 150 miles (250km) away from the capital when the American Airlines 757 hit the Pentagon. Flight 77 was in fact able to travel virtually undetected for more than half an hour, only being identified while airborne by the crew of an Air National Guard C-130 transport, who witnessed its crash.

No military assistance was ever requested from the FAA regarding Flight 93. The commission concluded that had its occupants not intervened, the United 757 probably would have reached Washington before the F-16s from Langley, then circling the city, had received any authorisation to engage the airliner, and at a time when the pilots of the fighters were unaware of the nature of the threat, not realising that the 'hostile' aircraft were commercial transports. Only after N591UA had crashed was authorisation given to shoot down any threatening aircraft. The commission concluded that the defence of US airspace on this day had not been conducted in accordance with existing training and protocols, but rather was improvised by both military personnel and civilians who were not prepared to deal with a situation that should have been predicted. And astonishingly, this catastrophic act of terrorism had been carried out by a small group of terrorists for only about half a million dollars.

The attack led to an unprecedented grounding of every commercial and civilian general aviation aircraft airborne over the US at the time, with the exception of those making flights considered absolutely essential, some 4,500 in number. Their landing at the nearest airport without incident marked one bright spot on this otherwise dark day in the nation's history.

But the effects of the 'nine-eleven' tragedy were more profound. The attack marked the true beginning of what would become known as the 'War on Terror', leading to military action in both Afghanistan, the home base of al-Qaeda, and Iraq, the latter primarily by American and British forces in what would become one of the most controversial wars in the history of either nation. There were also profound changes in airline security, particularly in the US, with heightened awareness of the threat posed by international terrorism and increased security procedures, including the use of many more air marshals and modifications in aircraft to reduce the chance of cockpit intrusions. Some of these changes resembled the procedures that had been adopted years earlier by the Israeli airline El Al, and which, had they been in use by US carriers at the time, would probably have guaranteed the failure of the terror plot.

The paths of the four jetliners hijacked on 11 September, including the assumed route taken by Flight 77. (Haynes Publishing)

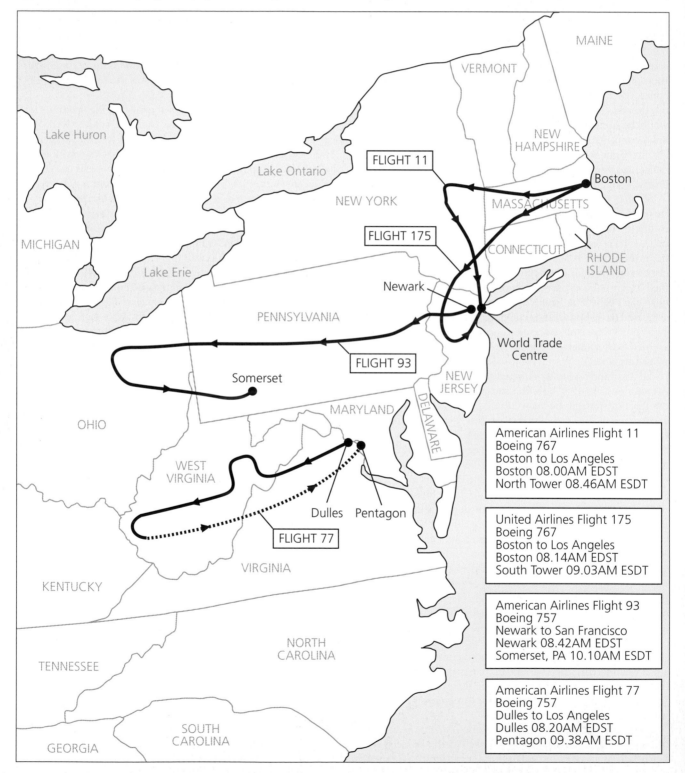

American Airlines Flight 11
Boeing 767
Boston to Los Angeles
Boston 08.00AM EDST
North Tower 08.46AM ESDT

United Airlines Flight 175
Boeing 767
Boston to Los Angeles
Boston 08.14AM EDST
South Tower 09.03AM ESDT

American Airlines Flight 93
Boeing 757
Newark to San Francisco
Newark 08.42AM EDST
Somerset, PA 10.10AM ESDT

American Airlines Flight 77
Boeing 757
Dulles to Los Angeles
Dulles 08.20AM EDST
Pentagon 09.38AM ESDT

6

Blood for money

Beginning in the late 1940s and continuing for more than a decade-and-a-half, the airlines of North America were plagued with a new terrorist threat, the destruction of an airliner with an underlying profit motive. The plot simply involved bringing down a commercial flight, usually with some type of explosive device, and making it appear to be an accident. Insurance could then be collected on one of the passengers, which in many cases was the suicidal suspect himself. Except for the first and last incidents recorded here,

which occurred in Canada, all the events covered in this chapter took place in the US.

The cracking of the 1949 Quebec Airways bombing case and the subsequent hanging of the three perpetrators should have taught all potential airline saboteurs that such crimes would be

Completely intact, the empennage of the United Air Lines DC-6B sabotaged in November 1955 rests in a field some some distance from where the main wreckage fell. (The Denver Post)

dealt with firmly. Nevertheless, in the next two decades such 'get rich quick' (or make somebody else rich quick) crimes would reach critical proportions, becoming as much of a menace to safe air travel in North America as midair collisions and bad weather conditions.

Interestingly, in only one case – that involving the National Airlines DC-7B over the Gulf of Mexico in 1959 – would insurance money actually be collected. But with nearly 300 lives being lost and a number of aircraft destroyed, the saboteurs involved in such crimes succeeded in injecting a new element of fear and risk into the air travel business.

The accounts in this chapter are confined to North American airline insurance scams that were either proven or strongly suspected, and which resulted in fatalities and/or destruction of the aircraft. Other acts of sabotage, such as those that were politically motivated or related to personal revenge, and insurance scams occurring in other parts of the world, are dealt with in other chapters.

9 SEPTEMBER 1949

THIS was a case of a love triangle degenerating into one of Canada's most horrific crimes, and ending with the offenders paying the ultimate price for their actions.

John Graham, 23, who was later convicted and executed for the bombing of United Air Lines Flight 629, in which 44 lives were lost. (AP/Press Association Images)

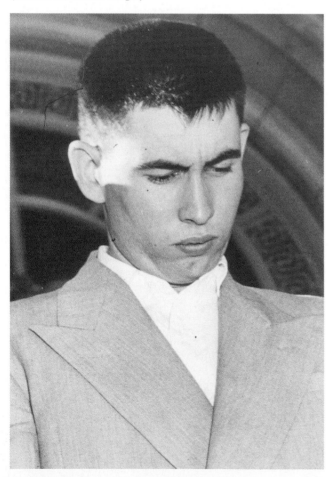

Operated by Quebec Airways, a subsidiary of Canadian Pacific Air Lines, a Douglas DC-3 (CF-CUA) had taken off from Quebec City at 10:25 local time on a scheduled domestic service originating at Montreal, with an ultimate destination of Comeau Bay. Some 20 minutes later, the twin-engine transport was observed over the St Lawrence River, near the town of St Joachim, when suddenly an explosion occurred in its front fuselage section, and the aircraft turned to the right and started to descend. It ultimately slammed into a hill on the northern side of the river, near the village of Sault-au-Cochon, Quebec, some 40 miles (65km) north-east of Quebec City. There was no fire, but all 23 persons aboard (19 passengers and four crew members) lost their lives. Investigation revealed that the violent blast had taken place in the forward luggage compartment, and probably either killed or incapacitated the two pilots, resulting in an uncontrolled descent.

A police investigation led to the subsequent arrest of two men and a woman in connection with the intentional destruction of an aircraft, under the guise of an accident. The mastermind of the plot was J. Albert Guay, a jeweller, whose wife had been a passenger on the flight and had been insured for $10,000, with her husband named as beneficiary. The woman with whom he was romantically involved was Marie Pitre, suspected of placing the bomb aboard the airliner, her brother Genereux Ruest also being implicated in the crime. All three were later hanged.

9 MAY 1953

A clerical error may have made the difference between success and failure in this attempted sabotage of an Aeronaves de México DC-3 airliner that was carrying seven persons on a scheduled domestic service to Mexico City from Ciudad Obregon, Sonora, but did not prevent the resulting accidental fatalities.

Sent by the wrong route, the bomb that had been hidden in a suitcase detonated after being taken off the aircraft at the airport serving Mazatlan, Sinaloa, which was an en-route stop. Including the airport manager, three persons lost their lives in the blast occurring shortly after noon in the terminal building, while seven others suffered injuries. Four suspects were apprehended in connection with the bombing, which was determined to have been a suicide-for-insurance plot.

1 NOVEMBER 1955

UNITED Air Lines Flight 629, a Douglas DC-6B (N37559), took off from Stapleton Airfield, serving Denver, Colorado, bound for Portland, Oregon, one segment of a transcontinental US domestic service originating at New York City, with an ultimate destination of Seattle, Washington. Approximately ten minutes later, or shortly after 19:00 local time, while climbing in visual meteorological conditions at an estimated above-ground height of 5,000ft (1,500m), the transport was shattered by an explosion. The loud blast was confirmed by eye-witnesses; tower controllers reported seeing lights in the night sky, then a flash on or near the ground that illuminated the base of the clouds, some 10,000ft (3,000m) above. Burning wreckage was scattered over a wide area in the vicinity of Longmont, about 40 miles (65km) north-west of Denver. All 44 persons aboard (39 passengers and five crew members) perished.

In the first hours following the crash, definite clues were uncovered indicating an explosion within, but foreign to, the aircraft. Chemical analysis revealed the residue of dynamite in the wreckage, while other pieces found could have originated from a dry cell battery, these being the two main components of a bomb. The blast had taken place in the No 4 baggage compartment, with a disintegrating force that tore the aft fuselage section to pieces. During its fall to earth, a more complete break-up of the aircraft occurred, including the separation of the wings and forward fuselage.

A criminal investigation conducted by the FBI was launched about a week into the Civil Aeronautics Board (CAB) probe, leading to the arrest on 14 November of John G. Graham, whose mother had been a passenger on the flight. He thereafter confessed to the mass murder. Before the aircraft had taken off, he took out $37,500 in life insurance on her – six policies purchased for 25 cents apiece from an airport vending machine (these would later be banned in the state of Colorado). He had planted the bomb, fashioned from 25 sticks of dynamite, in her suitcase. Convicted of the crime, he was executed in the Colorado gas chamber in 1957.

25 JULY 1957

BEFORE proceeding on towards its ultimate destination of Los Angeles, California, Western Air Lines Flight 39 landed at McCarran Field, serving Las Vegas, Nevada, its final en-route stop during a US domestic service that had originated at Rochester, Minnesota. It was here that Saul Binstock boarded, becoming one of the 13 passengers on the twin-engine Convair 240.

About 15 minutes after take-off, the 62 year-old retired jeweller entered the lavatory, located in the rear of the aircraft's cabin. Some 20 minutes later, or around 03:40 local time, as it was cruising in darkness at 10,000ft (3,000m) over the Mojave Desert of southern California, the Convair was rocked by an explosion, which resulted in an immediate decompression of the cabin and left a hole measuring approximately 6ft by 7ft (1.8m by 2m) near the tail assembly. The victim's body, which had been blasted out of the fuselage, would later be found along the route of the flight.

In what was believed to have been a suicide-for-insurance scheme on his part, he had set off dynamite after spending a considerable time trying to ignite the blasting cap. There were no injuries among the other 15 persons aboard, who included a crew of three, and the damaged Convair managed a safe emergency landing at a military airbase.

16 NOVEMBER 1959

THIS aviation mystery was widely believed to have been an act of aerial sabotage that could not be proven due to a lack of evidence.

Originating at Miami, National Airlines Flight 967 had landed at Tampa, Florida, before proceeding on towards New Orleans, Louisiana, its next scheduled stop during a transcontinental US domestic service with an ultimate destination of Los Angeles, California. Last reported cruising at 14,000ft (4,300m) in darkness and good weather conditions, the Douglas DC-7B (N4891C) had been about 120 miles (190km) east-south-east

Dr Robert Spears, suspected but never convicted in the destruction of a National Airlines DC-7B in November 1959. (AP/Press Association Images)

of New Orleans when radio and radar contact was lost shortly before 01:00 local time.

Search vessels combing the Gulf of Mexico subsequently recovered a small amount of debris, mostly cabin furnishings, as well as the bodies of nine victims and the remains of a tenth. There were no survivors among the 42 persons aboard the aircraft, including six crew members. Attempts to locate the main wreckage, which lay in water more than 200ft (60m) deep, were unsuccessful, preventing the US Civil Aeronautics Board (CAB) from being able to determine the cause of the crash.

The sabotage theory gained credibility two months later when Robert Vernon Spears, a naturopathic doctor first listed as a passenger on the downed DC-7B, showed up alive in Arizona. He reportedly told his wife that another man had taken his seat on the flight, leading to speculation that the aircraft had been sabotaged with some type of explosive device in an elaborate insurance swindle.

Dr Spears died in 1969, perhaps taking the solution to this mystery with him to the grave.

6 JANUARY 1960

NATIONAL Airlines had been using Boeing 707 jetliners on its New York to Florida route for more than a year, in a lease agreement with the major US international carrier Pan American World Airways. This time, however, the trip would take a little longer; the 707 being used had to be removed from

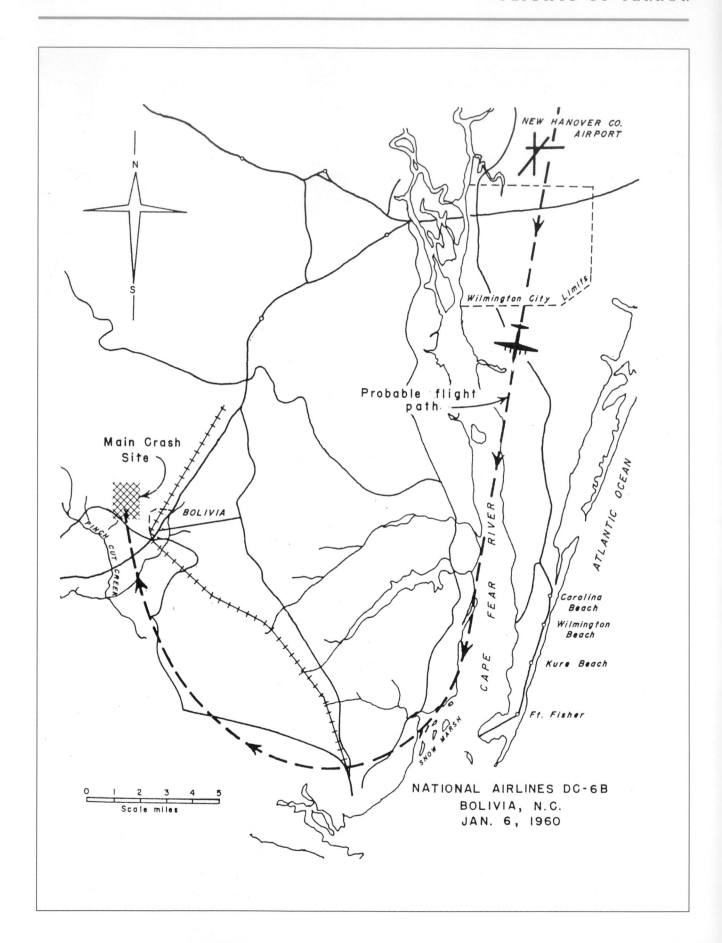

NATIONAL AIRLINES DC-6B
BOLIVIA, N.C.
JAN. 6, 1960

service due to a cracked cockpit window. Two other aircraft were brought in as replacements, a turboprop Lockheed Electra, which boarded most of the 105 passengers, and an older piston-engine Douglas DC-6B (N8225H), to which the rest were assigned. Designated as National Flight 2511, the latter had taken off from New York International Airport for Miami late the previous night.

Nearly three hours later, or around 02:40 local time, an explosion occurred in its passenger cabin as the transport was cruising at 18,000ft (5,500m) in darkness over south-eastern North Carolina. The blast, beneath the far right seat in row seven, compromised the structural integrity of the DC-6B, which made a descending right turn before it disintegrated and plummeted to earth. All 34 persons aboard, including a crew of five, were killed.

The main wreckage had fallen in a field near the town of Bolivia, located some 15 miles (25km) south-west of Wilmington, but additional debris and the body of one passenger was found on Kure Beach, some distance to the east of the main crash site. The mutilated body, in which were embedded wire fragments and foreign particles, was that of Julian A. Frank, a 33-year-old New York attorney who was known to be in serious financial trouble and who had taken out more than $1 million in life insurance. His wounds could only have resulted from the detonation of an explosive in close proximity to the victim. Amid the wreckage of the aircraft, there was further conclusive evidence of destruction by a foreign substance. Sodium nitrate found in the cabin air vent is a typical residue of dynamite; there were also traces of manganese dioxide, commonly found in a dry cell battery, which could have been used to set off the explosive.

The break-up of the DC-6B could not be attributed to any mechanical malfunction or structural failure, nor to the weather (although winds of 100 knots at the cruising altitude were responsible for the wide dispersion of many light pieces of cabin material; at the crash site there was rain and fog at the time).

22 MAY 1962

THE first confirmed successful sabotage of a commercial jet airliner involved Continental Air Lines Flight 11, which was en route from Chicago, Illinois, to Kansas City, Missouri, the first segment of a US domestic service scheduled to terminate at Los Angeles, California. The Boeing 707-124 (N70775) crashed along the Iowa/Missouri border around 21:20 local time, killing all 45 persons on board (37 passengers and eight crew members). One victim was actually removed alive from the wreckage but succumbed to his injuries about 1½ hours later.

Although the main wreckage fell into a field approximately five miles (8km) north-north-west of Unionville, Missouri, pieces were found over a path 40 miles (65km) long in a north-easterly direction, and some light debris was located up to 120 miles (190km) from the crash site. This evidence of an in-flight break-up could not be disputed. Early suspicions

OPPOSITE: The flight path of the National Airlines DC-6B sabotaged on 6 January 1960 included a descending turn after the detonation of the bomb in its passenger cabin. (Civil Aeronautics Board)

of sabotage were soon proven by the FBI, which established that dynamite had been detonated aboard the 707, apparently in the used towel bin underneath the washbasin in the right rear lavatory.

Flying in darkness and clear weather conditions at a height of around 37,000ft (11,300m), the jetliner had just circumnavigated some thunderstorm activity when the bomb exploded, causing severe structural damage. Subsequently, and after the flight crew had initiated an emergency descent, donned smoke masks, and lowered the undercarriage, the aircraft broke up at high altitude. Losing the aft 38ft (11.5m) of its fuselage, the 707 pitched down, causing most of its left wing, the outer portion of its right wing and all four engines to separate.

The explosive device was believed to have been carried aboard by a passenger in a suicide-for-insurance plot. A criminal investigation revealed that he had taken out two policies worth $275,000, with the intention of benefiting his wife and daughter. He had also purchased dynamite not long before the crash, and was facing a separate criminal charge in connection with a prior act of armed robbery.

7 MAY 1964

AMONG the passengers who boarded Pacific Air Lines Flight 773 at Reno, Nevada, was 27-year-old Francisco Gonzales. Deeply in debt and fraught with personal problems, he was also bent on self-destruction.

Following a scheduled stop at Stockton, California, the twin-engine turboprop Fairchild F-27A (N2770R) continued on towards its ultimate destination, San Francisco. It was last observed by ground radar while on a south-westerly heading and cruising at an altitude of 5,000ft (1,500m) before the Oakland approach control centre received a frantic, unintelligible message from the flight. Deciphered through laboratory analysis, the message, sent by co-pilot Ray Andress, was believed to have been 'Skipper's shot! We've been shot! I was trying to help.'

At around 06:50 local time, the aircraft crashed on a hill and disintegrated in a ball of fire some 15 miles (25km) east of Oakland. All 44 persons aboard, including a crew of three, perished. In the wreckage was found the remains of a recently-fired .357 Magnum revolver. This was the weapon the suspect had purchased the day before his trip to Reno, which he had reportedly showed to others. Also purchased by him the previous day, at San Francisco International Airport, were two insurance policies worth a total of $105,000. Found elsewhere in the remains of the aircraft was a piece of tubing from the pilot's seat containing a bullet indentation, evidence that a shooting had taken place in the cockpit.

The manner in which the gunman must have shot the two pilots could not be determined due to the condition of their remains, but it was believed that Captain Ernest Clark had been killed immediately. First Officer Andress may then have tried to save the aircraft and managed to pull up before the F-27 went into its final plunge from an approximate height of 3,000 feet (1,000m). Ironically, a rule requiring that the cockpit door be locked at all times in flight, which in this case might have protected the crew, was introduced only a week before the disaster, but was not to take effect until August.

A Fairchild F-27 of the type flown by Pacific Air Lines that crashed on 7 May 1964 after its two pilots were shot. (Fairchild Aircraft)

Francisco Gonzales, who had reportedly told others throughout the previous week of his intention to kill himself, was thus easily able to carry out his threat in a horrifying act of suicide and mass murder.

8 JULY 1965

A suicide-for-insurance scam was suspected in the destruction of a Canadian Pacific Air Lines Douglas DC-6B (CF-CUQ). All 52 persons aboard (46 passengers and six crew members)

Little remained of the twin-engine turboprop following its high-speed plunge to earth. (AP/Press Association Images)

perished when the transport exploded and plummeted to earth vertically near the Canadian town of 100 Mile House, in British Columbia.

Operating as Flight 21 en route from Vancouver to Prince George, the first segment of a service with an ultimate destination of Whitehorse, Yukon Territory, the aircraft was observed cruising in clear weather conditions at an approximate height of 15,000ft (4,500m) when witnesses reported a midair explosion that tore off its empennage. Its crew managed three 'May Day' distress messages before the DC-6B crashed and burned in a wooded area at around 17:40 local time.

The unknown saboteur was believed to have ignited a mixture of acid and gunpowder, which may have been poured into the toilet bowl in the left rear lavatory.

7
Skyjack by parachute

When the man known as D.B. Cooper leapt from a 727 into the darkness over the American Pacific Northwest, he opened a bizarre new chapter in the world of aerial piracy. The idea was actually quite ingenious, for it tackled the dilemma that had always faced the hijacker: where to go after the aircraft lands.

However, the success rate of the parachuting hijacker was very, very low – in fact, none of those who employed this daring gimmick escaped, with the single exception of D.B. Cooper (and there were indications that even he didn't make

it). Subsequent air pirates generally displayed less creativity than Cooper, in some cases not even realising that only certain types of aircraft had a rear stairway from which such a jump could be made with relative safety.

Skyjacking by parachute virtually disappeared after the early-1970s, and with such a high rate of failure it is easy to

Artist's concept of D.B. Cooper, the most famous of the parachuting air pirates. (AP/Press Association Images)

understand why. But whether he is seen as an almost-heroic figure, one who 'got away with it', or just another ruthless criminal, D.B. Cooper and the legend associated with him will probably remain an indelible part of aviation history.

The following is a list of actual or would-be parachuting hijackers, whether successful, unsuccessful or really unsuccessful (i.e. deadly).

12–13 NOVEMBER 1971

CONTRARY to popular belief, 'D.B. Cooper' was not the first air pirate to attempt a parachute escape from a hijacked airliner. That distinction goes to the lone assailant who commandeered Air Canada Flight 812, a DC-8 jet carrying 125 persons on a domestic service from Vancouver, British Columbia, to Toronto, Ontario. The hijacker, who claimed to be a member of the Irish Republican Army, was armed with a sawn-off shotgun, and had threatened to destroy the aircraft with dynamite

The DC-8 landed twice at Great Falls, Montana, the first time for refuelling and the acquisition of $50,000 – only a small part of the $1.5 million he was demanding – and the second time to release all of the passengers. Originally the gunman asked to be taken to Ireland, but he then had the aircraft zigzagging all over southern Canada and the northern US. He also demanded and was provided with a parachute, which he prepared to use as the jet neared Calgary, Alberta.

It was not known exactly how he planned to jump from one of the DC-8's side doors, but it never came to that anyway. As he bent over to put on the parachute, he was hit over the

20 January 1972: a stewardess pics up the money in a hijack-for-ransom involving a Hughes Airwest DC-9. (AP/Press Association Images)

head with the blunt end of a fire axe, wielded by the captain. Seriously injured, he was arrested, and later sentenced to life imprisonment.

24 NOVEMBER 1971

ONE of the passengers who boarded Northwest Airlines Flight 305 at Portland, Oregon, was about to make history; the other 41 persons aboard were to become a part of history. He had been booked on the flight under the name 'Dan Cooper'; due to an erroneous media report, he would become known as 'D.B. Cooper'. Claiming to have a bomb, he took over the Boeing 727-51 jet as it proceeded to Seattle, Washington, the final destination of a flight which had originated at Washington DC. He demanded $200,000 and four parachutes. A ransom request was rare in the history of US hijackings, but the demand for parachutes was a novelty.

The aircraft landed at Seattle, where all the passengers and two of the three cabin attendants were released, and the 727 then proceeded back south, followed by two military jet fighters. The aircraft had been ordered to Reno, Nevada, with the flight crew being asked to maintain a height of not over 10,000ft (3,000m) and a low airspeed, with the undercarriage and flaps extended. When the aircraft landed at Reno, the air pirate, the money and two of the parachutes were gone. Cooper had obviously opened and jumped out from the rear stairway over the Cascade Mountains in the area of southern Washington and northern Oregon.

Interest in the mystery waned until 1980, when it was renewed after some of the ransom money was unearthed along the bank of the Columbia River, near Vancouver, Washington. This find led many to believe that the hijacker had been killed in the jump. There were other reasons to believe this as well,

for one of the two parachutes he took with him was a ground training model, and could not be opened.

The case of 'D.B. Cooper' may forever remain a mystery; somewhat easier to understand was the ensuing spate of copycat hijackings, none of which would succeed.

24 DECEMBER 1971

A lone hijacker armed with a revolver and an alleged bomb, which turned out to be a fake, commandeered Northwest Airlines Flight 734, a Boeing 707 jetliner on a US domestic service to Chicago from Minneapolis, Minnesota, with 35 persons aboard. He demanded a ransom of $300,000 and two parachutes, but later surrendered. He was committed to a psychiatric facility and charges against him were dropped.

12 JANUARY 1972

DEMANDING $1 million and ten parachutes, a lone assailant hijacked Braniff International Airways Flight 38, a Boeing 727 jet carrying 101 persons on an intrastate service from Houston to Dallas, Texas. He subsequently surrendered and was sentenced to 20 years' imprisonment.

20 JANUARY 1972

A Hughes Airwest twin-jet DC-9, designated as Flight 800 and carrying 73 persons, was commandeered during an intrastate service from Las Vegas to Reno, Nevada. The hijacker, who had demanded half-a-million dollars and two parachutes, jumped from the aircraft in the vicinity of Denver, Colorado. He was captured, however, and later sentenced to prison for 40 years.

A Mohawk Airlines FH-227 of the type involved in failed hijack by parachute plot. (Fairchild Aircraft)

26–27 JANUARY 1972

IT was ten hours of terror for Eileen McAllister, the stewardess of Mohawk Airlines Flight 452, which was commandeered during a US domestic intrastate service from Albany, New York, to La Guardia Airport, serving New York City. The 45-year-old hijacker, an unemployed father of seven, held a pistol against the cabin attendant and also said he had a bomb.

The 42 other passengers disembarked safely when the twin-engine turboprop FH-227 landed at Westchester Airport, White Plains, New York. In this case of hijacking for ransom, the assailant demanded $200,000 and two parachutes, for himself and, to her surprise, the stewardess. As the aircraft type had no rear ramp, the jump would have to be made from a side door, adding to its difficulty and danger. The airline in fact offered to exchange a company vice president for the hostage. The money was finally delivered at around 01:30 local time on the second day, three hours past the hijacker's deadline. Finally, the aircraft took off and proceeded to circle the White Plains area.

In an act of defiance that probably saved her life, Stewardess McAllister refused to jump; her determination was enough for her captor to change his mind. He then ordered that the FH-227 should land at Poughkeepsie airport and that a car be made available for his getaway. An unmarked vehicle was waiting upon his arrival there, but so were FBI agents. After

The body of the hijacker lies beside his getaway car at Poughkeepsie, where he was killed following a 10-hour ordeal aboard a Mohawk Airlines FH-227 on 26–27 January 1972. (AP/Press Association Images)

placing his hostage in the front passenger seat, he got behind the steering wheel, whereupon he was immediately killed by a single shotgun blast. The ordeal of Eileen McAlister had ended with her escaping physical harm.

5 APRIL 1972

THE hijacker of a Merpati Nusantara Airlines Viscount was shot dead by the pilot at Maguwo Airport, Jogjakarta, Indonesia. Armed with two hand grenades, the assailant had commandeered the four-engine turboprop aircraft during a scheduled domestic flight from Surabaja to Djakarta, demanding a ransom of 20 million rupees and a parachute. He later lowered his ransom demand to five million rupees and released the other passengers.

During the siege, an army officer had slipped a pistol to the pilot, who then killed the hijacker.

7 APRIL 1972

A lone assailant armed with a pistol and an alleged bomb hijacked United Air Lines Flight 885, a Boeing 727 jet that had been on a US domestic service from Denver, Colorado, to Los Angeles, California, with 91 persons aboard. Demanding

$500,000, he parachuted from the aircraft near Provo, Utah, and was captured shortly thereafter. He was sentenced to 45 years in prison, and after escaping was killed resisting capture in 1974.

9 APRIL 1972

FLIGHT 942, a Pacific Southwest Airlines Boeing 727 jet on an intrastate service from Oakland to San Diego, California, with 92 persons aboard, was hijacked by a lone assailant who, claiming to have a hand grenade, demanded $500,000 and four parachutes, which he never used. He was subsequently captured and placed in a psychiatric facility for a year.

5 MAY 1972

AN Eastern Airlines Boeing 727 jet, operating as Flight 175 and carrying 55 persons on a US domestic service from Allentown, Pennsylvania, to Washington DC, was commandeered by a passenger who was armed with a pistol and also said he had a bomb. Carrying a ransom of more than $300,000, he parachuted from the aircraft over Honduras, but was later captured. He was sentenced to life imprisonment that September; the money was recovered about a year after the crime.

23 MAY 1972

A Compañia Ecuatoriana de Aviación SA Electra turboprop was commandeered and forced to return to Quito, Ecuador, from where it had taken off on a scheduled domestic service to Guayaquil. The hijacker demanded $40,000 ransom and a parachute. On the pretext of showing him how to use the parachute, a military officer boarded the aircraft and immediately opened fire, killing the assailant. The captain and a female passenger were slightly wounded.

2 JUNE 1972

IN the first of two US airline hijackings in a single day, a man and a woman commandeered a Western Air Lines Boeing 727 jetliner, operating as Flight 701, which had been on a domestic service from Los Angeles, California, to Seattle, Washington, with 97 persons aboard.

The hijackers received $500,000 in ransom money, which would later be recovered, and five parachutes, which would not be used. Switching to a longer-range Boeing 720 jet at San Francisco, the couple were flown to Algiers, where they surrendered. Arrested in France three years later, the man was given a prison sentence of five years, but his accomplice remained a fugitive.

2 JUNE 1972

THE second hijacking of the day involved a United Air Lines Boeing 727 jet, designated as Flight 239, which a lone gunman forcefully boarded at Reno, Nevada, as it was preparing for a domestic service to San Francisco, California. He parachuted from the aircraft in the vicinity of Lake Washoe, Nevada, some 25 miles (40km) south of Reno, with about three-quarters of the $200,000 ransom he had obtained, but was captured within two hours and subsequently sentenced to 30 years' imprisonment.

23 JUNE 1972

ARMED with a sub-machine gun, a hijacker commandeered American Airlines Flight 119, a Boeing 727 jet carrying 101 persons on a domestic service from St Louis, Missouri, to Tulsa, Oklahoma. Demanding more than half-a-million dollars in ransom, he parachuted from the aircraft in the vicinity of Peru, Indiana, but was caught five days later and was subsequently sentenced to life imprisonment.

30 JUNE 1972

A Hughes Airwest DC-9 twin jet airliner, which was operating as Flight 775 on a US domestic service from Seattle, Washington, to Portland, Oregon, with 42 persons aboard, was targeted for hijack by a lone assailant who turned out to be unarmed. His demand was for $50,000 and a parachute, though he was captured on the ground at the aircraft's intended destination. He was committed to a psychiatric facility five days later.

5 JULY 1972

THIS daring act of aerial piracy with a violent conclusion began about 10:00 local time, shortly after Pacific Southwest Airlines Flight 710 had taken off from Sacramento, California. There were 86 persons aboard the twin-jet Boeing 737, which was on a domestic intrastate service to Los Angeles, with an en-route stop at San Francisco.

The two young men who commandeered the aircraft, both armed with semi-automatic pistols, were demanding $800,000, two parachutes and a trip to the Soviet Union. Landing briefly at San Francisco International Airport, the 737 took off and proceeded to circle as the airline tried to meet these demands. It returned to the same airport around noon, which would mark the beginning of a four-hour stand-off with FBI agents, who surrounded the jetliner. One agent, posing as a pilot ostensibly bringing the ransom, parachutes and charts needed for the transcontinental flight, was asked to strip down to his underclothes to prove that he was unarmed before being allowed to re-dress and board the aircraft. The assailants did not know about the small pistol that he had stashed in a coat pocket.

Soon after the first agent had entered, a second one rushed aboard and almost immediately confronted one hijacker in the cockpit, killing him with two shotgun blasts. The second suspect in the rear of the cabin then opened fire, wounding three passengers, a 66-year-old man fatally. Emptying his weapon, the assailant was himself shot to death after threatening the agent with a knife. The gun battle was over moments after it began around 16:00 local time.

The family of the innocent man killed in the incident received a modest compensation for their loss: $100,000 in air travel insurance.

6 JULY 1972

FOR the second straight day, the same carrier was victimised by a hijacking-for-ransom incident during a service within the state of California, but this one ended peacefully. The lone gunman who commandeered Pacific Southwest Airlines Flight 389, a Boeing 727 jet en route from Oakland to Sacramento carrying 58 persons, first demanded a ransom of $455,000 and a parachute but later surrendered after the aircraft had returned to its point of origin. He was subsequently sentenced to prison for 30 years.

10 JULY 1972

A Lufthansa German Airlines twin-jet Boeing 737 was hijacked during a scheduled domestic service from Cologne to Munich, with the lone assailant demanding a ransom and a parachute. He was overpowered and captured by police.

12 JULY 1972

THE first of two US hijackings-for-ransom on the same day involved a National Airlines Boeing 727 jet, operating as Flight 496 on a domestic service to New York City from Philadelphia, Pennsylvania, with 120 persons aboard. The two assailants demanded three parachutes and $600,000, but they subsequently surrendered. They were sentenced to 50 and 60 years' imprisonment, respectively.

12 JULY 1972

A lone hijacker took over American Airlines Flight 633, a Boeing 727 jet carrying 57 persons on a domestic service from Oklahoma City, Oklahoma, to Dallas, Texas. He demanded a ransom of more than half-a-million dollars and a parachute, but then surrendered. He would later be sentenced to life imprisonment.

15 NOVEMBER 1972

ONE of Australia's rare cases of aerial hijacking involved Ansett Airlines of Australia Flight 232, a twin-engine turboprop Fokker F.27 on a domestic service from Adelaide to Darwin with 32 persons aboard. It was commandeered by a single assailant armed with a .22 calibre rifle, who, after landing at Alice Springs, Northern Territory, demanded a light aircraft and a parachute. He allowed one cabin attendant and all female passengers to disembark.

Subsequently, while walking to the single-engine Cessna provided, with the second stewardess as hostage, he was jumped by a plain-clothes detective, who was shot and wounded by the gunman. Running into nearby bushes the assailant then shot himself, and later succumbed in hospital.

12 MARCH 1974

A Japan Air Lines Boeing 747SR wide-bodied jetliner with 425 persons aboard was hijacked during a scheduled service from Tokyo to Okinawa by an 18-year-old assailant who demanded $55 million, 200 million yen, 15 parachutes, 15 pairs of handcuffs and mountain-climbing gear. He was captured on the ground at Naha, Okinawa, by police dressed as food handlers.

22 FEBRUARY 1975

A Viação Aérea São Paulo SA (VASP) Boeing 737 jetliner carrying 76 persons on a scheduled Brazilian domestic service from Goiana to Brasilia was commandeered by a gunman who set down an infant in the cockpit and grabbed a stewardess. During the eight hours of negotiations at Brasilia, he demanded 10 million cruzeiros, guns, parachutes, and the release by the Brazilian government of at least two prisoners.

After he had released the women and children aboard, the assailant was killed by police who had slipped onto the aircraft as the other passengers were leaving. One of the pilots suffered a hand wound.

20 OCTOBER 1977

DESIGNATED as Flight 101, a Frontier Airlines twin-jet Boeing 737 carrying 34 persons on an intrastate US domestic service from Grand Island to Lincoln, Nebraska, was commandeered on the ground by a shotgun-armed assailant who had stormed past the airport security checkpoint. He demanded more weapons, two parachutes and a large ransom, but released his hostages after the aircraft had landed at Atlanta, Georgia. There, following lengthy negotiations, the gunman shot and killed himself.

11 JULY 1980

SKYJACKINGS by parachute had almost faded to distant memory when a teenage boy commandeered Northwest Airlines Flight 608 on a US domestic service from Seattle, Washington, to Portland, Oregon. He demanded $100,000, a parachute and a light aeroplane, but was captured on the ground at Seattle-Tacoma International Airport. A prison sentence of 20 years was later deferred, and he underwent psychiatric treatment and vocational training.

18 JANUARY 1983

THREE men hijacked a Thai Airways Shorts 330 twin-engine turboprop that had been on a scheduled domestic service from Phitsanulok to Chiang Mai. When their demand for three parachutes was refused they escaped from the aircraft while it was on the ground, but two were subsequently captured.

21 OCTOBER 1991

A Czechoslovak Airlines (CSA) Tupolev Tu-134A jetliner on a scheduled domestic service from Bratislava to Prague with 17 persons aboard was commandeered by a teenage passenger who demanded one million German Marks and two parachutes. The aircraft landed at its intended destination, where the hijacker surrendered some 16 hours later.

4 SEPTEMBER 1992

MORE than 20 years after 'D.B. Cooper' leaped into the history books, the tactic of parachuting from a hijacked aircraft was brought back to the attention of the world with this bizarre incident, which rekindled memories of a bitter civil war that had lasted two decades but had ended years earlier.

Vietnam Airlines Flight 850, a wide-bodied, twin-jet Airbus A310 carrying 167 persons en route from Bangkok, Thailand, was nearing its destination, Ho Chi Minh City, Vietnam, when a lone assailant claiming to have an explosive device asked a cabin attendant to take him to the flight deck of the aircraft. Forcing the pilot to fly over the city at minimum airspeed and a height of only 500ft (150m), he would over a period of half-an-hour toss from the Airbus sackfuls of propaganda leaflets urging the citizens of Vietnam to overthrow the nation's Communist government. The former South Vietnamese fighter pilot then donned a parachute and jumped out of an emergency exit. The aircraft itself landed safely at its intended destination.

Captured outside the city two hours after making the jump, the hijacker would subsequently be sentenced to a prison term of 20 years. He was released by presidential amnesty after serving only six years, and two years later would be involved in another leaflet-dropping scheme, this time involving a light aeroplane.

25 MAY 2000

THE risks of parachuting from a commercial jet should have been understood, but perhaps were not fully realised until the death of the hijacker of Philippine Airlines Flight 812. Operating on a domestic service from Davao to Manila, the Airbus A330 wide-bodied jetliner, with 298 persons aboard, had been commandeered approximately one hour into its flight by an assailant armed with a pistol and a grenade, although the latter turned out to be a fake.

After robbing the passengers, the hijacker demanded that the aircraft's rear door be opened, which required the depressurisation of the cabin. Wearing a home-made parachute, he then jumped from the Airbus at an approximate height of 6,000ft (1,800m). His body was later found on Luzon, about 10 miles (16km) east of the capital city. Apparently his parachute had broken away during the descent. The aircraft landed safely, and there were no other casualties. For understandable reasons, no parachute hijackings have been attempted or even threatened since this incident.

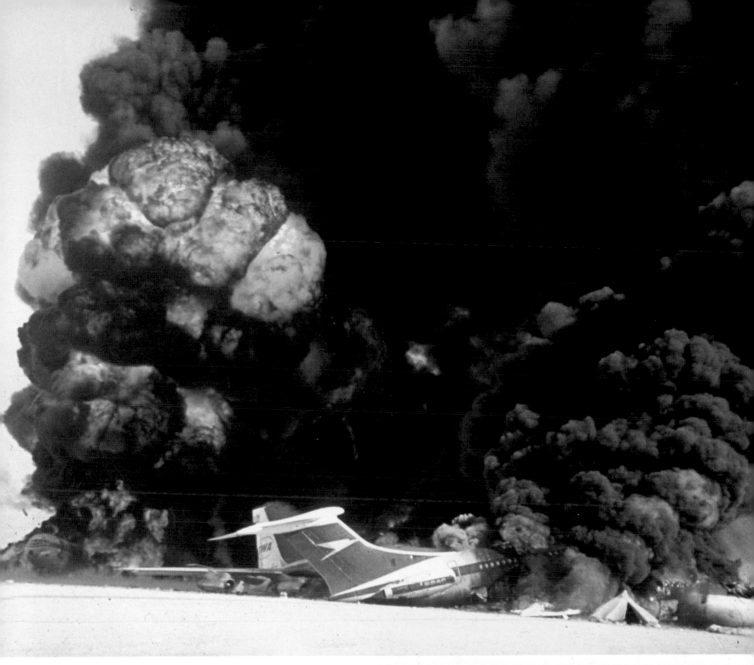

ABOVE: *Three of the four jetliners commandeered during mass hijacking incident 6–12 September 1970 burn in the Jordanian desert after being blown up by Palestinian guerrillas.* (Getty Images)

RIGHT: *The Pan Am aircraft hijacked with three other jets, and which was blown up 7 September 1970 at Cairo, Egypt, represented the first operational loss of a Boeing 747.* (Getty Images)

LEFT: *Hundreds of fragments of wreckage litter the countryside where Pacific Southwest Airlines Flight 1771 plummeted to earth on 7 December 1987 near Paso Robles, California.* (AP/Press Association Images)

OPPOSITE: *A huge crater marks the main fuselage impact of the Pan Am 747 destroyed by terrorist bomb on 21 December 1988 over Lockerbie, Scotland.* (AP/Press Association Images)

BELOW: *This Singapore Airlines A310 was the same aircraft involved in the hijacking incident 26–27 March 1991, which ended with the deaths of the four Pakistani assailants.* (Douglas Green)

LEFT: *The human side of aerial terrorism is reflected in this photo taken on 9 November 1995, wherein a hijacker holds a knife to the throat of a hostess aboard Olympic Airways Boeing 747 before the former was captured at Athens, Greece.* (Getty Images)

BELOW: *The wreckage of the Ethiopian Airlines Boeing 767 came to rest in shallow water in the Indian Ocean, off Grande Comoro Island, after the jetliner crashed during hijacking on 23 November 1996.* (AP/Press Association Images)

OPPOSITE TOP: *Negotiations continued for three days at Stansted Airport, near London, during a hijacking incident 6–10 February 2000, before the terrorist group that had commandeered the aircraft surrendered to the authorities.* (AP/Press Association Images)

OPPOSITE BOTTOM: *Vnukovo Airlines Tu-154 is stormed by security forces on 16 March 2001, the day after the hijacked Russian jetliner landed at Medina, Saudi Arabia.* (Getty Images)

OPPOSITE TOP: *A massive explosion shatters World Trade Center building No 2 in New York City after impact of United Airlines Boeing 767, one of four aircraft hijacked in day of terror 11 September 2001.* (AP/Press Association Images)

OPPOSITE BOTTOM: *The horrific destruction at the site of the World Trade Center, where two wide-bodied jetliners were intentionally crashed, resulting in most of the nearly 3,000 fatalities in the 'nine-eleven' terrorist attack.* (AP/Press Association Images)

RIGHT: *The fiery explosion occurring at the moment the hijacked American Airlines Boeing 757 struck the Pentagon building, located outside Washington, DC, is captured by a security camera on 11 September 2001.* (AP/Press Association Images)

BELOW: *The severely-damaged Pentagon is photographed after the terrorist attack on the US military complex, located outside Washington, DC, in which nearly 200 persons perished.* (AP/Press Association Images)

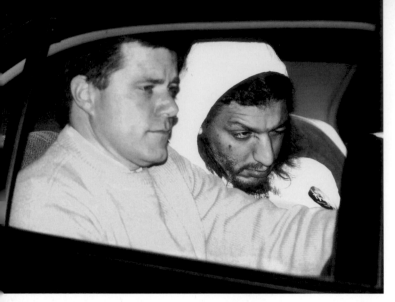

LEFT: *'Shoe bomber' Richard Reid is taken away in custody after an unsuccessful attempt to bring down an American Airlines Boeing 767 on a transatlantic flight 22 December 2001.* (AP/Press Association Images)

BELOW: *The remains of one of the two Russian jetliners destroyed in twin terrorist bombings on 24 August 2004, in which a total of 90 persons lost their lives.* (AP/Press Association Images)

BOTTOM: *Security personnel board an Aeromexico Boeing 737 at Mexico City International Airport, leading to the capture of a lone assailant in a hijacking incident on 9 September 2009.* (AP/Press Association Images)

8
Shot up and shot down

Not all violent acts against commercial aircraft are committed by greedy individuals or amoral terrorist groups – a number of aircraft have simply been shot down, even by established and democratic governments.

Commercial airliners have, on occasion, been mistaken for combat or other types of military aircraft, or have simply been victims of haste and faulty judgement. Israel, for instance, which lost a transport to hostile action in 1955, repeated the mistake itself with the downing of an off-course Libyan jetliner

nearly two decades later. A navigational error apparently precipitated the downing of Korean Air Lines Flight 007 by the Soviet Union in 1983.

The event sparked harsh criticism by the United States, which would find itself at the opposite end of a similar

A Korean Air Lines Boeing 747-200B of the type involved in history's most notorious incident of a commercial airliner being shot down, that of Flight 007 in September 1983. (Douglas Green)

controversy five years later, after shooting down an Iranian wide-bodied transport flying along a prescribed airway.

Occasionally aircraft have been targeted for destruction by ground forces, though sometimes it has simply been a matter of being in the wrong place at the wrong time.

As might be expected, all such events are more likely to occur during wartime, but they have occurred in peacetime too, especially during the uneasy era of 'the Cold War'.

Although arguably falling outside the technical definition of 'aerial terrorism', the following is a list of all air-to-air, surface-to-air and ground-to-ground attacks on commercial aircraft that were in operation at the time or which resulted in human casualties, excepting ground assaults by terrorist groups, which have been dealt with elsewhere.

26 MAY 1937

A British-built Airspeed Envoy operated by the French airline Air Pyrenees on a scheduled international service from Biarritz, France, to Bilbao, Spain, was attacked by German fighters over 'Basque country' near its destination, then crash-landed. Among the six occupants of the twin-engine commercial transport, the pilot and one passenger suffered injuries.

24 AUGUST 1938

A China National Aviation Corporation Douglas DC-2 (32) on a scheduled service from Hong Kong to Chungking was attacked by five Japanese military fighters, then strafed after it had ditched in the Pearl River near Wangmoon, China, located some 225 miles (360km) north-west of Macao. Among the 17 persons aboard, only one passenger and two members of its crew of four (the pilot and radio operator) survived. The wreckage was later salvaged, and the bodies of all but three of the victims were recovered.

6 MAY 1939

A Eurasia Aviation Corporation Junkers Ju.52/3M (XVII) was reportedly shot down near Hanchung, China, by Japanese aircraft. The number of casualties is not known.

14 JUNE 1940

A Junkers Ju.52/3m (OH-ALL) flown by the Finnish carrier Aero O/Y was shot down near Kar, Estonian SSR, USSR, by a Soviet military aircraft, and all nine persons aboard the trimotored transport were killed.

20 JUNE 1940

AN Air France Dewoitine D.338 three-engine airliner (F-ARTD) was inadvertently shot down by French anti-aircraft fire near Ouistreham, Normandy, and its pilot was killed.

7 JULY 1940

AN Air France Dewoitine D.338 (F-AQBA) was shot down by a Japanese fighter over the Gulf of Tonkin, off French Indo-China. The number of casualties is not known.

27 OCTOBER 1940

A Eurasia Junkers Ju.52/3m airliner (XXV) was attacked by a Japanese aircraft and crash-landed near Kunming, Yunnan, China. Among its four occupants, both crew members were injured, but the two passengers escaped unscathed.

29 OCTOBER 1940

NINE persons aboard were killed when a China National Aviation Corporation Douglas DC-2 (39) on a scheduled domestic flight from Chungking to Kunming was attacked by Japanese fighters, then strafed on the ground after crash-landing some 75 miles (120km) north-east of its destination. Three passengers and two crew members, one of them the co-pilot, survived.

27 NOVEMBER 1940

AN Air France Farman F-224 four-engine airliner (F-AROA) was shot down by an Italian aircraft over the Mediterranean. The number of casualties is not known.

3 JUNE 1941

A Great Western and Southern Air Lines de Havilland Dragon (G-ACPY), on a British domestic service from the Isles of Scilly to Penzance, Cornwall, was lost over the Atlantic with six persons aboard (five passengers and the pilot). The twin-engine commercial biplane was believed to have been shot down by German military aircraft shortly after its departure at around 17:00 local time.

24 JANUARY 1942

A Douglas DC-3 (PK-AFW) operated by the Dutch airline Koninklijke Nederlandsch-Indische Luchtvaart Maatschappij (KNILM) was reportedly shot down by the Japanese near Samarinda, on the island of Borneo. The number of casualties is not known.

26 JANUARY 1942

ANOTHER transport flown by KNILM, this one a Grumman Goose twin-engine amphibian (PK-AFS), was shot down by Japanese military aircraft near Kupang, on the Western Pacific island of Timor. The number of casualties is unknown.

30 JANUARY 1942

A British Overseas Airways Corporation (BOAC) Short S.23 'Empire Class' flying boat (G-AEUH), on a scheduled service for the Australian carrier Qantas Empire Airways from Darwin, in the Northern Territory of Australia, to Kupang, on the island of Timor, was reportedly shot down at sea by Japanese aircraft near its destination. Five survivors were rescued from among the 18 persons aboard the transport, including two members of its crew of five.

15 FEBRUARY 1942

A BOAC Consolidated Liberator four-engine transport (G-AGDR) was apparently shot down by accident and crashed in the English Channel south of Plymouth, England, in the vicinity of the Eddystone Lighthouse. All nine persons aboard (four passengers and a crew of five) were killed.

28 FEBRUARY 1942

A BOAC Short S.23 (G-AETZ) with 20 persons aboard (16 passengers and a crew of four) was lost over the Indian Ocean some 150 miles (250km) from Java, in the Dutch East Indies, from where it had taken off earlier on a scheduled flight to Broome, Western Australia. The four-engine flying boat was

believed to have been shot down by Japanese aircraft during a service undertaken by BOAC on behalf of the Australian carrier Qantas Empire Airways.

3 MARCH 1942

FOUR persons aboard were killed when a KNILM DC-3 airliner (PK-AFV) was shot down by Japanese fighters near Wyndham, Western Australia. Eight others aboard the Dutch airliner survived.

28 MARCH 1942

A Linee Aeree Transcontinentali Italiane SA (LATI) Savoia-Marchetti SM 82 (I-BURA) was shot down, apparently at sea, near Sicily. The number of casualties aboard the Italian trimotored airliner is not known.

13 AUGUST 1942

AN Air France Lioré et Olivier H.246 (F-AREJ) on a scheduled service from Marseille to Algiers was attacked by Royal Air Force Hurricane fighters some 50 miles (80km) from its destination. The damaged four-engine flying boat actually reached Algiers, but sank after landing in the water, with four of its passengers losing their lives.

15 NOVEMBER 1942

THE number of casualties and the location of the shooting-down of a Linee Aeree Transcontinentali Italiane SA (LATI) Savoia-Marchetti SM 75 tri-motor airliner (I-TELO) are not known. It was probably on an Italian domestic flight.

10 APRIL 1943

ANOTHER Linee Aeree Transcontinentali Italiane SA (LATI) Savoia-Marchetti SM 75 (I-BONI) was shot down, although the location and the number of casualties aboard the Italian trimotored airliner are not known.

1 JUNE 1943

ONE of the commercial air routes not disrupted by the Second World War was the one between Portugal and England.

A Short S.23 flying boat, two of which were believed shot down in the Pacific Theatre by Japanese forces in early 1942. (Philip Jarrett)

It was while on this service that one civil airliner met with a violent end.

The twin-engine Douglas DC-3 in question was operated by KLM Royal Dutch Airlines but, owing to the German occupation of The Netherlands, was registered in Great Britain as G-AGBB. Designated as Flight 2L272, the transport departed from Portela Airport, serving Lisbon, bound for an airfield at Whitchurch in Somerset, England. It was to follow the coasts of Portugal and Spain, staying clear of occupied France.

During its flight, eight Luftwaffe Junkers Ju.88 twin-engine fighters took off from France. Perhaps it was fate, or perhaps it was German intelligence gathering combined with good timing, but the paths of the fighters and G-AGBB intersected over the Bay of Biscay at around 13:00 local time.

Soon after visual contact with the airliner was established, an attack commenced. The radio operator of the DC-3 was able to transmit a message before the fighters struck, and moments later, the airliner, which had been set afire, plummeted into the sea. All 17 persons aboard perished, including a crew of four and British actor turned Hollywood star Leslie Howard. The German pilots reported seeing four parachutes, but this could not be explained as the airliner was not known to have been carrying such emergency equipment.

The German attack on an unarmed commercial transport may have been ruthless, but it was not unprecedented; twice in the previous six months aircraft flying along the same route had come under attack, though on both earlier occasions they had managed to escape.

11 AUGUST 1943

ALL three of its crew members (and only occupants) lost their lives when a China National Aviation Corporation Douglas DC-3 (48) was apparently shot down by a Japanese fighter over the Hertz Valley region, in the Chinese province of Yunnan, west of Kunming, which was its destination during a cargo service originating at Dinjan, India.

27 AUGUST 1943

A Douglas DC-3 (SE-BAF) flown by the Swedish carrier Aktiebolaget Aerotransport (ABA) was apparently shot down by German aircraft over the North Sea during a scheduled service to Sweden from England. There were no survivors among the seven persons (three passengers and four crew members) aboard.

13 OCTOBER 1943

FOR the second time in two months, a China National Aviation Corporation cargo transport, also a Douglas DC-3 (72), was apparently shot down by a Japanese fighter over Southern China while en route from Dinjan, India, to Kunming, in the Chinese province of Yunnan. All three members of the aircraft's crew (and its only occupants) were killed.

22 OCTOBER 1943

AN Aktiebolaget Aerotransport (ABA) DC-3 (SE-BAG) was shot down by German aircraft near Halla, Vasterbotten, Sweden, located about 60 miles (100km) north-west of Ornskoldsvik, possibly during a scheduled domestic service. All but two of the 15 persons aboard the airliner were killed in the incident.

27 SEPTEMBER 1944

ALL nine persons aboard (five passengers and a crew of four) were killed when a Deutsche Lufthansa AG Focke Wulf Fw.200 Condor (D-AMHL) was shot down by a British fighter near Dijon, Bourgogne, France. The German-built and registered four-engine airliner had been on a scheduled international service from Stuttgart, Germany, to Barcelona, Spain, when destroyed in darkness at around 20:30 local time.

29 NOVEMBER 1944

A Deutsche Lufthansa AG Focke Wulf Fw.200 Condor (D-ARHW) was shot down over the Baltic Sea near Falsterbo, Sweden, located some 25 miles (40km) west of Trelleborg, and all ten persons aboard (six passengers and a crew of four) were killed. The German airliner had been on a scheduled international service from Berlin to Stockholm, Sweden, when fired upon and hit, apparently accidentally, by a German patrol boat at around 10:30 local time.

21 APRIL 1945

IN the closing days of the Second World War, Allied forces shot down a Deutsche Lufthansa AG Focke-Wulf Fw.200 Condor (D-ASHH) near Piesenkofen, Germany. The German four-engine airliner was capable of carrying about two dozen passengers, but the casualties resulting from this incident are not known.

17 OCTOBER 1947

A Central Air Transport Corporation C-47 was shot down by Communist revolutionary forces near Pao-ting (Baoding), in the Chinese province of Hopei (Hebei), while on a domestic freight service from Peking to Shijiazhuang. All three crewmen of the aircraft were killed.

27 OCTOBER 1947

A China National Aviation Corporation C-46 cargo transport was brought down by Communist ground fire while approaching to land at the airfield serving Yulin, Shaanxi, China, which was an en-route stop during a non-scheduled domestic service from Peking to Shihchiachuang. Two of its three crew members were killed, and the surviving radio operator was taken prisoner.

29 APRIL 1948

IN an apparent attempt to kill one of its passengers, shots were fired at a Pan American World Airways DC-3 as it took off from San José, Costa Rica, on a scheduled international service. There were no injuries among the 12 persons aboard, including a crew of three, and the American-registered airliner was able to continue on to its intended destination despite suffering some damage in the attack.

25 OCTOBER 1948

A Douglas DC-3 (HS-PC103) cargo transport operated by the Thai carrier Pacific Overseas Airlines was believed to have been shot down at sea off Sumatra by Dutch aircraft. The fate of its occupants was not reported.

21 DECEMBER 1948

A Douglas DC-3 (OK-WDN), designated as Ceskoslovenske Aerolinie (CSA) Flight 584 and on an international service from Rome to Athens, was reportedly shot down by Greek insurgents, the incident occurring around 15:00 local time some 100 miles (150km) south-west of its destination. Struck by ground fire, the transport fell into the Tavgetos Mountains near Kalamata, in the province of Peloponnisos, and all 24 persons aboard (19 passengers and five crew members) were killed.

24 JULY 1950

AFTER refusing its order to land, a DC-3 flown by the Lebanese carrier Compagnie Générale de Transports, on a non-scheduled service from Jerusalem to Beirut, was attacked by an Israeli Air Force Spitfire fighter over Israeli territory north of Rosh Pinna, near the Sea of Galilee. Among the 28 persons aboard the airliner, one passenger and the radio operator were killed by the Spitfire's guns, while seven others suffered injuries.

Following the attack, which occurred at around 19:15 local time, the DC-3 flew back across the border and the fighter gave up the pursuit. Lebanese officials insisted that their aircraft never entered Israeli airspace and had been flying three miles (5km) north of the border when attacked.

29 APRIL 1952

AN Air France DC-4, on a scheduled service to (West) Berlin from Frankfurt, (West) Germany, was attacked by two Soviet MiG jet fighters near Konnern, (East) Germany, some 100 miles (150km) from its destination. Among the 17 persons aboard the airliner, including a crew of five, two passengers and a steward were injured.

The attack occurred at around 10:00 local time, at an approximate height of 7,000ft (2,100m), although the damaged transport subsequently landed safely at Templehof Airport, in Berlin. Western powers rejected the Soviet contention that the DC-4 had strayed from the designated air corridor laid out over Communist territory.

Ironically, the same aircraft would be successfully shot down over Laos 20 years later (see page 111).

3 MAY 1952

A Société de Transports Aériens en Extrême Orient DC-3 (F-BEIB) was fired upon by rebel fighters while taking off at around 17:00 local time from Phan Thiet, Indochina (Vietnam), on an internal service to Saigon, located some 100 miles (150km) to the west. The French-registered airliner caught fire and was destroyed in the attack, and among its 14 occupants a steward was killed and some of the passengers suffered injuries.

29 NOVEMBER 1952

A Douglas C-47 operated by the Taiwanese carrier Civil Air Transport was reportedly shot down over the Chinese region of Manchuria (Jilin) while on a special service. Two of the aircraft's four occupants were killed in the incident.

27 JULY 1953

IN what proved to be the last military action of the Korean War, a twin-engine Ilyushin Il-12 operated by the Soviet airline Aeroflot was shot down by a US Air Force F-86 jet fighter, about ten miles (16km) south of the Yalu River, North Korea. All 21 persons aboard (15 passengers and six crew members) were killed. The Soviet Union claimed the attack had occurred over China.

According to the US Air Force, the Il-12, which it identified as a transport 'assigned to Communist Air Forces in China', was flying in an easterly direction at 6,000ft (1,800m) when spotted some 35 miles (55km) north-east of Kanggye. The Soviets identified it as a regular commercial flight to Vladivostok, in the USSR, from Lushun, Liaoning, China.

After one firing pass by the F-86 both engines of the Ilyushin transport caught fire, and soon afterward, at around 12:30 local time, the aircraft exploded and plummeted to earth.

3 JUNE 1954

A Belgian Airlines (SABENA) DC-3 cargo transport carrying a load of pigs was attacked by a MiG jet fighter in Soviet markings while flying at 11,500ft (3,500m) just inside the Yugoslav border, over the town of Murska Sobata. Its radio operator was

killed and two of its other three crew members were wounded, though the damaged DC-3 managed a forced landing near Graz, Austria.

The transport had been on a scheduled service from London to Belgrade, Yugoslavia, when the fighter reportedly dived out of the clouds and tried to force it towards Hungarian airspace at around 10:00 local time. When the airline crew ignored the action, the MiG opened up with cannon fire.

23 JULY 1954

AT around 09:45 local time, a Cathay Pacific Airways Douglas DC-4 (VR-HEU) on a scheduled service from Singapore to Hong Kong was shot down by two Communist Chinese MiG jet fighters, ditching off Hainan Island in the South China Sea. Ten persons aboard the Hong Kong-registered airliner lost their lives, including two of its six crew members. A US Navy amphibious aircraft rescued the eight survivors.

27 JULY 1955

THE risks of breaching the 'Iron Curtain' surrounding Eastern Europe were fully realised in this disastrous incident. El Al Israel Airlines Flight 402/26, a Lockheed 049 Constellation (4X-AKC), had stopped at Vienna, Austria, as scheduled, before proceeding on towards Tel Aviv, the second segment of a service originating at London.

After passing over Belgrade, Yugoslavia, the aircraft began to stray to the east of the prescribed airway. An Israeli investigative commission attributed the deviation to an incorrect radio compass indication, the instrument apparently having been affected by thunderstorm activity in the area. This must have misled the crew into believing that they had reached the reporting point at Skopje, Yugoslavia, when in fact the flight was seven minutes from that position. The course would then have been altered to a heading of 142° in order to stay within

Shown in the livery of another airline, this Ilyushin Il-12 is the type operated by Aeroflot that was shot down during the Korean War. (Philip Jarrett)

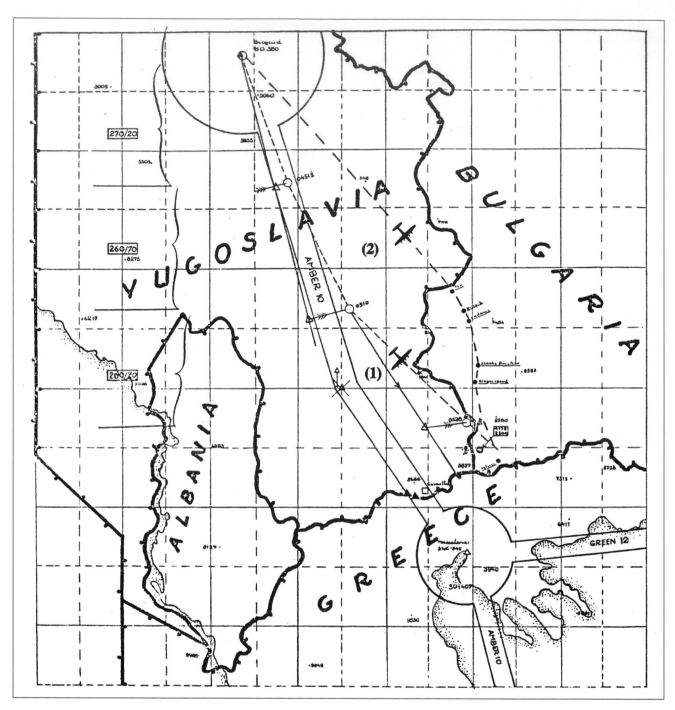

The route taken by the El Al Constellation shot down on 27 July 1955, (1) according to the Israeli Commission, and (2) according to the Bulgarian authorities. (International Civil Aviation Organisation)

the airway. Considering the heavy cloud coverage, westerly winds of 70 knots – 50 knots above those forecast – and the absence of navigational aids between Belgrade and Skopje, the crew could not have been aware of their drift.

The Constellation entered Bulgarian airspace some 40 miles (65km) east of the proper track. Shortly thereafter, it radioed the distress message 'SOS DE 4X-AKC'. The first attack by two jet fighters was at the cruising altitude of 18,000ft (5,500m), and set the airliner afire. As it was descending, the crew apparently looking for a place to land, a second attack occurred at approximately 8,000ft (2,500m), and a third at about 2,000ft (600m), whereupon an explosion occurred in the right wing, and the aircraft then broke up and plummeted to earth near Petrich, Bulgaria. All 58 persons aboard (51 passengers and a crew of seven) perished. The disaster took place at around 07:40 local time.

Israel rejected Bulgaria's contention that the Constellation had been notified within the established regulations but refused to land before the fighters opened fire. Bulgaria maintained it had flown much deeper into its airspace, though this contradicted the accounts of ground witnesses in both Yugoslavia and Greece. It also expressed regret over the incident, admitting that its defence forces had exhibited 'a certain haste' in downing the aircraft. In August 1957 Israel also rejected Bulgaria's offer to compensate for the downing of the Constellation.

1 JUNE 1959

A twin-engine Curtiss Wright C-46 (TI-1022) flown by the Costa Rican carrier Aerolíneas Nacionales SA crashed and burned in Nicaragua after reportedly being 'forced down' by Nicaraguan Air Force fighters. There were an estimated 50 to 60 persons aboard the airliner, all of whom were killed.

4 AUGUST 1961

AN Iranian Airways DC-4 (EP-ADK), which had become lost due to faulty navigation during a non-scheduled freight service from Tehran to Beirut, was fired on by an unidentified aircraft. The attack took place in early morning darkness at an approximate altitude of 15,000ft (4,500m) over or near the Caspian Sea, presumably in Soviet airspace. Subsequently, the transport managed a successful wheels-up landing without injury to its three crew members (and only occupants). Damaged in the attack, EP-ADK was destroyed in the crash-landing.

20 SEPTEMBER 1962

Chartered by the United Nations, a Transair Sweden AB DC-3 airliner (UN-202) was shot down by Congolese forces near the railway station at Kamonza, in the Congo, some 180 miles (290km) north of Kamina. Among its ten occupants, two crew members were killed and four of the survivors suffered injuries.

16 SEPTEMBER 1965

AFTER apparently being hit by ground fire, an Air Vietnam Douglas DC-3 (XV-NIC) crashed and burned in a rice paddy at around 10:30 local time, or some four minutes after its departure from Quang Ngai, (South) Vietnam, located approximately 340 miles (550km) north-east of Saigon, where the scheduled domestic service was destined. Including the crew of three and one passenger who was found alive at the crash site but later succumbed to injuries, all 39 persons aboard were killed.

10 APRIL 1969

THE three crew members (and only occupants) of an Ethiopian Airlines DC-3 (ET-AAQ) were killed when the cargo transport, being operated for United Arab Airlines on a non-scheduled cargo service, was reportedly shot down near Suez, Egypt.

25 APRIL 1969

A Pan African Airlines DC-4 on a troop transport flight was hit by anti-aircraft fire while descending to land at Enugu, Biafra, Nigeria. Among the 86 persons aboard, six passengers were seriously injured, but the Nigerian aircraft returned safely to Lagos, where the non-scheduled domestic service had originated. The DC-4 had been struck at around 15:20 local time while at an approximate height of 6,000ft (1,800m), with the shell producing a hole measuring 5ft (1.5m) in the starboard side of its fuselage.

18 JUNE 1969

AN Ethiopian Airlines Boeing 707-360C jetliner sustained damage in an attack by three members of the Eritrean National Liberation Front, who used automatic weapons and hand grenades, during a transit stop at the airport serving Karachi, (West) Pakistan. The passengers were at the time in the terminal, and there were no injuries in the attack. The three young assailants were captured and detained.

19 AUGUST 1969

FLOWN by Air America, a civilian airline operated by the US Central Intelligence Agency, and on charter to the US Agency for International Development, a single-engine Pilatus PC-6C Porter (N196X) crashed and burned in mountainous terrain during an internal Laotian service from Long Tieng to Sam Thong after the pilot was reportedly shot, presumably by someone firing at the aeroplane from the ground. All 13 persons aboard the Porter were killed in the incident, which occurred at around 17:00 local time.

26 JUNE 1970

IT was a lucky day for the 104 persons aboard Alitalia Flight 713, a DC-8 Series 43 jet airliner that had been on a service from Tehran to Rome.

While cruising at an approximate height of 30,000ft (9,000m) over Syria, about five miles (8km) east of Damascus, the Italian-registered aircraft experienced a heavy jolt, dropping some 3,000ft (900m). Its No 1 power plant having been shut down, the DC-8 landed safely at Beirut, Lebanon, which was a scheduled en-route stop. There were no casualties, but damage to the aircraft was frighteningly serious. In its left wing was found a hole approximately 2ft (0.6m) in diameter, and both port engines were peppered with hundreds of metal fragments. It was concluded that the aircraft had miraculously survived being struck by a missile launched during an Israeli air attack on Syrian positions along the Golan Heights.

11 FEBRUARY 1972

A Royal Air Lao DC-4 (XW-TDE) was apparently shot down near Vientiane, Laos, where it was to have landed during a scheduled service originating at Saigon, (South) Vietnam. All 23 persons aboard (17 passengers and a crew of six) were killed. In its last radio transmission, received at 13:20 local time, the airliner was reported to be flying at 10,000ft (3,000m).

2 OCTOBER 1972

NINE persons aboard were killed, including two pilots, when a Cambodia Air Commercial DC-3 (XW-TDA) was hit by a mortar shell and crashed while approaching to land at Kampot, Cambodia, during a scheduled domestic passenger service. There were no survivors.

21 FEBRUARY 1973

A number of intentional acts of aggression had soured Arab-Israeli relations even before this deadly blunder over the Sinai Peninsula.

Operating as Flight 114, a Libyan Arab Airlines Boeing 727-224 jetliner (5A-DAH) had taken off from Tripoli and

A Libyan Arab Airlines Boeing 727-224 like the one downed over the Sinai by Israeli fighters in February 1973. (Douglas Green)

stopped at Banghazi before proceeding on towards its ultimate destination, Cairo.

Although the aircraft generally assumed the correct heading, its track was displaced to the east, then to the south, of the normal flight route to the Egyptian capital. Significantly, low cloud cover obscured the ground during much of the trip, and it was only when they were over the Sinai Peninsula, and the terrain had become visible, that the crew realised their incorrect position. By now, however, the 727 had already been spotted on radar by Israeli defence forces, which sent up two F-4 Phantom II jet fighters.

Using hand gestures, rocking their wings and, eventually, by firing their cannons across the nose of the intruder, the military pilots tried to get the commercial transport to land. The airline crew apparently did not understand the actions of the fighter pilots, and when they turned back and raised their undercarriage, which had been lowered, this was construed by the Israelis as an attempt to escape. At an approximate height of 5,000ft (1,500m), 5A-DAH was attacked and hit with tracers, touching off a fire. The jetliner subsequently crashed and exploded some 10 miles (16km) to the east of the Suez Canal while attempting a belly-landing in the desert, and 108 persons aboard were killed, including eight crew members. Four passengers and the aircraft's co-pilot survived with injuries.

The navigational error that led to the shooting down of the 727 probably resulted from a strong tailwind, and in its report on the tragedy the International Civil Aviation Organisation (ICAO) ruled it 'probable' that the Cairo non-directional beacon had not been functioning properly at the time. In addition, the Cairo approach control radar was out of order, making it impossible for controllers to detect the deviation.

Israeli Defence Minister Moshe Dayan admitted an 'error in judgement' in the downing of the Libyan transport, and his country agreed to compensate the families of the victims.

4 MAY 1973

THREE persons aboard were killed and eight injured when a Khmer Hansa aircraft, possibly a DC-3, was hit by a mortar shell and crashed as it was taking off from Kampot, Cambodia, about 100 miles (160km) south-west of Phnom Penh.

19 MAY 1973

A Cambodia Air Commercial DC-3 airliner (XW-TDM) was apparently hit by ground fire shortly after it had taken off from Svay Rieng, Cambodia, crashing some 60 miles (100km) southeast of Phnom Penh. All 11 persons aboard (nine passengers and two pilots) were killed.

28 NOVEMBER 1974

AN Air Cambodge Douglas DC-4 cargo transport on a service from Cambodia to Hong Kong was apparently shot down near An Loc, (South) Vietnam, some 60 miles (100km) north of Saigon, at around 15:00 local time. All five persons aboard were killed.

16 DECEMBER 1974

A Korean Air Lines DC-8 Super 63 jetliner that had accidentally strayed into restricted airspace was fired at by South Korean anti-aircraft units near Seoul. The aircraft was not hit, but shrapnel falling into the city killed one person and injured 27.

12 MARCH 1975

AN Air Vietnam Douglas DC-4 (XV-NUJ) was apparently shot down by North Vietnamese or Viet Cong forces over the Central Highlands of (South) Vietnam, approximately 15 miles (25km) south-west of Pleiku, and all 26 persons aboard (20 passengers and a crew of six) were killed.

The airliner was last reported cruising along a prescribed airway at 11,000ft (3,400m) on a scheduled service to Saigon from Vientiane, Laos, when it was believed to have been hit by anti-aircraft fire or a hand-held surface-to-air missile in twilight conditions, around 18:30 local time.

8 APRIL 1975

A South African Airways Boeing 747 wide-bodied jetliner carrying 287 persons on a scheduled service from Johannesburg to London was hit by ground fire and damaged while landing at Luanda, Angola, an en-route stop. There were no injuries.

11 APRIL 1975

TWO of its three crew members (and only occupants) lost their lives when a Sorya Airlines DC-3 crashed and burned while attempting a forced landing after being hit by ground fire as it took off from Phnom Penh, Cambodia, on a domestic flight to Kompong Chhnang,

27 JUNE 1976

A Middle East Airlines Boeing 720B jetliner (OO-AGE) parked at the international airport serving Beirut was destroyed by a rocket hit and shellfire. One member of its flight crew was killed and two others injured in the attack, which occurred after the arrival of the Lebanese-registered aircraft on a scheduled international service from Amman, Jordan. The passengers had fortunately already disembarked.

26 NOVEMBER 1977

AN African Lux C-54B cargo transport (9Q-CAM), on a non-scheduled service from Rhodesia to Zaire, was shot down by Mozambique ground forces over Tete Province, Mozambique. Its two crew members (and only occupants) were reportedly captured.

20 APRIL 1978

THOUGH overshadowed in history by the Soviet downing of KAL Flight 007 five years later, the following was a headline-grabbing incident in its own right.

The bizarre saga of Korean Air Lines Flight 902 began at Orly Airport, serving Paris, from where the Boeing Advanced 707-321B jetliner (HL-7429) took off, bound for Seoul, South Korea. This polar trip would include an en-route stop at Anchorage, Alaska. Built more than a decade earlier, the aircraft lacked a modern inertial navigational system, and as a magnetic compass is useless in this part of the world, and with a scarcity in ground aids, the crew would have to rely upon the older but well-proven method of celestial navigation.

Trouble first arose in the vicinity of Iceland, when atmospheric conditions prevented the aircraft from communicating with the corresponding ground station. Approximately over Greenland, and following the instructions of the navigator, the 707 inexplicably initiated a turn of 112°, heading in a south-easterly direction towards the USSR. A while later, the pilot, Captain Kim Chang Kyu, sensed something was amiss by the rather obvious fact that the sun was on the wrong side of the aircraft!

Before the crew could take any corrective action, the transport was intercepted by at least two Soviet Su-15 jet fighters, one of which flew just off its starboard wing for 10 to 15 minutes before veering away. (The Soviets would later claim that the fighter pilots had tried in vain to contact the jetliner, though this was refuted by the Korean crew.) Moments later, the 707 was under attack; one of the fighters raked it with cannon fire, blasting away its left wingtip and causing a rapid decompression of its cabin.

Descending rapidly from 35,000 to 5,000ft (10,700 to 1,500m), the damaged aircraft was kept under control, the pilot then skilfully crash-landing it on a frozen lake in moonlit darkness, at about 22:15 local time, near Kem', RSFSR, located some 280 miles (450km) south of Murmansk. Among the 109 aboard, two passengers were killed and 13 other persons seriously wounded, all during the aerial attack. Numerous minor injuries were also reported.

The passengers and most of the crew were released two days afterwards, the captain and navigator about a week later. It was learned in 1991 that the Soviet pilot had ignored orders to destroy the 707.

3 SEPTEMBER 1978

FLIGHT 825, an Air Rhodesia four-engine turboprop Vickers Viscount 782D (VP-WAS), had taken off shortly after 17:00 local time from Kariba, on a domestic service to Salisbury. About five minutes later it sent a distress message reporting the failure of both starboard power plants, the airliner having been struck near the right in-board engine by a heat-seeking missile fired by nationalist guerrillas.

The following day its burned wreckage was located in bush country some 35 miles (55km) south-east of Kariba. Eight passengers were found alive from the 56 persons, including a crew of four, who had been aboard. The world also learned with horror that ten others who had survived the crash-landing had been murdered, being allegedly shot by the guerrillas.

17 NOVEMBER 1978

A Zambia Airways Hawker Siddeley 748 Series 2A was damaged by guerrilla ground fire as it was on its final approach to land at the international airport serving Lusaka, Zambia. There were no injuries, however, and the twin-engine turboprop landed safely.

12 FEBRUARY 1979

FOR the second time in less than six months, an Air Rhodesia airliner was destroyed by nationalist guerrilla forces. All 59 persons aboard (54 passengers and a crew of five) perished when the Vickers Viscount 748D turboprop (VP-YND), designated as Flight 827, was hit by two surface-to-air missiles. It crashed shortly before 17:00 local time approximately 30 miles (50km) east of Kariba, from where it had taken off about five minutes earlier after making an en-route stop during a domestic service originating at Victoria Falls, with an ultimate destination of Salisbury.

September 1978: Rhodesian security forces recover the remains of victims from a Viscount airliner shot down by Joshua Nkomo's guerrilla forces. (AP/Press Association Images)

The downing was described as a 'mistake' by a guerrilla spokesman, resulting from an erroneous belief that the Rhodesian Army commander had been aboard. In order to reduce the threat posed by terrorist-launched missiles, Air Rhodesia introduced a new matt grey colour scheme on its aircraft and fitted their engine exhausts with baffles, in addition to adopting new flying procedures.

8 JUNE 1980

HAVING been reportedly misidentified as a foreign aircraft, a Líneas Aéreas de Angola (TAAG-Angola Airlines) Yakovlev Yak-40 (D2-TYC) was accidentally brought down by anti-aircraft fire at around 15:30 local time near Matala, Huíla, Angola, during a scheduled domestic service from Jamba to Lubango. All 19 persons aboard the tri-jet airliner (15 passengers and a crew of four) perished.

23 SEPTEMBER 1980

ALL four crew members (its only occupants) were killed when an Iraqi Airways Ilyushin Il-76T (YI-AIO) was apparently shot down during an Iranian air raid as the four-engine cargo jet was approaching to land at Baghdad at the end of an international service from Paris.

16 MAY 1981

A Líneas Aéreas de Angola (TAAG-Angola Airlines) Lockheed L-100-20 Hercules (D2-EAS) was shot down near Menongue, Angola, its four crew members (and only occupants) being killed. The four-engine turboprop cargo aircraft was approaching to land when its No 4 power plant was hit by a heat-seeking missile at an approximate height of 4,000ft (1,200m).

19 JANUARY 1982

A Boeing 707-348C jet transport (70-ACJ) operated by Alyemda Democratic Yemen Airlines was fired upon over Syria by an unidentified jet fighter during a non-scheduled freight service to Aden, (South) Yemen, from Tripoli, Libya. The aircraft managed a safe emergency landing at Damascus, its five occupants escaping serious injury. The airline elected not to have the damaged 707 repaired.

1 SEPTEMBER 1983

THE Cold War never experienced any direct exchanges between the Super Powers, although there were a number of 'flashpoints', during which tensions reached the brink. The most infamous of these was the Cuban missile crisis in 1962, but also standing out in history was the downing by Soviet defence forces of Korean Air Lines Flight 007.

This international incident began as a routine trip from New York City to Seoul, South Korea. Making the flight would be a Boeing 747-230B (HL7442), which made its departure from John F. Kennedy International Airport on the evening of 31 August. Stopping for refuelling and a change of crew at Anchorage, Alaska, the wide-bodied jetliner proceeded on the second leg of its transpacific service. Aboard were 240 passengers, 20 cabin attendants, six off-duty company personnel and three flight crewmen.

Only ten minutes out of Anchorage the aircraft began to stray from the prescribed airway, assuming a track that would ultimately take it into the restricted airspace of the Soviet Union. A military radar recording captured this deviation, but it was of little use, since at the time there was no interaction between military and civilian air traffic control services; furthermore, such a deviation was not considered abnormal.

Entering Soviet territory while at a point some 250 miles (400km) to the right of assigned route R-20, the 747 passed over the southern Kamchatka Peninsula, then the location of both missile and submarine bases. Fighters that were scrambled into action failed to locate the transport, and it proceeded out over the Sea of Okhotsk. Defence forces would get a second opportunity as the jetliner again entered Soviet territory, this time over the southern tip of Sakhalin Island, another militarily sensitive area.

Shortly after 03:00 local time, the pilot of a Soviet Air Force Sukhoi Su-15 jet fighter radioed that in the pre-dawn darkness he had made visual contact with what he referred to as the 'target'. During the ensuing pursuit, which lasted some 20 minutes, the Russian was believed to have implemented the IFF (identification friend or foe) code procedure, and then to have fired his cannon in an attempt to get the attention of the airline crew. Unable to make contact with the 747, he ultimately launched two air-to-air missiles, at least one of which struck the transport, possibly in the area of the left wing. The first officer was able to transmit a distress message, reporting cabin decompression and that the aircraft had initiated a descent. Moments later, at about 03:35, the 747 plummeted into the Sea of Japan an estimated 50 miles (80km) south-west of Sakhalin, near the island of Moneron, in international waters, possibly after a midair explosion. There was no chance of survival for the 269 persons aboard the aircraft. A small amount of debris was later recovered, as were the remains of several victims.

A report on the tragedy released in 1993 by the newly-established Commonwealth of Independent States (CIS) largely supported the actions of the Soviet defence forces a decade earlier. Using information from the aircraft's digital flight data recorder (DFDR) and cockpit voice recorder (CVR), this new inquiry was able to determine that the crew of Flight 007 had either left the autopilot in the heading mode, or switched it to the inertial navigation system (INS) when already too far off course to capture the desired track. (This was one of two plausible explanations considered by the International Civil Aviation Organisation in its own investigation, the second being the faulty programming of the INS as the 747 sat on the ground at Anchorage.)

Flying with the autopilot in the heading mode should have caused the illumination of lights on the instrument panel indicating that the INS was not engaged. Furthermore, there would have been other ways for the crew to determine the position of the aircraft, even by using the ground-mapping mode of the weather radar installed on HL7442. Nevertheless, the ICAO admitted that such inattentiveness was not 'unknown in international civil aviation'.

The CIS report further stated that the aircraft had been misidentified as an RC-135 reconnaissance jet, one of which the US Air Force had been operating in the area before Flight 007 came along (but which had returned to its base more than an hour before the latter was attacked).

It should be added that the North Pacific route, still widely used by commercial air traffic, is a lot safer today, not just because of what has subsequently happened within the Societ bloc, but also due to the establishment of a long-range radar system designed to monitor the region, which went into operation in December 1984.

8 NOVEMBER 1983

A Línhas Aéreas de Angola (TAAG-Angola Airlines) Boeing Advanced 737-2M2 (D2-TBN) which crashed near Lubango, Huila, Angola, was thought to have been a victim of hostile action. All 130 persons aboard (126 passengers and a crew of four) were killed when the twin-jet transport crashed at around 15:20 local time, immediately after it had taken off on a scheduled domestic service to the capital, Luanda. Climbing to an approximate height of 200ft (60m), the aircraft made a steep turn to the left before it plummeted to the ground about half a mile (0.8km) beyond the end of the airport runway, exploding on impact

The cause of the disaster given by the Angolan authorities was a 'technical failure during weather conditions described as very bad', but it was widely believed that the 737 had been shot down by anti-government guerrillas, probably by means of a surface-to-air missile.

21 SEPTEMBER 1984

AN Ariana Afghan Airlines DC-10 Series 30 wide-bodied jetliner, with more than 300 persons aboard, was hit by explosive bullets while in flight near Kabul, Afghanistan, where it was to have landed. En route from Kandahar, the domestic segment of a scheduled service originating at Mecca, Saudi Arabia, the aircraft safely reached Kabul's international airport without injury to its passengers and crew, despite damage to its No 1 and No 3 hydraulic systems.

On 10 September 1983, more than a week after its destruction, police officers continue to search for debris from KAL Flight 007, some of which was washed ashore on beaches in northern Japan. (AP/Press Association Images)

Correct route and, as indicated by silhouette, the course believed taken by the Korean Air Lines Boeing 747 that was shot down. (International Civil Aviation Organisation)

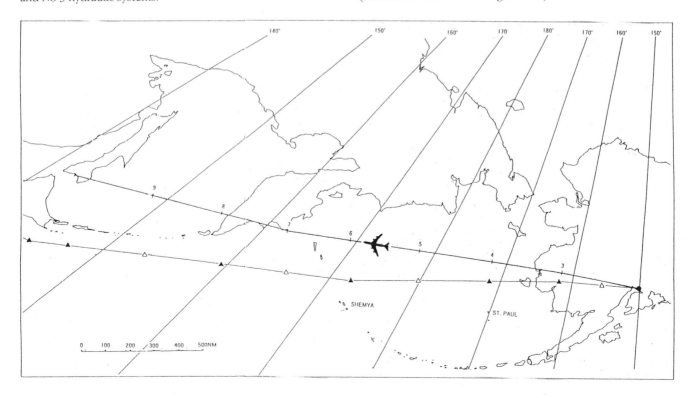

4 SEPTEMBER 1985

A Bakhtar Afghan Airlines Antonov An-26 (YA-BAM) was shot down over western Afghanistan, about 12 miles (20km) west of Kandahar, from where it had taken off minutes earlier on a scheduled domestic service to Farah province. All 52 persons aboard (47 passengers and a crew of five) were killed in the crash, which occurred shortly after 11:00 local time.

According to the Afghan government, the Soviet-built twin-engine turboprop was hit at an approximate height of 13,000ft (4,000m) by a surface-to-air missile fired by guerrillas.

20 FEBRUARY 1986

AN Iran Aseman Airlines Fokker F.27 Friendship Mark 600 twin-engine turboprop, on a non-scheduled domestic service from Tehran to Ahwaz, in the province of Khuzestan, was damaged about 20 miles (30km) north-east of its destination in an attack by an Iraqi jet fighter. Though hit by at least one air-to-air missile at about 12:25 local time, some 330 miles (530km) south-west of the Iranian capital, the aircraft landed safely without injury to its 49 passengers and crew members. An earlier report that the F.27 had been destroyed and all aboard killed may have been an anti-Iraqi propaganda ploy by Iran.

16 AUGUST 1986

A Sudan Airways Fokker F.27 Mark 400M Friendship turboprop airliner (ST-ADY) was shot down at around 10:30 local time shortly after it had taken off from Malakal, Sobat, on a scheduled domestic service to the Sudanese capital of Khartoum. Its pilot having declared an emergency, the F.27 was attempting to return to Malakal when it plunged to earth in flames, and all 60 persons aboard (57 passengers and three crew members) perished.

The aircraft was reportedly struck by a SAM-7 surface-to-air missile fired by Sudanese rebels. The airline subsequently suspended flights to the southern part of the country.

15 OCTOBER 1986

IRAQI warplanes attacked an Iran Air Boeing Advanced 737-286 (EP-IRG) as the jet airliner was discharging passengers on the ground at Shiraz airport in Iran's Fars Province at about 17:00 local time. Of the estimated 80 persons aboard, three passengers lost their lives in the attack and some 30 others were injured. The 737 was destroyed.

31 DECEMBER 1986

A United Airlines Boeing 737 jet, operating as Flight 1502, was hit by ground fire while approaching to land at Raleigh-Durham airport, North Carolina. A male passenger was wounded, but the aircraft reached its intended destination safely. An FBI investigation indicated that the gunman responsible for the attack was aiming at the pilot; the assailant was later sentenced to prison for 20 years.

8 JANUARY 1987

A Middle East Airlines Boeing 707-323C jetliner (OD-AHB) was destroyed by shellfire at the international airport serving Beirut, the incident occurring during fighting between Christian and Muslim forces. There were no injuries as the 707 was unoccupied at the time of its destruction, having landed

about an hour and a half earlier at the end of a scheduled service from Abidjan, Côte-d'Ivoire.

9 MARCH 1987

ALL three occupants were killed when an Aero Express DC-3 (N49454) was shot down by the Honduran Air Force in early morning darkness near Cucuyagua, located in western Honduras near the Guatemalan border. Reportedly, the aircraft was downed after failing to respond to several warnings.

11 JUNE 1987

An Antonov An-26 (YA-BAL), which was registered to Ariana Afghan Airlines and may have been operating on behalf of the Afghan Republican Air Force, was shot down by guerillas some 120 miles (190km) north-east of Kandahar, Afghanistan, from where it had taken off earlier on an internal flight to Kabul. There were only two survivors among the 55 persons aboard the twin-engine turboprop, both of whom suffered serious injuries. The An-26 had been brought down at around 06:30 local time, reportedly by a Stinger missile. According to the guerrillas, the aircraft was a military Ilyushin Il-14, and the crash killed the five members of its crew.

14 OCTOBER 1987

A Zimex Aviation Lockheed L-100-30 Hercules four-engine turboprop cargo transport (HB-ILF), which had been chartered by the Red Cross, was hit by a heat-seeking surface-to-air missile about five minutes after take-off from Cuito, Cuando Cubango, Angola. Struck in its No 3 power plant at an approximate height of 2,000ft (600m), which resulted in an uncontrollable fire, the Swiss-registered aircraft crashed at around 08:00 local time while trying to return to its point of departure, killing its six occupants as well as two persons on the ground.

6 NOVEMBER 1987

TEN persons (eight passengers and two pilots) were killed when an Air Malawi Shorts Skyvan Series 3 (7Q-YMB) was shot down near Ulonque, Tete, Mozambique. There were no survivors. The twin-engine turboprop had been on a domestic charter service from Blantyre to the capital city, Lilongwe. Mozambique military forces had received no advance information about the flight, and destroyed the aircraft at around 08:30 local time.

It was subsequently recommended that aircraft intending to fly over or land in Mozambique should first apply for authorisation from competent government authorities to avoid a repetition of this tragedy.

21 APRIL 1988

BOTH crew members (its only occupants) lost their lives when an African Air Carriers DC-3 (N47FE) crashed near Quelimane, Mozambique. The cargo transport was believed to have been shot down.

3 JULY 1988

FIVE years after the downing of KAL Flight 007, for which it had verbally lashed the USSR, the United States found itself on the opposite side of a similar controversy when one of its navy ships destroyed an Iranian wide-bodied jetliner over the Persian Gulf.

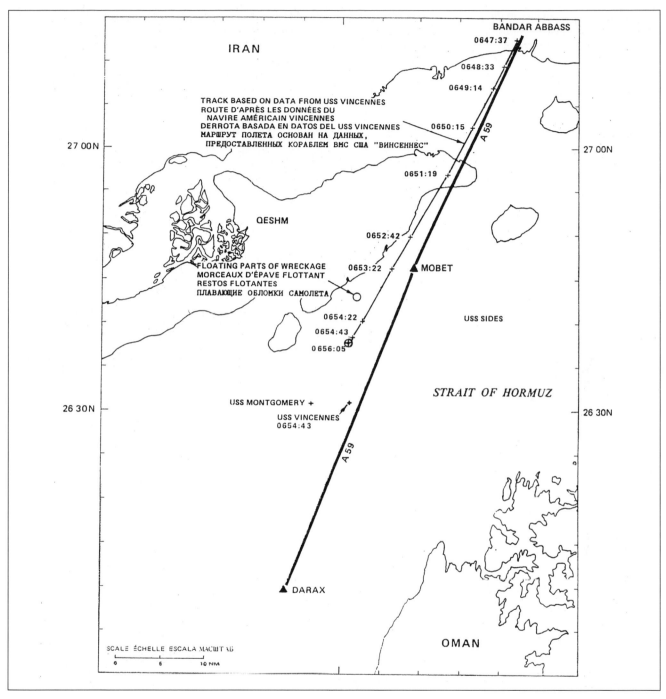

IRAN

BANDAR ABBASS
0647:37
0648:33
0649:14

TRACK BASED ON DATA FROM USS VINCENNES
ROUTE D'APRÈS LES DONNÉES DU
NAVIRE AMÉRICAIN VINCENNES
DERROTA BASADA EN DATOS DEL USS VINCENNES
МАРШРУТ ПОЛЕТА ОСНОВАН НА ДАННЫХ,
ПРЕДОСТАВЛЕННЫХ КОРАБЛЕМ ВМС США "ВИНСЕННЕС"

0650:15

A 59

27 00N   27 00N

0651:19

QESHM

0652:42

FLOATING PARTS OF WRECKAGE   0653:22   ▲ MOBET
MORCEAUX D'ÉPAVE FLOTTANT
RESTOS FLOTANTES
ПЛАВАЮЩИЕ ОБЛОМКИ САМОЛЕТА

0654:22   USS SIDES
0654:43
0656:05

STRAIT OF HORMUZ

USS MONTGOMERY +
                          +
26 30N   USS VINCENNES   26 30N
             0654:43

A 59

▲ DARAX

OMAN

SCALE ÉCHELLE ESCALA МАСШТАБ
0   5   10 NM

The genesis of this tragedy dated back more than a year, when US Naval forces began convoying Kuwaiti oil tankers to counter the attacks on civilian ships that had grown out of the Iran-Iraq War. The risks soon became apparent when, in May 1987, a missile – fired supposedly 'accidentally' by an Iraqi jet fighter – struck the frigate *Stark*, killing 37 American sailors.

In the wake of the *Stark* incident, a new set of 'rules of engagement' was formulated in order to clarify the authority of US commanders to take protective measures when facing 'hostile intent'.

American forces were alerted to the probability of significant Iranian military activity during the weekend that encompassed

A map showing the slight displacement from the airway centreline of the Iran Air A300 destroyed on 3 July 1988, and its position relative to the Vincennes, *which shot it down, and other US Navy ships.* (International Civil Aviation Organisation)

the American Independence Day holiday. On the morning of Sunday 3 July, the US Navy cruiser *Vincennes* and the frigate *Elmer Montgomery* had become involved in a skirmish with some Iranian gunboats in the Strait of Hormuz. During this time, Iran Air Flight 655, a twin-jet Airbus A300B2-203 (EP-IBU), took off from the Bandar Abbas international airport (which was used by both civilian and military aircraft), bound for Dubai in the United Arab Emirates. In the confusion of the moment, *ie* with the surface battle continuing and with an Iranian P-3 patrol aircraft in the vicinity, conceivably providing targeting information, the Airbus was misidentified as an F-14 jet fighter. As the commercial jet proceeded on a heading of 200°, its flight path generally along the prescribed airway but slightly to the right of its centreline, the crew was given a number of warnings from the *Vincennes* and the American frigate *John Sides*. Faced with the potential of another disaster such as that suffered by the *Stark*, the commanding officer of the *Vincennes* ordered the launch of two Standard surface-to-air missiles. At a position about ten miles (16km) from the vessel, the aircraft was hit around 10:25 local time and at an approximate altitude of 13,500ft (4,100m). One wing and its tail having been broken off, it plummeted into the water near the island of Henqam. All 290 persons aboard (274 passengers and 16 crew members) perished.

Conducting its own inquiry into the tragedy, the US Navy revealed the underlying factor in the misidentification. The atmospheric conditions in the Persian Gulf at the time, with a high level of evaporation, were conducive to radar ducting, or the bouncing of the signal. The ship had apparently picked up a Mode II signal emanating from a military aircraft, perhaps an F-14 or even a C-130 transport, which was on the ground around the same time and at the same airport from which EP-IBU had taken off. Interestingly, however, tape recordings of the ship's defence system clearly indicated a Mode III transponder code, normally associated with a civilian aircraft.

Pivotal in the decision to destroy the A300 was a report that the target was descending towards the ship, when in reality its altitude was increasing. This could have happened had the tactical information co-ordinator passed on only range values, which were interpreted as height, or if he misread his read-out and interchanged altitude and range. Also, due to the weather conditions actual visual contact with the airliner was never made.

Radio challenges had been made to Flight 655, including the threat of defensive action, on both military air defence (MAD) and international air defence (IAD) frequencies. Although EP-IBU was not equipped to receive the MAD frequency, its pilots

An Aeroflot Il-76 of the type struck by missile over Afghanistan and later destroyed in crash-landing. (Aeroflot)

should have been monitoring IAD when flying in the Gulf area. They either may not have been doing so, or perhaps did not identify theirs as the challenged aircraft.

The Navy report referred to the downing as a 'tragic and regrettable accident', placing some of the blame on Iran itself for allowing an airliner to operate in a 'war zone'. Conceding its error, the US would some eight years later agree to pay more than $60 million in damages to the families of those killed aboard Flight 655.

8 APRIL 1989

DURING its approach to land at Luena, Moxico, Angola, fire erupted in the No 2 power plant of a Lockheed L-100-20 Hercules (S9-NAI) of São Tomé and Principe registry, and operated by Transafrik Corporation Ltd. The four-engine turboprop cargo transport landed in scrub approximately one mile (1.6km) from the airfield, where it burnt out. Its crew of three escaped unscathed.

The wreckage showed evidence of small arms fire, but it could not be determined whether the aircraft had been struck before or after its forced landing.

28 JUNE 1989

A Somali Airlines Fokker F.27 Friendship Mark 600RF (60-SAZ) was believed to have been shot down by rebels near Borama, Woqooyi Galbeed, Somalia, and all 30 persons aboard (24 passengers and a crew of six) were killed. Apparently hit by a surface-to-air missile, it crashed shortly before 09:30 local time, about ten minutes after the twin-engine turboprop had taken off from Hargeysa, on a scheduled domestic service to Mogadishu.

29 JUNE 1989

DURING an internal flight from Malema to Lioma, an Empresa Nacional de Transporte e Trabalho Aéreo (TTA) BN-2A Islander was struck by gunfire near Mutuali, Nampula, Mozambique, located some 150 miles (250km) west-north-west of the city of Nampula. Though mortally injured, the pilot managed to set down the twin-engine aeroplane before succumbing to his wound.

3 SEPTEMBER 1989

A Henson Airlines twin-engine turboprop, operating on a US Air commuter service from the Bahamas, was either deliberately or accidentally struck by a bullet while approaching to land at Fort Lauderdale/Hollywood International Airport in Florida. One passenger of its 19 occupants was slightly injured, but the aircraft landed safely.

5 JANUARY 1990

AN Angola Air Charter Lockheed L-100-30 Hercules (D2-THB) was hit in its No 4 power plant by a heat-seeking missile after taking off from Menongue, Cuando Cubango, Angola. The four-engine turboprop cargo transport, its right wing ablaze, managed to return to its point of origin, but on landing ran off the airfield runway on to rough terrain and was destroyed. There were no serious injuries among the seven persons aboard.

12 JUNE 1990

AN Aeroflot Ilyushin Il-76MD jet transport (SSSR-86905) was hit by a Stinger surface-to-air missile at a height of

25,500ft (7,800m) over Afghanistan, suffering an explosive decompression and other damage, and subsequently belly-landed at Kabul. The Soviet aircraft was destroyed and two of the ten persons aboard were seriously injured.

2 OCTOBER 1990

AN Iraqi Airways Il-76 jet transport, believed to have been carrying military personnel, was shot down near Kuwait City, Kuwait, killing approximately 130 persons aboard. There were no survivors. The aircraft was hit by a surface-to-air missile fired by Kuwaiti resistance fighters, the downing occurring during the occupation of Kuwait by Iraqi forces.

13 FEBRUARY 1991

A DC-8 Series 33F cargo jet operated by the São Tomé and Principe-based carrier Transafrik Corporation Ltd and carrying relief supplies was hit in its left wing and one engine by ground fire while approaching to land at Menongue, Cuando Cubango, Angola. There were no injuries, however, and the aircraft landed safely.

16 MARCH 1991

NINE persons aboard (five passengers and a crew of four) perished when a Lockheed L-100-30 Hercules (CP-1564) flown by Transafrik Corporation Ltd was shot down some 20 miles (30km) from the town of Malanje, Angola, apparently by rebel forces. There were no survivors. The four-engine turboprop cargo aircraft was reportedly hit by a surface-to-air missile at a height of 17,000ft (5,200m) while on an internal service from Luanda to the province of Lunda Norte.

25 MARCH 1991

AN Ethiopian Airlines Boeing 707-385C jet (ET-AJZ) was struck by shellfire on the ground at Yohannes IV Airport, serving Asmara, Ethiopia, where it had landed at the end of a freight service. A number of loaders were killed in the attack, and the aircraft itself was destroyed.

29 MARCH 1991

CHARTERED by the Red Cross from the Swiss firm Zimex Aviation, and on an internal Angolan service from Luena, Moxico, to Cuito Cuanavale, Cuando Cubango, a de Havilland Twin Otter Series 300 was damaged by a surface-to-air missile near its destination. There were no injuries among the 11 persons aboard the twin-engine turboprop, which landed safely despite some damage.

10 JULY 1991

AN Aeroshasqui SA CASA 212-200 Aviocar (OB-1218) was shot down by members of Peru's national police force near Bellavista, Loreto. All 15 persons aboard the Peruvian-registered twin-engine turboprop (13 passengers and two pilots) were killed. The police officers, who reportedly had been drinking, had tried to stop the airliner from taking off from the local airport so that it could be searched, and opened fire when it returned to land. Both pilots were shot and the aircraft then plummeted to the ground at around 16:50 local time. Six officers would later be charged with homicide in connection with the incident.

10 SEPTEMBER 1991

A twin-engine turboprop Fokker F.27 Friendship Mark 400M (9Q-CBE) operated by the Congolese carrier Scibe Airlift was reportedly struck by gunfire while en route from Kigali, Rwanda, to Goma, Congo, and one passenger among its 17 occupants was seriously injured. Although it managed to reach Goma, the airliner was badly damaged in the attack and had to be removed from service.

17 SEPTEMBER 1991

LEASED from Aviation Leasing GmbH by the Swiss firm Zimex Aviation and on a Red Cross-chartered relief flight over Somalia, from Mogadishu to Berbera, a twin-engine turboprop Dornier 228 was struck by a missile at an approximate height of 10,000ft (3,000m) in the vicinity of Galcaio. There were no serious injuries among its five occupants, and the damaged aircraft landed safely at Djibouti.

27 MARCH 1992

AN Aeroflot Yak-40 jet airliner was hit by a heat-seeking missile shortly after it took off from Stepanakert, Azerbaijan, on a scheduled service to Yerevan, Armenia. The damaged aircraft landed safely despite a fire that was subsequently extinguished. Among the 34 persons aboard the Yak-40, including a crew of four, ten passengers suffered minor injuries.

9 MAY 1992

AN Armenian Airlines Yak-40 jet airliner was attacked by an Azeri jet fighter during a scheduled service from Stepanakert, Azerbaijan, to Yerevan, Armenia. Damaged in one wing and set afire, the aircraft was able to land at Sisian, Armenia, where it burned out after its passengers and crew were evacuated to safety.

29 MAY 1992

AN Ariana Afghan Airlines Tu-154M jetliner, carrying Afghanistan's just-named President Sibghatullah Mujadidi and 16 other persons on a non-scheduled international service, was targeted for destruction as it was arriving at Kabul, Afghanistan. A rocket apparently launched from behind or atop a hill overlooking the city's airport exploded as the Tu-154 was at an approximate height of 600ft (180m) while approaching to land. Shrapnel struck the aircraft and wounded one of its pilots, but the jetliner was able to land safely.

27 AUGUST 1992

A Turkish Airlines (THY) Airbus A310 wide-bodied jetliner with 128 persons aboard was struck by gunfire during its departure from Adana, Turkey, on a scheduled international service to Jiddah, Saudi Arabia. There were no injuries in the incident. Later in the year a militant group would claim responsibility for the attack, with the purpose of creating 'a sensational act in Turkey'.

5 DECEMBER 1992

AN Ariana Afghan Airlines twin-engine turboprop, probably either an Antonov An-24 or An-26, was reportedly struck by an anti-tank missile as it was approaching to land at Kabul at the end of a service from Peshawar, Pakistan. There were no injuries, and the aircraft landed safely.

22 JANUARY 1993

AN American Airlines A300 wide-bodied jetliner was struck by gunfire while taxiing at Jorge Chávez International Airport, serving Lima, Peru, but there were no casualties among its passengers and crew.

23 JANUARY 1993

A Lockheed L-100-30 Hercules four-engine turboprop cargo transport operated by Transafrik was damaged by mortar fire as it was taking off from Luena, Moxico, Angola. The aircraft returned for a safe landing, its crew escaping injury.

26 APRIL 1993

A Komiavia An-12V cargo aircraft (RA-11121) was hit in its No 4 power plant by a surface-to-air missile at a height of around 15,000ft (4,500m) over Angola. The Russian-built and registered four-engine turboprop crash-landed in a field near Luena, in the province of Moxico, from where it had taken off earlier on an internal Angolan service to Catumbela. Although there had been no fatalities as a result of either the missile-strike or the crash, one crew member was killed when he stepped on a landmine; a second suffered injuries.

25 JUNE 1993

AN Orbi Georgian Airways Tu-154B jetliner was struck in its No 3 power plant by a missile believed to have been fired by Abkhazi rebels during its approach to land at Sukhumi, Georgia, following a non-scheduled domestic service from Tbilisi. There were no injuries among the more than 100 persons aboard the aircraft, which landed safely.

22 JULY 1993

ANOTHER Georgian Tu-154 jetliner was struck by a missile while on a domestic service from Sukhumi to Tbilisi, although the damaged aircraft returned safely to its departure point without injury to its passengers or crew.

20 SEPTEMBER 1993

AN Orbi-Georgian Airlines Tu-134A jetliner (SSSR-65809) was reportedly struck by small arms fire, or possibly a missile, while taking off from Babusheri Airport, serving Sukhumi, Georgia, and although the aircraft was destroyed there were no reported casualties.

21 SEPTEMBER 1993

A Transair Georgia Airlines twin-jet Tupolev Tu-134A (SSSR-65893) was allegedly shot down by Abkhazi separatist forces over the Black Sea near Sukhumi, Georgia. All 27 persons aboard (22 passengers and crew of five) were killed. The aircraft had been on a non-scheduled service from Sochi, Russian Federation, and was on its approach when reportedly hit at an altitude of around 1,000ft (300m) by a missile fired from a patrol boat, which sent it plunging into the water about 2.5 miles (4km) from Babusheri Airport, serving Sukhumi, where it was to have landed.

22 SEPTEMBER 1993

WHILE landing at Babusheri Airport, serving Sukhumi, a Transair Georgia Airlines Tupolev Tu-154B jetliner (SSSR-85163), which had been on a Defence Ministry of Georgia domestic charter service from Tbilisi and was carrying mostly military personnel, was hit by a missile apparently fired by Abkhazi separatists. Of the 132 persons aboard the aircraft, 106 were killed in the subsequent crash, including half of its 12 crew members. All the survivors suffered serious injuries. The Tu-154 was just about to touch down in twilight conditions when the missile-strike occurred at about 18:30 local time.

23 SEPTEMBER 1993

THE pilot was killed when a Transair Georgia Airlines Tupolev Tu-134A (SSSR-65001), which was on the ground boarding soldiers and refugees at Babusheri Airport, serving Sukhumi, was hit by a mortar or artillery shell that had apparently been fired from offshore in the Black Sea. Numerous passengers suffered injuries and the twin-engine jet, which was on a non-scheduled domestic service to Tbilisi, was destroyed.

27 JULY 1994

ALL seven occupants of an Avialinii Ukrainy (Air Ukraine) twin-engine turboprop Antonov An-26B (UR-26207) were killed when the cargo aircraft was shot down as it approached to land, crashing in a minefield near Bihac, in Bosnia-Herzegovina, located some 150 miles (250km) north-west of Sarajevo.

28 JANUARY 1995

A twin-engine turboprop Beechcraft Super King Air 200 (D2-ECH), flown by the Angolan operator Aviação Ligeira, crashed shortly after take-off from Kafunfo, Luanda Norte, Angola, apparently after being hit by a missile. Two of the aircraft's six occupants were killed.

21 FEBRUARY 1995

A Twin Otter turboprop operated by the Papua New Guinea carrier Airlink was fired upon as it took off from Oria, on Bougainville Island, after dropping off medical supplies. One passenger was killed and a second wounded in the attack, although the damaged aircraft subsequently landed safely on the nearby island of Buka. Flights into Bougainville were suspended as a result of the attack, which was believed to have been carried out by rebel fighters.

28 APRIL 1995

OPERATED by the Sri Lankan carrier Helitours, a British Aerospace BAe 748 Series 2A (4R-HVB) crashed near Jaffna, Sri Lanka, killing all 45 persons aboard (42 passengers and a crew of three). The twin-engine turboprop had just taken off from Palaly Air Base, on a non-scheduled domestic trooping flight to Colombo, when the pilot requested permission to return due to a fire in its left power plant. However, the flames spread to its wing before a safe landing could be made, and the aircraft crashed some 700ft (200m) short of the runway. A surface-to-air missile was believed to have been responsible for bringing down the airliner.

29 APRIL 1995

ANOTHER Helitours aircraft, a British Aerospace BAe 748 Series 2B (4R-HVA), was shot down near Jaffna, and all 52 persons aboard (49 passengers and a crew of three) were

A de Havilland Twin Otter, the type flown by the carrier Airlink that was targeted in an attack in Papua New Guinea. (Philip Jarrett)

killed. The twin-engine turboprop, on a domestic military charter service from Anuradhapura, crashed and burned some five miles (8km) from Palaly Air Base, where it was to have landed, after reportedly being struck by a surface-to-air missile while descending from a height of 3,000ft (900m).

15 MAY 1997

AN Azerbaijan Airlines Yakovlev Yak-40 jetliner (4K-87504) got shot down near Gyandzha, Azerbaijan, while on a training flight, and all six of its crew members (and only occupants) were killed.

The aircraft had been approaching to land and was apparently hit after flying over a military training area, resulting in an in-flight fire and loss of control. It then plunged to earth some three miles (5km) short of the airport runway. The incident occurred in daylight and in an area where a number of soldiers, who had just completed firing practice, had been shooting at a road sign. The downing must therefore have been accidental.

13 FEBRUARY 1998

A Delta Air Lines Boeing 727 jetliner was hit by a gunshot while taxiing at Hartsfield International Airport, serving Atlanta, Georgia, in preparation for take off on a scheduled US domestic flight to Mobile, Alabama. There were no injuries.

29 SEPTEMBER 1998

DESIGNATED as Flight 602 and on a Sri Lankan domestic service to Colombo, an Antonov An-24RV (EW-46465) operated by the carrier Lionair, which had been leased from the Belarus-based carrier Gomelavia, crashed in the Gulf of Mannar some 15 minutes after its departure from Palaly Air Base, near Jaffna. All 55 persons aboard the twin-engine turboprop (49 passengers and a crew of six) were killed. The crash occurred shortly before 14:00 local time, after the pilot had declared an emergency and reported cabin depressurisation while at an approximate height of 8,000ft (2,500m). According to one source, the airliner was shot down by rebels.

10 OCTOBER 1998

A Lignes Aériennes Congolaises (Congo Airlines) Boeing 727-30 (9Q-CSG) jetliner was shot down over the Congo shortly after it had taken off from Kindu, Maniema, on a non-scheduled domestic service to the capital city of Kinshasa, located some 750 miles (1,200km) to the west. All 41 persons aboard lost their lives in the crash, including a crew of three; the passengers were civilian evacuees. Apparently struck in one engine by a missile fired by rebel forces, the 727 plummeted into a dense jungle area after the pilot reported experiencing control difficulties and that he would be attempting an off-airport forced landing.

14 DECEMBER 1998

OWNED by the Ukrainian carrier Khors Air Company and chartered by the government of Angola, a four-engine turboprop Antonov An-12BP (UR-11319) was shot down shortly after its departure from Cuito Cuanavale, Cuando Cubango,

An Antonov An-12 such as this was one of the three aircraft shot down over Angola during a three-week period in 1998–1999. (Philip Jarrett)

Angola, located some 300 miles (480km) south-east of Luanda, which was its destination. All ten persons aboard (five passengers and a crew of five) were killed. The Russian-built aircraft was reportedly struck at a height of 15,000ft (4,500m) by a surface-to-air missile apparently fired by National Union for the Liberation of Angola (UNITA) rebels.

26 DECEMBER 1998

Chartered by the United Nations from the airline Transafrik International and on an internal Angolan service to Saurimo, Luanda Sul, a Lockheed L-100-30 Hercules (S9-CAO) of São Tomé and Principe registry was shot down, apparently by UNITA rebels, shortly after taking off from the city of Huambo. The four-engine turboprop plunged to earth in flames at around 12:00 local time near the village of Vila Nova, some 300 miles (480km) south-east of Luanda, killing all 14 persons aboard (ten passengers and a crew of four).

2 JANUARY 1999

FOR the second time in less than a week, a Transafrik International Lockheed L-100-30 Hercules four-engine turboprop that had been chartered by the United Nations was shot down near Bailundo, Huambo, Angola, probably by UNITA rebels. All nine persons aboard the Angolan-registered aircraft (D2-EHD), including its crew of four, were killed. The Hercules was struck by ground fire, burst into flames and fell to earth some 50 miles (80km) north of the city of Huambo, from where it had taken off about 20 minutes earlier on a non-scheduled internal service to Luanda.

    The UN subsequently suspended all its flights within Angola.

12 MAY 1999

A twin-engine turboprop Antonov An-26 (D2-FBN) chartered by the Angolan company Avita Serviços Aéreos and being used to transport food and other supplies was shot down, reportedly by UNITA rebels, shortly after taking off on an internal flight from Luzamba to Luanda. The aircraft crash-landed some 20 miles (30km) from its departure point, and of its six occupants the three members of its Russian crew were reported by UNITA to have been captured alive.

1 JULY 1999

ONE of its five crew members (and only occupants) was killed when a Russian-built and registered four-engine turboprop Antonov An-12V (RA-12951), operated by the Angolan firm Savanair and on a non-scheduled domestic cargo service from Luanda to Saurimo, was apparently hit by ground fire, then crash-landed in the bush near Luzamba.

9 DECEMBER 2000

HAVING nearly completed a scheduled service from Brussels, a Belgian SABENA Airbus A330 wide-bodied jet airliner was struck by automatic weapon fire while landing at the international airport serving Bujumbura, Burundi. The aircraft was hit in the left side of its fuselage and its port wing at an estimated height of 300ft (90m) above the ground during its approach to Runway 17, the incident occurring in darkness at around 20:00 local time. Despite damage to its hydraulic system the landing was completed safely, and there were no serious injuries reported among the 172 persons who had been aboard.

8 JUNE 2001

WHILE being operated on behalf of the United Nations' World Food Programme, a Transafrik International Boeing 727-90C cargo jet was struck by a missile in its No 2 power plant while at a height of 15,000ft (4,500m) and some ten miles (16km) from Luena, Moxico, Angola, where it was to have landed. The airliner was damaged in the attack, which occurred in predawn darkness at around 04:30 local time, but nevertheless landed safely at its intended destination, its three crew members (and only occupants) escaping injury.

4 OCTOBER 2001

THIS peacetime case of 'friendly fire' had the same consequences as it would have in wartime, since it led to the destruction of a commercial transport. The Tupolev Tu-154M jetliner (RA-85693) of the Russian carrier Sibir Airlines had been on a non-scheduled international service from Tel Aviv, Israel, to Novosibirsk, Russia, before it crashed in the Black Sea some 110 miles (180km) south-west of Sochi, Russia. All 78 persons aboard (66 passengers and 12 crew members) perished.

The finding of pellets in the remains of the victims that were recovered and of shrapnel holes in wreckage retrieved from the water confirmed that RA-85693 had been struck by a missile, one of two that had been fired at drone aircraft during an exercise being conducted by Ukrainian military forces on the Crimean peninsula. After missing the target, the Almaz S-200 anti-aircraft missile flew for about 150 miles (250km), which was near the maximum range for the type, and was believed to have then detonated approximately 50ft (15m) above the jetliner, which was cruising at 36,000ft (11,000m), at around 12:45 local time.

This blunder led to a shake-up within Ukraine's military forces, with the commander of its air defence forces and his deputy later resigning. Additionally the country's defence minister was suspended, and would also resign.

8 OCTOBER 2001

AN Air Chayka International Ltd Mil Mi-8T turbine-engine helicopter (UR-24229), being operated by the Ukrainian company on behalf of the United Nations, was shot down in the vicinity of the Kodori Gorge, in Abkhazia, an independent region of Georgia. All nine occupants of the aircraft (its crew of three and six UN observers) were killed. The Mi-8 was reportedly struck by a surface-to-air missile about 15 minutes after its departure from Sukhumi.

28 NOVEMBER 2002

THIS miss, but potentially catastrophic hit, involved an Arkia Israel Airlines Boeing 757 jet airliner on a non-scheduled international service to Tel Aviv with 271 persons aboard. The transport had just taken off from Moi International Airport, serving Mombasa, Kenya, when the pilot observed two flashes of light off its port side, the incident occurring around 07:30 local time. There were no injuries, and the 757 proceeded on to its intended destination without further incident.

It was determined that terrorists had fired two shoulder-launched missiles at the jet, the launchers being subsequently found near the airport. Almost five years later a suspect who had admitted having a role in the attempted downing was turned over to the American authorities and transferred to the Guantanamo Bay prison in Cuba. As a preventative measure,

Israel would later equip commercial aircraft in its registry with anti-missile defence systems.

22 NOVEMBER 2003

DURING the occupation of Iraq by Western forces, an Airbus A300B4 wide-bodied cargo jet owned by the Belgian firm European Air Transport and being operated by Bahrain-based DHL Aviation was hit by a surface-to-air missile shortly after its departure from Baghdad. Struck in its port wing at an approximate height of 8,000ft (2,500m) at around 09:30 local time, the aircraft experienced an in-flight fire and also lost its hydraulic system. It was able to return to Baghdad International Airport, veering off the runway after landing. Although the Airbus sustained substantial damage, its three crew members (and only occupants) escaped injury.

21 APRIL 2005

A Heli Air Services Mil Mi-8P turbine-engine helicopter (LZ-CAV) was shot down some ten miles (16km) north of Baghdad. None of its 11 occupants, including the three members of its crew, were found alive; however, the pilot apparently did survive the crash, only to be murdered on the ground by guerrilla forces.

Reportedly, the Bulgarian-registered aircraft was struck by a rocket-propelled grenade or surface-to-air missile during an internal flight to Tikrit, and plummeted to earth in flames, the incident occurring in good weather conditions at around 14:00 local time.

9 MARCH 2007

AN Ilyushin Il-76MD jet transport operated by the Belarusian carrier Transaviaexport Airlines and chartered to carry Ugandan peace-keeping forces was struck by ground fire while approaching to land at the international airport serving Mogadishu, Somalia. Despite an in-flight fire, the aircraft got down safely, and its 15 occupants escaped serious injury.

23 MARCH 2007

ONLY two weeks after another company aircraft was struck by ground fire, a second Transaviaexport Ilyushin Il-76MD jet transport (EW-78849) was attacked over Somalia, this time successfully.

After bringing in equipment to be used to repair the first aircraft, EW-78849 was returning to Minsk, Belarus. Immediately after the Il-76 had taken off from Mogadishu International Airport, it was apparently struck by a surface-to-air missile at an estimated height of 500ft (150m), around 14:00 local time, then crashed. All 11 persons aboard the aircraft were killed. Somali officials reported that this was an accident resulting from a technical failure.

29 SEPTEMBER 2008

A Badr Airlines Mil Mi-8T turbine-engine helicopter (ST-BDD), which had been chartered from the Sudanese carrier by the United Nations' African Union mission, was shot down near Nyala, in Sudan, from where it had taken off shortly before, on an internal relief flight to Muhagiriya. All four crew members (the only occupants of the aircraft) were killed in the incident, which occurred at around 09:30 local time.

9

Miscellaneous acts of terror

Through advances in procedures and security equipment, commercial aviation has made great strides in the war against aerial terrorism. It is now possible, for example, to detect firearms and explosives going aboard aircraft. Consequently, in 2005 only three hostile acts against airlines were recorded around the world, compared to more than 80 such incidents in 1970.

A number of airliners from Soviet bloc countries were hijacked to the West in the late 1960s and early 1970s, including this Polish Il-18. (AP/Press Association Images)

There has also been progress in the diplomatic arena in dealing with such terrorism. Nations have become far less receptive to the concept of 'good' versus 'bad' hijackings, and have been returning perpetrators for punishment regardless of political sympathies, and in some cases prosecuting them on their own behalf.

But no security system is infallible, and hijackers and saboteurs alike continue to demonstrate originality in their modus operandi. Thus, even with sophisticated preventative measures in place, a bomb was allowed to go aboard a jumbo

jet crossing the Atlantic in 1985, resulting in history's worst act of aerial sabotage. And despite the screening of its regular passengers, one airline was shocked in 1987 when one of its own employees was able to bring down an aircraft using a weapon that had been smuggled past detection equipment.

The following is a list of miscellaneous acts of terror that have occurred since 1969 which do not fall into any of the categories covered in previous chapters.

6 JANUARY 1970

THE would-be hijacker of a Delta Air Lines DC-9 jet, operating as Flight 274 on an intrastate service from Orlando to Jacksonville, Florida, with 65 persons aboard, was overpowered and captured after demanding to be taken to Switzerland. He spent five years in prison, part of a 25-year sentence for air piracy, before his deportation in 1975.

7 JANUARY 1970

A twin-engine Convair 440 flown by the Spanish airline Iberia on a scheduled domestic service from Madrid to Zaragoza with 46 persons aboard was commandeered by a lone assailant using a toy pistol, who wanted to go to Albania. He surrendered when the aircraft landed at its intended destination and was subsequently sentenced to a prison term of six years and one day.

10 MARCH 1970

TWO armed 'bandits', later identified as a married couple, reportedly committed suicide after failing in their attempt to hijack a twin-engine turboprop Antonov An-24 operated by the East German airline Interflug, which had been on a scheduled domestic flight from (East) Berlin to Leipzig.

12 MARCH 1970

A man committed suicide aboard a United Air Lines Boeing 727 as the jetliner was in flight over Nebraska, on a scheduled US domestic service from San José, California, to Chicago, Illinois. The victim's automatic pistol, triggered by a reflex, fired a second time and seriously wounded another passenger.

An Eastern Airlines DC-9 Series 31, identical to the aircraft involved in the fatal hijacking in March 1970. (McDonnell Douglas)

17 MARCH 1970

THE first fatality in a US airline hijacking since the dawn of the jet age involved an Eastern Airlines DC-9 Series 31, designated as Flight 1320, which was on a domestic service from Newark, New Jersey, to Boston, Massachusetts, with 77 persons aboard. During the landing approach to Logan International Airport, a male passenger, identified as 27-year-old John DiVivo, showed a stewardess a .38 calibre revolver as she was collecting fares, then asked to see the captain.

Shortly after the gunman entered the flight deck, at around

The wounded gunman who shot the pilots of Eastern Flight 1320 is taken to hospital after the safe landing of the jetliner. (UPI/Corbis-Bettmann)

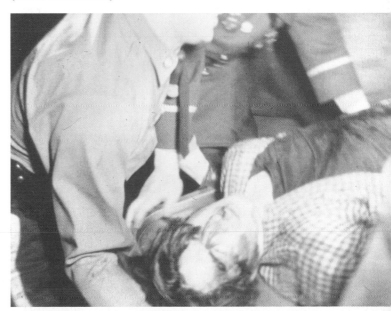

20:00 local time, shots were heard. It was later revealed that after the captain announced his intention to land despite the demands of the assailant 'to fly east', the latter opened fire. First Officer James Hartley, though mortally wounded, managed to disarm the gunman and shoot him with the same weapon. The hijacker was wounded, as was Captain Robert Wilbur, who nevertheless managed to land the twin-engine jet safely. Convicted of the crime, John DiVivo committed suicide in prison in October 1970.

31 MARCH–3 APRIL 1970

NINE Japanese student radicals armed with swords, members of the infamous 'Red Army', commandeered Japan Air Lines Flight 351, a Boeing 727 jet carrying 138 persons on a domestic service from Tokyo to Fukuoka, and demanded to be taken to North Korea. The aircraft instead landed at Kimpo airport, Seoul, South Korea, where a stand-off went on for 79 hours. The hijackers finally agreed to release the passengers and four cabin attendants in return for Japan's Deputy Minister of Transport, and the aircraft flew on to Pyongyang, North Korea.

In 2002, one member of the group who had commandeered the 727 and had been arrested in Cambodia was sentenced to 12 years' imprisonment in Japan for his involvement in the act of piracy. Previously two men not directly involved in the hijacking had also received prison sentences in Japan, one for conspiracy and the other for providing the weapons used.

21 APRIL 1970

A Philippine Air Lines Hawker Siddeley 748 Series 2 (PI-C-1022), operating as Flight 215 on a domestic service to Manila from Cauayan, Isabela, was blown up with a bomb about 100 miles (160km) north-north-east of the capital. The twin-engine turboprop crashed and burned in a mountainous region near Pantabangan, on Luzon, and all 36 persons aboard, including four crew members, perished.

A Philippine Air Lines Hawker Siddeley 748 of the type destroyed by an explosive device during an intra-island flight on 21 April 1970. (British Aerospace)

The aircraft was last reported at 10,500ft (3,200m), and was awaiting clearance to begin its descent when the explosion in the cargo compartment ripped away its tail assembly shortly after 11:30 local time.

The bombing may have been a suicidal act by one of the passengers, or was perhaps aimed at the assassination of Colonel Filemon Lagman, who had been leading the drive to stop illegal logging and mining operations in Isabela province and was on the flight.

23 APRIL 1970

A lone assailant with a toy pistol and an alleged bomb, which was also a fake, commandeered a bus to the airport at Pellston, Michigan, where he forced his way aboard a North Central Airlines twin-jet DC-9, operating as Flight 945, and demanded to be taken to Detroit. He was subdued by the crew and subsequently committed to a psychiatric facility.

10 MAY 1970

AFTER a telephone threat had been received warning of the attack, a suitcase bomb exploded aboard a DC-9 of the Spanish carrier Iberia before its planned departure from Geneva, Switzerland, on a scheduled service to Palma de Mallorca, in the Spanish Balearic Islands. There were no injuries. Sabotage attempts were also made against Spanish airliners at London, Amsterdam and Frankfurt, but in these cases the devices failed to reach their intended targets.

14 MAY 1970

AN Ansett Airlines of Australia DC-9 jet was commandeered by a man with a cap pistol while it was on the ground at Kingsford-Smith Airport, serving Sydney, preparing for a scheduled domestic service to Brisbane, Queensland. The 60 passengers escaped and the hijacker then surrendered; he was sentenced to a prison term of five years.

30 MAY 1970

USING a real-looking toy pistol, an otherwise unarmed hijacker commandeered an Alitalia DC-9 jetliner that had been on a scheduled domestic service from Genoa to Rome with 35 persons aboard. It landed at Cairo, Egypt.

2 JUNE 1970

THE third bombing of a Philippine Air Lines aircraft in less than a year involved Flight 537, which was on a domestic service from Manila to Bacolod, on the island of Negros. The twin-engine turboprop Fokker F.27 Friendship Mark 100 had been cruising at an altitude of 13,000ft (4,000m) near Roxas, located on Panay, when it was rocked by an explosion shortly after 06:00 local time. The detonation of a fragmentation grenade that had apparently been placed in a briefcase occurred between rows 4 and 5 on the left side of the aircraft, and created a hole in the fuselage about 3ft (1m) in diameter. One of the 44 persons aboard – the suspected saboteur – was killed, succumbing in hospital later that morning.

Twelve other passengers and one of the four crew members assigned to the flight suffered injuries. Following the blast, the pilot initiated an emergency descent and landed the Friendship safely at Roxas airport.

In view of these three acts of sabotage, airlines in the Philippines announced plans to physically search hand-carried and checked-in luggage, and regulations were also implemented requiring the shippers of unaccompanied baggage to present proper identification.

4 JUNE 1970

FLIGHT 486, a Trans World Airlines a Boeing 727-231 jet carrying 58 persons on a US domestic service from Phoenix, Arizona, to St Louis, Missouri, was hijacked by a lone assailant armed with a revolver, a razor blade, and a bottle of gasoline, who demanded a ransom of $100 million. He was given about $100,000 when the aircraft landed at Dulles International Airport, near Washington DC. On discovering that he had been short-changed, he ordered the 727 to return to Dulles. After wounding the pilot in a scuffle while on the ground, the assailant was himself shot by an FBI agent. Charges against the hijacker were later dropped, and he was committed to a psychiatric facility.

5 JUNE 1970

A Polish Airlines (LOT) An-24 turboprop with 23 persons aboard was commandeered during a scheduled domestic service from Stettin to Gdansk, and landed at Copenhagen. The hijacker was sentenced to 3½ years in prison by a Danish court.

8 JUNE 1970

A group of eight Czechs, accompanied by an infant, took control of a Czechoslovak Airlines (CSA) Il-14 that was carrying 27 persons on a scheduled domestic flight to Prague from Karlovy Vary, diverting it to Nuremberg, (West) Germany, where the hijackers asked for political asylum. The adult members of the band were instead tried and convicted in a German court, receiving prison terms ranging from eight months to 2½ years. However, five of them had their sentences suspended.

9 JUNE 1970

TWO hijackers were foiled by the crew in an attempt to take over a Polish Airlines (LOT) An-24 turboprop that was on a scheduled domestic service from Katowice to Warsaw. They were sentenced, respectively, to four and five years' imprisonment.

22 JULY 1970

AFTER it had landed at Tan Son Nhut Airport, serving Saigon, (South) Vietnam, during a scheduled domestic service from Pleiku, an American serviceman held the pilot of an Air Vietnam DC-4 at knifepoint for two hours. He subsequently surrendered.

3 AUGUST 1970

A lone assailant armed with a starter pistol tried to hijack to Hungary a Pan American World Airways Boeing 727 jetliner, designated as Flight 742, which was on a service from Munich, (West) Germany, to (West) Berlin with 125 persons aboard. The crew convinced him that the aircraft did not have enough fuel to make the trip, and he subsequently surrendered. Charges against him were dropped, and he was committed to a psychiatric facility.

7 AUGUST 1970

ARMED with a hand grenade, a lone assailant tried to hijack to (West) Germany a Polish Airlines (LOT) twin-engine turboprop An-24 that had been on a scheduled domestic service from Szczecin to Katowice. It instead landed in (East) Berlin. The hijacker was sentenced to eight years' imprisonment for the hijacking and additional time for the crimes of rape and blackmail.

8 AUGUST 1970

TWO brothers, one of them accompanied by his son, hijacked a Czechoslovak Airlines Il-14 that was on a scheduled domestic flight from Prague to Bratislava with 27 persons aboard. Having landed at Vienna, two of the assailants were sentenced to a year's imprisonment and the other to 15 months.

19 AUGUST 1970

A lone assailant armed with what would later be found to be a toy pistol commandeered an All Nippon Airways Boeing 727 jetliner during a Japanese domestic service from Nagoya to Sapporo. He ordered the aircraft to land at a military base and demanded a rifle and ammunition in what may have been a suicide plot. During the confusion brought about by the feigned pregnancy pains of a passenger he was overpowered by police, and was subsequently sentenced to seven years' imprisonment.

19 AUGUST 1970

THREE men accompanied by two women commandeered a Polish Airlines (LOT) Il-14 on a scheduled domestic service from Gdansk to Warsaw. The transport landed on the Danish island of Bornholm, where the hijackers asked for asylum. Their leader was expelled back to Poland nearly a decade later.

26 AUGUST 1970

A would-be hijacker and ten other persons aboard were injured when a bomb he was carrying accidentally exploded during an attempt to commandeer a Polish Airlines (LOT) An-24 turboprop. The aircraft returned safely to Katowice, Poland, from where it had taken off earlier on a scheduled domestic flight to Warsaw with 31 persons aboard. The assailant was sentenced to 25 years' imprisonment.

31 AUGUST 1970

THREE hijackers armed with pistols and waving a Molotov cocktail commandeered an Air Algérie twin-engine turboprop Convair 640 that had been on a scheduled domestic service from Annaba to Algiers. After landing on Sardinia, where 11 passengers were released, and then at Brindisi, Italy, the aircraft proceeded on to Albania, where it was refused permission to land. They instead went on to Yugoslavia, where they asked for asylum.

10 SEPTEMBER 1970

A passenger threatened to hijack an Aer Lingus-Irish International Airlines Boeing 707 jetliner that was on a scheduled transatlantic service, but after trying to stab the first officer with a knife and fork he was subdued, then fell asleep. After the aircraft had reached New York City the assailant was charged with the lesser crime of interfering with an airline crew.

14 SEPTEMBER 1970

FOUR hijackers accompanied by two children took over a Romanian Airlines (TAROM) BAC One-Eleven jetliner that was on a scheduled service from Bucharest, Romania, to Prague, Czechoslovakia, with 89 persons aboard. The aircraft landed in (West) Germany, where one of the assailants was acquitted and the other three were sentenced to 2½ years' imprisonment.

15 SEPTEMBER 1970

A lone assailant who attempted to hijack to North Korea a Trans World Airlines Boeing 707-131B jetliner was shot and wounded by a private security guard on the ground at San Francisco International Airport, where the aircraft, operating as Flight 15 and carrying 62 persons, had just arrived from Los Angeles on the intrastate segment of a domestic transcontinental service originating at New York City. He would later be sentenced to 12½ years' imprisonment for kidnapping.

15 OCTOBER 1970

THOUGH several attempts had been reported, no successful hijacking of a Soviet airliner ever occurred until this incident, which involved an Aeroflot Antonov An-24V on a scheduled domestic service from Batumi to Sochi carrying 51 persons.

According to the hijacker, Proinas Brazinskas, who was accompanied by his 14-year-old son Algirdas, the pilot ignored his orders and instead put the twin-engine turboprop into an 'acrobatic' manoeuvre, causing him to lose his balance and fire the shotgun he was carrying. A stewardess was hit and killed. A subsequently declassified Russian report indicated that the stewardess had been shot while trying to stop one assailant from entering the cockpit. The captain later said that the hijackers burst into the cockpit when the flight crew tried to radio the ground, shooting and wounding three of its members.

The aircraft managed a safe landing at Trabzon, Turkey,

The commandeered Aeroflot An-24 on which a stewardess was killed sits on the apron at Trabzon after being seized by a father-and-son hijacking team in October 1970. (Wide World Photos/AP/ Press Association Images)

located on the Black Sea. The Turkish authorities refused the two hijackers political asylum due to the nature of their crime, and they spent two years there before moving to the US. But freedom does not always equal bliss. In 2002 Algirdas Brazinskas, at the age of 46, was sentenced to prison for the murder his 77-year-old father in Santa Monica, California, marking a tragic end to the hijacking team that had made news more than three decades earlier.

27 OCTOBER 1970

TWO students commandeered an Aeroflot L-200 Morava that was on a scheduled Soviet domestic service from Kerch to Krasnodar with a total of four persons aboard. After the twin-engine light aircraft landed at Sinop, Turkey, the authorities returned both hijackers to the USSR, where they received prison sentences of 10 and 12 years, respectively.

13 NOVEMBER 1970

A married couple, reportedly drunk at the time, tried to commandeer an Aeroflot Il-14 airliner that was on a scheduled domestic service from Vilnius to Palanga, in the Soviet Republic of Lithuania. They were overpowered by the crew and other passengers and the flight landed safely at its intended destination. The husband subsequently received a death sentence, which, largely due to world reaction, was later commuted to 15 years' imprisonment; his wife was given three years.

10 DECEMBER 1970

AN attempt to hijack a Czechoslovak Aero Taxi L-200 Morava on a domestic service from Bratislava to Brno ended when the other passengers overpowered the lone assailant while in the air. One person was wounded but the aircraft returned safely to Brno.

21 DECEMBER 1970

A Puerto Rico International Airlines Heron, operating as Flight 157 on an intra-island service from San Juan to Ponce with 21 persons aboard, got hijacked by a lone assailant who was overpowered by the crew. He would later spend more than two years in a psychiatric facility.

10 JANUARY 1971

AN armed assailant who said he wanted to be taken to Las Vegas, Nevada, was dissuaded by a stewardess from hijacking a Trans World Airlines Boeing 707 during a domestic service from New York City to Denver, Colorado. He was taken into custody when the aircraft landed at its intended destination.

22 JANUARY 1971

AN Ethiopian Airlines DC-3 was hijacked during a scheduled domestic flight from Bahir Dar to Gondar with 23 persons aboard and diverted to Banghazi, Libya, where the four assailants were taken into custody.

30 JANUARY–2 FEBRUARY 1971

IN India's first commercial aviation hijacking, two young Kashmiris commandeered an Indian Airline Corporation Fokker F.27 Friendship Mark 100 (VT-DMA), designated as Flight 422, during a domestic service from Srinagar to Delhi, forcing it to fly to Lahore, (West) Pakistan. It was there that they set afire and destroyed the twin-engine turboprop after the Indian authorities refused to release three dozen detainees being held in Kashmir, although their 38 hostages were released unharmed. The two assailants, who suffered minor injuries in sabotaging the aircraft, would later be deported to the US.

8 MARCH 1971

AT the airport serving Mobile, Alabama, a 16-year-old boy armed with a pistol forced his way aboard National Airlines Flight 745, which was en route to New Orleans, Louisiana, with 46 persons aboard. He ordered the Boeing 727 jet to Miami, Florida, where he surrendered. Due to his age he was sentenced to a correctional facility.

19 MARCH 1971

AN armed assailant who demanded to be taken to Sweden commandeered a KLM Royal Dutch Airlines DC-8 jetliner at Zanderij Airport, serving Paramaribo, Suriname, prior to its departure on a scheduled service to Amsterdam, but he was captured by two police officers.

30 MARCH 1971

HALF-A-DOZEN young men commandeered a Philippine Air Lines twin-jet BAC One-Eleven carrying 50 persons on a scheduled domestic service from Manila to Davao. Landing for refuelling in Hong Kong, where more than half of the passengers were released, the aircraft proceeded on to Canton, China. Two of the hijackers returned to the Philippines six years later and both were subsequently indicted in a military court.

13 APRIL 1971

THREE youths who attempted to hijack a Transair Ltd (Midwest Division) Piper Navajo, which was on a scheduled Canadian domestic commuter service within the province of Manitoba, from Dauphin to Winnipeg, were duped by the crew, who remained in the clouds until reaching their intended destination. In a subsequent struggle, the captain held off the juveniles while the co-pilot landed the twin-engine aeroplane, after which the young assailants were taken into custody by the authorities.

The light twin-engine L-200 flown by Soviet airline Aeroflot, which was commandeered to Turkey by two students in October 1970. (AP/Press Association Images)

21 APRIL 1971

A single assailant who said he had a pistol and a hand grenade, but was in fact unarmed, failed in his attempt to hijack to Italy an Eastern Airlines DC-8 jet, which had been operating as Flight 403 en route from Newark, New Jersey, to Miami, Florida, with 59 persons aboard. He was sentenced to three years' imprisonment, although the sentence was suspended.

8 MAY 1971

A DC-4 of the Colombian airline AVIANCA, on a scheduled domestic flight from Montería to Cartagena, was hijacked by a lone assailant, who was detained when the transport landed at Maracaibo, Venezuela.

13 MAY 1971

AN All Nippon Airways YS-11 turboprop was commandeered and forced to return to Tokyo, from where it had taken off earlier on a scheduled domestic service to Sendai. The lone assailant offered no resistance and was arrested by police.

17 MAY 1971

THE attempted hijacking of a Scandinavian Airlines System (SAS) DC-9 jetliner, on a scheduled domestic service to Stockholm, was averted on the ground at Malmö, Sweden, with the lone assailant being taken into custody.

27 MAY 1971

A Romanian Airlines (TAROM) Il-14 on a scheduled domestic service from Oradea to Bucharest with 24 persons aboard was commandeered by six hijackers, all of whom were taken into custody when the transport landed in Vienna. They were sentenced to prison terms ranging from two years to 30 months.

28 MAY 1971

A former policeman who claimed to have wrapped himself in explosives hijacked Eastern Airlines Flight 30, a Boeing 727 jetliner carrying 138 persons en route to New York City from Miami. The aircraft was flown to Nassau in the Bahamas, where, after landing, the assailant was overpowered by an airline pilot and taken into custody. Deported to the US, he was later committed to a psychiatric facility.

4 JUNE 1971

A United Air Lines Boeing 737 jet, designated as Flight 796 and carrying 72 persons on a US domestic service from Charleston, West Virginia, to Newark, New Jersey, was commandeered by a lone gunman who wanted to be taken to Israel. Stopping at Dulles International Airport, serving Washington DC, to switch to a longer-range aircraft, the hijacker was captured. He was later sentenced to concurrent 20-year prison terms for air piracy and interference with an airline crew.

11 JUNE 1971

THE first instance of a US airline passenger being killed in a hijacking involved Trans World Airlines Flight 358, a Boeing 727-231 on a domestic service to New York from Albuquerque, New Mexico.

Armed with a .38 calibre pistol, the 23-year-old assailant forced his way aboard the jetliner after it had landed at Chicago's O'Hare International Airport, an en-route stop. Seizing one of the stewardesses as a hostage, he released the passengers, though a 65-year-old man was shot and killed when he went back into the cabin, apparently to retrieve his coat. The aircraft then took off and headed east, the air pirate not only demanding to be flown to North Vietnam but also $75,000 in ransom money.

Gunman holds stewardess Maria Concepcion hostage while transferring from the TWA Boeing 727 to another aircraft on 23 July 1971, moments before being shot. (AP/Press Association Images)

Unbeknown to the gunman, a deputy US marshal had been smuggled in through a cockpit window at O'Hare, and about 30 minutes after the 727 had departed from Chicago, when the stewardess stepped away from her captor, he shot and wounded the hijacker. The aircraft later landed in New York City.

The hijacker committed suicide by hanging himself in a psychiatric hospital in 1978.

29 JUNE 1971

A woman who tried to hijack a Finnair DC-9 jet airliner on a scheduled service from Helsinki, Finland, to Copenhagen, Denmark, was overpowered by the crew.

2 JULY 1971

TWO assailants, a man and a woman armed with four pistols and alleged explosives, hijacked a Braniff International Airways Boeing 707 jet, operating as Flight 14, en route from Mexico City to San Antonio, Texas, one segment of a service originating at Acapulco, Mexico, with an ultimate destination of New York City. They were demanding a ransom of $100,000 and to be taken to Algeria.

Landing at Lima, Peru, and Rio de Janeiro, Brazil, the US aircraft, with 110 persons aboard, later touched down at Buenos Aires, Argentina, where the authorities refused to refuel it for the transatlantic trip. The passengers were released and, following a stand-off, the two hijackers gave themselves up. Both of them were sentenced to prison terms in Argentina and in 1975 were extradited to Mexico, where they served additional time.

11 JULY 1971

AFTER an unsuccessful attempt by two assailants to hijack an Empresa Consolidada Cubana de Aviación aircraft, possibly a twin-engine Ilyushin Il-14, which was operating as Flight 740 on a domestic service from Havana to Cienfuegos, a hand grenade was detonated. One passenger was killed and three persons were wounded, although the transport landed safely.

23 JULY 1971

IN this incident, a pistol-wielding suspect would lose his life after commandeering Trans World Airlines Flight 335, which had taken off from New York City on a domestic service to Chicago, Illinois. He asked to be taken to Milan, Italy, but was convinced by the pilot that the tri-jet Boeing 727 could not make the transatlantic trip.

After the aircraft had returned to La Guardia Airport, the gunman and the stewardess he was holding hostage were driven to nearby John F. Kennedy International Airport, where a longer-range Boeing 707 stood by for the flight to Italy. But it was never needed, the hijacker being felled by an FBI sharpshooter at around 14:00 local time as he walked about 20ft (6m) behind his hostage; he died approximately half-an-hour later. There were no other casualties.

24 AUGUST 1971

AN Alia Royal Jordanian Airlines Boeing 707 jetliner was extensively damaged by a bomb that detonated in an aft lavatory as the aircraft was parked on the ground at Madrid, Spain. There were no injuries.

24 SEPTEMBER 1971

WITH the intention of freeing two prisoners and escaping with them to Algeria, a woman commandeered an American Airlines Boeing 727 jetliner, operating as Flight 124 and en route to New York City from Detroit, Michigan, with 76 persons aboard. Armed with a pistol and dynamite, she was captured by police and subsequently given probation for assaulting a federal officer.

26 OCTOBER 1971

AN Olympic Airways DC-6B carrying 64 persons on a scheduled domestic service from Athens to the Greek island of Crete was hijacked to Rome, where the lone assailant was overpowered and captured.

20 NOVEMBER 1971

SABOTAGE with an explosive device was suspected in the crash of a China Airlines Sud-Aviation Caravelle III (B-1852), which occurred in the Formosa Strait. Designated as Flight 825 and en route to Hong Kong from T'aipei, Taiwan, the second leg of a service that had originated at Osaka, Japan, the Taiwanese-registered twin-engine jet was last reported cruising in darkness at 26,000ft (8,000m) when it vanished from radar contact at around 21:30 local time, at a position some 200 miles (320km) from its intended destination and in the vicinity of the Pescadores.

Subsequently, a small amount of debris washed ashore on one of the islands, but no survivors or bodies were found of the 25 persons who had been aboard the aircraft (17 passengers and a crew of eight).

3 DECEMBER 1971

A lone assailant who had the intention of securing supplies for Pakistani refugees commandeered a Pakistan International Airlines Boeing 720B jetliner, operating as Flight 712 on an international service to Karachi, Pakistan, while it was on the ground at Orly Airport, serving Paris. The suspect was overpowered by police, with one of the officers being slightly wounded, and subsequently received a five-year prison sentence, which was suspended.

16 DECEMBER 1971

THE hijacker of a Lloyd Aéreo Boliviano SA Fairchild F-27 was shot and killed by police and military troops at Cochabamba, Bolivia, where the twin-engine turboprop airliner had landed for refuelling. He had already killed the pilot of the aircraft after commandeering it while on a scheduled domestic service from Sucre to La Paz, ordering the co-pilot to fly to Arica, Chile.

22 DECEMBER 1971

AN attempt to commandeer a BN-2A Islander operated by the Dominican Republic carrier Alas Del Caribe Air, which had been on a scheduled domestic service from Santiago to Santo Domingo with seven persons aboard, was foiled when the lone assailant was overpowered by the pilot and other passengers after the aircraft had landed at Dajabon, in the north-western part of the Dominican Republic. The twin-engine aircraft sustained damage when it swerved off the airport runway and ploughed into rough terrain during the failed hijacking.

26 DECEMBER 1971

FLIGHT 47, an American Airlines Boeing 707 jet carrying 85 persons on a domestic service from Chicago, Illinois, to San Francisco, California, was taken over by a lone assailant, who demanded $200,000. The hijacker, who had used a knife, a pistol that turned out to be a toy and a fake bomb, was overpowered and subsequently served three years' imprisonment for air piracy and interference with an airline crew.

26 JANUARY 1972

A Jugoslovenski Aerotransport (JAT) McDonnell Douglas DC-9 Series 32 (YU-AHT) was blown up by a bomb over north-western Czechoslovakia, falling into a mountainous region near the town of Hermsdorf. All but one of the 28 persons aboard (22 passengers and five crew members) were killed.

Originating at Stockholm, Sweden, Flight 364 had stopped at Copenhagen before proceeding on towards Zagreb and ultimately Belgrade. The jet airliner had been cruising in darkness and clear weather conditions at an approximate altitude of 31,000ft (9,500m) when the explosion occurred in its forward baggage compartment, shortly after 18:00 local time. Croatian Nationalist activists were suspected of the act of sabotage.

The one remarkable aspect of the tragedy was the almost miraculous survival of 22-year-old stewardess Vesna Vulovic, who remained in the aircraft's tail assembly as it spun to earth like a falling leaf, and tumbled out when it struck the ground.

In January 1972, 22-year-old stewardess Vesna Vulovic miraculously survived the bombing of a Yugoslav DC-9 over Czechoslovakia. (UPI/Corbis-Bettmann)

It was theorised that the impact on sloping terrain was similar to a ski-jumping effect, with deceleration forces within human tolerance. She would later recover from the critical injuries suffered in the crash, which included brain damage, a fractured spine and paralysis from the waist down.

29 JANUARY 1972

DESIGNATED as Flight 2, a Trans World Airlines Boeing 707 jet was on a transcontinental domestic service from Los Angeles to New York City with 101 persons aboard when it was commandeered by a gunman who demanded some $300,000 in ransom and the release of prisoners. He was shot and wounded by an FBI agent on the ground at John F. Kennedy International Airport, and subsequently sentenced to life imprisonment on multiple charges.

7 MARCH 1972

ARMED with a pistol, a teenage boy three weeks short of his 15th birthday forced his way aboard a National Airlines Boeing 727 jetliner, operating as Flight 67 on an intrastate service to Miami, which was on the ground at Tampa, Florida. Demanding to be taken to Sweden, he was overpowered by a US federal marshal, and charges against him were later dismissed.

7–8 MARCH 1972

IN an extortion plot, Trans World Airlines was informed that bombs were on four of its aircraft. One bomb was actually found, aboard Flight 7, a domestic transcontinental service from New York City to Los Angeles, and about 04:00 local time on 8 March another exploded in the cockpit of a Boeing 707-331 (N761TW) jetliner that was on the ground at McCarran Airport, serving Las Vegas. There were no injuries, but the latter aircraft was damaged beyond repair.

Although $2 million was demanded, no money was ever collected and no suspects were apprehended.

11 MARCH 1972

A lone female assailant hijacked an Alitalia Caravelle, operating as Flight 68 on an Italian domestic service from Rome to Milan with 36 persons aboard, and the jetliner landed at Munich, (West) Germany. She was later charged with air piracy.

13 APRIL 1972

A lone gunman tried to hijack to Mexico a Frontier Airlines twin-jet Boeing 737, designated as Flight 91 and on a US domestic service from Albuquerque, New Mexico, to Tucson, Arizona, with 33 persons aboard. Surrendering at Los Angeles International Airport after a six-hour stand-off, he was sentenced to life imprisonment for air piracy but was paroled after serving six years.

16 APRIL 1972

AN attempt to hijack a Puerto Rico International Airlines Heron, operating as Flight 179 on an intra-island service from Ponce to San Juan, failed when the lone assailant, allegedly carrying a bomb but actually unarmed, was overpowered on the ground by another passenger and a mechanic. He served two years in prison after being convicted of conveying false information concerning attempted air piracy.

17 APRIL 1972

AT Seattle, Washington, an unarmed assailant who claimed to have a pistol forced his way aboard an Alaska Airlines Boeing 727 jetliner, carrying 92 persons and designated as Flight 1861, but was later captured. He was committed to a psychiatric facility for approximately a year.

17 APRIL 1972

A Swissair DC-9 carrying 20 persons was hijacked during a scheduled service from Geneva to Rome, but the lone assailant was captured after the jetliner had landed at its intended destination. He was sentenced to more than two years' imprisonment in 1973, but was released six days later after posting bail.

17 APRIL 1972

AS part of an extortion plot, a lone assailant who said he had a pistol but was in fact unarmed commandeered Delta Air Lines Flight 952, a Convair 880 jet carrying 78 persons. He surrendered at Chicago, Illinois, after a service from West Palm Beach, Florida, and was later sentenced to 20 years' imprisonment for air piracy.

18 APRIL 1972

THE co-pilot of a Slov-Air Let 410 twin-engine turboprop was shot and wounded during the hijacking of a scheduled Czechoslovakian domestic service from Prague to Marienbad with nine persons aboard. The aircraft landed at Nuremberg, (West) Germany, where the two assailants were sentenced to seven years' imprisonment. One of them would later commit suicide.

3 MAY 1972

WITH the intention of releasing three imprisoned members of the Turkish Liberation Army, four assailants hijacked a Turkish Airlines (THY) twin-jet DC-9 that was on a scheduled domestic service from Ankara to Istanbul with 68 persons aboard. They surrendered after landing at Sofia, Bulgaria, and later in the year were sentenced to three years' imprisonment.

24–26 MAY 1972

A South African Airways Boeing 727 jetliner carrying 66 persons was hijacked during a scheduled service from Salisbury, Rhodesia (Zimbabwe), to Johannesburg, South Africa, landing at Blantyre, Malawi, where, the following day, the passengers and crew escaped. The two assailants were overpowered by troops and subsequently sentenced to prison; both were deported to Zambia in 1974.

25 MAY 1972

A home-made pipe bomb exploded in the ice water service compartment of a LAN-Chile Boeing 727-116 as the jetliner was on a scheduled service from Panama to Miami, Florida, with 50 persons aboard. The blast, which occurred at around 01:20 local time at an approximate height of 30,000ft (9,000m), caused extensive damage and a rapid depressurisation of the cabin, but there were no injuries, and the aircraft landed safely at Montego Bay, Jamaica.

28 MAY 1972

A lone assailant with the objective of receiving medical treatment in London commandeered an Olympic Airways Boeing 707 jetliner that was on a scheduled domestic service from Crete to Athens with 130 persons aboard. After landing at its intended destination, police rushed the aircraft and captured the hijacker, who was later sentenced to two years' imprisonment.

30 MAY 1972

AN SA Empresa de Viação Aérea Rio Grandense (VARIG) Lockheed Electra was hijacked while on a scheduled Brazilian domestic flight from São Paulo to Curitiba with 92 persons aboard. The gunman released all of the passengers and the cabin attendants after receiving a ransom of $254,000 from the airline. Subsequently, the flight crew escaped through the cockpit of the four-engine turboprop and federal troops rushed the aircraft, with the hijacker shooting and killing himself before he could be captured.

8 JUNE 1972

A group of ten Czechs – seven men and three women, accompanied by a child – hijacked a Slov-Air Let 410 twin-engine turboprop commuter airliner that was carrying them, along with six other persons, on a scheduled domestic service from Marianske Lazne to Prague. The pilot was shot and killed when he resisted, and two others aboard also suffered injuries. The aircraft landed safely in (West) Germany, where the hijackers asked for asylum. One of them later committed suicide in prison, while the other nine adults were sentenced to prison terms of between three and seven years.

15 JUNE 1972

FIRST thought to have been an incidental act of war, the destruction of Cathay Pacific Airways Flight 700Z turned

A chart indicating the breaking-up points of the Cathay Pacific Airways Convair 880 jetliner blown up over South Vietnam on 15 June 1972. (International Civil Aviation Organisation)

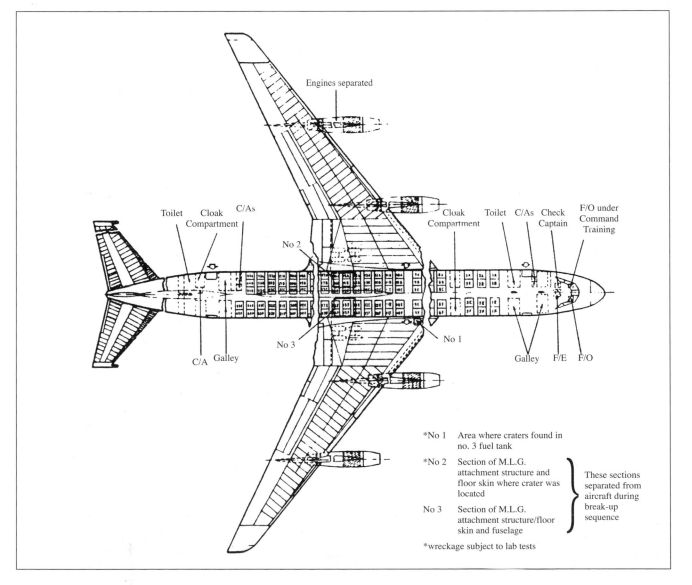

Toilet   Cloak Compartment   C/As

Engines separated

Cloak Compartment   Toilet   C/As   Check Captain   F/O under Command Training

No 2

No 3

C/A   Galley

No 1

Galley   F/E   F/O

*No 1   Area where craters found in no. 3 fuel tank

*No 2   Section of M.L.G. attachment structure and floor skin where crater was located

No 3   Section of M.L.G. attachment structure/floor skin and fuselage

} These sections separated from aircraft during break-up sequence

*wreckage subject to lab tests

out to be an act of sabotage, possibly motivated by personal profit. The Convair 880M jetliner (VR-HFZ) flown by the Hong Kong-based carrier had stopped at Bangkok, Thailand, before proceeding on towards Hong Kong, one segment of a service originating at Singapore. Some two hours after the loss of radio contact with the aircraft, just before 14:00 local time, its burning wreckage was located in the Central Highlands of (South) Vietnam, near Pleiku. All 81 persons aboard (71 passengers and a crew of ten) perished.

The sudden and catastrophic nature of the disaster, coupled with the fact that it had occurred in a war-torn region, led to early speculation that VR-HFZ had been shot down. But the metallic particles found in the debris and in some of the victims' bodies were too small and light to be associated with military missiles or projectiles. The outward travel of the fragments also indicated an internal rather than external explosion, pointing to a bomb.

Its flight data recorder (FDR) read-out showed the aircraft had been cruising at 29,000ft (8,800m) at an indicated air speed of approximately 350mph (560kph) and on a heading of about 70° when the high-explosive device detonated within its passenger cabin, in or near the centre section. The vertical stabiliser broke off after being hit by at least one victim who had been ejected from the cabin and, possibly, by some seats, also blown out. In-flight fire also occurred when the blast ruptured a right wing fuel tank. Damage probably inflicted on the flying controls routed beneath the cabin floor together with the loss of the vertical tail fin must have caused erratic, high-speed manoeuvres that led to the progressive break-up of the jetliner, with the various components striking the ground after a vertical descent. Those occupants not killed in the initial blast were probably rendered unconscious in the resulting explosive decompression.

Suspected of the mass murder was a Thai police lieutenant whose fiancée and daughter by a previous marriage were

A dead hijacker is taken away at Saigon after beign shot during an attempt to commandeer a Pan Am 747. (UPI/Corbis-Bettmann)

passengers on the flight. Both had been insured prior to their departure, prompting the investigative board to recommend that the sale of such insurance at airports be discouraged. Owing to insufficient evidence, the suspect was acquitted of the charges two years later.

2 JULY 1972

FLIGHT 841, a Pan American World Airways Boeing 747-121 wide-bodied jet with 153 persons aboard, was hijacked by a knife-wielding Vietnamese man about 45 minutes after it had taken off from Manila, the Philippines, an en-route stop during a service originating at San Francisco, California, with an ultimate destination of Saigon, (South) Vietnam. The assailant sent the captain a note stating that he was carrying explosives and would blow up the aircraft unless flown to Hanoi, (North) Vietnam. A second note written in blood reiterated his demand. Nevertheless, the captain landed at Tan Son Nhut Airport, serving Saigon.

As they were negotiating in the aircraft once it was on the ground, the captain jumped the hijacker, who had been holding a stewardess at knifepoint. Grasping the assailant by the throat, the captain ordered another passenger, who was armed, to shoot him; the dead hijacker was then tossed out of the cabin door. During the hasty disembarkation of the aircraft that ensued, numerous passengers suffered minor injuries.

The armed passenger who shot the hijacker was a civilian security officer who, at the beginning of the flight, had checked in his weapon with the crew. They were able to smuggle it back to him after the attempted hijacking commenced.

5 JULY 1972

A knife-wielding assailant who had already seriously wounded his estranged wife boarded an American Airlines Boeing 707 jet that was parked at the Buffalo, New York, airport, holding hostage his 14-month-old daughter and demanding to be flown out of the area. He surrendered after three hours and, the following year, was given five years' probation.

12 JULY 1972

AN attempt to hijack a DC-8 jetliner operated by the French carrier Union de Transports Aériens (UTA), which was on a scheduled service to Paris from Abidjan, Côte-d'Ivoire, was foiled, the gunman being shot and captured after wounding his wife.

18 JULY 1972

AN Aerolíneas TAO Viscount 785D, designated as Flight 511 and carrying 51 persons, was on a Colombian domestic service from San Andrés Island to Cartagena, with an ultimate destination of Bogotá, when a passenger went berserk. Forcing his way into the cockpit of the turboprop airliner, he shot both pilots, the captain fatally. He was subdued by others aboard after emptying his gun, the shooting taking place at around 18:00 local time.

Though wounded in the face and bleeding, the first officer managed to land the aircraft safely at Crespo Airport, serving Cartagena, where the assailant was taken into custody.

31 JULY 1972

FIVE assailants commandeered Delta Air Lines Flight 841, a DC-8 jetliner carrying 101 persons, during a US domestic service to Miami, Florida, from Detroit, Michigan. Their demands for a million dollars and a trip to Algeria were met. Three children who accompanied them were returned to the US, as was the money. Four of the hijackers were arrested in Paris, and although extradition to the US was denied, all spent between three and five years behind bars in France.

17–18 AUGUST 1972

A lone assailant rode up on a bicycle to the airport serving Reno, Nevada, and then, armed with a shotgun, commandeered United Air Lines Flight 877, a Boeing 727 jet bound for San Francisco, California, with 32 persons aboard.

He forced the aircraft to fly to Vancouver, British Columbia, and demanded an assortment of weapons, 15 gold bars, and $2 million, which he said was destined for children crippled in the Vietnam War. He released the passengers and cabin staff and ordered the 727 on to Seattle, Washington, where an FBI agent, using a weapon smuggled through a cockpit window, shot and wounded him. He was later sentenced to 30 years' imprisonment.

15 SEPTEMBER 1972

AN Air Manila Fairchild F-27 twin-engine turboprop, which had taken off minutes earlier from Romblon on a scheduled domestic service within the Philippines with 42 persons aboard, was cruising at an altitude of 11,000ft (3,400m) when what was believed to be a hand grenade was detonated on board. The possibly inadvertent blast occurred at 18:45 local time, the lightly damaged aircraft landing safely at Roxas. Two unexploded hand grenades were found on the floor of the cargo compartment.

15–16 SEPTEMBER 1972

A Scandinavian Airlines System (SAS) twin-jet DC-9 carrying 90 persons on a scheduled service from Göteborg to Stockholm, Sweden, was commandeered by three terrorists, who demanded a ransom and also secured the release of six Croatian

nationalists. All nine were then flown to Madrid, where the three responsible for the hijacking were later sentenced to 12 years' imprisonment. However, they were subsequently pardoned by Spanish leader General Francisco Franco.

6 OCTOBER 1972

OPERATING on a scheduled Italian domestic service with an ultimate destination of Bari, an Aero Trasporti Italiani SpA (ATI) Fokker F.27 Friendship Mark 200 was hijacked by a young man and forced to return to Ronchi dei Legionari Airport, serving Trieste, from where it had taken off earlier. The assailant demanded 200 million lire and a flight to Cairo.

After the six passengers had been released, the three crew members of the twin-engine turboprop managed to escape. Shortly thereafter the hijacker hurled an explosive device from the cockpit window, and police opened fire. Early the next morning they stormed the airliner and found him shot to death.

11 OCTOBER 1972

A lone assailant who claimed to have a bomb commandeered a Lufthansa German Airlines Boeing 727 jetliner that was on a scheduled service to Frankfurt from Lisbon, Portugal, with 58 persons aboard. He was shot and wounded by a sharpshooter while walking towards a getaway car.

22–23 OCTOBER 1972

A Turkish Airlines (THY) Boeing 707 jet, carrying 81 persons, was hijacked during a scheduled domestic service from Istanbul to Ankara, landing at Sofia, Bulgaria. The four air pirates threatened to blow up the aircraft unless the Turkish government released prisoners and instituted reforms; the pilot and a passenger were wounded and, the following day, the hijackers surrendered. They were sentenced to terms of 2 to 2½ years' imprisonment in Bulgaria, and the ringleader was later sentenced to 20 years in Turkey.

24 NOVEMBER 1972

A previous hijacking was an important element in this attempted act of air piracy, which led to the death of the assailant. The gunman kidnapped a stewardess and boarded an Air Canada DC-8 Super 63 jetliner that was parked at Rhein-Main Airport, serving Frankfurt, (West) Germany. Operating as Flight 807, the aircraft had been preparing for a transatlantic service with an ultimate destination of Montreal, Canada.

The hijacker had threatened to set off dynamite unless the German authorities released several Czech prisoners, including one of those who, on 8 June of the same year, had participated in the take-over of a Czech airliner, the pilot of which had been killed. However, he was himself killed by a police marksman.

8 DECEMBER 1972

IN a blazing gun-battle with security guards, seven members of the Eritrean Liberation Front, two of them women, were killed after the attempted hijacking of an Ethiopian Airlines Boeing 720B. Designated as Flight 708 and carrying 101 persons, the jetliner was en route from Addis Ababa to Asmara, the domestic segment of a service with an ultimate destination of Paris, when the terrorists, armed with pistols and hand grenades and intent on holding the passengers and crew members for ransom, put their ill-fated plan into effect.

During the assault, a courageous American passenger picked up a grenade that had been dropped by a wounded hijacker and tossed it into an unoccupied section of the cabin. The blast damaged the aircraft substantially, knocking out one engine and briefly causing a loss of control. Nine persons were wounded, most in the explosion, but the 720B returned safely to Addis Ababa.

14 DECEMBER 1972

A Quebecair twin-jet BAC One-Eleven, carrying 62 persons on a scheduled Canadian domestic service to Montreal, Quebec, from Wabush, Newfoundland, was hijacked by a lone assailant armed with a rifle. He required the pilot to proceed on to his intended destination, then shuttle between Montreal and Ottawa. He released the passengers and later surrendered, being subsequently sentenced to 20 years' imprisonment.

2 JANUARY 1973

ARMED with a pistol, a lone assailant who wanted to be taken to Canada boarded a Piedmont Airlines twin-engine turboprop YS-11, operating as Flight 928, which had just landed at Friendship International Airport, serving Baltimore, Maryland. He surrendered after several hours of negotiations and was later sentenced to 20 years' imprisonment.

4 JANUARY 1973

DEMANDING $2 million and passage to (North) Vietnam, a lone assailant commandeered a Pacific Western Airlines twin-engine turboprop Convair 640 at the airport serving Vancouver, British Columbia, from where it was about to take off on a Canadian scheduled domestic service to Penticton. After releasing the passengers he was arrested by police.

19 JANUARY 1973

A young US Army soldier who was absent without leave fired about 20 rounds from a shotgun at Standiford Field, serving Louisville, Kentucky, then commandeered a parked Ozark Air Lines DC-9 jet, holding a mechanic hostage aboard the aircraft. The assailant was subdued by a policewoman and then captured.

19 MARCH 1973

AN Air Vietnam Douglas DC-4 (XV-NUI) was sabotaged while on a scheduled domestic service from Saigon to Ban Me Thuot, crashing in the Central Highlands of (South) Vietnam near its destination and some 150 miles (250km) north-east of the capital. All 59 persons aboard, including a crew of five, perished. The airliner had been on its landing approach when, at about 10:05 local time, it plunged to earth from an approximate altitude of 2,000ft (600m) after an explosive device detonated in its cargo hold near the main wing spar.

30 MAY–3 JUNE 1973

A Sociedad Aeronáutica de Medellín Consolidada SA (SAM) Electra turboprop airliner was hijacked during a scheduled Colombian domestic service from Pereira to Medellín, with the two assailants demanding a ransom plus the release by the government of 140 prisoners. None were released and the hijackers received only a quarter of the amount requested.

The Electra landed several times, where passengers were either released or escaped, and four days into the siege the hijackers themselves escaped. Both were captured about a week later.

10 JUNE 1973

A Royal Nepal Airlines Twin Otter turboprop with 21 persons aboard was commandeered during a scheduled domestic service from Biratnagar to Kathmandu. It landed at Forbesganj, Bihar, India, where the three assailants escaped into the jungle with three million rupees that were being transported on the flight by a Nepalese bank.

8 JULY 1973

A lone assailant sent a note to the captain of an Aeroflot Il-18 turboprop, which had earlier taken off from Moscow on a scheduled international service, stating that he wanted the aircraft to proceed directly to its ultimate destination of Hanoi, (North) Vietnam, without landing as planned at Tashkent, USSR. Claiming to have an explosive device, he locked himself in a lavatory. The crew tricked him into believing they were setting down in Afghanistan for refuelling when in fact they had landed at Tashkent, where the man was arrested. Found to be mentally disturbed, he was committed to a psychiatric facility.

26 JULY 1973

WHILE on a scheduled domestic service originating at Vilnius, with an ultimate destination of Palanga, USSR, a passenger rushed into the cockpit of an Aeroflot Il-14 and, striking the captain in the head with a screwdriver, demanded to be flown to Sweden. He was overpowered by members of the crew. Exempted from criminal charges due to his mental state, he was committed to a psychiatric hospital.

2 OCTOBER 1973

THE hijacker of a KLM Royal Dutch Airlines DC-9, who commandeered the twin-engine jet during a scheduled service from Düsseldorf, (West) Germany, to Amsterdam, The Netherlands, was disarmed while talking with the pilot. He was later taken into custody.

10 OCTOBER 1973

THE lone assailant who tried to hijack a Compañia Mexicana de Aviación SA Boeing 727 jetliner on the ground at Mexico City was captured by a security officer dressed as a crew member.

11 OCTOBER 1973

THREE hijackers commandeered a Philippine Airlines twin-jet BAC One-Eleven that was on a scheduled domestic service from Davao to Bacolod. They exchanged the 49 passengers for the president of the airline and then flew to Hong Kong. After being granted amnesty by the government of the Philippines they surrendered.

18 OCTOBER 1973

AN Air France Boeing 727-228 jet airliner on a scheduled domestic service from Paris to Nice was hijacked by a woman who wanted to go to Cairo; she also demanded that all air traffic in France be halted for 24 hours. The aircraft landed at the airport serving Marseille, ostensibly for refuelling, where she allowed the 110 passengers and most of the crew to disembark. Following a subsequent attempt to overpower her she opened fire with a rifle and was then killed by police.

2 NOVEMBER 1973

FOUR young men commandeered an Aeroflot Yak-40 as the Soviet-built and registered three-engine jet airliner, designated as Flight 19, was on a domestic service from Moscow to Bryansk, and demanded half-a-million dollars' ransom. The flight engineer and one passenger were wounded in the take-over, although the aircraft managed to land at Vnukovo Airport, serving the capital. One assailant who had also been wounded later died, while a second shot himself before he could be arrested.

1 DECEMBER 1973

THE hijacker of a Swissair DC-8 jetliner, which was commandeered during a scheduled domestic service from Geneva to Zürich, demanded money to fight starvation in Africa, a ticket to New York City, and safe conduct. He released all of the occupants except for four crew members. He was subsequently arrested by police posing as the newsmen he had requested aboard.

3 JANUARY 1974

A lone assailant who claimed to have a hand grenade wrapped in a handkerchief tried to hijack to Miami an Air Jamaica DC-9 jetliner while it was at the airport serving Kingston, Jamaica, but he was overpowered and captured by security guards.

20 FEBRUARY 1974

TRICKERY by the pilot foiled this attempt to hijack an Air Vietnam DC-4 to (North) Vietnam. The airliner was taken over minutes after its departure from Dalat, (South) Vietnam, on a scheduled domestic service to Qui Nhon with 52 persons aboard. Shortly before noon local time, it landed at Hue, also in the South, but the hijacker was fooled into believing that it was in the Communist North.

During a scuffle with the co-pilot, which ensued when the hijacker learned of the truth, he dropped the live hand grenade he had been carrying, and it detonated in the cabin, killing him and two other passengers. Another 15 persons were injured, and the aircraft was extensively damaged in the blast.

22 FEBRUARY 1974

A gunman who was also carrying an incendiary bomb shot dead a security guard at Baltimore-Washington International Airport, near Baltimore, Maryland, then stormed aboard a Delta Air Lines twin-jet DC-9, designated as Flight 523, which was boarding passengers in preparation for a domestic service to Atlanta, Georgia. The assailant then shot both pilots, the first officer fatally, when they refused his demand to take off. He was himself wounded by police and subsequently committed suicide with his revolver. The incident was over minutes after it began, at approximately 07:00 local time.

American newspaper columnist Jack Anderson would later reveal that the man who committed the crime had, more than

a month earlier, sent him a tape-recording detailing plans to hijack an airliner and crash it into the Presidential White House in Washington DC.

20 MARCH 1974

A married couple hijacked an East African Airways Fokker F.27 Friendship twin-engine turboprop that was carrying 35 persons on a scheduled internal service from Nairobi to Malindi, Kenya, and ordered it to Libya. The airliner landed for refuelling at Entebbe, Uganda, where the hijackers gave themselves up after negotiations.

22 MARCH 1974

AN Air Inter Aérospatiale Caravelle III jet airliner (F-BSRY) was destroyed by an explosive device while parked unattended at Poretta Airport, serving Bastia, on French Corsica. There were no injuries in the early morning attack, the responsibility for which was claimed by a Corsican separatist group.

30 MARCH 1974

AN assailant armed with a shotgun and holding two hostages boarded a National Airlines Boeing 727 jet that was parked at the airport serving Sarasota, Florida, demanding to be flown out of the area. He was disarmed by a maintenance man, the only other occupant of the aircraft, and was later sentenced to 15 years' imprisonment for kidnapping.

15 JULY 1974

A youth armed with a knife who said he also had a bomb commandeered Japan Air Lines Flight 124, a DC-8 jetliner that was on a domestic service from Osaka to Tokyo with 90 persons aboard. The hijacker was captured after the aircraft landed at Nagoya, and, in 1977, was sentenced to ten years' imprisonment.

24 JULY 1974

A man who hijacked a flight to Cuba in 1969 had considerably less success in this attempted take-over of an AVIANCA Boeing 727-24C jetliner. Operating on a scheduled domestic service from Bogotá to Barranquilla and carrying 129 persons, the aircraft had last stopped at Pereira, where the assailant got aboard armed with a revolver. After it had, as ordered, landed at Cali, two passengers suffered injuries evacuating the 727. Only the flight crew and a young woman with an infant, who had accompanied the assailant, remained aboard. Subsequently the hijacker was shot by police, and later died in hospital.

6 AUGUST 1974

A bomb destroyed an Air Inter twin-engine turboprop Fokker F.27 Friendship Mark 500 (F-BPNF) that was parked unattended at Pluguffan Airport, serving Quimper, Brittany, France. There were no injuries in the attack, the responsibility for which was claimed by the Breton Liberation Front.

4 SEPTEMBER 1974

AN Eastern Airlines DC-9 jet, operating as Flight 1160 and completing a US domestic service from New York City with 100 persons aboard, was commandeered by a lone assailant after it had landed at Boston, Massachusetts. Taking the captain hostage,

Great Britain's only domestic airline hijacking to date, which occurred in January 1975, involved a British Airways BAC One-Eleven like this one. (British Aerospace)

with a razor blade and a nail, he demanded $10,000, but after more than three hours he was persuaded to surrender. He was subsequently committed to a psychiatric facility.

7 OCTOBER 1974

A Far Eastern Air Transport Viscount 810 turboprop airliner on a scheduled domestic flight from T'ainan to T'aipei, Taiwan, was hijacked by a single assailant carrying a knife and four bottles of gasoline. He demanded to be flown to mainland China, but was captured by a security guard and a cabin attendant.

23 NOVEMBER 1974

A 16-year-old boy, brandishing what resembled a stick of dynamite, seized an All Nippon Airways Boeing 727 jetliner on a scheduled domestic service from Tokyo to Sapporo, but was overpowered by a member of the flight crew.

29 NOVEMBER 1974

A CP Air twin-jet Boeing 737, designated as Flight 71 and on a Canadian domestic service from Winnipeg, Manitoba, to Edmonton, Alberta, with 86 persons aboard, got hijacked by a lone assailant who held and slightly wounded a stewardess with a knife. Demanding to be taken to Cyprus, he allowed the aircraft to land at Saskatoon, Saskatchewan, for refuelling, and later surrendered to the pilot. He was sentenced to seven years in prison.

2 DECEMBER 1974

A Swissair DC-8 Super 62 jet carrying more than 100 persons on a scheduled service from Bombay, India, to Karachi, Pakistan, was commandeered by a teenager armed with what turned out to be a toy pistol. Overpowered by the crew after the aircraft had landed for refuelling to Karachi, he was later sentenced to three years' imprisonment.

25 DECEMBER 1974

OPERATING as Flight 105 and carrying 170 persons, an Air-India Boeing 747 wide-bodied jet airliner was commandeered during an international service from Bombay to Rome, with the lone assailant brandishing a pocket knife and claiming to have bombs aboard. He demanded passage to a place of his choice, but was subsequently overpowered by the flight crew.

3 JANUARY 1975

TRYING to draw attention to himself, a lone assailant armed with a rifle boarded an out-of-service National Airlines Boeing 727 jet at the airport serving Pensacola, Florida. He was subsequently disarmed and overpowered by two aircraft cleaners. The following month he committed suicide in prison.

7 JANUARY 1975

THE United Kingdom's first and, to date, only domestic airline hijacking involved a British Airways BAC One-Eleven jet, designated as Flight 4069 from Manchester to London with 52 persons aboard. Carrying a pistol and a hand grenade (both of which turned out to be fakes), the assailant demanded £100,000 and a trip to Paris. He was tricked, however, the aircraft actually landing at Stansted Airport in Essex, and was later arrested while trying to escape with a hostage.

Subsequently convicted of the crime, the hijacker was sentenced to a prison term of seven years. The airline, meanwhile, announced stepped-up security measures to prevent future acts of air piracy.

13 JANUARY 1975

A would-be hijacker ordered Eastern Airlines Flight 140 to San Juan, Puerto Rico, during a US domestic service from Atlanta, Georgia, to Philadelphia, Pennsylvania. However, after the Boeing 727 jet, with 60 persons aboard, had landed for refuelling at Dulles International Airport, serving Washington DC, he locked himself in a lavatory. He was found to be unarmed when apprehended, and was subsequently committed to a psychiatric facility.

3 FEBRUARY 1975

A passenger who had ignited gasoline poured from a whisky bottle in the lavatory of a Pan American World Airways Boeing 747 wide-bodied jetliner was injured in the resulting flash fire, the incident occurring as the aircraft was over the Bay of Bengal some 60 miles (100km) west of Rangoon, Burma, on a scheduled international service from Bangkok to Delhi. The blaze was extinguished by the crew, and there were no other casualties.

25 FEBRUARY 1975

DEMANDING that one of them be pardoned for a previous offence, two men commandeered a Philippine Airlines DC-3 carrying 32 persons on a scheduled domestic service from Pagadian to Zamboanga. After ten hours of negotiations they both surrendered, but received no pardon, instead being sentenced to death by firing squad.

2 MARCH 1975

A knife-wielding assailant boarded an Air New England Twin Otter turboprop that was on the ground at Hyannis, Massachusetts, the pilot being its only other occupant. He demanded to be flown to New Haven, in neighbouring Connecticut, but was later captured by police and convicted on a weapon-possession charge.

9 APRIL 1975

A Japan Air Lines Boeing 747 wide-bodied jet on a scheduled domestic service from Sapporo to Tokyo was commandeered by a lone gunman who demanded 30 million yen, but after it had landed at its intended destination he was overpowered by police while talking with the pilot.

15 MAY 1975

SAYING that she did not want to land at its intended destination, an unarmed 16-year-old girl attempted to seize a United Airlines Boeing 727 jetliner, operating as Flight 509 on a US domestic service to San Francisco, California, from Eugene, Oregon, with 80 persons aboard. Captured and held by a crew member until taken into custody by police, she was subsequently returned to the psychiatric facility from which she had escaped.

3 JUNE 1975

DEPENDING on one's viewpoint, RP-C-1184 may be one of the unluckiest or luckiest commercial airliners to have ever carried passengers. Twice the Philippine Airlines BAC One-Eleven Series 500 was targeted in suicide bombings, resulting in death and injury. But both times, despite substantial damage, the twin-engine jet managed a safe landing.

The first case involved Flight 126, a domestic service to Manila from Legaspi. Having just begun its descent, the aircraft was at an approximate height of 20,000ft (6,000m) over Alabat Island when it was jolted by a bomb blast in its right rear lavatory around 15:30 local time. The alleged saboteur was killed; among the other 63 persons aboard, including a crew of five, 45 were injured, three passengers seriously.

After the pilot had descended to a lower altitude, the One-Eleven continued on towards its intended destination, setting down at Manila's international airport. Utilising plastic explosive, the bomb had left a hole measuring approximately 4ft (1.2m) wide in the top of the aircraft's fuselage. Subsequently repaired, RP-C-1184 would experience a remarkably similar incident three years later (see page 144).

28 JUNE 1975

A Balkan Bulgarian Airlines twin-engine turboprop An-24 was hijacked during a scheduled domestic service from Varna to Sofia and forced to land at Thessaloniki, Greece, where the armed assailant asked for political asylum.

5 JULY 1975

AFTER its passengers had disembarked, a Pakistan International Airlines Boeing 707 jetliner was damaged in a bomb blast on the ground at the airport serving Islamabad, Pakistan, where it had landed following a scheduled domestic service from Karachi. The detonation of the explosive device, which had been planted under a passenger seat, blasted a hole measuring 3ft by 4ft (0.9m by 1.2m) in the aircraft's fuselage, but there were no injuries.

15 JULY 1975

IN a fiery act of suicide, a passenger started a blaze in the aft right lavatory of a National Airlines DC-10, which was operating as Flight 1601 on a US domestic service from Miami to New York City. None of the other 69 persons aboard were injured in the incident, which occurred around 22:40 local time, and the wide-bodied jet landed safely at Jacksonville, Florida.

28 JULY 1975

A youth feigning that he had a knife seized an All Nippon Airways L-1011 wide-bodied jetliner on a scheduled domestic service from Tokyo to Sapporo with 286 persons aboard. After the aircraft returned to its point of origin, the passengers and crew disembarked and the hijacker was then arrested by police.

3 SEPTEMBER 1975

THE captain was reportedly shot and killed aboard an Aeroflot Il-62 shortly before the Soviet jetliner was scheduled to land at London, an en-route stop during a service from New York City to Moscow.

14–15 SEPTEMBER 1975

WHAT began as a hold-up led to kidnapping, the attempted hijacking of a commercial jet and, ultimately, to the death of the assailant. After trying to rob a grocery store, where a woman was stabbed, the gunman commandeered an automobile and its driver, then took a doctor hostage at a hospital before finally kidnapping a security guard at Reid-Hillview Airport in San José, California. Switching vehicles, he drove with his three captives to San José Municipal Airport, where he took hostage two maintenance personnel before herding all five of them on to a Continental Air Lines Boeing 727.

The gunman had the maintenance workers start the jetliner and taxi it into position for take-off, but police shot out its tyres. Subsequently, the doctor was shot and tumbled down the rear stairway, critically wounded. After the aircraft had stopped, the assailant emerged and was himself shot dead after pointing his gun at one of the more than two dozen police officers who had surrounded the 727. The drama ended around 01:30 local time, some two hours after it began.

27 SEPTEMBER 1975

A lone assailant holding a spray bottle that he claimed contained nitric acid tried to take over an Olympic Aviation SC.7 Skyvan twin-engine turboprop during a scheduled Greek domestic service from Athens to the island of Mikonos, but he was overpowered by the crew and turned over to the authorities after landing.

5 OCTOBER 1975

A band of guerrillas commandeered an Aerolíneas Argentinas Boeing 737 jet airliner during a scheduled domestic service from Buenos Aires to Corrientes, landing at the city of Formosa, where the passengers were released and more guerrillas boarded. Low on fuel, the 737 landed at Rafaela, in the province of Santa Fe, where the assailants escaped.

7 OCTOBER 1975

A lone assailant armed with a pistol and a hand grenade who wanted to be taken to Libya tried to commandeer a Philippine Airlines BAC One-Eleven jetliner that had been on a scheduled domestic service from Davao to Manila with 71 persons aboard. After the aircraft had landed at its intended destination, and a stand-off lasting several hours, he surrendered to the authorities.

22 DECEMBER 1975

THE hijacker of a Sociedad Aeronáutica de Medellín Consolidada SA (SAM) Beechcraft Queen Airliner, who had commandeered the twin-engine aircraft during a Colombian domestic air-taxi service from Barrancabermeja to Medellín, demanded three million pesos and safe conduct to an unspecified location, but was shot and wounded by secret police on the ground at its intended destination and then taken into custody.

5 JANUARY 1976

TWO armed men seized a Japan Air Lines DC-8 Super 61 jetliner with 219 persons aboard on the ground at Manila, the Philippines, an en-route stop during a scheduled service to Tokyo from Bangkok. They later surrendered to the Philippine authorities after Japan refused them entry into the country.

26 JANUARY 1976

HAVING obtained signal rockets and seven small pyrotechnic devices, a lone assailant attempting to flee from the USSR to avoid punishment for a previous crime threatened to blow up an Aeroflot Il-62 jet airliner – designated as Flight 614, on a scheduled domestic service – unless he was taken to Tel Aviv, Israel. However, the aircraft instead landed at Moscow, and he was captured and sentenced to ten years' imprisonment.

29 FEBRUARY 1976

POLICE shot and killed the hijacker of an Aerolíneas Centrales de Colombia (ACES) twin-engine turboprop Saunders ST-27 on the ground at the airport serving Medellín, Colombia, from where it had taken off earlier. He had commandeered the aircraft during a scheduled domestic service to Apartado, demanding $300,000 but releasing the 15 passengers.

5 APRIL 1976

A Cuban soldier commandeered a Transportes Aéreos Portugueses (TAP) Boeing 747 wide-bodied jet airliner on the ground at Luanda, Angola, but surrendered his rifle after the aircraft was airborne and the crew had agreed not to return to its departure point. The 747, with 380 persons aboard, then proceeded on to Lisbon, Portugal. Under the circumstances, the Portuguese authorities allowed the Cuban to stay in their country.

7–13 APRIL 1976

THREE men commandeered a Philippine Airlines twin-jet BAC One-Eleven that was carrying 79 persons on a scheduled domestic service from Cagayan de Oro to the island of Mactan, and demanded a ransom and the release of numerous prisoners. Over a period of six days, the aircraft stopped in Malaysia, then Thailand – where the hijackers switched to a longer-range DC-8 jetliner – then Pakistan, and finally Libya, where they requested, but were refused, political asylum.

18–19 APRIL 1976

A lone assailant facing charges of vehicular homicide and larceny commandeered a twin-engine Piper Navajo, with its pilot and a mechanic aboard, at Grand Island, Nebraska. Forced to fly to Denver, Colorado, the Navajo set down at that city's Stapleton International Airport, then took off and circled for about half an hour before landing again.

To satisfy the gunman's demand for a flight to Mexico, the authorities offered the use of a larger aircraft, a Convair 990A Coronado four-engine jet operated by Denver Ports of Call. Waiting aboard it were FBI agents, who shot and killed him in the passenger cabin shortly after midnight of the second day. His two hostages escaped harm.

24 APRIL 1976

TO protest at 'the neglect of the peasants', an armed man commandeered an AVIANCA Boeing 727 jetliner during a scheduled Colombian domestic service to Bogotá from Pereira. He surrendered after it had landed at its intended destination.

30 APRIL 1976

A Turkish Airlines (THY) DC-10 wide-bodied jet carrying 253 persons was on a scheduled service from Paris to Istanbul when a man threatened a stewardess with a knife and tried to force it to land at either Marseille or Lyon, France. The aircraft instead returned to its point of origin, where the unsuccessful hijacker surrendered without further incident.

2 JULY 1976

IN an attack possibly related to strained race relations, an Eastern Airlines four-engine turboprop Lockheed 188A Electra (N5531) was set afire and destroyed by a bomb while parked at Logan International Airport, serving Boston, Massachusetts. There were no injuries in the incident, which occurred in early morning darkness after a telephoned threat.

7 SEPTEMBER 1976

AN Air France Boeing 707-328 jet airliner (F-BHSH) was destroyed in a night-time terrorist attack while parked at Campo dell'Oro Airport, serving Ajaccio, French Corsica, in readiness for a domestic service to Paris. The passengers and crew had been ordered off the aircraft. before at least two bombs were set off in its cabin, and there were no injuries. Subsequently, 18 suspects were charged with involvement in the attack, with at least some of them facing prison time.

10 SEPTEMBER 1976

AN Indian Airlines twin-jet Boeing 737, designated as Flight 491 and carrying 84 persons, was commandeered during a domestic service from New Delhi to Bombay, subsequently landing at Lahore, Pakistan. There, the six alleged hijackers were taken into custody, but all were later released on grounds of insufficient evidence.

10 SEPTEMBER 1976

FIVE terrorists allegedly carrying plastic explosives (which turned out to be clay) commandeered Trans World Airlines Flight 355, a Boeing 727-231 jetliner en route from New York City to Chicago with 92 persons aboard, with the intention of distributing propaganda regarding Croatian independence. Stopping in Newfoundland and Iceland, the aircraft eventually landed in Paris. As another part of their demands, leaflets were dropped over London from another aircraft.

The hijackers were returned to the US to face charges of not only air piracy but also the murder of a police officer, killed by a bomb found at Grand Central Station, New York City. Three were sentenced to 30 years' imprisonment, plus additional time on state charges, and the other two received life prison terms, although the lead hijacker was paroled in 2008 and returned to Croatia.

26 SEPTEMBER 1976

IN a bizarre case of personal rage, the pilot who had stolen an Aeroflot Antonov An-2 crashed the Soviet-built and registered single-engine biplane into an apartment building where his ex-wife lived in Novosibirsk, USSR. She was not a victim of the kamikaze-type attack, but 11 other persons on the ground were killed, as was the pilot, the sole occupant of the aircraft.

6 OCTOBER 1976

EMPRESA Consolidada Cubana de Aviación Flight 455, a Douglas DC-8 Series 43 (CU-T1201), departed from Seawell International Airport, serving Barbados, bound for Kingston, Jamaica, one segment of a service that had originated at Georgetown, Guyana, with an ultimate destination of Havana, Cuba. About ten minutes after take-off, the crew transmitted a radio distress message reporting an on-board explosion, and were granted a request for an immediate landing. Turning back towards its point of departure, the jetliner was observed to be trailing smoke before it entered a steep climb while banked to the left, and then plummeted into the Caribbean Sea some ten miles (16km) off the southern coast of Barbados, in water more than 1,000ft (300m) deep, at around 13:30 local time. All 73 persons aboard perished, including ten off-duty crew members riding as passengers and a regular crew of 15.

The tragedy was believed to have resulted from the detonation of an explosive device in the rear of the aircraft's cabin. This led to an uncontrollable fire producing toxic fumes that must have eventually incapacitated the flight crew. A decade later, two men were sentenced to 20 years' imprisonment by a Venezuelan court for their involvement in the crash.

28 OCTOBER 1976

A lone assailant armed with a sub-machine gun and a pistol hijacked a Czechoslovak Airlines (CSA) Il-18 turboprop that was on a scheduled domestic service from Prague to Bratislava carrying 111 persons. The aircraft landed at Munich, (West) Germany, the hijacker being later sentenced to eight years' imprisonment in that country. However, he hanged himself in prison in 1980.

4 NOVEMBER 1976

USING a dummy bomb, a lone assailant commandeered a Polish Airlines (LOT) Tu-134A jetliner that was on a scheduled service from Copenhagen to Warsaw. The aircraft landed at Vienna, where the hijacker surrendered. He was later sentenced to four years' imprisonment.

21 DECEMBER 1976

A United Airlines employee armed with two revolvers and a knife boarded one of the carrier's empty DC-8 jetliners at San Francisco International Airport. Holding two hostages, he demanded a crew to fly him to the US East Coast. He then surrendered. He was later ruled legally insane and committed to a psychiatric facility.

11 JANUARY 1977

A Trans World Airlines Boeing 747 wide-bodied jetliner, designated as Flight 700 on a transatlantic service from New York City to London with 349 persons aboard, was targeted for hijack by a man who claimed to have a hand grenade and wanted to be taken to Uganda. He was overpowered by other passengers and members of the crew. After being returned to the US, he was sentenced to prison on misdemeanour assault charges and also ordered to receive psychiatric treatment.

13 FEBRUARY 1977

AN attempt to hijack to Yugoslavia a Turkish Airlines (THY) DC-9 jet, which was on a scheduled domestic service from Istanbul to Izmir with 62 persons aboard, ended when the 17-year-old assailant surrendered to security forces at a military airbase near its intended destination. The pilot and a stewardess were shot and wounded.

14–16 MARCH 1977

A Boeing 727 jet operated by the Spanish airline Iberia was commandeered by a single assailant during a scheduled domestic service from Barcelona to Palma de Mallorca with 37 persons aboard. The aircraft was flown to Algeria, Côte-d'Ivoire, back to Spain, then to Italy, Switzerland and Poland, and finally back to Switzerland, where the hijacker was arrested after an odyssey that had lasted 44 hours and covered some 10,000 miles (16,000km). He was sentenced to ten years' imprisonment, and after failing to return from prison leave and threatening to commandeer another aircraft was apprehended in Italy, and sentenced to another nine years.

17 MARCH 1977

TWO All Nippon Airways Boeing 727 jetliners were targeted on this day, with both hijackings failing and one ending in death. Flight 724, which was carrying 43 persons on a Japanese domestic service to Sendai from Chitose Airport, located near Sapporo, was commandeered by a single assailant who was overpowered by other passengers and turned over to police after the aircraft landed at Hakodate. Later in the day, another lone assailant took over Flight 817, on a domestic service from Tokyo to Sendai with 180 persons aboard, but shortly before the aircraft returned to its point of origin he entered a lavatory and swallowed poison. Two passengers had been slightly wounded by this would-be hijacker.

31 MARCH 1977

THE pilot of a Swiftair DC-3 that had been on a Philippine non-scheduled domestic service from Zamboanga to the Tawitawi group of islands suddenly went berserk and opened fire with an M-16 rifle. Killed in the attack, which occurred about five minutes before the transport was to have landed, at approximately 11:45 local time, were the stewardess and six of the 34 passengers; 16 other persons aboard were wounded. The pilot was nevertheless subdued, and the co-pilot landed the aircraft safely.

Most of the occupants were military personnel, the weapon used belonging to one of the soldiers. The assailant, who may have been infatuated with the stewardess he killed, was later detained at a stockade.

24 APRIL 1977

POLICE overpowered a lone assailant on the ground at the airport serving Kraków, Poland, after he tried to take over a Polish Airlines (LOT) Tu-134 jet that had been on a charter service to Nuremberg, (West) Germany.

25 APRIL 1977

TWO members of the Eritrean Liberation Front were shot and killed by the crew after attempting to hijack an Ethiopian Airlines DC-3, which had been on a scheduled domestic service from Makele to Gondar. Several passengers were reportedly wounded, although the transport landed safely.

2 MAY 1977

A Boeing 727 jetliner of Spain's airline Iberia, on a scheduled service from Madrid, was seized by a lone hijacker after landing at Rome, but he was overpowered and arrested.

8 MAY 1977

A passenger armed with a razor blade tried to commandeer to the USSR a Northwest Airlines Boeing 747 wide-bodied jet that was operating as Flight 22 on a service from Tokyo to Honolulu, with 262 persons aboard. He was overpowered and tied up. Ruled insane, he was committed to a psychiatric facility for two years.

26 MAY 1977

AN Aeroflot An-24B turboprop carrying 23 persons on a scheduled Soviet domestic service within Latvia, from Riga to Daugavpils, was successfully commandeered to Sweden, which refused to extradite the lone hijacker and instead sentenced him to a four-year prison term.

17 JUNE 1977

ARMED with a bottle of dark liquid (which turned out to be coloured water), a lone assailant tried to hijack to Sweden an Aeroflot twin-jet Yak-40 that had been on a scheduled Soviet domestic service from Tallin to Kaliningrad. It instead landed at Ventspils, Latvia, where he was arrested.

18 JUNE 1977

A Balkan Bulgarian Airlines An-24 turboprop on a scheduled domestic flight from Vidin to Sofia with 47 persons aboard was hijacked by a lone assailant, who was captured after the aircraft had landed at Belgrade, Yugoslavia.

21 JUNE 1977

A LAN-Chile Boeing 727 jetliner, carrying 78 persons on a scheduled domestic service to Santiago from Antofagasta, was commandeered to Mendoza, Argentina, where the lone hijacker was taken into custody by military personnel.

28 JUNE 1977

A knife-wielding Turk who was being returned to his country tried to seize a Lufthansa German Airlines Boeing 727 jetliner that had taken off from Frankfurt on a scheduled international service to Istanbul, with approximately 90 persons aboard. The aircraft instead landed at Munich and the assailant was overpowered.

5 JULY 1977

A Línea Aérea del Cobre SA (Ladeco) Boeing 727 jet airliner on a scheduled Chilean domestic service from Arica to Santiago with 60 persons aboard was commandeered to Lima, Peru. The four air pirates were subsequently deported to Cuba for asylum.

10–12 JULY 1977

AN Aeroflot Tu-134 jet airliner carrying 79 persons on a scheduled domestic service from Petrozavodsk to Leningrad, USSR, was hijacked to Helsinki, Finland. The two assailants held the other passengers and members of the crew hostage, demanding that the aircraft be released to Sweden, but they were returned to the Soviet Union, where they received prison terms of eight years and 15 years, respectively.

20 AUGUST 1977

FLIGHT 550, a Western Air Lines Boeing 707 jet carrying 31 persons on a US domestic service from San Diego, California, to Denver, Colorado, was hijacked by a lone assailant who claimed to have a bomb and demanded to be taken to Mexico and several other locations. He surrendered to the authorities when the aircraft landed at Salt Lake City, Utah. Criminal charges against him were subsequently dismissed on grounds of mental incompetency.

5 SEPTEMBER 1977

A lone assailant held a stewardess at gunpoint aboard a Garuda Indonesian Airways twin-jet DC-9 that was on a scheduled domestic service from Jogjakarta to Surabaja, East Java, but he was overpowered by other members of the crew.

28 SEPTEMBER–1 OCTOBER 1977

OPERATING as Flight 472 on an international service to Tokyo from Bombay, a Japan Air Lines DC-8 Super 62 jet with 156 persons aboard was commandeered by five members of the self-proclaimed Japanese 'Red Army', armed with guns and grenades. On the ground at Dacca, Bangladesh, the assailants released about 60 passengers in exchange for ransom money and six prisoners held in Japan. They finally surrendered to Algerian authorities when the aircraft reached Algiers, although they were reportedly expelled from the country a week later.

The mastermind behind this and a previous Japan Air Lines hijacking would later be sentenced to life imprisonment by a Japanese court.

30 SEPTEMBER 1977

AN Air Inter Caravelle 12 jetliner, carrying 107 persons on a scheduled French domestic service to Lyon, was commandeered and forced to return to Paris, from where it had taken off earlier, landing at Orly Airport. A stewardess was shot and wounded trying to stop the lone air pirate from entering the flight deck.

When police stormed the aircraft at around 14:00 local time, the assailant tossed a hand grenade, the resulting explosion killing one passenger and injuring four other persons, as well as causing considerable damage to the aircraft. He was nevertheless captured, and later sentenced to 18 years' imprisonment.

11 OCTOBER 1977

A Czechoslovak Airlines (CSA) twin-jet Yak-40 was hijacked by two employees of the carrier during a scheduled domestic service from Karlovy Vary to Prague, Czechoslovakia, and landed at Frankfurt, (West) Germany. They received prison terms of 3½ years and 6 years, respectively.

17 OCTOBER 1977

TWO gunmen stormed aboard an Air Djibouti Twin Otter turboprop at the airport serving Tadjoura, Djibouti. Among the 11 persons aboard the aircraft, the pilot and one passenger were killed in the attack and five others wounded.

18 OCTOBER 1977

AN attempt to commandeer a Polish Airlines (LOT) An-24B turboprop, carrying 50 persons on a scheduled domestic flight from Katowice to Warsaw, was reportedly foiled by the crew.

A Japan Air Lines DC-8 Super 62 of the type hijacked and held for three days in the autumn of 1977 by members of the Japanese 'Red Army'. (McDonnell Douglas)

29 OCTOBER 1977

TWO crew members were killed and a third wounded in the hijacking of an Air Vietnam DC-3, which occurred as the airliner, carrying 40 persons, was on a scheduled service from Ho Chi Minh City, Vietnam, to Phu Quoc Island, Thailand. The twin-engine transport was diverted to Singapore, where the four assailants were sentenced to 14 years' imprisonment each.

20–21 JANUARY 1978

ARMED with a pistol and what he said was a suitcase of explosives, a lone assailant seized a Pakistan International Airlines Fokker F.27 turboprop carrying 42 persons on a scheduled domestic service from Sukker to Karachi. He demanded a cash ransom for cancer treatment. The aircraft landed at its intended destination, where the hijacker was overpowered; an airline employee was shot and wounded in the incident. The assailant would lose his life three years later, not to disease but to the hangman's noose.

6 FEBRUARY 1978

FALSELY claiming to have a bomb, a single hijacker commandeered a Czechoslovak Airlines (CSA) Tu-134 jet that was on a scheduled service to Prague from (East) Berlin. The aircraft, with 46 persons aboard, landed at Frankfurt, (West) Germany, where the assailant surrendered and asked for political asylum. He was subsequently sentenced to four years' imprisonment.

2 MARCH 1978

A hijacking attempt was made by a single assailant against a Pakistan International Airlines Boeing 747 wide-bodied jetliner carrying 357 persons on a scheduled domestic service from Islamabad to Karachi. Three other passengers who overpowered him were injured in a grenade blast. The hijacker lost his hand in the explosion, and, convicted of air piracy, he was hanged in 1979.

9 MARCH 1978

THE flight engineer of a China Airlines Boeing 737 tried to hijack the jetliner as it was on a scheduled service to Hong Kong from Kaohsiung, Taiwan, with 101 persons aboard, attacking the pilot and co-pilot with a hammer and scissors. However, he was shot dead by a security guard and the Taiwanese aircraft landed safely at its intended destination.

1 APRIL 1978

ARMED with a rifle, a 15-year-old boy jumped a fence at Byrd International Airport, Richmond, Virginia, and forced his way aboard a Piedmont Airlines Boeing 737 jet, designated as Flight 66 and on a domestic intrastate service to Norfolk with 66 persons aboard. He demanded a million dollars in ransom and a trip to France, but subsequently surrendered. Convicted of multiple charges, he was remanded to the care of a psychiatrist.

9 APRIL 1978

FIRING shots and spilling gasoline in the cabin and threatening to start a fire, a lone assailant tried to hijack to Sweden an Aeroflot Yak-40 jetliner that was on a scheduled Soviet domestic service originating at Palanga, with an ultimate destination of Tallinn. The aircraft instead landed at Pyarnu, Estonian SSR, where he was captured. Found to be mentally disturbed, he was committed to a psychiatric hospital.

1 MAY 1978

AN attempt to hijack an Aeroflot Il-18 turboprop airliner to Iran during a scheduled Soviet domestic service from Ashkhabad to Mineral'nyye Vody ended with the assailant, who was carrying a training grenade, being shot dead by the co-pilot.

10 MAY 1978

THREE adults accompanied by two children hijacked a Czechoslovak Airlines (CSA) Il-18 turboprop carrying 46 persons on a scheduled domestic flight from Prague to Brno. All were taken into custody when the aircraft landed at Frankfurt, (West) Germany.

11 MAY 1978

TWO men armed with a toy pistol and a home-made nitro-glycerine device commandeered an AVIANCA Boeing 727

The bombing, in August 1978, of a Philippine Airlines BAC One-Eleven Series 500 such as this was the second sabotage attack on the same aircraft. (British Aerospace)

jetliner on a scheduled Colombian domestic flight from Santa Marta to Bogotá with 109 persons aboard. They then took a real revolver from a customs official, which was used to shoot and wound the flight engineer.

After the aircraft had landed at Curaçao, Netherlands Antilles, the assailants were disarmed by other passengers and members of the crew. Four persons, including two police officers, suffered injuries.

16 MAY 1978

TWO men aboard an Aeroméxico DC-9 jetliner, carrying 99 persons on a scheduled domestic service from Torreon to Mexico City, handed a stewardess a note on which was written an incoherent message, stating they were carrying explosives and demanding 'justice' for themselves and certain others. Both were taken into custody after the aircraft had landed at its intended destination.

17 MAY 1978

AN attempt to hijack a Czechoslovak Airlines (CSA) Yak-40 jet, which was on a scheduled domestic service from Brno to Prague, failed when the lone assailant was overpowered.

29 MAY 1978

A lone hijacker tried to take over a Czechoslovak Airlines (CSA) Yak-40 jet that was on a scheduled domestic flight from Brno to Karlovy Vary, demanding to be taken to (West) Germany, but he was overpowered by members of the crew.

6 AUGUST 1978

ARMED with a pistol that turned out to be a toy, a lone assailant seized a KLM Royal Dutch Airlines DC-9 jet carrying 68 persons on a scheduled service from Amsterdam to Madrid, demanding to be taken to Algeria. He was overpowered by a stewardess and three passengers, and subsequently extradited to The Netherlands for prosecution.

18 AUGUST 1978

A Philippine Airlines BAC One-Eleven Series 500 (RP-C-1184), the same aircraft damaged in a 1975 suicide bombing (see page 139), was targeted in this amazingly similar incident. Operating as Flight 148 on a domestic run to Manila from Cebu, the jetliner

was cruising at 24,000ft (7,300m) in the vicinity of Sibuyan Island when an explosive device detonated in its left rear lavatory. The blast, which took place shortly after 07:00 local time, resulted in the death of the saboteur, who was ejected from the aircraft and lost at sea. Three passengers were injured, while the other 80 persons aboard, including the crew of six, escaped unscathed. Following the explosion the pilot descended to 12,000ft (3,700m) in order to equalise pressure, and the One-Eleven proceeded on to Manila, landing safely despite a hole measuring 2ft by 3ft (0.6m by 0.9m) in the rear fuselage area.

The bomber was found to have purchased a one-way ticket and taken out an insurance policy worth 50,000 pesos the night before the flight.

25 AUGUST 1978

A lone assailant claiming to have explosives handed a note to a stewardess aboard Trans World Airlines Flight 830, a Boeing 707 jet on a service from New York City to Geneva with 89 persons aboard. The note demanded the release of a number of individuals imprisoned in the US and elsewhere. After the aircraft had landed at its intended destination, a seven-hour stand-off ensued until the assailant surrendered. He was subsequently sentenced to seven years' imprisonment for interference with an airline crew and making a false bomb threat.

26 AUGUST 1978

A Burma Airways Corporation de Havilland Twin Otter Series 300 (XY-AEI) was apparently destroyed by explosives and crashed near Papun, Kayin, Burma, killing all 14 persons aboard (11 passengers and a crew of three). The twin-engine turboprop was on a scheduled domestic service from Moulmein to Pa-an, and crashed seconds after taking off from Runway 18 at the local airport following a blast in its cabin at an approximate height of 400ft (120m). It was not known if the explosion was an intentional act of sabotage or an accident.

27 AUGUST 1978

A United Airlines DC-8 Super 61 jetliner, designated as Flight 179, en route from Denver, Colorado, to Seattle, Washington, and carrying 159 persons, was diverted to Vancouver, British Columbia, by a female passenger claiming in a note to have a bomb. She was declared mentally incompetent by a government psychiatrist.

30 AUGUST 1978

A lone assailant armed with a starter pistol hijacked a Polish Airlines (LOT) Tu-134 jetliner on a scheduled service from Gdansk, Poland, to (East) Berlin with 71 persons aboard, ordering it to land in (West) Berlin. There, he and eight other passengers asked for political asylum. The hijacker was sentenced to nine months' imprisonment.

7 SEPTEMBER 1978

THE detonation of an explosive device in the fuselage mid-section of an Air Ceylon Hawker Siddeley 748 Series 2 (4R-ACJ) that was on the ground at Ratmalana Airport, near Colombo, Sri Lanka, resulted in a fire that destroyed the twin-engine turboprop airliner. The blast occurred at around 08:40 local time, as the aircraft was being prepared for a ferry flight.

The pilot and co-pilot, who had been carrying out their pre-departure checks, were the only occupants and escaped injury.

30 SEPTEMBER 1978

A Finnair Super Caravelle jet airliner was seized by a pistol-armed assailant during a scheduled domestic service from Oulu to Helsinki, Finland, with 48 persons aboard. The aircraft proceeded to its intended destination, then returned to its point of origin, with a stop at Amsterdam, The Netherlands. The gunman, who was paid a ransom during the hijacking, was allowed to go home but was arrested the following day. He was subsequently fined and sentenced to seven years' imprisonment.

1 OCTOBER 1978

IN a suspected sabotage attempt, a passenger apparently started a fire in the aft lavatory of a Toa Domestic Airlines DC-9 jetliner that had been on a scheduled Japanese domestic service. Although he suffered serious injuries, there were no casualties among the other 111 persons aboard the aircraft, which landed safely at the city of Oita at around 11:45 local time, some ten minutes after the incident.

The passenger had taken into the lavatory a suitcase that was found to contain, among other items, three bottles of liquid propane gas and two empty bottles of benzene. The hazardous materials had not been detected during the pre-flight screening because the airport security guard in charge of the metal detection equipment had not been properly instructed.

22 OCTOBER 1978

THE pilot of a Transportes Aéreos Portugueses (TAP) Boeing 727 jetliner on a scheduled service from Lisbon to the Portuguese Island of Madeira, having correctly ascertained that the two pistols held by his assailant were fakes, overpowered a passenger who had been demanding to be flown to Morocco.

31 OCTOBER 1978

THREATENING to blow it up, a lone assailant tried to hijack to Norway an Aeroflot twin-jet Tu-134 that had been on a scheduled Soviet domestic flight from Leningrad to Murmansk, but the crew instead landed at Petrozavodsk, Karel'skaya ASSR, where he was arrested. He was subsequently sentenced to six years' imprisonment.

9 NOVEMBER 1978

AN armed passenger rushed into the cockpit of an Aeroflot An-24 turboprop, which had been on a scheduled Soviet domestic service originating at Krasnodar and ultimately destined for Baku, firing off a few shots and wounding the flight engineer before being locked in the baggage compartment, where he subsequently killed himself.

10 NOVEMBER 1978

FALSELY claiming to have an explosive device, a passenger tried to divert to Turkey an Aeroflot An-24 turboprop that had been on a scheduled Soviet domestic service originating at Kharkov, with an ultimate destination of Sukhumi. He was arrested after it instead landed at Batumi, Georgian SSR, and was later sentenced to eight years' imprisonment.

23 NOVEMBER 1978

A would-be hijacker drove his car through a fence at Mitchell Field, serving Madison, Wisconsin, and up to a North Central Airlines twin-jet DC-9, which was operating as Flight 468. He then boarded the aircraft, claiming to have a bomb (which turned out to be a fake) in a trash bag. He was later captured by police on the flight deck of the DC-9, but charges against him were subsequently dropped on grounds of mental incompetency.

20 DECEMBER 1978

TWO assailants brandishing what appeared to be a pistol and a hand grenade commandeered Indian Airlines Flight 410, a Boeing 737 jet on a domestic service to New Delhi from Lucknow, and forced it to land at Varanasi, in Pradesh. They were demanding the release of former Indian Prime Minister Indira Gandhi, who at the time was in jail.

After releasing the passengers and crew the hijackers were flown by light aircraft to Lucknow, where they were taken into custody by police. The gun was a toy and the grenade actually a cricket ball.

21 DECEMBER 1978

A 17-year-old girl who said she had dynamite strapped to her body commandeered a Trans World Airlines DC-9 jet, designated as Flight 541, on an intrastate service from St Louis to Kansas City, Missouri, with 89 persons aboard. She was demanding the release of a prisoner serving a life sentence for a 1972 hijacking. The aircraft landed at Marion, Illinois, where a nine-hour stand-off ensued until she was arrested by two law enforcement officers.

The hijacker, who actually had three railroad flares, was convicted of air piracy as a juvenile, and placed in a foster home until her 21st birthday, then put on probation.

27 JANUARY 1979

A woman claiming to have nitro-glycerine in her possession seized United Airlines Flight 8, a Boeing 747 wide-bodied jet, during a transcontinental US domestic service from Los Angeles to New York City with 131 persons aboard. She demanded that certain personalities read on television a message she had written. After six hours of negotiations at John F. Kennedy International Airport, which was the aircraft's intended destination, she was arrested and found not to have any explosives. The assailant was subsequently given five years' probation after being convicted of first degree coercion.

19 FEBRUARY 1979

A bomb was suspected in the destruction of an Ethiopian Airlines DC-3 (ET-AFW), which crashed near Barentu, located in the disputed Ethiopian province of Eritrea some 200 miles (320km) west-south-west of Asmara, during a scheduled domestic service. All five persons aboard the twin-engine transport were killed.

27 FEBRUARY 1979

THREE hijackers, one of whom lit a Molotov cocktail, tried to seize an Aeroflot Tu-154 that was on a scheduled service to Moscow from Oslo, Norway. The assailants were overpowered by other passengers and members of the crew, and the Soviet aircraft landed as planned at Stockholm, Sweden. A Swedish court sentenced two of the hijackers to three years' imprisonment and the third to 18 months.

1 APRIL 1979

TWO assailants tried to divert to Turkey an Aeroflot twin-jet Yak-40, operating as Flight 546, after it had taken off from Simferopol, Ukraine, an en-route stop during a scheduled Soviet domestic service from Odessa to Kutaisi. Both were detained and turned over to the police, being subsequently sentenced to respective prison terms of five and seven years.

4 APRIL 1979

A lone assailant commandeered Pan American World Airways Flight 816, a Boeing 747 wide-bodied jet on a service to Auckland, New Zealand, while it was on the ground at Kingsford-Smith Airport, serving Sydney, Australia. A woman and a police officer suffered stab wounds. The hijacker was shot dead by police before the aircraft could take off.

26 APRIL 1979

A high explosive device detonated in the area of the forward lavatory of an Indian Airlines Boeing Advanced 737-2A8 (VT-ECR) after the twin-engine jet, on a scheduled domestic service from Trivandrum, had initiated a descent from 27,000ft (8,200m) in preparation for landing at Madras airport. Following the blast the aircraft experienced a total electrical and instrument failure, and its cockpit and front cabin area filled with smoke.

A gear-down but flapless landing was accomplished some 2,500ft (760m) beyond the threshold of Runway 25. Due to its high speed when it touched down, and the non-availability of reverse thrust and the anti-skid system due to damage suffered in the blast, the aircraft ran off the end of the pavement and ploughed into a field. Among the 61 passengers and six crew members aboard, eight persons were seriously injured. The aircraft itself was destroyed by the in-flight explosion and the subsequent crash, which occurred at around noon local time.

8 JUNE 1979

A lone assailant armed with a shotgun seized a Trans-Australia Airlines twin-jet DC-9 that was on a scheduled domestic service from Coolangotta to Brisbane, Queensland. He allowed the aircraft to land at its intended destination and then released the 41 passengers. He was subsequently overpowered by members of the cabin and flight crew and arrested by the police.

20 JUNE 1979

FLIGHT 293, an American Airlines Boeing 727 jetliner on a domestic service from New York City to Chicago with 136 persons aboard, was seized by a lone assailant using two ground-burst simulator projectiles and what he said was a bag of dynamite. He demanded the release of a US federal prisoner and a trip to Peru, which he then changed to South Africa and finally Ireland.

The air pirate, who had been joined by his attorney, switched to a longer-range Boeing 707 in New York for the transatlantic flight. He surrendered in Ireland and was extradited back to the US, where he was sentenced to more than 40 years in prison on multiple charges.

9 JULY 1979

IT was a bad day all round for the would-be hijacker of a Cóndor Aerovías Nacionales twin-engine turboprop Fairchild F-27 that was on a scheduled Ecuadorean domestic service from Tulcan to Quito. Though he had ordered the aircraft to be flown to Costa Rica, it nevertheless set down at Quito, where the passengers escaped through a cabin door. After firing two shots, apparently accidentally, the assailant's gun jammed. He then tried to ignite a stick of dynamite he was holding, but his cigarette lighter failed to operate, after which he was finally overpowered and taken into custody.

25 JULY 1979

A lone assailant armed with a knife and what later proved to be a toy pistol hijacked a Biman Bangladesh Airlines Fokker F.27 turboprop carrying 43 persons on a scheduled domestic flight from Jessore to Dacca, and diverted it to Calcutta, India. He demanded a ransom and also an escape aircraft, but after ten hours of negotiations he agreed to surrender. Later in the year he was returned to Bangladesh for prosecution.

5 AUGUST 1979

THREE deserters from the Spanish Foreign Legion commandeered an Iberia DC-9 jet that had just landed and was disembarking passengers at Puerto Del Rosario, Fuerteventura, in the Canary Islands. The Spanish aircraft flew to Lisbon, Portugal – where all the hostages except the two flight crew members were released – and ultimately to Geneva, Switzerland, where the hijackers surrendered. They were later sentenced to 20 months' imprisonment by a Swiss court.

22 AUGUST 1979

A twin-engine turboprop Hawker Siddeley HS 748 Series 2A (FAC-1101), operated by the Colombian carrier Servicio de Aeronavegación a Territorios Nacionales (SATENA), crashed in a residential area of Bogotá, Colombia, after being stolen by a mechanic and a companion. Both occupants of the aircraft and three persons on the ground were killed.

22 AUGUST 1979

A United Airlines Boeing 727 jet, designated as Flight 739 and carrying 120 persons on a US domestic service from Portland, Oregon, to Los Angeles, California, was seized by a passenger who claimed to have a bomb. His demand that the aircraft return to Portland having been satisfied, the hijacker subsequently gave himself up. He was sentenced to 60 years in prison for kidnapping.

12 SEPTEMBER 1979

ARMED with a very real-looking toy pistol, a lone hijacker took control of a Lufthansa German Airlines Boeing 727 jet that was on a scheduled domestic service from Frankfurt to Cologne with 128 persons aboard. Following seven hours of negotiations, he read a long statement calling for a more humane world; after more negotiations, he surrendered.

30 OCTOBER 1979

A Pacific Southwest Airlines Boeing 727-214 jetliner, operating as Flight 784 on a short-haul service from Los Angeles to San Diego with 108 persons aboard, got hijacked over Southern California by a passenger who claimed to have a bomb and wanted to be taken to Mexico City. He was apprehended during a refuelling stop at Tijuana, Mexico, and sent back to the US, where he was sentenced to prison for 16 months on the charge of interfering with an airline crew.

13 NOVEMBER 1979

THE pilot of a Japan Air Lines DC-10, which had been seized during a scheduled domestic service from Osaka to Tokyo with 356 persons aboard, overpowered the hijacker of the wide-bodied jet after he had threatened a stewardess with a can-opener and demanded to be flown to Moscow.

15 NOVEMBER 1979

AN American Airlines Boeing 727 jet, designated as Flight 444 and on domestic service from Chicago to Washington DC, landed safely at Washington National Airport after the pilot had reported smoke, later determined to have resulted from the detonation of an explosive device in the baggage compartment. There were no serious injuries among the 78 persons aboard.

Investigation traced this attempted act of sabotage to Theodore Kaczynski, the so-called Unabomber, who for 17 years terrorised the US with numerous bombings that claimed a total of three lives. Pleading guilty to these crimes, he was sentenced to life imprisonment in 1998.

24 NOVEMBER 1979

AN 18-year-old man armed with a hunting knife tried to hijack to Iran an American Airlines Boeing 727 jet, operating as Flight 395 and carrying 74 persons on an intrastate service from San Antonio to El Paso, Texas. On the ground in El Paso he was overpowered by FBI agents and was later given a ten-year prison sentence.

21 JANUARY 1980

THE risks to aviation of even a false threat were realised in this incident involving United Airlines Flight 199, a DC-8 Super 61 jetliner on a transoceanic service from Los Angeles, California, to Honolulu, Hawaii, with 125 persons aboard, including a crew of eight.

Copying the plot of a 1960s made-for-television movie, an extortionist demanded money from the airline by claiming that a pressure-activated bomb would detonate aboard the aircraft if it descended below 5,000ft (1,500m). The DC-8 therefore landed at Colorado Springs, Colorado, which is higher than that elevation. The bomb, which was found in an aft lavatory, turned out to be a fake, but the emergency evacuation of the aircraft at Colorado Springs resulted in real casualties, with seven passengers suffering minor injuries.

30 JANUARY 1980

TWO men were overpowered by other passengers and members of the crew after trying to hijack an Interflug Il-18 turboprop that had been on a scheduled (East) German domestic service from Erfurt to (East) Berlin.

29 FEBRUARY 1980

ARMED with an arsenal of weapons, including a rifle and two sticks of dynamite, a lone assailant took four hostages and tried to board a Compañia Ecuatoriana de Aviación SA Boeing 707 jetliner on the ground at Guayaquil, Ecuador, but was unable to gain entry. He subsequently surrendered to the authorities.

20 MARCH 1980

DEMANDING to be flown to Turkey, a knife-wielding hijacker aboard an Aeroflot Tu-134 jetliner designated as Flight 6647, on a Soviet domestic service from Baku to Yerevan, was overpowered by other passengers and crew members. He was later sentenced to eight years' imprisonment.

14 APRIL 1980

AT Stapleton International Airport, serving Denver, Colorado, a knife-wielding assailant boarded Continental Air Lines Flight 11, a Boeing 727 jet carrying 78 persons on a US domestic service to Ontario, California. He demanded that it take off, but gave himself up on hearing of a possible mechanical problem with the aircraft. He was sentenced to 20 years' imprisonment for air piracy.

1–2 MAY 1980

FLIGHT 818, a Pacific Southwest Airlines Boeing 727 jet that was preparing to take off from Stockton, California, was targeted for hijack by a pistol-armed assailant. He was disarmed by the flight engineer and surrendered early the next morning, being later sentenced to 15 years' imprisonment.

6 MAY 1980

OPERATING as Flight 131, an Air Portugal-TAP Boeing 727 jetliner carrying 90 persons on a domestic service from Lisbon to Faro was seized by a 16-year-old boy who demanded a ransom and wanted to be taken to Switzerland. On the ground at Madrid, Spain, he dropped his demands, and was taken into custody after returning to Lisbon.

15 MAY 1980

ARMED with a handgun and a rifle, a lone assailant commandeered a Chalk's International Airline Grumman 73 Mallard amphibian on the ground at Miami, Florida, taking a company employee hostage and demanding to be flown to South Africa. He later surrendered and, subsequently, was found not mentally competent to stand trial.

6 JUNE 1980

AN explosive device that apparently failed to detonate was found in the luggage compartment of a Transavia twin-jet Boeing 737 after the Dutch-registered aircraft had landed on the Greek island of Rhodes at the end of a non-scheduled service from Amsterdam with 96 persons aboard.

27 JUNE 1980

EARLY suspicions of sabotage would, many years later, be confirmed in this disastrous airliner crash.

Aerolinee Italia SpA Flight 870, a twin-jet Douglas DC-9 Series 15 (I-TIGI), had departed from Bologna on a domestic service to Palermo, Sicily. It had been cruising on an almost due southerly heading in darkness at an approximate height of 25,000ft (7,600m) over the Tyrrhenian Sea when, shortly before 20:00 local time, something of a sudden and catastrophic nature happened to the aircraft. The bodies of more than 40 victims were subsequently found; there was no hope of survival among the 81 persons aboard (77 passengers and a crew of four). The scene of the crash was some 15 miles (25km) north-east of the Italian island of Ustica, in water about 12,000ft (3,700m) deep.

Tests performed on recovered debris and pathological examinations of the deceased seemed to indicate that the airliner had either collided with, or suffered damage from the nearby explosion of, a missile. In 1990, an investigative commission was unable to agree on whether the loss of the DC-9 resulted from a missile strike or an internal explosion. Later, an international commission was formed to probe the mystery of Flight 870, and its findings were released in 1994.

A considerable amount of additional wreckage was raised from the seabed as part of the second investigation, which led to a determination of the probable cause of the tragedy. Particularly revealing was the damage and distortion around the right rear lavatory, which the commission found had preceded the more general in-flight disintegration of the aircraft. It was concluded that only the detonation of an explosive device could have caused such internal damage. Structural failure due to fatigue, corrosion or overload was dismissed. Also ruled out was the original missile theory, which seemed tenable when little wreckage was available for examination but would not have explained the interior damage.

The commission determined that the blast produced a shock wave that tore off a considerable amount of aircraft skin atop the rear fuselage area, with internal parts and passengers being flung out of the cabin. Both engines then broke away, followed by the separation of the empennage. The resulting pitch-down of the rest of the aircraft caused a download that snapped off the left outer wing. The break-up sequence occurred in a matter of only a few seconds, after which the jet plummeted almost vertically into the water.

The bomb that destroyed I-TIGI must have been a relatively small amount of explosive, probably wrapped only in plastic; the absence of penetration marks or pitting in recovered structures indicated that it was not in a hard container. Most likely, the device had been placed between the outer wall of the lavatory and the skin of the aircraft, access to which would have been available several ways, and where it would have been difficult to detect.

No claim of responsibility was ever made in connection with the Itavia disaster, though it may have been related to a wave of terrorism, blamed largely on right-wing extremists, that plagued Italy from the late 1960s into the 1980s. The most serious such case was the bombing of Bologna railway station some five weeks after the destruction of Flight 870, which claimed 85 lives.

30 JUNE 1980

ARMED with a pistol and a hand grenade, a lone assailant commandeered an Aerolíneas Argentinas twin-jet Boeing 737 that was on a scheduled domestic service from Mar del Plata to Buenos Aires, demanding a ransom and a trip to Mexico. After the aircraft had landed at its intended destination, he was convinced by the pilot to give himself up.

12 JULY 1980

A hijacking extortionist used a bomb threat against a Philippine Airlines Boeing 727 jet that was on a scheduled domestic flight from Manila to Cebu, demanding $6 million. However, he was duped by the crew, who locked the cockpit door and returned to the capital, where he was arrested by security personnel.

15 AUGUST 1980

ANGER that the aircraft had to land for refuelling prompted a passenger to cause a disruption aboard a Trans World Airlines Boeing 747 wide-bodied jetliner that had been on a scheduled transatlantic service to New York City from Madrid, Spain. His behaviour was viewed as more than a display of temper, and would lead to his prosecution for interference with a flight crew.

29–30 AUGUST 1980

A mob of Cuban refugees forced their way aboard Braniff International Airways Flight 920 when the DC-8 jetliner was on the ground at Lima, Peru. Three persons were injured after the police fired shots and pulled the ramp away from the US aircraft. After a siege lasting 23 hours, and after being convinced that they would be prosecuted if flown to the US, the 168 refugees surrendered.

9 SEPTEMBER 1980

TWO baggage handlers suffered injuries when an explosive device contained in a small cardboard package detonated in the cargo hold of a United Airlines Boeing 727 jetliner that was on the ground at Sacramento Municipal Airport, serving California's capital city.

The incident occurred around 09:50 local time, minutes after the aircraft, designated as Flight 291, had landed at the end of a domestic service originating at Seattle, Washington, and after its passengers had disembarked. The crew was still aboard at the time but escaped unscathed, and the 727 itself sustained only moderate damage.

17 SEPTEMBER 1980

A French Army ordnance specialist trying to deactivate a bomb placed on the outside of an Air France Boeing 737 on the ground at Le Raizet Airport, serving Pointe-a-Pitre, Guadeloupe, was killed when the device detonated, badly damaging the jet airliner.

13 OCTOBER 1980

A Turkish Airlines (THY) Boeing 727-200 jet, operating as Flight 890 and carrying 148 persons, was commandeered during a domestic service from Istanbul to Ankara. Landing at Diyarbakir, Turkey, the aircraft was stormed by troops. One passenger was killed and about a dozen persons wounded in the assault, the latter including the four hijackers, who were all captured.

4 DECEMBER 1980

A lone assailant commandeered a Polish Airlines (LOT) An-24B turboprop, designated as Flight 770 on a domestic service from Zielona Góra to Warsaw with 25 persons aboard, diverting it to (West) Berlin. He asked for asylum there but instead received a four-year prison sentence.

5 DECEMBER 1980

REPORTEDLY to protest the acquittal in Venezuela of those suspected of blowing up a Cuban airliner in 1976, four hijackers commandeered a Línea Aeropostal Venezolana DC-9 jet carrying 120 persons on a scheduled domestic service from Porlamar to Caracas. After it had landed at Higuerote, Venezuela, they stole from it two chests containing 7.5 million bolivars. The money was subsequently located and 35 persons were arrested in connection with the crime.

10 DECEMBER 1980

A threat by a passenger to physically harm a cabin attendant and 'wreck' the aircraft led to the diversion of an Eastern Airlines DC-9 jetliner that had been on a scheduled US domestic service from Atlanta, Georgia, to Orlando, Florida. The assailant was taken into custody when the DC-9 landed at Jacksonville, Florida, and placed in the psychiatric ward of a hospital, but charges against him were later dismissed.

21 DECEMBER 1980

AN Aerovías del Cesar (Aerocesar Colombia) Sud-Aviation Caravelle VI-R (HK-1810) crashed some 15 miles (25km) south of the airport at Riohacha, Guajira, from where it had taken off about five minutes earlier on a scheduled domestic service to Medellín. All 70 persons aboard (63 passengers and seven crew members) perished.

There appeared to have been a fire in its right-hand aft section before the twin-jet airliner plunged into the Guajira Desert at around 14:25 local time, scattering wreckage over a distance of about half a mile (0.8km). The weather at the time was good. All Caravelles registered in Colombia were subsequently grounded for the purpose of an airworthiness check. But the crash did not result from a technical fault. It was subsequently determined that an explosive substance, apparently nitro-glycerine, had detonated in the vicinity of its cargo hold and caused damage, primarily in the aircraft's hydraulic system, apparently leading to a loss of control.

A telephone threat had been made against the flight at the carrier's office in Valledupar, which was a stop-off point prior to Riohaca, with the message that it 'will not arrive at its destination'.

23 DECEMBER 1980

FOR the second time during the year, a fake bomb threat against a US commercial flight resulted in real casualties. This threat involved Eastern Airlines Flight 225, an L-1011 TriStar wide-bodied jetliner carrying 293 persons on a transcontinental domestic service from New York to Los Angeles. Nine passengers suffered minor injuries in the emergency evacuation of the aircraft, which was carried out in darkness shortly after midnight, and after the TriStar had diverted to Dulles International Airport, serving Washington DC. No bomb was found.

10 JANUARY 1981

FOUR men tried unsuccessfully to hijack to the West a Polish Airlines (LOT) An-24B turboprop on a scheduled domestic service from Katowice to Warsaw. After it had landed at its intended destination, supposedly for refuelling, the assailants were captured as they tried to switch to another aircraft.

6 FEBRUARY 1981

PROTESTING against the Colombian political system, two men hijacked an AVIANCA Boeing 727 jet airliner that was on a scheduled domestic service from Bucaramanga to Cúcuta with 77 persons aboard, but after a siege lasting ten hours they surrendered on the ground at the intended destination.

5 MARCH 1981

A lone assailant took seven hostages aboard a Continental Air Lines Boeing 727 jet, operating as Flight 72, at Los Angeles International Airport. He demanded $3 million, but after hours of negotiations he released the hostages and then surrendered. He would later be sentenced to 20 years' imprisonment.

27 MARCH 1981

CLAIMING to be terrorists opposed to the Honduran government, three men and a woman commandeered a Servicio Aéreo de Honduras SA Boeing 737 jet, designated as Flight 414, on a domestic service from Tegucigalpa to San Pedro Sula with 87 persons aboard. Landing first at Managua, Nicaragua, the aircraft proceeded on the following day to Panama City, where the hijackers surrendered. Technically this was not a Cuban hijacking, but that's where the assailants ended up fleeing to, along with a number of activists whose release they had demanded.

28–30 MARCH 1981

GARUDA Indonesian Airways Flight 206, a twin-jet DC-9 carrying 57 persons on a domestic service from Palembang to Medan, was hijacked by five assailants and ultimately flown to Bangkok, Thailand. Shortly after 02:30 on the third day of the siege that ensued at Don Muang Airport, Indonesian commandos rushed the aircraft. All five hijackers were killed, as well as one soldier and the pilot; two other persons had earlier been shot and wounded.

2 MAY 1981

WITH the intention of getting newspapers to publish a lengthy religious statement, a lone assailant carrying bottles of gasoline commandeered an Aer Lingus-Irish International Airlines Boeing 737 jet, operating as Flight 164 on a service from Dublin with 118 persons aboard, just before it was to have landed at London. The aircraft landed at Le Touquet, France, where a police unit boarded it secretly and arrested the hijacker.

24–25 MAY 1981

FOUR men commandeered Turkish Airlines (THY) Flight 104, a twin-jet DC-9 on a domestic service from Istanbul to Ankara with 84 persons aboard, forcing it to land at Burgas, Bulgaria, and demanding a ransom and the release by Turkey of 47 imprisoned fellow terrorists. The following day two of the hijackers were arrested after getting off to give a press conference, and the remaining two were overpowered by passengers, both of them and four other persons being injured in the process. Bulgaria sentenced the hijackers to three years' imprisonment.

21 JULY 1981

USING a dummy hand grenade, a lone assailant hijacked a Polish Airlines (LOT) An-24B turboprop to (West) Berlin. It had been on a scheduled domestic service from Katowice to Gdansk with 55 persons aboard. The hijacker was later sentenced to three years' imprisonment by the German authorities.

5 AUGUST 1981

A lone assailant attempting to hijack a Polish Airlines (LOT) An-24B turboprop, on a scheduled domestic service from Katowice to Gdansk with 49 persons aboard, was arrested after it landed at its intended destination.

11 AUGUST 1981

THE hijacker of another Polish Airlines (LOT) An-24B turboprop on a scheduled domestic service from Katowice to Gdansk was tricked by the pilot into believing that it had landed in (West) Berlin, when in fact it had set down at Warsaw. There, the assailant was arrested.

22 AUGUST 1981

THIS successful hijacking of a Polish Airlines (LOT) An-24B turboprop, which was carrying 43 persons on a scheduled domestic flight from Wroclaw to Warsaw, ended with the sole assailant surrendering in (West) Berlin. The German authorities subsequently sentenced him to 5½ years' imprisonment.

18 SEPTEMBER 1981

A dozen youths aged 17 to 22 commandeered a Polish Airlines (LOT) An-24B turboprop on a scheduled domestic service from Katowice to Warsaw with 49 persons aboard. After the aircraft had landed in (West) Berlin they surrendered to the American authorities. Eight of the hijackers were sentenced to between one and four years' imprisonment by a German court.

22 SEPTEMBER 1981

THREE men and a woman tried to hijack a Polish Airlines (LOT) An-24B turboprop to (West) Berlin, but they were captured, one of them having been wounded, after the pilot landed at Warsaw, from where the flight had taken off earlier on a scheduled domestic service to Koszalin.

26 SEPTEMBER 1981

A Jugoslovenski Aerotransport (JAT) Boeing 727 jet carrying 101 persons on a scheduled Yugoslavian domestic service from Titograd to Belgrade was commandeered by three assailants who wanted to go to Italy and then Israel. Both countries refused them entry and the airliner landed at Larnaca, Cyprus, where the hijackers surrendered. They were given prison terms ranging from 3½ to 8½ years.

29–30 SEPTEMBER 1981

USING daggers that they had been allowed to carry for religious reasons, seven Sikh assailants took over Indian Airlines Flight 425, a Boeing 737 jet carrying 117 persons on a domestic service from New Delhi to Srinagar, forcing it to Lahore, Pakistan. Their demands included a ransom of half a million dollars and the release of other Sikh separatists by India. Shortly before 08:00 local time on the second day, as two of the hijackers were negotiating, disguised Pakistani Army personnel boarded the aircraft and captured the others.

All seven air pirates would subsequently be sentenced to life imprisonment.

29 SEPTEMBER 1981

A lone assailant armed with a razor blade tried to commandeer a Polish Airlines (LOT) An-24B turboprop that was on the ground at Okecie Airport, serving Warsaw, preparing for a scheduled domestic service to Szczecin, but he was threatened by other passengers and then arrested by police.

5 OCTOBER 1981

A passenger who claimed to have a bomb tried to hijack to the USSR a US Air BAC One-Eleven jet, which was operating as Flight 455 on a domestic intrastate service from Albany to Buffalo, New York, with 66 persons aboard. He was captured at the intended destination of the flight, and charges against him were later dismissed on grounds of mental illness.

21 OCTOBER 1981

TWO men and two women commandeered an Aeropesca Colombia C-46 airliner that had been on a domestic service from Medellín to Barranquilla. After landing in the Guajira Peninsula, it was loaded with weapons and took off again, later to be ditched in a river in the province of Caquetá. Taken hostage, five employees of the company were released the following month. The aircraft was wrecked in the crash-landing.

23 OCTOBER 1981

WHILE en route to New York City from San Juan, Puerto Rico, American Airlines Flight 676, a DC-10 wide-bodied jet carrying 109 persons, was targeted for hijack by a lone assailant who claimed to have a bomb and wanted to be taken to Quebec. He surrendered when the aircraft landed at its intended destination to refuel. Air piracy charges against him were later dismissed.

29–30 OCTOBER 1981

A Servicios Aéreos Nacionales (SAN) CASA-212 twin-engine turboprop airliner was commandeered by five assailants just after landing at San José, Costa Rica, on a scheduled domestic service from Quepos. They demanded the release of seven prisoners, six of whom joined the hijackers on the second day (the seventh prisoner choosing to remain in Costa Rica). They then flew to El Salvador, where they were taken into custody with plans to extradite them back to Costa Rica for prosecution.

25 NOVEMBER 1981

FORTY-FIVE men, part of a group that had tried to take over Seychelles airport, located on Mahe Island, boarded an Air-India Boeing 707 jetliner, designated as Flight 224, which had just landed during a service to Bombay from Salisbury, Zimbabwe, with 79 persons aboard. It was ordered to be flown to Durban, South Africa. After about six hours of negotiations there, the hostages were released and the hijackers surrendered. All but three of the assailants were successfully prosecuted, with the leader being sentenced to 20 years' imprisonment for air piracy, seven others receiving terms of from one to five years, and the rest being sentenced to six months.

5 DECEMBER 1981

A lone assailant who claimed to have a gun and a bomb, but was actually unarmed, brushed his way past ticket agents and boarded a Trans World Airlines Boeing 707 jetliner, operating as Flight 534, as it was preparing to take off from Cleveland-Hopkins International Airport, Ohio, on a domestic service to New York City with 88 persons aboard. He demanded to be taken to Iran. During a struggle, he and the flight engineer fell down the stairway and were injured, and he was then arrested. He was committed to a psychiatric facility the following year.

12 DECEMBER 1981

WHILE it was on the ground at the Mexico City international airport, an explosive device rocked an Aerolíneas Nicaraguenses (Aeronica) Boeing 727-25 jet airliner, which was designated as Flight 527 and carrying 117 persons. Three crew members aboard the aircraft and three baggage handlers outside suffered injuries in the blast, which occurred at around 12:40 local time as it was preparing to take off, bound for San Salvador, El Salvador, one segment of a service originating at Managua, Nicaragua. The bomb had detonated between the rearmost seat on the left side and the cabin wall, and blew a hole in the 727's fuselage.

7 JANUARY 1982

IN an attempt to release his brother, imprisoned for a failed hijacking four years earlier, a lone assailant carrying a bottle of gasoline and a stick of dynamite tried to hijack an Aerotal Colombia Boeing 727 jetliner on a scheduled domestic flight from Santa Marta to Barranquilla. This hijacker had no better luck, being overpowered by other passengers and later arrested.

8 FEBRUARY 1982

One person was killed and six others were wounded when an explosive device detonated on or near a Sociedad Aérea del Caquetá (SADELCA) DC-3 as the Colombian airliner was boarding passengers at Miraflores, Guaviare, Colombia, some 250 miles (400km) south-east of Bogotá, prior to its planned departure. The bomb had been placed in a suitcase belonging to the passenger killed, in what might have been some type of suicide plot.

12 FEBRUARY 1982

FALSELY advising ground controllers that the aircraft had been hijacked, the pilot of a Polish Airlines (LOT) twin-engine turboprop An-24B, on a scheduled domestic service from Warsaw to Wroclaw with 22 persons aboard, himself diverted the aircraft to (West) Berlin, where he, his family and the co-pilot requested asylum. Since no threat of force was employed in the diversion, potential criminal charges facing the pilot were dismissed by the German authorities.

13 FEBRUARY 1982

DEMANDING a pilot, an unarmed assailant boarded an out-of-service Braniff International Airways Boeing 727 jetliner that was parked at Amarillo airport, Texas. He later surrendered, and charges against him were subsequently dismissed on grounds of mental incompetency.

20 FEBRUARY 1982

THREE baggage handlers were killed and four other persons suffered injuries when an explosive device hidden in a suitcase detonated on a conveyor belt at the international airport serving Managua, Nicaragua. The suitcase containing the bomb had just been unloaded from a Servicio Aéreo de Honduras SA (SAHSA) Boeing 737 jetliner, which had landed some 15 minutes earlier on a scheduled service from Tegucigalpa, Honduras.

26 FEBRUARY–1 MARCH 1982

FIVE hijackers who claimed to be members of the Tanzanian Revolutionary Youth Movement took over Air Tanzania Flight 206, a Boeing 737 jet on a domestic service from Mwanza to Dar-es-Salaam with 99 persons aboard. They demanded the resignation of the President of Tanzania. During the hijacking the co-pilot was shot and wounded, and the aircraft finally landed at Stansted Airport, Essex, England. The assailants were subsequently sentenced to prison terms ranging from three to eight years by a British court.

30 APRIL 1982

EIGHT men disarmed the six security guards aboard a Polish Airlines (LOT) An-24B, injuring two of them in the process, and then hijacked the twin-engine turboprop to (West) Berlin; it had been on a scheduled domestic flight from Wroclaw to Warsaw at the time, with 52 persons aboard. More than half of the other passengers, who were related to the hijackers, got off with them in Berlin, where the air pirates were sentenced to prison terms of from 2½ to 4 years for 'endangering air traffic'.

10 MAY 1982

DURING a Nicaraguan domestic service from Bluefields to Great Corn Island, an Aerolíneas Nicaraguenses (Aeronica) twin-engine C-46 was hijacked to Limón, Costa Rica, where the two air pirates responsible requested political asylum.

21 MAY 1982

ARMED with a hand grenade, a lone hijacker commandeered a Philippine Airlines twin-jet BAC One-Eleven that was carrying 114 persons on a scheduled domestic service from Bacolod to Cebu. Besides 60,000 pesos he demanded various government reforms, but was overpowered and captured.

9 JUNE 1982

TWO men who tried to hijack a Polish Airlines (LOT) An-24 turboprop to (West) Berlin during a scheduled domestic service from Katowice to Warsaw were captured by police.

23 JUNE 1982

A woman who claimed to be armed confronted the co-pilot of Henson Airlines Flight 611, a four-engine turboprop Dash 7, at Shenandoah Valley Regional Airport, serving Staunton, Virginia. She first demanded to be flown out, but when the crew member escaped she went back into the terminal building and was subsequently apprehended by police. Charges against her were later dismissed.

30 JUNE 1982

AN Alitalia Boeing 747 with 261 persons aboard was commandeered during a scheduled international service of the Italian-registered wide-bodied jet airliner from New Delhi to Bangkok. The lone assailant demanded a ransom and wanted to be reunited with his wife and child in Italy. They arrived the following day in Bangkok, and the three were then flown to Sri Lanka, where he was later arrested and sentenced to a prison term of 20 years to life.

3 JULY 1982

IN a note to the crew, a passenger of Aeroflot Flight 8690, a Tu-154 jetliner on a Soviet domestic service from Murmansk to Leningrad, asked for 250,000 roubles and for the aircraft to fly 'in a direction we'll give'. He was instead arrested and later sentenced to five years' imprisonment.

25 JULY 1982

FIVE hijackers experienced the harshness of Chinese law when they tried to commandeer to Taiwan a Civil Aviation Administration of China (CAAC) Il-18, which, operating as Flight 2502, was on a domestic service to Shanghai from Xian, Shaanxi, with 80 persons aboard. They wounded two flight crew members, and about a dozen others were also injured, mostly when an explosive device detonated, but the assailants were nevertheless overpowered and the four-engine turboprop landed safely at its intended destination. The five hijackers were executed the following month.

4 AUGUST 1982

INDIAN Airlines Flight 423, a twin-jet Boeing 737 carrying 135 persons on a domestic service from New Delhi to Srinagar, with an en-route stop at Amritsar, was hijacked by a lone assailant holding what he said was a bomb. Denied permission to land at Lahore, Pakistan, the aircraft set down at Amritsar, where the hijacker was subsequently overpowered. His bomb turned out to be a rubber ball.

20 AUGUST 1982

INDIAN Airlines Flight 492, a Boeing 737 jet with 71 persons aboard, was hijacked during a domestic service from Jodhpur to New Delhi and forced to fly to Pakistan, which denied it clearance to land. Subsequently it set down at Amritsar, India, where the lone assailant was shot dead by police when he stuck his head out of the cabin door.

25 AUGUST 1982

A Polish Airlines (LOT) Il-18 turboprop that had been on a scheduled service to Warsaw from Budapest, Hungary, with 70 persons aboard, was successfully diverted to Munich, (West) Germany, by two men. There they were each sentenced to 4½ years in prison.

25 SEPTEMBER 1982

ALITALIA Flight 871, a Boeing 727 jetliner en route to Rome from Algiers with 109 persons aboard, was hijacked by a lone assailant armed with a knife. The Italian-registered aircraft was denied entry by both Libya and Malta, and finally landed at

Catania, Sicily. The hijacker was subsequently overpowered and injured; a police officer was also hurt.

14 OCTOBER 1982

A married couple commandeered a Balkan Bulgarian Airlines twin-jet Tu-134 that was on a scheduled service from Burgas, Bulgaria, to Warsaw, Poland, demanding to be flown to (West) Germany. Because it was low on fuel, the aircraft instead landed at Vienna. There the man was sentenced to two years' imprisonment for air piracy and the woman was given a one-year suspended sentence.

27 OCTOBER 1982

AT Los Angeles International Airport a man forced his way aboard Trans World Airlines Flight 72, an L-1011 wide-bodied jet carrying 109 persons, in an apparent hijacking attempt. However, he was shoved out of the door by a passenger and was injured in the fall. Convicted of air piracy, he was sentenced to 12 years' imprisonment.

7 NOVEMBER 1982

INJURING the flight engineer and one passenger in the process, three men commandeered an Aeroflot An-24 as the Soviet twin-engine turboprop airliner was on a scheduled domestic service from Novosibirsk to Odessa. They surrendered when it landed at a NATO airbase in Turkey and were later sentenced to prison terms of from eight to nine years.

22 NOVEMBER 1982

ONE of three security guards assigned to a Polish Airlines (LOT) An-24B turboprop, which was on a scheduled domestic service from Wroclaw to Warsaw with 38 persons aboard, ended up hijacking the aircraft to (West) Berlin. Though he was shot and wounded, and suffered further injury when he jumped out after the aircraft had landed, he survived to be taken into custody by the US authorities.

27 NOVEMBER 1982

A uniformed man who appeared to be a security guard tried to hijack to (West) Berlin a Tu-154B jetliner operated by the Hungarian airline MALEV, which was on a scheduled international service from Warsaw to Budapest, but he was overpowered.

30 DECEMBER 1982

A passenger who claimed to have a bomb aboard United Airlines Flight 702, a Boeing 727 jet carrying 77 persons on a US domestic service from Chicago, Illinois, to Pittsburgh, Pennsylvania, demanded to be taken to Washington DC. Convinced by the flight engineer that it did not have enough fuel, he allowed it to land at its intended destination, where he subsequently surrendered. Prosecution was deferred and he was enrolled in a mental health programme.

7 JANUARY 1983

AN emotionally disturbed passenger aboard Delta Air Lines Flight 177, a Boeing 727 jet carrying 30 persons on a US domestic service from Portland, Maine, to Boston, Massachusetts, asked to be taken to Las Vegas, Nevada. A bag that he said contained explosives was taken away from him and he was taken into custody. Charges against him were later dismissed on grounds of mental incompetency.

20 JANUARY 1983

A convicted hijacker, on probation for a crime committed three years earlier, commandeered a Northwest Airlines Boeing 727 jetliner operating as Flight 608 on a US domestic service from Seattle, Washington, to Portland, Oregon, with 41 persons aboard. He wanted to be taken to Afghanistan. However, he was shot and killed by FBI agents after the aircraft had landed at its scheduled destination.

13 FEBRUARY 1983

A Trans-Australia Airlines A300 wide-bodied jet, designated as Flight 5 on a domestic service from Perth, Western Australia, to Melbourne, Victoria, with 204 persons aboard, was targeted for hijack by a lone assailant who claimed to have a bomb and wanted to be taken to Adelaide, South Australia. He allowed it to land at its intended destination, and while on the ground at Tullamarine Airport he surrendered. His 'bomb' was not real.

18 FEBRUARY 1983

SECURITY guards shot and killed the would-be hijacker of a Czechoslovak Airlines (CSA) Tu-134 jet after he attacked a stewardess and tried to enter the flight deck as the aircraft was on a scheduled domestic service from Poprad to Prague.

7 MARCH 1983

FOUR assailants who demanded to be taken to Turkey hijacked a Balkan Bulgarian Airlines twin-engine turboprop An-24 that had been on a scheduled domestic service from Sofia to Varna. Tricking them in the darkness, however, the pilot landed the aircraft at its intended destination, where one of the hijackers was killed by security personnel and the other three were captured.

15 APRIL 1983

A lone assailant armed with a knife and what he said was a bottle of liquid explosive commandeered a Turkish Airlines (THY) Boeing 727 jet carrying 115 persons on a scheduled domestic service from Istanbul to Izmir, and demanded to be taken to Australia. After it landed for refuelling at Athens, he was captured by police. He was sentenced to a prison term of 13½ years by a Greek court.

5 MAY 1983

FIVE hijackers commandeered a Civil Aviation Administration of China (CAAC) Trident 2E jet airliner that was on a scheduled domestic service to Shanghai from Shenyang, Liaoning, with 102 persons aboard. Shooting their way into the cockpit, and in the process injuring two crew members, the assailants forced the aircraft to land at a military airbase in South Korea. Sentenced to jail terms, they were expelled by South Korea and taken to Taiwan the following year.

5 JULY 1983

TWO men carrying a tape-recorder made to resemble a bomb tried to hijack an Aeroflot Tu-134A jetliner, designated as Flight 2113, during a Soviet domestic service from Moscow to

A Civil Aviation Administration of China Trident, similar to the aircraft hijacked to South Korea in May 1983. (British Aerospace)

Tallinn. They were fooled by the pilot, who instead landed at a military airfield near Leningrad, where a military courier killed one of the assailants and wounded the other.

26 AUGUST 1983

AN incendiary device detonated in the cabin lavatory of an Air France Boeing 747 wide-bodied jet airliner that had been on a scheduled transatlantic service from Paris to Montreal, Canada. There were no injuries, and the 747 landed safely in Ireland.

1 SEPTEMBER 1983

THE hijacker of a Compañia Mexicana de Aviación SA Boeing 727 jetliner, which had been on a scheduled service from Mexico City to Miami carrying 144 persons, was arrested by disguised security personnel when he allowed the aircraft to land for refuelling at Mérida, Yucatan.

21 SEPTEMBER 1983

AN Empire Airlines Swearingen Metro II twin-engine turboprop, carrying 17 persons on a scheduled international service from Washington DC to Montreal, was targeted in a bizarre, possibly suicidal attack when a passenger stormed into the aircraft's cockpit at around 17:00 local time and began interfering with the controls during its approach to land at Syracuse, New York, which was an en-route stop. Though he was subdued by the co-pilot and another passenger, his actions caused the failure of the left power plant and a temporary loss of control of the aircraft. The Metro landed safely at Hancock Airport, where the assailant was captured; he would later be charged with attempted murder, although a judge ordered that he should also undergo psychiatric evaluation.

25 SEPTEMBER 1983

THE detonation of an explosive device started a fire in the cargo hold of an RN Air Cargo of Nigeria Boeing 707-336C jet transport (5N-ARO) during a non-scheduled international freight service from Lagos, Nigeria, to Accra, Ghana. Although it landed safely at its intended destination and its four crew members (and only occupants) were evacuated safely, the aircraft was destroyed by fire. The device must have been hidden among the 707's cargo.

15 OCTOBER 1983

A lone assailant, allegedly carrying a gun but in fact unarmed, hijacked a People Express Airlines Boeing 737 jetliner, operating as Flight 104, carrying 107 persons on a US domestic service from Buffalo, New York, to Newark, New Jersey. He ordered it to land at Atlantic City, New Jersey, and was arrested in the airport terminal there after demanding a taxi. The following year he was committed to a psychiatric facility.

28 OCTOBER 1983

A passenger jumped to his death from a Pennsylvania Airlines Shorts 330 in a bizarre act of suicide that occurred south of Harrisburg, Pennsylvania, from where the aircraft had taken off earlier.

Operating as Flight 1231 on a domestic service to Washington DC with 30 persons aboard, including a crew of three, the twin-engine turboprop was at an approximate height of 3,500ft (1,050m) and climbing when the victim, who had earlier in the day resigned as an employee of the same carrier, opened the right rear door and jumped out at around 13:30 local time. After boarding the flight, he had asked the cabin attendant for a seat located near the door through which he departed the aircraft, having previously told a ground crew member that he was headed for 'DC or some place in between'.

21 NOVEMBER 1983

A single assailant 'disrupted' Republic Airlines Flight 277, a twin-jet DC-9 on a US domestic intrastate service from Detroit to Kalamazoo, Michigan, with 41 persons aboard. He shouted incoherently and threatened to blow up the aircraft, and after it had set down at its intended destination he ordered it to Chicago, Illinois.

During the trip there he struck a number of passengers until one hit him back, whereupon he was overpowered.

Charged with air piracy, he was convicted on the lesser crimes of assault and intimidation and sentenced to eight years' imprisonment.

18 JANUARY 1984

A suitcase containing what was described as a 'combustible material' detonated in the cargo hold of an Air France Boeing 747 wide-bodied jet airliner some 70 miles (110km) west of Karachi, Pakistan, from where it had taken off shortly before on a scheduled international service with an ultimate destination of Paris. There were no injuries among the 261 persons aboard the aircraft, which landed safely despite the blast having punched a hole in the bottom of its No 4 cargo hold, with consequent loss of cabin pressure.

20 JANUARY 1984

ONE passenger among the five persons aboard was killed when a Douglas DC-6BF (YS-37C) operated by the Salvadorian carrier Atlantida Línea Aérea Sudamericana (ALAS) struck a landmine and was blown up while landing at San Miguel, El Salvador. The survivors suffered various injuries. The mine had apparently been planted in an attempt by Salvadorian guerrillas to destroy a transport carrying US advisors and officers of El Salvador's army.

9 FEBRUARY 1984

SHORTLY after it had taken off from the Angolan city of Huambo on a scheduled domestic service to Luanda, and while at an approximate height of 8,000ft (2,500m), an explosive device detonated in the forward cargo hold of a Línhas Aéreas de Angola (TAAG-Angola Airlines) twin jet Boeing Advanced 737-2M2 (D2-TBV), causing structural damage and engine control difficulties. Due to this damage, the aircraft overran the airport runway during a forced landing after returning to Huambo. Although the 737 was destroyed, there were no serious injuries among its 147 passengers and crew members.

10 FEBRUARY 1984

AN Olympic Airways Boeing 707 jetliner on a scheduled domestic service to Athens from the island of Crete was commandeered by a lone assailant who claimed to have an explosive device and wanted to be flown to the US. The aircraft landed at its intended destination for refuelling, where the hijacker was overpowered and arrested.

11 FEBRUARY 1984

AT Port-au-Prince, Haiti, a corporal in the Haitian Army boarded an American Airlines Boeing 727 jet, designated as Flight 658 and carrying 152 persons. Armed with an automatic weapon, he asked to be taken to New York City, which was the intended destination of the aircraft. During the trip there he surrendered his weapon to the crew and later asked for political asylum, but he was convicted in the US of air piracy and sentenced to ten years' imprisonment.

7 MARCH 1984

A knife-wielding hijacker commandeered an Air France twin-jet Boeing 737 that was on a scheduled service to Paris from Frankfurt, (West) Germany, demanding to be taken to

Libya. The aircraft instead landed at Geneva, where he was overpowered by police.

10 MARCH 1984

AN explosive device detonated in the aft cargo compartment of a Union de Transports Aériens (UTA) DC-8 Super 63PF jet airliner (F-BOLL), which, operating as Flight 772, was preparing to take off from N'Djamena, Chad, on a service with an ultimate destination of Paris. All 23 persons aboard at the time (18 passengers and five crew members) were evacuated safely before the French-registered aircraft was destroyed in the resulting fire.

22 MARCH 1984

FLIGHT 003, a British Airways Boeing 747 wide-bodied jet carrying 354 persons on a service from Hong Kong to Beijing, was commandeered by a lone assailant who claimed to have explosives and wanted to be taken to Taiwan. Upon landing at T'aipei, he was arrested and subsequently received a suspended prison sentence of 1½ years for the crime of 'endangering aviation safety'.

25 JUNE 1984

AN attempt to commandeer a Civil Aviation Administration of China (CAAC) An-24 turboprop airliner during a scheduled domestic service from Nanch'ang, Jiangxi, to Fuzhou, Fujian, ended in failure when the lone hijacker was overpowered.

5–6 JULY 1984

AN Indian Airlines A300 wide-bodied jet, designated as Flight 405 and carrying 264 persons on a domestic service from Srinagar to New Delhi, was commandeered by eight assailants demanding the release of Sikhs arrested during a siege the previous month and also restitution for damage done to their temple. Their demands were not met and the hijackers surrendered the second day at Lahore, Pakistan. Two of them were later sentenced to life prison sentences and three condemned to death, although the latter sentences were subsequently commuted.

29–30 JULY 1984

A Línea Aeropostal Venezolana twin-jet DC-9 was commandeered during a scheduled Venezuelan domestic service from Caracas to Curaçao with 87 persons aboard. Landing at its intended destination, the airliner was stormed by commandos in the early hours of the second day of the incident, and both hijackers were killed.

6 AUGUST 1984

A DC-8-55F cargo jet operated by the French carrier SF Air and en route to Algeria from Marseille, France, was commandeered by a lone assailant who had hidden himself in its freight area. He ordered the aircraft to return to its departure point, where he was overpowered by police.

10 AUGUST 1984

A lone assailant, armed with what turned out to be a toy gun and unclear about his intended destination, commandeered an Indian Airlines Boeing 737 jet that was on a scheduled

An Indian Airlines Boeing 737, two of which were hijacked on scheduled domestic flights in August 1984. (Douglas Green)

domestic flight from Mangalore to Bangalore. He gave himself up when it landed at its intended destination.

24 AUGUST 1984

SEVEN Sikh terrorists hijacked Indian Airlines Flight 421, a Boeing 737 jet with 88 persons aboard on a domestic service originating at New Delhi with an ultimate destination of Srinagar, demanding the release of cohorts from Indian prisons. The aircraft was first diverted to Lahore, Pakistan, and ultimately reached Dubai, where the hijackers surrendered. All received life prison terms.

24–27 NOVEMBER 1984

THREE Somali soldiers armed with sub-machine guns and grenades took over a Somali Airlines Boeing 707 jet, operating as Flight 414 on a service from Mogadishu, Somalia, to Jiddah, Saudi Arabia, with 111 persons aboard. Diverting it to Addis Ababa, Ethiopia, they demanded the release of political prisoners held in Somalia and stays of execution for seven condemned men. The latter demand having been met, the hijacking ended after 75 hours of negotiations, with the air pirates being granted political asylum. A security guard was wounded in the incident.

29 NOVEMBER 1984

A lone assailant who claimed to be carrying dynamite seized Eastern Metro Express Flight 1962, a twin-engine turboprop Jetstream on an intrastate commuter service from Augusta to Atlanta, Georgia, with 13 persons aboard. He demanded to speak with designated friends and relatives, but after a radio conversation with one of these he surrendered. He was sentenced to six years' imprisonment for interference with an airline crew.

4 JANUARY 1985

A ticket-less woman who wanted to go to South America forced her way aboard a Pan American World Airways Boeing 727 jetliner, operating as Flight 558, which was on the ground at Cleveland, Ohio, preparing for a domestic service to New York City. Having shot and wounded a ticket agent in the process, she was herself subsequently wounded by police and captured. She was later found not guilty by reason of insanity.

23 JANUARY 1985

IN an ironic twist of fate, the saboteur who tried to destroy a jet airliner in an apparent suicide-for-insurance plot may have inadvertently saved it. The incident involved a Lloyd Aéreo Boliviano SA Boeing Advanced 727-2K3 in the air near Santa Cruz, Bolivia. Designated as Flight 900, the aircraft was at an approximate height of 10,000ft (3,000m) and descending for a landing at Viru-Viru International Airport, serving Santa Cruz, when the passenger set off a stick of dynamite in the forward lavatory at 22:15 local time. He was the only fatality among the 127 persons aboard, including a crew of seven, his body having apparently absorbed much of the blast and prevented what could have been catastrophic damage to the 727. Three other passengers suffered injuries.

The aircraft had been en route from La Paz, Bolivia, with an ultimate destination of Asunción, Paraguay, and after this incident new security measures were recommended for the boarding of local (transit) passengers on such international flights.

27 FEBRUARY 1985

WIELDING knives and broken bottles, two men being deported from (West) Germany commandeered a Lufthansa German Airlines Boeing 727 jet after it had taken off from Frankfurt with 43 persons aboard. The aircraft was diverted to Vienna, where both gave themselves up. They were sentenced in Austria to five years in prison.

27 MARCH 1985

A Lufthansa German Airlines Boeing 727 jet with 151 persons aboard, on a scheduled service from Munich to Athens, was hijacked by a lone assailant armed with a knife and a broken bottle. Demanding to be taken to Libya, he allowed the aircraft to land for refuelling at Istanbul, where security personnel disguised as airline employees went aboard and overpowered him. He was sentenced in Turkey to a prison term of eight years and four months.

29 MARCH 1985

A mentally disturbed assailant who claimed to have a gun commandeered a Lufthansa German Airlines Boeing 737 jetliner that had been on a scheduled service to London from Hamburg, (West) Germany, carrying 114 persons. He demanded to be taken to Hawaii, but after about an hour at Heathrow Airport he surrendered. The hijacker would be confined for approximately one year before being released.

26 APRIL 1985

A disgruntled Taiwanese Air Force sergeant who said he was carrying a bottle of sulphuric acid tried to hijack to Hong Kong a China Airlines Boeing 737 jet that was carrying 80 persons on a scheduled domestic flight from T'aipei to Kaohsiung. The pilot ignored his order and proceeded on to his intended destination, where the assailant surrendered. The bottle was found to contain water.

18 MAY 1985

ANNOUNCING that he had planted a bomb on board, a lone assailant tried to hijack to North Korea a (South) Korean Air Lines Boeing 727 jet on a scheduled domestic service from Seoul to Cheju carrying 118 persons. He was overpowered by security guards and other passengers, and a search revealed no explosive device.

21 JUNE 1985

NORWAY'S first case of aerial hijacking involved a Braathens SAFE Boeing 737 jetliner, operating as Flight 139 on a domestic service from Trondheim to Oslo with 121 persons aboard. Armed with a handgun, the assailant spoke about his personal problems and dissatisfaction with society in general before releasing his hostages and giving himself up at the aircraft's intended destination. He would have three years to deal with his personal issues – the prison term he received from a Norwegian court.

23 JUNE 1985

TWO ground workers were killed and four injured when a bomb contained within a suitcase exploded in the tourist area at Narita Airport, serving Tokyo. The suitcase had just been unloaded from CP Air Flight 003, arriving from Vancouver, British Columbia, and was to have been placed aboard Air-India Flight 301, which was bound for Bangkok.

Investigation revealed that four days earlier a man with an Indian accent had made bookings for two men with the same surname as his own on two CP Air flights, one of which was 003. The other was Flight 60, which interconnected with Air-India 181/182, a Boeing 747 that would crash in the Atlantic Ocean only about an hour after the blast at Narita (see next entry).

The bomb intended for Air-India 301 was apparently in retaliation for the Indian Army's attack the previous year on the Golden Temple, the Sikh religious shrine located in Amritsar, Punjab. Its premature detonation probably resulted from an incorrectly-set timer. One man would later be sentenced to ten years' imprisonment in Canada for involvement in the Narita Airport explosion.

23 JUNE 1985

THE worst single case of aerial sabotage, which would also result in the worst aviation disaster occurring over water, involved Air-India Flight 182, a Boeing 747-237B (VT-EFO) making a transatlantic trip from Montreal, Canada, to London, one segment of a service with an ultimate destination of Bombay. The wide-bodied jet airliner crashed about 110 miles (175km) east of Cork, Ireland, and all 329 persons aboard (307 passengers and 22 crew members) were killed.

As Flight 181, the doomed aircraft had originated at Toronto, Canada. At Montreal it was redesignated Flight 182. It was last observed on radar as it cruised above a solid overcast at flight level 310 before suffering catastrophic structural failure at around 07:15 local time, falling in an area where the depth of the ocean was about 7,000ft (2,000m). Searchers eventually recovered the bodies of 132 victims and between three and five per cent of the aircraft's structure. A photographic and video-graphic map made of the wreckage on the seabed confirmed that the 747 had broken up in the air. Further investigation, including examination of recovered debris and the flight data and cockpit voice recorders, pointed

A piece of wreckage from the downed Air-India Boeing 747, floating in the Atlantic Ocean off the Irish coast in June 1985. (AP/Press Association Images)

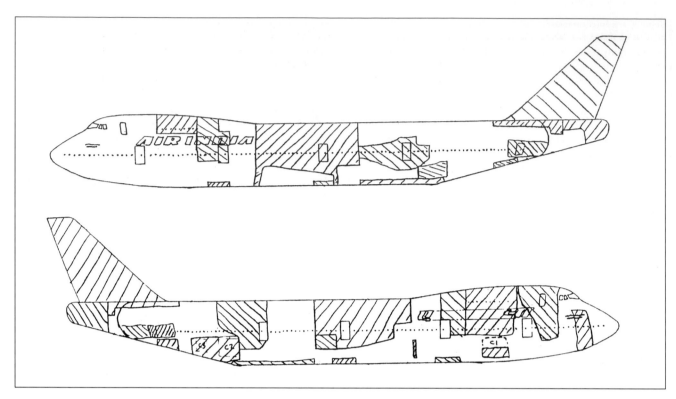

*The lined portions indicate the pieces of the Air-India
Boeing 747 that were identified on the ocean floor.*
(Canadian Aviation Safety Board)

to an explosion in its forward cargo hold, leading to the
conclusion by the Indian investigative commission that the
aircraft had been sabotaged.

The blast which had earlier taken place at Tokyo's Narita
Airport further substantiated the sabotage theory, as did the
story of the simultaneous bookings of a man with the same
surname on two CP Air flights that interconnected with Air-
India Flights 181/182 and 301, the apparent target of the bomb
that exploded in Japan. The suspected device that destroyed
VT-EFO may also have originated at Vancouver, British
Columbia, where, the day before, a passenger booked on
Toronto-bound CP Air Flight 60 had requested that his suitcase
be interlined through to the doomed Air-India 747.

Since his seat on the latter was only stand-by and not
reserved, the ticket agent explained that this was not possible.
The man persisted, and the agent gave in to his demands. Due
to equipment and personnel shortcomings at Air-India, luggage
was not properly inspected, and the explosive device may have
been loaded aboard Flight 182 in an unaccompanied suitcase,
which was contrary to company policy.

Seven years later, a 30-year-old suspected Sikh terrorist
believed responsible for the bombing was arrested in Bombay.
It was announced without further elaboration in June 1997 that
he had been killed while still in police custody.

In February 2003 one man who pleaded guilty to acquiring
the materials used in the destruction of the 747 was sentenced
to five years' imprisonment by a court in Vancouver. Two other
suspects were acquitted in 2005 of first-degree murder and
conspiracy charges in connection with the bombing.

28 JUNE 1985

A lone assailant rushed into the cockpit of a Turkish Airlines
(THY) Boeing 727 jet on a scheduled service to Istanbul from
Frankfurt, shouting that he wanted to blow up the aircraft and
spraying its instruments and the flight crew with foam. Several
of the 81 passengers subdued him, and he was arrested after
a safe landing at the intended destination. He would later be
sentenced to eight years' imprisonment in Turkey.

4 JULY 1985

A woman armed with a knife demanded that the Air Niugini
A300 wide-bodied jetliner on which she was a passenger, and
which had been on a scheduled international service from Papua
New Guinea to Brisbane, Australia, should instead continue on
to Sydney. She was dissuaded from her demand and the Airbus
landed at its intended destination. Known to have been mentally
ill, she was charged with endangering an aircraft.

26 SEPTEMBER 1985

AN explosive device was found in the suitcase of a passenger
who got off an Air Haiti Boeing 737 jetliner minutes before
its scheduled departure from John F. Kennedy International
Airport, serving New York City, as Flight 34, on a service to
Port au Prince, Haiti. He and two accomplices would later be
charged with the attempted destruction of an aircraft.

27 OCTOBER 1985

FOUR armed assailants assaulted and robbed passengers
aboard an Aerolíneas Centrales de Colombia SA (ACES) Twin
Otter turboprop on a scheduled domestic service from El
Bagre to Medellín with 20 persons aboard. They then forced
the aircraft to land at Amalfi, Colombia, where they fled.

30 OCTOBER 1985

AN apparently small explosive device that had been contained in a tote bag detonated in the baggage compartment of an American Airlines Boeing 727-200 after the jetliner – operating as Flight 203 on a domestic intrastate service from Austin, Texas, with 154 persons aboard – had landed at Dallas/Fort Worth International Airport.

There were no injuries in the incident. The bag in which the bomb had been planted belonged to a woman whose husband, who did not accompany her on the flight, subsequently pleaded guilty to attempted murder and other charges.

10 NOVEMBER 1985

TWO men commandeered a Uganda Airlines Fokker F.27 Friendship turboprop carrying 49 persons on a scheduled domestic service from Entebbe to Arua, the aircraft landing in rebel-held Kasese. It and the hostages were released over a period of approximately one month.

19 NOVEMBER 1985

A lone assailant wielding a lighter and an electrical switch threatened to hijack America West Airlines Flight 261, a twin-jet Boeing 737 with 63 persons aboard, which was preparing to take off at Phoenix Sky Harbor International Airport, serving Arizona's capital city, on a domestic service to Ontario, California. He was removed from the aircraft, charges against him subsequently being dismissed on grounds of mental incompetency.

19 DECEMBER 1985

AN Aeroflot An-24 turboprop, carrying 44 persons on a Soviet scheduled domestic service originating at Yakutsk, with an ultimate destination of Irkutsk, was commandeered by its first officer. Low on fuel, the aircraft force-landed in a pasture near Gannon, Heilongjiang, China. The hijacker was sentenced to eight years' imprisonment.

8 JANUARY 1986

IN a harrowing incident that may have been an attempted suicide, a known psychiatric patient who had been asked to extinguish his cigarette went berserk aboard a Southern Jersey Airways Twin Otter turboprop, on a scheduled Allegheny Commuter air-taxi service from Atlantic City, New Jersey, to Islip, New York. His interference with the two pilots sent the aircraft plunging from 5,000 to 1,500ft (1,500–450m) before he was knocked out by two other passengers and later taken into custody. He was taken to a psychiatric facility for evaluation and would later be charged with the crime of interfering with an aircraft crew.

5 FEBRUARY 1986

A knife-wielding assailant took a stewardess hostage aboard Delta Air Lines Flight 139, an L-1011 wide-bodied jetliner with 232 persons aboard that had just landed at Dallas/Fort Worth International Airport, Texas, an en-route stop during a domestic service from Fort Lauderdale, Florida, to Los Angeles, California. He gave himself up and was later found not guilty by reason of insanity.

25 FEBRUARY 1986

A group of soldiers commandeered a Philippine Airlines twin-jet BAC One-Eleven after landing at Cotabato, the Philippines, and were flown to Manila to join other rebel forces. All were captured after it had landed.

27 FEBRUARY 1986

DURING a US domestic service to New York City from Miami, a woman with a history of psychiatric problems began to display erratic behaviour in the cabin of Trans World Airlines Flight 348, a Boeing 727 jetliner carrying 56 persons, mentioning the word 'hijacking' while wielding a steak knife. She was taken into custody when the aircraft landed at its intended destination, then taken to a hospital for observation. Considering her history, there were no plans for her prosecution.

4 MARCH 1986

AN attempt to hijack an Olympic Airways Boeing 737 jet, on a scheduled domestic service from Athens with 76 persons aboard, ended with the aircraft landing on the Greek island of Thira (Santorini), its intended destination, where the lone assailant was arrested.

14 MARCH 1986

A lone gunman boarded a Delta Air Lines DC-9 jet at the airport serving Daytona Beach, Florida, where it had just landed and unloaded its passengers, and ordered the co-pilot to take off. After police had shot out the aircraft's tyres the hijacker gave himself up.

2 MAY 1986

A Horizon Air Metro III turboprop, on a scheduled intrastate commuter service from Medford to Portland with 14 persons aboard, was hijacked by a man who said he had a gun and forced to land at Hillsboro, Oregon. He released his hostages and gave himself up after a siege lasting about three hours. He would later kill himself while in custody.

3 MAY 1986

A Taiwanese-registered China Airlines Boeing 747 wide-bodied cargo jet on a scheduled service to Hong Kong from Bangkok was flown to Guangzhou, on mainland China, by the pilot, who subdued his two fellow flight crewmen. He took the action because he wanted to see his 82-year-old father.

3 MAY 1986

TAMIL separatist activity was suspected in the bombing of an AirLanka Lockheed L-1011-100 TriStar (4R-ULD) on the ground at Bandaranaike International Airport, located at Katunayake, Sri Lanka, and serving Colombo. Operating as Flight 101, the wide-bodied jet airliner was preparing for its departure on a service to Male, in the Maldives, when the blast occurred in a rear cargo hold shortly after 09:00 local time. Killed in the explosion were 16 of the 128 persons aboard the TriStar, including one member of the crew of 16. More than 40 others suffered injuries and the aircraft itself was destroyed, its fuselage being broken in two.

The fuselage of the AirLanka L-1011 was broken in two by the blast at the Colombo airport. (AP/Press Association Images)

The single suspect later arrested was a customs employee; he allegedly placed the explosive device aboard in a consignment of tea.

20 MAY 1986

A passenger tried to hijack a Finnair DC-9 jet airliner that had been on a scheduled domestic service from Oulu to Helsinki with 100 persons aboard, but the pilot landed anyway at its intended destination, where the assailant was arrested.

23 MAY 1986

A Swissair DC-10, operating as Flight 125 and preparing for a service to Zürich, was boarded by a man at O'Hare International Airport, Chicago, who held a knife at a woman's throat for half-an-hour before he surrendered. The victim was slightly injured.

6 JUNE 1986

A lone assailant commandeered an Aerolíneas Nicaraguenses (Aeronica) Boeing 727 on the ground at Managua, Nicaragua, as the jetliner, designated as Flight 726, was preparing to take off on a service to El Salvador. He held the passengers and crew hostage until arrested by police.

2 AUGUST 1986

IN an apparent attempt to make a connecting flight in Roanoke, Virginia, a passenger commandeered an Atlantic Southeast Airlines twin-engine turboprop EMB-110 Bandeirante that had been on a scheduled US domestic service from Atlanta, Georgia, with six persons aboard. But he never made his connection; the aircraft instead diverted to Greenville, South Carolina, where the assailant was arrested.

28 AUGUST 1986

IN the attempted hijacking of a Polish Airlines (LOT) Tu-134 jet, which had been on a scheduled domestic service from Wroclaw to Warsaw, a passenger held a razor blade to the throat of a stewardess. He was seized by security guards and later sentenced to five years' imprisonment.

20 SEPTEMBER 1986

TWO policemen were killed in a crime spree by three heavily-armed assailants in Ufa, USSR, and after one had run away the other two seized an Aeroflot Tu-134 jetliner at the city's airport, where it had made a scheduled en-route stop during a domestic service from Kiev to Nizhnevartovsk. Two passengers were killed in the attempted hijacking. One assailant was captured after 12 hours of negotiations, while the other was killed in a subsequent police operation. The third man, who had run away earlier, was also captured.

18 OCTOBER 1986

A Suriname Airways Twin Otter Series 300 turboprop, on a domestic flight from Paramaribo, was commandeered after its arrival at the Raleighvallen Votsberg nature reserve, in Suriname, whereupon its contents were ransacked by five armed men who were apparently seeking medical supplies. The aircraft would not be returned until the following May.

26 OCTOBER 1986

A Thai Airways International Airbus A300B-600 wide-bodied jetliner, operating as Flight 620 and carrying 249 persons, had just been authorised for descent from 33,000ft (10,050m) when an explosion occurred in a rear lavatory while the aircraft was flying in darkness and poor weather conditions over Tosa Bay, in the vicinity of Kochi, Shikoku, Japan, and south of Osaka, where it was scheduled to land. Occurring around 20:00 local time, the blast was followed by a rapid decompression of its cabin.

The Airbus, which had been on a service originating at Bangkok, landed safely at its intended destination despite the loss of two hydraulic systems that made it difficult for the crew to maintain control. Injured either in the explosion, the decompression, the uncontrolled flight deviations or the high loads imposed during an emergency descent, were a total of 109 persons, eight of them (five passengers and three crew members) seriously. Among the former was the assailant, who was attempting to smuggle a hand grenade into Japan and dropped it in a waste basket when the pin accidentally fell out.

10 JANUARY 1987

SHORTLY after it had taken off from Newark, New Jersey, bound for Washington DC, a New York Air DC-9 jet, designated as Flight

681 and carrying 50 persons, was taken over by a man who threatened to set it on fire. He surrendered after it had landed at Dulles International Airport, which was its intended destination.

10 MARCH 1987

A lone assailant tried to hijack an Empresa Consolidada Cubana de Aviación twin-engine turboprop An-24, carrying 48 persons, while it was preparing to take off from José Martí Airport, serving Havana, on a scheduled Cuban domestic service to Nueva Gerona, located on the Isla de la Juventud. When the pilot refused to fly him to the US, the hijacker let loose a hand grenade, the resulting explosion injuring 13 persons. The hijacker was then shot and killed by an off-duty police officer.

19 MAY 1987

AN Air New Zealand Boeing 747 wide-bodied jetliner, carrying 129 persons on a service as Flight 24 to Auckland from Tokyo, was commandeered on the ground after it had landed at Nadi International Airport, Suva, Viti Levu, Fiji. Claiming to have dynamite strapped to his body, the assailant, an airport worker, demanded the release of the 11-member government of Timoci Bavadra, which had been overthrown and placed under house arrest. He was overpowered by the flight crew and taken into custody.

6 SEPTEMBER 1987

A lone assailant was thwarted by other passengers in an attempt to hijack to (West) Germany a Polish Airlines (LOT) An-24 turboprop, which had been on a scheduled domestic service from Warsaw to Kraków.

13 SEPTEMBER 1987

AN attempt was made by a lone assailant to hijack to Paris an Aeroflot twin-jet Tu-134 that was on a scheduled Soviet domestic service from Minsk to Rostov. The pilot agreed to his demands, but instead landed at Rostov, where the hijacker was arrested. Found to be mentally unstable, the assailant was subsequently committed to a psychiatric hospital.

6 NOVEMBER 1987

AN Air Canada Boeing 767 wide-bodied jet that had just landed on a scheduled service from Toronto and disembarked its passengers was commandeered at San Francisco International Airport, California, by a lone assailant, who threatened the pilot with an axe. He first demanded to be taken to either the UK or Ireland, but after about three hours surrendered. He was subsequently ruled not mentally competent to stand trial.

29 NOVEMBER 1987

KOREAN Air, which had found itself thrust into the world political arena four years earlier when its Flight 007 was shot down by the Soviet Union, was the target in this terrorist attack that also had international ramifications.

Flight 858, a Boeing 707-358C (HL-7406), had originated at Baghdad, Iraq, with an ultimate destination of Seoul, South Korea, and en-route stops at Abu Dhabi and Bangkok. During the second leg of the service, the jet airliner, with 104 passengers and crew of 11 aboard, vanished over the Andaman Sea off the western coast of Burma (Myanmar).

No survivors or bodies were ever found, though a partially-inflated life-raft identified as belonging to HL-7406 and part of a folding meal-table from the back of a passenger seat were recovered some 30 miles (50km) south-west of the mouth of the Ye River. Eye-witnesses who had been fishing in the area later reported seeing a bright flash in the sky followed by a trail of smoke descending into the sea, then black smoke rising from the site of impact, which was fixed as being about 70 miles (110km) north-west of the city of Tavoy.

The sudden and catastrophic nature of the crash seemed to indicate foul play, stirring airline personnel into almost immediate action, starting with a review of the passenger manifest. Two of the passengers who had disembarked at Abu Dhabi were an elderly man and a woman in her 20s who said they were Japanese, ostensibly travelling as father and daughter, but an inquiry showed that the woman's passport had been forged. As they were being detained by immigration authorities in Bahrain, to where they had flown two days after the disappearance of Flight 858, the couple swallowed cyanide ampoules concealed in cigarette filters. The man, later identified as 70-year-old Kim Sung-il, died, but his accomplice, Kim Hyon Hui, 24, survived the suicide attempt. She later confessed to sabotaging the aircraft, and said they were acting under orders from North Korean officials in what may have been an attempt to frighten other countries away from attending the 1988 Olympic Games in Seoul.

The attack was carried out with a time bomb, using the composition C-4 hidden within a portable radio and a bottle of PLX liquid explosive, which had been left in an overhead rack above seat row No 7 within the passenger cabin. It was possible that the blast, the explosive decompression of the cabin at the cruising altitude of 37,000ft (11,300m), and the accompanying flash fire, could have caused instant death to the occupants of the 707.

The surviving saboteur, who at her trial exclaimed 'It is natural that I be punished and killed a hundred times for my sin,' was sentenced to death but was later pardoned by the President of South Korea. She was freed in 1993.

7 DECEMBER 1987

IN a disaster reminiscent of the 1964 Pacific Air Lines crash (see page 89), which also took place in California, this case of suicide and mass murder stemmed from an employer-employee dispute.

The genesis of this tragic tale dated back some three weeks, to 19 November, when David Burke, a 35-year-old customer service agent for US Air, the parent company of Pacific Southwest Airlines (PSA), was fired for allegedly pilfering petty cash from in-flight cocktail sales. Directly responsible for his dismissal was his supervisor, 48-year-old Ray Thomson, who was stationed at Los Angeles but lived in the San Francisco Bay area, commuting by air to and from work every weekday. He was on his way home when, on this Monday afternoon, he boarded PSA Flight 1771 at Los Angeles International Airport.

At around 16:15 local time, the British Aerospace BAe 146 Series 200 (N350PS) was cruising in clear weather conditions at 22,000ft (6,700m), about halfway to San Francisco. It was then that the Oakland air-traffic control centre received an ominous 'squawk' from the aircraft's transponder, indicating an on-board emergency. The pilot also reported by radio that gunshots had been fired in the cabin. Less than 30 seconds later, eye-witnesses observed the four-engine jetliner descending in a steep nose-down attitude. It crashed on the sloping terrain of a cattle ranch near Paso Robles.

All 43 persons aboard perished, including the crew of five. Much of the evidence of what had transpired aboard Flight 1771 was destroyed in the crash, but amid the shattered, burned wreckage and pitiful human remnants lay some of the answers.

Written on an air-sickness bag was an unsigned note that read, 'Hi Ray. I think it's sort of ironical that we end up like this.' It went on, 'I asked for some leniency for my family, remember. Well I got none and you'll get none.' Also found in pieces was a .44 calibre Smith & Wesson revolver, with all six rounds expended. A portion of a human finger was found in the trigger of the weapon; prints identified it as belonging to David Burke. He had also left a prophetic message on his girlfriend's telephone answering machine stating that he was on his way to San Francisco on Flight 1771 and ending with, 'I really wish I could say more but I do love you.'

The rest of the story was told by the aircraft's cockpit voice recorder, which survived the crash. Two shots were heard, apparently in the passenger cabin, and a stewardess then entered the flight deck and announced, 'Captain, we have a problem.' A male voice then interjected, 'I'm the problem.' The sounds of a scuffle ensued, and three more shots were fired in or near the cockpit presumably at the two pilots and, possibly,

A Pacific Southwest Airlines British Aerospace BAe 146 Series 200, identical to the aircraft brought down on 7 December 1987 by the shooting of its flight crew. (Douglas Green)

a flight attendant. A final shot was believed to have been the suicide of the gunman.

The US Federal Aviation Administration (FAA) rules then in effect permitted employees to bypass security check-points, which could account for how the pistol was smuggled aboard the aircraft. Two weeks after the tragedy, procedures were changed so that even crew members had to be screened prior to boarding.

23 DECEMBER 1987

A 15-year-old boy who said he had a bomb hijacked KLM Royal Dutch Airlines Flight 343, a twin-jet Boeing 737 with 97 persons aboard, which was en route from Amsterdam to Milan. He forced it to land at Rome and demanded a million dollars, but after releasing about half of the passengers was overpowered by police. The following November he was acquitted of the hijacking charge on account of his age.

4 JANUARY 1988

An Aeroméxico DC-9 Series 32 jetliner, operating as Flight 179 on a domestic service from Tijuana to Mexico City with 119 persons aboard, was hijacked by a man who claimed to have an explosive device and wanted to be taken across the US border to Brownsville, Texas. He surrendered after the aircraft landed for refuelling at Monterrey, Mexico, and subsequently committed suicide while in custody.

13 FEBRUARY 1988

DEMANDING to be flown to London, four young men armed with knives commandeered an Air Tanzania Boeing 737 jetliner that had been on a scheduled domestic service from Dar-es-

Salaam to Mount Kilimanjaro with 76 persons aboard. Tricking the hijackers, the pilot landed the aircraft at a darkened Dar-es-Salaam airport; he and the co-pilot were attacked and injured when the act of deception was realised. However, the assailants were overpowered and captured, and were subsequently sentenced to 15 years' imprisonment.

22 FEBRUARY 1988

AN attempt to hijack to the mainland a China Airlines A300 wide-bodied jet, which had been on a scheduled Taiwanese domestic service from T'aipei to Kaohsiung, ended in failure, with the lone assailant being overpowered.

1 MARCH 1988

A mineworker with both marital and financial difficulties and who had recently taken out a large life insurance policy was considered a suspect in the destruction of a Commercial Airways (Comair) Ltd EMBRAER EMB-110P1 Bandeirante (ZS-LGP). Designated as Flight 206, the Brazilian-built twin-engine turboprop, which had been leased from Bophuthatswana Air and was on an internal South African service from Phalaborwa to Johannesburg, crashed and burned about eight miles (13km) south-west of Jan Smuts Airport, where it was scheduled to land. All 17 persons aboard perished, including a two-member flight crew.

The commuter airliner was last reported on the instrument landing system (ILS) localiser on an approach course to Runway 03-Left in conditions of reduced visibility, with scattered clouds, when it was shattered by an explosion at an approximate height of 7,500ft (2,300m), or about 2,500ft (760m) above the terrain elevation. Its cockpit section, containing the two pilots, was torn away from the rest of the fuselage by the force of the blast; the aircraft then fell in pieces into the grounds of a factory.

The local time of the crash was fixed at 17:28. Tests confirmed the presence of an explosive consisting of nitro-glycerine and ammonium nitrate. It was perhaps significant that a briefcase known to have been placed aboard at Phalaborwa could not be located, despite an extensive search.

At the time there were no requirements to screen carry-on baggage at the point of departure. In the wake of this tragedy the urgent implementation of measures designed to prevent dangerous goods from being placed aboard commercial aircraft at airports lacking sufficient security services was recommended.

12 MARCH 1988

A lone assailant who wanted to be taken to either India or Afghanistan commandeered Pakistan International Airlines Flight 320, an A300 wide-bodied jet carrying 156 persons on a domestic service from Karachi to Quetta. He shot and wounded a guard before being subdued and captured.

29 MARCH 1988

A gunman demanding to be taken to either India or Afghanistan commandeered a Pakistan International Airlines Boeing 707 jet that was on a scheduled domestic service from Karachi to Quetta with 143 persons aboard. He was subdued and captured, although one person was shot and wounded.

EMBRAER Bandeirante, shown in the livery of another carrier but of the type blown up over South Africa. (EMBRAER)

30 MARCH 1988

IT was no laughing matter aboard Aeroflot Flight 38422, a Tu-134 jetliner on a Soviet domestic service from Frunze to Moscow, when a passenger handed a note to a stewardess that read 'Divert to Istanbul'. The passenger who wrote it later explained that he had been kidding; he was nevertheless arrested when the aircraft landed at Moscow.

13 APRIL 1988

IN an act of 'personal' terrorism, or perhaps rage, a man wielding a pair of scissors who said he was terminally ill disrupted a Korean Air Boeing 747 wide-bodied jetliner that had been on a scheduled international service to New York City from Seoul, South Korea. He and five other passengers suffered minor injuries during a struggle, and the aircraft was diverted to Anchorage, Alaska, after which the assailant was taken to a hospital for observation.

12 MAY 1988

A Xiamen Airlines Boeing 737 jet, on a scheduled Chinese domestic flight from Xiamen to Canton with 118 persons aboard, was commandeered by two defectors and forced to land in Taiwan, where they were granted asylum.

1 AUGUST 1988

WITH the intention of robbing their fellow passengers, two gunmen commandeered an Aerolíneas Centrales de Colombia (ACES) Twin Otter turboprop that had been on a scheduled domestic service from Bagre to Medellín with 24 persons aboard. The aircraft was ordered to land at an isolated airstrip, after which the assailants escaped.

5 AUGUST 1988

A mentally-disturbed passenger tried to force his way into the cockpit of a Delta Air Lines DC-9, designated as Flight 925 and carrying 47 persons, as the jetliner was approaching to land at the Greenville-Spartanburg airport, South Carolina, near the end of an interstate service from Atlanta, Georgia. Throwing a cabin attendant to the floor before he was subdued, he was subsequently found not guilty by reason of insanity.

29 SEPTEMBER 1988

A Viação Aérea São Paulo (VASP) Boeing 737 jet, operating as Flight 375 on a Brazilian domestic service from Porto Velho to Rio de Janeiro with 105 persons aboard, got hijacked by a mentally-disturbed assailant who wanted to crash the airliner into a government building in the capital city of Brasilia. He shot dead the first officer and wounded two other crew members before the 737 landed at Santa Genoveva Airport, serving Goiania, in the state of Goias. As he was transferring to another aircraft with the captain, police opened fire, and he then shot and wounded his hostage. Also wounded, the hijacker died two days later.

1 OCTOBER 1988

THREE Haitian soldiers boarded and temporarily commandeered American Airlines Flight 658, an A300, on the ground at Port-au-Prince, Haiti. They surrendered their weapons after the wide-bodied jet had taken off, bound for New York City with 233 persons aboard, and requested asylum on arrival at its intended destination.

1–2 DECEMBER 1988

FOUR heavily armed men who seized a school bus in Ordzhonikidze, USSR, and asked for $2 million and transportation to any capitalist country that had no diplomatic relations with the Soviet Union, were provided with an Aeroflot Il-76 jet, which flew them to Israel. They were returned to the USSR by the Israeli authorities and subsequently sentenced to prison terms of 14 to 15 years.

20 JANUARY 1989

THREATENING that, unless he was flown to Bucharest, Romania, he would blow the aircraft up, a lone assailant commandeered an Aeroflot Tu-134 jetliner that was on a scheduled Soviet domestic service originating at Arkhangel'sk, with an ultimate destination of Odessa. He was arrested when it nevertheless landed at Odessa.

21 JANUARY 1989

IN what may have been an attempted hijacking, a passenger aboard an Aeroflot An-24 got up holding a bottle of gasoline and a lit cigarette-lighter while the twin-engine turboprop was still on the ground at the airport serving Ivano-Frankovsk, Ukraine, USSR, about to take off on a scheduled domestic flight to Kiev. He was detained and subsequently found to have been schizophrenic for nearly a decade.

31 JANUARY 1989

AN Aerolíneas Centrales de Colombia SA (ACES) Boeing 727 jet airliner, carrying 123 persons on a scheduled domestic service to Medellín from San Andrés Island, was commandeered by an assailant who doused another passenger with gasoline and threatened to start a fire. The aircraft landed at San José, Costa Rica, where the principal hijacker and three accomplices were arrested.

29 MARCH 1989

FLIGHT 640 of Hungarian airline MALEV, a Tu-154B jetliner carrying 116 persons, was commandeered by two teenage boys at Prague, Czechoslovakia, where it had stopped during an international service from Budapest to Amsterdam, and was forced to fly to Frankfurt. The youthful hijackers would each be subsequently sentenced in Germany to 24 months' probation.

30 MARCH 1989

A lone assailant claiming to have an explosive device tried to hijack to Pakistan or Nepal an Aeroflot Tu-154 jetliner that had been on a scheduled Soviet domestic service originating at Astrakhan. He also demanded $500,000. He was arrested when the aircraft landed at Baku, Azerbaijan, which was its intended destination. No bomb was found.

24 APRIL 1989

A Shanghai Oriental Airlines Xian Y-7 (Yunshuji-7) twin-engine turboprop (a Chinese-built An-24), carrying 50 persons on a scheduled Chinese domestic service from Ningbo, Zhejiang, to

Xiamen, Fujian, was targeted for hijack by a lone assailant who wanted to be taken to Taiwan. When he learned that the aircraft had instead landed at Fuzhou, on the mainland, he detonated a bomb, killing himself and injuring two other passengers. A stewardess had been stabbed and wounded earlier in the hijack.

18 MAY 1989

AN attempt by a member of the African National Congress to commandeer an Aeroflot Il-62 jet airliner ended with the lone assailant being shot, wounded and captured. The Soviet aircraft, carrying 174 persons, had been on a charter service from Luanda, Angola, to Dar-es-Salaam, Tanzania, and reached its intended destination safely. The would-be hijacker was later convicted of multiple charges and sentenced to a lengthy prison term.

24 MAY 1989

CARRYING 13 persons, a Bell 212 turbine-engine helicopter operated by the Colombian firm Helico was hijacked after leaving Medellín on a domestic service to the town of Antioquia. The six assailants, who may have been cocaine traffickers, robbed the other passengers and then escaped after ordering the aircraft to land at a site where a number of accomplices were waiting.

26 MAY 1989

AN attempt to hijack to (West) Germany a Czechoslovak Airlines (CSA) Yak-40 jet that had been on a scheduled domestic flight from Prague to Karlovy Vary, using an inert hand grenade, would end in the capture of the lone assailant, who would later be sentenced to prison for the crime.

31 MAY 1989

TWO men who said they had a bomb and wanted to be taken to Israel commandeered an ALM Antillean Airlines twin-jet MD-82 that had been on a scheduled service originating at Miami, Florida, with an ultimate destination of Curaçao, Dutch Antilles. The aircraft landed at New York City, where both hijackers were taken into custody.

An Aeroflot Il-62, one of which was targeted for hijack during an African internal service. (Douglas Green)

19 SEPTEMBER 1989

A Royal Air Maroc ATR-42 turboprop airliner carrying ten persons was hijacked during a scheduled service from Casablanca to El Aaiún (Laâyoune), Western Sahara, and forced to fly to Gran Canaria, in the Spanish Canary Islands, where the lone assailant surrendered.

6 OCTOBER 1989

TWO students protesting political repression in their country commandeered a Myanmar Airways Fokker F.28 Fellowship jetliner that had been on a scheduled domestic service from Mergui to Yangon (Rangoon) with 85 persons aboard. They surrendered after it landed at a military airbase in Thailand, and both would later be imprisoned for air piracy.

27 NOVEMBER 1989

FIVE police informants flying as passengers were marked for death by a drug cartel and would perish along with everyone else aboard Aerovías Nacionales de Colombia SA (AVIANCA) Flight 203.

The Boeing 727-21 jetliner (HK-1803) took off from El Dorado Airport, serving Bogotá, Colombia, on a domestic service to Cali, Valle del Cauca. Some five minutes later, or around 07:15 local time, it plunged to earth in flames in hilly terrain about 12 miles (20km) south-west of the capital city. The death toll of 110 included six crew members and three unidentified victims who were either passengers not on the manifest or persons killed on the ground.

The detonation of an explosive device apparently placed in a seat on the right hand side of the aircraft's passenger cabin had ruptured its fuel tanks and caused other serious damage. A passenger who may have brought the bomb aboard the 727 probably disembarked before its departure. The terrorist leader who was believed responsible for arranging this act of sabotage was himself killed in a police raid in 1992. A fellow conspirator in the bombing was captured and brought to trial in the US, where in 1994 he was convicted of this and other crimes and sentenced to a life prison term.

16 DECEMBER 1989

A Civil Aviation Administration of China (CAAC) Boeing 747 wide-bodied jetliner, operating as Flight 981 and carrying 223 persons, was hijacked during an international service to New York City from Beijing, landing at Fukuoka, Japan. The lone assailant, who had carried out the hijacking while accompanied by his wife and son, was injured in the process, and was returned to China by the Japanese authorities the following April.

3 JANUARY 1990

A twin-engine Cessna 402C operated by the Paraguayan carrier Líneas Aéreas de Transporte Nacional (LATN) was commandeered by six assailants after its departure from Asunción, Paraguay, on a charter service. The pilot and co-pilot were released before the aeroplane took off from a remote airstrip in Paraguay and headed in a northerly direction.

14 JANUARY 1990

IN an apparent act of suicide, an American tourist threw himself into an engine of a British Airways Boeing 747 wide-bodied jetliner that was preparing to take off at Port-of-Spain, Trinidad. He had first stolen a jeep and rammed it into the aircraft, subsequently smearing grease on his bleeding shoulder before killing himself.

The charred remains of an AVIANCA Boeing 727 destroyed in an apparently drug-related act of sabotage in November 1989. (Reuters/Corbis-Bettmann)

18 JANUARY 1990

A passenger's threat to detonate an explosive device led to the diversion of United Airlines Flight 705, a Boeing 727 jetliner on a US domestic service from San Francisco to Seattle, with the aircraft instead landing at Vancouver, British Columbia. Motivated to make his false threat by his anger over a delay in landing at Seattle due to bad weather, the passenger was arrested by Canadian police.

24 JANUARY 1990

AFTER it had landed and its ten occupants had been ordered off the aircraft, a North Solomons Air Services BN-2A Islander was set afire and destroyed by armed rebels at Wakunai, on the island of Bougainville, Papua New Guinea.

2–5 APRIL 1990

A Haitian Army private commandeered an empty American Airlines A300 wide-bodied jet at Port au Prince, Haiti, before its scheduled departure as Flight 658, and demanded to be flown to the US. Early on the morning of the third day of the stand-off, he escaped into the darkness.

18 APRIL 1990

A passenger claiming to have biological weapons commandeered an Aeroflot Tu-134 jet on a scheduled domestic service from Moscow to Leningrad, demanding to be taken to Kaunas, Lithuania. The aircraft instead landed at the Lithuanian city of Vilnius, where the assailant, who in fact had no weapons, surrendered.

26 APRIL 1990

A candidate for Colombia's presidency was assassinated by a member of the rebel group M-19 aboard an AVIANCA Boeing

727 jetliner shortly after it had taken off from Bogotá, as Flight 527, on a domestic service to Barranquilla. The gunman was then himself killed by a bodyguard, but there were no injuries among the approximately 120 other passengers.

9 JUNE 1990

USING a grenade that turned out to be only a training device, a teenager commandeered to Stockholm, Sweden, an Aeroflot Tu-154 jet that had been on a scheduled Soviet domestic service from Minsk to Murmansk with 121 persons aboard. He was subsequently returned to the USSR and sentenced to a four-year prison term.

19 JUNE 1990

CLAIMING to have an explosive device, a lone assailant hijacked an Aeroflot Tu-134 jetliner during a scheduled Soviet domestic service from Riga, Latvia, to Murmansk. The aircraft, with 60 persons aboard, landed at Helsinki, Finland, and the air pirate was returned to the USSR for prosecution. He was later sentenced to four years' imprisonment.

24 JUNE 1990

ANOTHER Aeroflot Tu-134 jetliner on a scheduled service within the USSR, from Tallinn, Estonia, to L'vov, Ukraine, was hijacked by an assailant who demanded to be taken to Sweden, but agreed to land at Helsinki, Finland, due to the aircraft's fuel situation. Denied asylum by the Finnish authorities, he was returned to the USSR.

30 JUNE 1990

AN Aeroflot Tu-154 jetliner on a scheduled Soviet domestic service from L'vov to Leningrad with 159 persons aboard was commandeered to Stockholm by a passenger carrying a grenade that turned out to be a harmless imitation. He was returned by the Swedish authorities and later sentenced to three years' imprisonment in the USSR.

4 JULY 1990

A passenger accompanied by her two-year-old daughter attempted to hijack to Turkey an Aeroflot Tu-134 jetliner that had been on a scheduled domestic service within the USSR, from Sochi to Rostov-na-Donu. She was overpowered and arrested when the aircraft landed at its intended destination.

5 JULY 1990

A Twin Otter Series 300 (HP-759) turboprop operated by the Panamanian carrier AeroPerlas on a scheduled domestic

An Aeroflot Tu-154, the type involved in numerous hijackings during the early 1990s. (Douglas Green)

service from Colón to the city of Panama with ten persons aboard was hijacked by five of its passengers, landing in Colombia. The hostages were released, but the aircraft was then stolen for use by the Colombian revolutionary organisation FARC.

5 JULY 1990

DURING a scheduled Soviet domestic flight from Leningrad to L'vov, yet another Aeroflot Tu-154 jet, this one carrying 178 persons, was hijacked to Sweden by a lone assailant, whose motive was to avoid military service. He was sentenced to four years' imprisonment in Sweden.

10 JULY 1990

A lone assailant attempted to hijack to Paris an Aeroflot Tu-154 jetliner after it took off from Leningrad, an en-route stop during a scheduled Soviet domestic service from Nikolaev to Murmansk. An explosive device he was purported to have was deemed harmless by the crew, who returned to Leningrad. The hijacker was later sentenced to a prison term of eight years.

12 JULY 1990

ONE or possibly two teenagers failed in their attempt to divert to Finland an Aeroflot Tu-154 jetliner, which instead landed at Leningrad, from where it had taken off earlier on a scheduled Soviet domestic flight to Murmansk.

18 JULY 1990

AN attempt to divert to Turkey an Aeroflot Tu-134 jetliner failed when the lone hijacker was overpowered and captured, the incident occurring during a Soviet scheduled domestic service from Odessa, Ukraine, to Sukhumi, Georgia.

23 JULY 1990

TWO assailants who wanted to be taken to Sweden commandeered an Aeroflot Tu-134 jetliner on a scheduled domestic service within the USSR, from Riga, Latvia, to Murmansk with 74 persons aboard. The aircraft instead landed at Petrozavodsk, where the assailants were captured.

28 JULY 1990

THREATENING to release poisonous gas, a teenage boy tried to hijack to Turkey an Aeroflot Tu-154 jet that had been on a scheduled Soviet domestic service from Krasnodar to Krasnoyarsk. He was convinced by the crew that the aircraft had to land at Orenburg, its intended en-route stop, where he was arrested.

16 AUGUST 1990

TWO passengers hijacked an Ethiopian Airlines aircraft that had been on a domestic flight, but were overpowered and arrested – one of them suffering injuries – when it landed at Aden, Yemen.

19 AUGUST 1990

A group of 11 convicts who were supposedly being guarded by three police officers seized an Aeroflot Tu-154 jetliner after it had taken off from Neryungri on a scheduled Soviet domestic service to Yakutsk with 101 persons aboard. Eventually the aircraft landed at Karachi, Pakistan, were they all gave themselves up. Plans were made by Pakistan to prosecute the hijackers there.

28 AUGUST 1990

THIS seizure by the passengers of an Aeroflot turboprop An-24 was apparently motivated by their frustration over four days of delays in the aircraft's scheduled departure from Yuzhno-Sakhalinsk, on the Soviet island of Sakhalin. The twin-engine turboprop instead returned to its departure point after finally taking off, whereupon the passengers abandoned their efforts to get where they were going.

30 AUGUST 1990

A vintage An-2 biplane believed to have been operated by Aeroflot on a domestic flight within the USSR was commandeered by a knife-wielding assailant who wanted to be taken to Afghanistan. The would-be hijacker was captured when the aircraft landed at Livny, some 200 miles (320km) south of Moscow.

30 AUGUST 1990

A second attempted hijacking in the USSR on the same day, this one by a passenger who demanded to be flown to (West) Germany, targeted an Aeroflot Yak-42 jet airliner that had been on a scheduled domestic service from Moscow to Voronezh. He was arrested when the aircraft landed at its intended destination.

2 SEPTEMBER 1990

TWO men who demanded to be taken to South Africa were overpowered and arrested after their attempt to hijack an Aeroflot Tu-134 jet that had been on a scheduled flight within Kyrgyzstan, USSR, from Przheval'sk to Frunze. During his capture, one of the assailants stabbed and wounded himself.

13 SEPTEMBER 1990

AN attempt to hijack Indian Airlines Flight 534, as the Boeing 737 jet was on a domestic service from Coimbatore to Bangalore with 97 persons aboard, was made by a young man who wanted to go to Australia. The pilot was able to convince him that the aircraft needed to land for refuelling at its intended destination, and there the assailant surrendered.

25 SEPTEMBER 1990

DEMANDING to be taken to Sweden, a lone hijacker commandeered an Aeroflot jetliner that had been on a scheduled domestic service within the USSR, from Leningrad to Arkhangel'sk, but the assailant was captured after the aircraft had landed at its intended destination, ostensibly for refuelling.

5 OCTOBER 1990

THE hijacker of an Aeroflot Yak-40, who commandeered the jetliner during a scheduled domestic service within the USSR, from Novgorod to Petrozavodsk, and demanded to be flown to Stockholm, ended up surrendering to the authorities in Helsinki, Finland, because the aircraft had insufficient fuel to reach Sweden. He ended up where he began when Finland extradited him back to the USSR.

7 OCTOBER 1990

A lone assailant attempted to divert to Sweden an Aeroflot An-24 that had been on a scheduled Soviet domestic service from Perm' to Arkhangel'sk, but was overpowered and captured when the turboprop airliner landed for refuelling at Kotlas, RSFSR.

10 NOVEMBER 1990

THAI Airways International Flight 305, an A300 wide-bodied jetliner carrying 221 persons, was hijacked during an international service from Bangkok to Yangon (Rangoon), Myanmar. Landing at Calcutta, the two assailants demanded the release of a pro-democratic leader under house arrest in Myanmar, and two others jailed in Thailand for a hijacking the previous year. A few hours later they surrendered.

15 NOVEMBER 1990

AN Aeroflot Tu-134 jetliner was diverted to Finland by a lone hijacker, who surrendered to the authorities after the aircraft had landed at Helsinki international airport. The Soviet aircraft had been on a domestic service from Leningrad to Moscow when commandeered.

16 NOVEMBER 1990

A lone assailant attempted to hijack to Sweden an Aeroflot Tu-134 jet that had been on a scheduled Soviet service bound for Moscow from Tallinn, Estonia, but he was arrested when the aircraft returned to its point of departure.

23–25 NOVEMBER 1990

ON a service to Tahiti from Santiago, Chile, a LAN-Chile Boeing 707 jet airliner, designated as Flight 33, was seized after it had landed on Easter Island in the South Pacific, an en-route stop, by scores of islanders protesting an increase in air fares and other issues. The bizarre protest ended two days later when the 90 persons who had been aboard the aircraft were released.

29 NOVEMBER 1990

DURING a scheduled domestic service within the USSR, from Moscow to Syktyvkar, a feeble attempt was made to hijack to Iraq an Aeroflot Tu-134 jetliner by a passenger who passed a note to a stewardess. Confident that the luggage aboard the aircraft had been properly screened, the crew completely disregarded his threat of having some type of weapon and landed at the flight's intended destination. There, the assailant was arrested.

2 DECEMBER 1990

AN Aeroflot Tu-154 jet airliner with 127 persons aboard, on a scheduled domestic flight from Murmansk to Leningrad, was targeted for hijack by a lone assailant who wanted to be taken to Sweden. The would-be hijacker was captured when the aircraft landed instead at its intended destination.

6 DECEMBER 1990

AN airliner possibly operated by the Civil Aviation Administration of China (CAAC) was targeted for hijack as it was preparing to take off from Baiyun Airport, serving Canton, on a scheduled domestic service to Qingdao, Shandong, but the assailant was overpowered by the crew.

11 DECEMBER 1990

AN attempt was made to hijack to Turkey an Aeroflot Yak-40 jetliner that had been on a Soviet scheduled service from Baku, Azerbaijan, to Tbilisi, Georgia, but the lone assailant was arrested when the aircraft landed, ostensibly for refuelling, at its intended destination.

15 DECEMBER 1990

AN AIRES Colombia EMB-110P Bandeirante (HK-3195X) was seized by guerrillas after landing at Villa Garzon, Colombia. After its eight occupants had been forced off, the twin-engine turboprop was doused with gasoline, set on fire, and destroyed.

21 DECEMBER 1990

AN apparent stowaway on an Aeroflot Tu-154 jet that had been on a scheduled domestic service within the USSR, from Rostov-na-Donu to Nizhnevartovsk, threatened to detonate an explosive device unless she was taken to the US, the incident occurring while the aircraft was on the ground at Volgograd, an en-route stop. She was instead arrested by the authorities.

24 DECEMBER 1990

AN Aeroflot Ilyushin Il-86 wide-bodied jetliner with 351 persons aboard was targeted for hijack during a scheduled domestic service within the USSR, from Moscow to Sochi, but the lone assailant, who wanted to be flown to London, was taken down by commandos when the aircraft landed at its intended destination.

28–30 DECEMBER 1990

AN Air Algérie twin-jet Boeing 737, designated as Flight 6201 and on a domestic service from Ghardaria to Algiers with 88 persons aboard, was hijacked by two young men who were apparently protesting against a crackdown on Muslim fundamentalists in Tunisia. That nation and Egypt both refused the aircraft entry, and it ultimately landed at Annaba, Algeria. Two days later the stand-off there ended, and the hijackers were taken into custody, later to be charged with, among other crimes, air piracy.

4 JANUARY 1991

IN what could be described as a case of employee 'self-flagellation', 15 ground crew members who were on strike commandeered an Air France Boeing 727 jetliner at Poretta Airport, serving Bastia, on French Corsica, before its scheduled departure on a domestic service to Marseille. The siege lasted 20 hours until it was ended by police.

7 JANUARY 1991

A Compañia de Aviación Faucett SA DC-8, operating as Flight 339 and carrying 125 persons, was commandeered during a domestic service from Trujillo to Lima, Peru. After proceeding to Jorge Chávez International Airport, serving the Peruvian capital, the jet airliner was stormed by police in darkness at around 21:00 local time, with the lone assailant, who had demanded a ransom, being killed. One passenger and a security officer were wounded in the incident.

13 JANUARY 1991

A purported 'explosive device' that was actually a can of hair spray was found by a cabin attendant aboard an Aloha Airlines Boeing 737 jetliner which, designated as Flight 115 and carrying 64 persons, had to turn back to its point of departure during a scheduled domestic intrastate service within Hawaii, from Honolulu to the island of Maui. The source of the device turned out to be the crew member who found it, who may have been trying to draw attention to himself. If so, it was the wrong kind of attention, leading to him being incarcerated for six months and having to pay $4,500 in damages.

21 JANUARY 1991

AN Aeroflot Tu-154 jetliner with 159 persons aboard on a scheduled domestic service from Tashkent, Uzbek SSR, to Odessa, Ukraine, was commandeered by a lone assailant armed with a fake bomb, and landed at Burgas, Bulgaria, after being refused entry into Turkey. The hijacker would later be returned to the USSR for prosecution.

4 FEBRUARY 1991

A passenger who reportedly had 'some business to settle' with the Indian government and claimed to have a bomb disrupted an Indian Airlines domestic flight from Calcutta to Agartala, but he was overpowered and later arrested when the aircraft landed at its intended destination.

13 FEBRUARY 1991

OPERATING as Flight 30 on a domestic service within the USSR, with an ultimate destination of Moscow, an Aeroflot Tu-154 jetliner with 171 persons aboard was targeted for hijack by a passenger who wanted to be taken to Turkey and claimed, falsely, to possess an explosive device. The aircraft returned to Tbilisi, Georgia, from where it had taken off earlier, where the hijacker surrendered.

13 FEBRUARY 1991

AN intoxicated passenger aboard United Airlines Flight 58, a Boeing 747 wide-bodied jetliner on a transpacific service from Tokyo to San Francisco, informed cabin attendants that he had a bomb. The aircraft returned safely to its point of departure, and the passenger later claimed that his threat was only a joke. But it was a bad joke, and would cost him a fine of nearly $30,000.

18 FEBRUARY 1991

SHORTLY after it had landed at Otu, Antioquia, Colombia, on a scheduled domestic service from Medellín, located some 30 miles (50km) to the north-west, an Aerolíneas Centrales de Colombia (ACES) de Havilland Twin Otter Series 300 (HK-2758) was seized by guerrillas, who ordered the 12 persons aboard the twin-engine turboprop to get off. The aircraft was then set afire and destroyed.

3 MARCH 1991

AFTER releasing his hostages, a lone hijacker killed himself by setting off an anti-tank grenade aboard an Aeroflot twin-engine turboprop An-24 that was on the ground at the airport serving Leningrad, USSR. He had demanded to be taken to Sweden after commandeering the aircraft, which was on a scheduled Soviet domestic service originating at Arkhangel'sk.

6 MARCH 1991

THREE armed men commandeered a Transportes Aéreos da Bacia Amazónica (TABA) EMB-110 twin-engine turboprop, operating as Flight 835 on a Brazilian domestic service to Manaus, forcing it to land at São Gabriel da Cachoeira. After the other passengers and the two crew members were released, the aircraft took off and headed towards Colombia.

14 MARCH 1991

AN attempt was made to hijack an Aeroflot Yak-42 jetliner that had been on a domestic service from Moscow to Naberezhnye Chelny, USSR, but it failed when the lone assailant was overpowered. He was arrested when the aircraft returned to Moscow.

18 MARCH 1991

A passenger who was identified as a 'psychiatric patient' threw a gasoline bomb in the cabin of an Aeroflot Ilyushin Il-86

An Aeroflot Ilyushin Il-86, the type involved in the fire-bombing incident during a Soviet domestic flight. (Douglas Green)

wide-bodied jetliner in flight near Sverdlovsk, USSR, during a scheduled domestic service from Moscow to Novosibirsk. The Il-86 landed safely at Sverdlovsk, and there were no serious injuries among the 380 persons aboard.

26–27 MARCH 1991

A Singapore Airlines A310 wide-bodied jetliner, designated as Flight 117 and carrying 129 persons, was commandeered while en route to Singapore from Kuala Lumpur, Malaysia. The hijackers were demanding the release of the jailed husband of former Pakistani Prime Minister Benazir Bhutto.

The aircraft landed at Changi Airport, Singapore, where it was attacked by commandos shortly before 07:00 local time on the second day, with all four Pakistani hijackers – who had been armed with explosives and knives – being killed. Two stewards had been injured when tossed from the aircraft before the commando assault, but there were no other casualties.

28 MARCH 1991

FOLLOWING an attempt to hijack to Sweden an Aeroflot twin-jet Tu-134 that had been on a scheduled Soviet domestic flight originating at Arkhangel'sk, the pilots tied up the unarmed assailant and kept him in the luggage compartment until the aircraft landed, as planned, at Kaliningrad, RSFSR. There, he was arrested.

31 MARCH 1991

IN an apparent protest over an election in Algeria, an Air Algérie Boeing 737 jet carrying 54 persons was hijacked during a scheduled domestic service from Bechar, but the lone assailant gave himself up after the aircraft had landed at Algiers, its intended destination, following several hours of negotiations.

29 APRIL 1991

AN Aeroflot Tu-154 jet with 72 persons aboard was commandeered during a scheduled Soviet domestic service from Barnaul to Moscow. The aircraft landed at Domodedovo Airport, serving the capital city, where the three hijackers, who wanted to be flown to the US, were captured by police commandos. One of the assailants was injured in the assault.

13 JUNE 1991

A passenger demanding to be taken to the Persian Gulf region and threatening to detonate an explosive device commandeered an Aeroflot Tu-154 jetliner carrying 111 persons on a Soviet scheduled domestic service from Rostov-na-Donu to Moscow. He surrendered after the aircraft landed at its intended destination.

17 JUNE 1991

AN Aeroflot Tu-154 jetliner with more than 100 persons aboard on a scheduled domestic service within the USSR, which originated at Krasnodar and had an ultimate destination of Krasnoyarsk, was targeted for hijack by a passenger who wanted to be flown to Turkey. After the aircraft landed at its intended destination the assailant fled into a nearby wooded area, but was subsequently apprehended.

30 JUNE 1991

A Somali Airlines Dornier 228 twin-engine turboprop on a scheduled service from Djibouti to Mogadishu was hijacked, unbelievably, by the aircraft's security agent, who threatened to detonate an explosive device. The Dornier landed safely in southern Somalia, where the passengers and two crew members were released unharmed.

9 AUGUST 1991

A Singaporean passenger who was denied additional alcohol became unruly aboard an American Airlines jetliner, operating as Flight 56 and bound for London from Miami, Florida, making several references to himself as a hijacker. The threat was treated as a potential hijacking, and the aircraft diverted to Boston, Massachusetts, where the passenger was arrested. He was convicted of interfering with an aircraft crew, fined and deported back to his native country.

2 SEPTEMBER 1991

A Lockheed L-100-20 Hercules four-engine turboprop cargo transport (N521SJ), operated by the US carrier Southern Air Transport and on a Red Cross relief flight, struck a landmine while taxiing in preparation for take-off at Wau, in the Sudanese state of Western Bahr el Ghazal, and in the subsequent explosion the aircraft was destroyed and its five crew members (and only occupants) were injured. Buried towards the centreline of the airport runway and some 500ft (150m) from its threshold, the mine had been struck by the nose gear of the Hercules.

6–7 SEPTEMBER 1991

WITH the apparent intention of avoiding having to attend school in the US and of returning to his native Egypt, a 17-year-old passenger left a threatening note concerning a bomb in the lavatory of a Trans World Airlines Boeing 747 wide-bodied jetliner, designated as Flight 841 and on a transatlantic service to New York City from Rome. This necessitated its diversion to Ireland. When no explosives were found the aircraft resumed its trip the following day, but during this segment of the flight a fire erupted in a lavatory. The youth would later admit to both writing the note and starting the blaze.

7 SEPTEMBER 1991

A single-engine turboprop Cessna 208 Caravan operated by the Colombian airline Servicio Aeronavegación a Territorios Nacionales (SATENA) was hijacked during a domestic flight from Bogotá to San José del Guaviare by the passengers who had chartered the aeroplane. The crew was released by the hijackers, who then stole the Cessna, although the aircraft was later recovered in south-eastern Colombia.

19 SEPTEMBER 1991

AN attempt to hijack to Algeria an Alitalia MD-80 jetliner, designated as Flight 864 and en route from Rome to Tunis with 137 persons aboard, ended with the Italian-registered aircraft landing at its intended destination and one assailant being captured by security forces. The hijacker was identified as a 'disgruntled Tunisian national', who had a companion who was also subsequently apprehended.

16 OCTOBER 1991

AN Ethiopian Airlines Twin Otter turboprop on a scheduled domestic flight from Debre Markos to Bahir Dar was hijacked to Djibouti, where the lone hijacker was taken into custody.

27 OCTOBER 1991

A twin-engine Beechcraft, operated by the Peruvian carrier Juan Leguía Jiménez and carrying 11 persons, was hijacked during a domestic commuter service from Trujillo to Tocache, with the pilot being forced to change course to another destination.

9 NOVEMBER 1991

IN the waning days of the USSR, an Aeroflot Tu-154 jetliner with 171 persons aboard was commandeered by four armed men, identified as Chechen separatists, during a scheduled domestic service from Mineral'nyye Vody to Ekaterinberg, and flown to Ankara, Turkey. The aircraft then proceeded to Groznyy, RSFSR, where the hijackers were believed to have surrendered.

13 NOVEMBER 1991

AN Aeroflot Tu-154 jetliner carrying 162 persons on a scheduled domestic service within the USSR, from Irktusk to St Petersburg, was targeted for hijack by a passenger who wanted to be taken to the West. The suspect was arrested when the aircraft landed at its intended destination.

25 NOVEMBER 1991

TWO assailants commandeered a Papua New Guinea aircraft that had been on a domestic service, then stole its cargo after it landed at a remote airstrip. The other occupants were unharmed.

25 NOVEMBER 1991

THREE suspects who were reportedly seeking political asylum hijacked an Ethiopian Airlines Boeing 737 jetliner, operating as Flight 616 on a domestic service from Addis Ababa to Dire Dawa with 91 persons aboard. They surrendered after the aircraft landed in Djibouti.

1 DECEMBER 1991

DURING a scheduled stop at New Delhi, a crude incendiary device hidden in a food container was found aboard an Air-India Boeing 747 wide-bodied jetliner, designated as Flight 111 and en route to New York City from Madras with 416 persons aboard. The device had apparently been planted by the supervisor of an in-flight catering business, possibly for some personal reason or as part of a larger terrorist plot.

3 JANUARY 1992

A Mil Mi-8 turbine-engine helicopter operated by the carrier Cubana de Aviación was stolen in Cuba, and then used to transport 34 Cubans fleeing their country. The aircraft landed at an airport near Miami, Florida, and the occupants then asked for political asylum. Their custody would be handed over to relatives living in the US.

31 JANUARY 1992

AN Aero Taxi Internacional Cessna 208B Grand Caravan single-engine turboprop on a Panamanian domestic commuter service from the city of Panama to El Porvenir with 13 persons aboard was commandeered by four of its passengers, who forced it to land at a remote airstrip near Turbo, Antioquia, Colombia. There the hijackers disembarked, allowing the aircraft and its other occupants to return to Panama.

5 FEBRUARY 1992

TWO assailants who wanted to be flown to Kenya commandeered an Ethiopian Airlines Twin Otter turboprop that was on a scheduled domestic service from Addis Ababa to Bahir Dar with 18 persons aboard. Due to insufficient fuel, the aircraft instead landed in Djibouti, where the hijackers surrendered.

12 MARCH 1992

THREE passengers hijacked an Aero Taxi Internacional BN-2A Islander that was on a Panamanian domestic commuter service from El Porvenir to the city of Panama, forcing it to land at some unspecified location before releasing the twin-engine aircraft and its pilot.

1 APRIL 1992

IN an attempt to escape the unsettled conditions in Ethiopia, a lone assailant hijacked to Yemen an Ethiopian Airlines Boeing 727 jetliner that had been on a scheduled domestic flight from Dire Dawa to Addis Ababa with 135 persons aboard. The hijacker surrendered after the aircraft landed in Aden.

12 APRIL 1992

DESIGNATED as Flight 574 and on a domestic service originating at Addis Ababa, an Ethiopian Airlines Boeing 727 jetliner with 105 persons aboard was commandeered by two assailants, both reportedly Ethiopian presidential guards who had escaped from prison. After the 727 had landed at Nairobi, Kenya, the hijackers requested a $5 million ransom and additional fuel for the aircraft to take them to Canada. However, they surrendered after four hours of negotiations.

17 APRIL 1992

A Mesaba Airlines Fairchild-Swearingen Metro III twin-engine turboprop was damaged in a freak ground attack at Blue Grass Airport, serving Lexington, Kentucky. The aircraft had just landed and was taxiing to the gate when the crew observed a vehicle approaching them. After being stopped by the pilots, the Metro was rammed by the automobile, whose driver was injured in the collision, although the four occupants of the aircraft escaped unscathed. The motorist later said that he had been drinking and wanted to kill himself.

25 APRIL 1992

FOR the third time in less than three months, an aircraft operated by the Panamanian carrier Aero Taxi Internacional was targeted for hijack. In this case, a single-engine turboprop Cessna 208B Grand Caravan was commandeered at Carti, in the San Blas Islands of Panama, by two individuals armed with semi-automatic weapons. After the passengers had been released the pilot was forced to fly the assailants to an unspecified location in Colombia. He was then freed to return to Panama, but without the Cessna, which was not recovered.

16 MAY 1992

THREE passengers, identified as members of a military intelligence unit, were reportedly tortured and then killed when thrown out while airborne by the four hijackers of an Aerotaxi Casanare Ltda (Aerotaca) Twin Otter Series 300 turboprop, carrying 16 persons, which had been on a scheduled Colombian domestic service originating at Bogotá, with an ultimate destination of Bucaramanga. The aircraft was forced to land at Fortul, Colombia, where six other passengers were released unharmed, then took off again, and was later found at a rural landing strip. However, the suspected National Liberation Army guerrillas may have taken hostage the three Aerotaca crew members, who were reported missing.

8 JUNE 1992

A man armed with a hand grenade was killed by security forces at Vnukovo Airport, serving Moscow, after attempting to hijack to Turkey an Aeroflot Tu-154 jetliner that had been on a scheduled domestic service to the Russian capital from Groznyy with 115 persons aboard.

13 AUGUST 1992

A passenger who displayed ampoules of a liquid that he said was acid, but was actually oil, tried to commander a Lvovskie Avialinii Yak-42 jet airliner that had been on a scheduled Ukrainian domestic service from Simferopol to L'vov with 88 persons aboard, but he was overpowered and captured.

28–30 AUGUST 1992

FIVE men armed with pistols and hand grenades commandeered Ethiopian Airlines Flight 551, a Boeing 727 jet carrying 86 persons on a domestic service from Addis Ababa to Bahir Dar. The aircraft first landed at Djibouti, where the passengers were released, and ultimately flew to Rome, where the hijackers, who claimed to be political dissidents, surrendered. They would later be sentenced to prison terms of just under five years.

4 SEPTEMBER 1992

AN Ethiopian Airlines Boeing 727 jetliner, operating as Flight 555 on a domestic service from Dire Dawa to Addis Ababa with 58 persons aboard, was commandeered by three assailants armed with hand grenades, who demanded to be taken to Djibouti. There, the hijackers surrendered after a period of negotiations with the authorities.

29 DECEMBER 1992

AN Aerocaribbean An-26 turboprop airliner, designated as Flight 360 on a Cuban domestic service from Havana to Varadero, was flown to Miami, Florida, by its pilot, who physically immobilised his fellow crew members. All but five of the 53 persons aboard requested asylum in the US. His 'flight to freedom' was greeted less than enthusiastically by American authorities, who considered prosecution of the pilot for air piracy. However, charges against him were later dropped on account of the 'exceptional circumstances' of the case.

22 JANUARY 1993

A passenger who claimed to have a chemical bomb, which turned out to be two balls of twine covered with flowers, commandeered Indian Airlines Flight 810, a Boeing 737 jetliner on a domestic service to New Delhi from Lucknow, Uttar Pradesh, with 53 persons aboard. He was demanding the release of Hindi activists being held by the Indian government for their involvement in rioting the previous month. After the aircraft had returned to its departure point, the assailant was persuaded by a leader of the Hindu nationalist opposition party to surrender to the authorities.

23 JANUARY 1993

A Korean Air Fokker 100, designated as Flight 388 and on a domestic service from Mokpo to Seoul, was disrupted by a passenger who threatened to blow up the jetliner and said he wanted to defect to Switzerland. The aircraft diverted to Kwangju, also in South Korea, where the assailant, who had been overpowered by members of the crew, was turned over to the police. He was classified as 'mentally disturbed', and also found to have not been carrying any explosives.

11 FEBRUARY 1993

A Lufthansa German Airlines A310 wide-bodied jet, operating as Flight 592 and carrying 104 persons on an international service from Frankfurt to Cairo, was hijacked by a sole assailant armed with a starter pistol. The aircraft completed a transatlantic journey and ultimately landed at Kennedy Airport, New York City, where the hijacker surrendered. He was later given a prison sentence of 20 years by a US Federal Court judge.

18 FEBRUARY 1993

A vintage Douglas DC-3 operated by Missionary Flight International was commandeered at Cap Haitien, Haiti, before it could take off on a scheduled service to West Palm Beach, Florida. The aircraft, with 11 persons aboard, safely reached Florida, landing at Miami, where the hijacker surrendered to the American authorities.

Charged with air piracy, the assailant was released on a $100,000 bond guaranteed by prominent Haitian exile activists.

20 FEBRUARY 1993

A man armed with two hand grenades and accompanied by his wife and infant child hijacked an Aeroflot Tu-134, designated as Flight 2134 and on a Russian domestic service from Tyumen' to St Petersburg with 82 persons aboard, surrendering when the twin-engine jet landed at Stockholm, Sweden. Reportedly, the hijacker paid off ground personnel to avoid a security check. However, the hijacker's quest for a new life in a new land was not successful, as the entire family was subsequently returned to Russia.

25 FEBRUARY 1993

AS it was preparing to take off from the airport serving Rzeszów, Poland, as Flight 702, a Polish Airlines (LOT) ATR 72 was boarded by an individual who tried to enter its cockpit and to detonate a hand grenade aboard the twin-engine turboprop. The assailant was shot and wounded by security personnel and captured.

12–18 MARCH 1993

AN Ethiopian Airlines ATR 42 twin-engine turboprop on a scheduled domestic service from Gambela to Addis Ababa was commandeered by four assailants who demanded to be taken to Djibouti. The aircraft landed in Dire Dawa to refuel, but remained on the ground there for six days, during which time 15 persons managed to escape. On the final day of the ordeal, Ethiopian security forces boarded the ATR and, in an exchange of gunfire, two of the hijackers were killed and one other passenger was wounded. The other two assailants were captured, one of them having been wounded earlier while trying to escape with some of the other passengers.

27 MARCH 1993

DESIGNATED as Flight 439 on a domestic service originating at New Delhi, with an ultimate destination of Madras, an Indian Airlines A300 wide-bodied jetliner with 204 persons aboard was commandeered by a lone assailant who demanded to be taken to Lahore, Pakistan, where it was denied permission to land. The aircraft then landed at Amritsar, India, after which the hijacker demanded political asylum in Pakistan. He subsequently surrendered, and was found to have strapped to his body a hair dryer that he had claimed was a bomb.

6 APRIL 1993

A China Southern Airlines Boeing 757 jetliner was hijacked during a scheduled domestic service to Beijing from Shenzhen, Kwangtung, with 200 persons aboard. It landed on Taiwan, where the two assailants asked for political asylum. They were instead sentenced to more than ten years' imprisonment in Taiwan, although a request to extradite them back to the mainland was denied.

10 APRIL 1993

FOUR students from the Government Arts College of Lucknow protesting, among other issues, the school's existing curriculum, demonstrated their dissatisfaction by hijacking an Indian Airlines Boeing 737 jetliner that had been on a scheduled domestic service to New Delhi with 59 persons

An Air China Boeing 767, one of which was hijacked to Taiwan during an international service. (Douglas Green)

aboard. After the aircraft returned to the city of Lucknow, Uttar Pradesh, from where it had taken off earlier, the assailants were overpowered by other passengers, then arrested by police. One passenger was injured in the hijacking.

18 APRIL 1993

AN Intercontinental de Aviación DC-9 jet airliner, operating as Flight 217 on a Colombian domestic service from the city of Arauca to Bogotá with 81 persons aboard, was commandeered by a lone assailant whose only demand was to speak to César Gaviria Trujillo, then the President of Colombia. After the aircraft had landed at its intended destination, the hijacker was overpowered by the guards of a congressman who had been on the flight, and he was then arrested.

24–25 APRIL 1993

THE lone assailant who had hijacked Indian Airlines Flight 427, a twin-jet Boeing 737 carrying 141 persons on a domestic service from New Delhi to Srinagar, was killed in a commando attack at around 01:00 local time on the second day of the incident at Amritsar, Punjab, where the aircraft had set down after being denied permission to land in Pakistan. There were no other casualties. One month after the hijacking, India signed an agreement with Israel allowing the latter country's experts to train its security personnel in new techniques for screening passengers at airports, and in the use of advanced systems for detecting explosive devices.

24 JUNE 1993

A passenger armed with a pistol that was a toy and a knife that was real commandeered a Xiamen Airlines Boeing 737 jetliner carrying 76 persons on a scheduled Chinese domestic service from Changzhou, Jiangsu, to Xiamen, Fujian, in the process injuring a cabin attendant and a security guard. The aircraft landed safely at T'aipei, Taiwan, where the hijacker surrendered to the authorities and requested political asylum.

4 JULY 1993

AN attempt was made to hijack to Australia a Royal Swazi National Airways twin-jet Fokker F.28, which had taken off from Maputo, Mozambique, on a scheduled service to Manzini, Swaziland, but ended with the lone assailant being shot and wounded at Jan Smuts International Airport, serving Johannesburg, South Africa, where the aircraft had landed for refuelling. The pilot and one passenger were also wounded. The hijacker, identified as an army deserter already wanted for the murder of two police officers, had managed to smuggle a military-type rifle aboard the jet.

25 JULY 1993

AN Ethiopian Airlines Boeing 757 jetliner with 134 persons aboard on a scheduled domestic service from Dire Dawa to Addis Ababa was hijacked to Djibouti by two Ethiopian soldiers. Seeking political asylum, the assailants surrendered there after a relatively short period of negotiations.

10 AUGUST 1993

AN Air China Boeing 767 wide-bodied jet airliner, operating as Flight 973 on an international service from Beijing to Jakarta, Indonesia, with 150 persons aboard, was hijacked to Taiwan by a lone assailant. Though he fled China seeking freedom, the hijacker would end up being sentenced to prison in Taiwan for the method used in escaping his country.

14 AUGUST 1993

AEROFLOT Flight 2422 had nearly completed a Russian domestic service from St Petersburg to Moscow when a lone assailant attempted to hijack the Tu-154 jetliner to Sweden. The aircraft landed at its intended destination, after which the would-be hijacker surrendered to the authorities, while apologising to his fellow passengers.

1 SEPTEMBER 1993

A teenager armed with several blocks of TNT, a knife and a tear gas canister commandeered an Aeroflot Tu-154 jetliner that was preparing to take off from Vladivostok, Russia, on a scheduled domestic service to Yekaterinburg with 170 persons aboard. The authorities refused the aircraft permission to depart, however, and a police officer was able to sneak aboard the jetliner and knock unconscious the would-be hijacker, who was then arrested.

15 SEPTEMBER 1993

DESIGNATED as Flight 3100, an Aeroflot Tu-134 jet airliner carrying 51 persons on a service from Baku, Azerbaijan, to Perm', Russia, was diverted to Norway, where the three hijackers surrendered. Two of the assailants were Iranian nationals, although the hijacking was apparently not related to Middle East affairs.

30 SEPTEMBER 1993

TRAVELLING with his wife and eight-year-old son, a man seized a Sichuan Airlines Tupolev Tu-154M jetliner carrying 69 persons on a scheduled Chinese domestic service to Canton from Jinan, Shandong, and asked for political asylum when it landed in Taiwan. The couple would later be sentenced to prison in Taiwan, then returned separately to the mainland. In 1999 the husband unsuccessfully tried to hijack the aircraft returning him to China.

25–28 OCTOBER 1993

A Nigeria Airways A310 wide-bodied jetliner, carrying 153 persons, was commandeered during a scheduled domestic service from Lagos to Abuja. The four hijackers, who were armed with firearms and knives and had splashed petrol around in the passenger cabin, wanted to be taken to Frankfurt, Germany. The aircraft landed for refuelling at Niamey, where 125 hostages were subsequently released. Early on the final day of the hijacking, the aircraft was stormed by security forces and the four assailants were captured. However, one crew member was caught in the crossfire and killed, while five other persons were wounded, including two of the hijackers.

6 NOVEMBER 1993

A Boeing 737 jetliner of China's Xiamen Airlines, carrying 140 persons on a scheduled domestic flight from Canton to Xiamen, Fujian, was hijacked to Taiwan by a lone assailant who claimed to be armed with a bomb that turned out to be toothpaste tubes and soap. He also claimed to have been motivated by his desire to see his maternal grandfather, living in Taiwan. The hijacker was subsequently returned to the mainland.

8 NOVEMBER 1993

A lone assailant carrying a fake bomb hijacked a Zhejiang Airlines Dash 8 twin-engine turboprop that had been on a Chinese scheduled domestic service from Hangzhou, Zhejiang, to Fuzhou, Fujian, diverting the aircraft to T'aipei, Taiwan, where he surrendered. It is believed that the hijacker was returned to the mainland.

12 NOVEMBER 1993

TWO men, one of them a doctor, commandeered a China Northern Airlines twin-jet MD-82 that was on a scheduled Chinese domestic service from Changchun, Jilin, to Fuzhou, Fujian, with 82 persons aboard, diverting it to Taiwan. Both were later returned to China.

27 NOVEMBER 1993

A China Eastern Airlines twin-jet Fokker 100 was targeted for hijack by a lone assailant, who wanted to be flown to Taiwan, during a scheduled domestic service from Nanjing, Jiangxi, to Fuzhou, Fujian. The hijacker was overpowered by the crew, and the aircraft landed safely at its intended destination.

8 DECEMBER 1993

A China Northern Airlines MD-82 jetliner was commandeered during a scheduled domestic flight from Qingdao, Shandong, to Fuzhou, Fujian, with 137 persons aboard. The lone assailant slightly wounded a cabin attendant before the aircraft landed in Taiwan, where he surrendered. In line with Taiwan's policy at the time concerning Chinese hijackers, he was returned to the mainland.

10 DECEMBER 1993

AN Air France Airbus A320 jet airliner, operating as Flight 2306 on a domestic service from Paris with 129 persons aboard, was seized just before its scheduled landing at Côte d'Azur Airport, serving Nice, by a previously convicted robber who claimed to

An Air France Airbus A320, the type targeted in an unsuccessful hijacking during a domestic flight. (Airbus Industrie)

have an explosive device and wanted to be taken to Libya. After the aircraft had landed at its intended destination, the assailant released the other passengers before being captured by police. No explosive was found.

28 DECEMBER 1993

ANOTHER hijacking of a Chinese scheduled domestic flight involved a Fujian Airlines twin-engine turboprop Xian Y-7 (Yunshuji-7) en route from Ganzhou, Jiangxi, to Xiamen, Fujian, carrying 50 persons, which was commandeered and diverted to Taiwan by a couple accompanied by their child. The 'bomb' the assailants carried actually consisted of such items as batteries and nails contained in a bottle. The hijackers would be charged with air piracy by the Taiwanese authorities.

As a result of this and other recent hijackings, China would ban on its airline flights all items that could simulate or be used as weapons, including hammers and even toy firearms.

28 DECEMBER 1993

IN an event considered rare in Chinese international airline operations, an Air China Boeing 747 wide-bodied jet airliner on a scheduled service originating at Beijing, with an ultimate destination of New York City, was targeted for hijack by a lone assailant who claimed to have explosives aboard the aircraft. A search discovered no such weapons, and the jetliner landed at Shanghai as scheduled. After touching down the pilot threw the hijacker off balance by braking the aircraft suddenly.

28 DECEMBER 1993

THE third Chinese hijacking on this day involved a Xiamen Airlines Boeing 737 jetliner that was on a scheduled domestic service from Ninghe, Tianjin, to Xiamen, Fujian. An inadequate amount of fuel prevented the aircraft from proceeding to Taiwan, where the hijacker wanted to go, and it landed at its intended destination, where he was arrested.

13 JANUARY 1994

A lone assailant making rambling statements about India's alcohol, tobacco and trade policies commandeered Indian Airlines Flight 995, probably an Airbus A320 jetliner, which was carrying 60 persons on a domestic service from Madras to Calcutta. Disguising its course, the crew instead diverted to Bangalore, where the would-be hijacker was arrested.

23 JANUARY 1994

AN Ethiopian Airlines Boeing 757 jetliner carrying 43 persons on a scheduled international service from Dakar, Senegal, to Bamako, Mali, was commandeered by a former Ethiopian soldier who claimed dissatisfaction with unemployment and the political situation in his country. The hijacker surrendered after the aircraft landed at Rome, Italy.

29 JANUARY 1994

TWO men attempted to hijack to Taiwan a China Eastern Airlines aircraft, designated as Flight 5513, shortly after it had taken off from Shanghai, on a domestic service to Hangzhou, Zhejiang. The aircraft landed at its intended destination,

and while they were disembarking the two assailants – who apparently believed they were in Taiwan – were arrested. One of the hijackers would later be sentenced to life imprisonment and the other to ten years.

9 FEBRUARY 1994

AN Ethiopian Airlines Boeing 737 jetliner on a scheduled domestic service from Bahir Dar to Addis Ababa with 123 persons aboard was commandeered by two assailants who later claimed they were seeking employment in Europe. The aircraft landed to refuel in Djibouti, and after four hours of negotiations there the hijackers surrendered.

18 FEBRUARY 1994

CLOTHED in a riot police officer's uniform and accompanied by his wife, two children and foster mother, a Chinese businessman commandeered a China Southwest Airlines Boeing 737 jetliner during a scheduled domestic service from Changsha, Hunan, to Fuzhou, Fujian. The aircraft reached Taiwan, but the hijacking could hardly be considered successful. The assailant was charged with air piracy there, while the other members of his family were forcibly returned to the mainland.

28 FEBRUARY 1994

THREE Algerian police officers fleeing their country hijacked Air Algérie Flight 6165, which had been on a domestic service from Oran to Annaba with 131 persons aboard. They surrendered after the aircraft landed in southern Spain. There, they were taken into custody, but not granted political asylum.

21 MARCH 1994

A twin-jet MD-82 operated by the Italian carrier Meridiana and designated as Flight 1132 was commandeered shortly after its departure from Palermo, Sicily, on a domestic service to Rome with 160 persons aboard. It subsequently landed at its intended destination, where the lone hijacker, who was reportedly protesting 'injustices' against him by the Italian government, was arrested by police.

7 APRIL 1994

IN an apparent suicide-for-insurance scheme, an off-duty pilot who had been facing a disciplinary hearing for falsifying his employment application attacked the three regular flight crew members of Federal Express Flight 705 shortly after the DC-10 Series 30F wide-bodied cargo jet had taken off from Memphis, Tennessee, on a US domestic service to Los Angeles, California. All four men were injured, but the aircraft returned safely to its point of departure. The assailant, who had wielded a hammer and a spear-gun in the assault, was later convicted of attempted murder and attempted air piracy and sentenced to life imprisonment.

8 MAY 1994

LOCKING his fellow crew members out of the cockpit, the pilot of a Cubana de Aviación An-24 turboprop airliner that had been on a scheduled international service from Havana, Cuba, to Nassau, in the Bahamas, intentionally diverted to Miami, Florida. The pilot requested asylum in the US, while the six other crew members returned to Cuba and the 16 passengers continued on their way.

26 MAY 1994

A Vietnamese refugee being returned to his country from Indonesia splashed gasoline near the cockpit of a Garuda Indonesia jetliner and threatened to immolate himself unless taken to Australia. He was overpowered by other passengers, and the aircraft reached its intended destination safely, where the would-be hijacker was taken into custody.

7 JUNE 1994

A China Southern Airlines Boeing 737 jetliner carrying 139 persons on a scheduled domestic flight from Fuzhou, Fujian, to Canton, Kwangtung, was commandeered by a lone assailant who claimed to have a bomb. The aircraft landed at T'aipei, Taiwan, where the hijacker, whose 'bomb' consisted of a radio, surrendered, later to be returned to the mainland.

23 JUNE 1994

A lone assailant demanding to be taken to either Djibouti or Italy tried to hijack an Ethiopian Airlines ATR 42 twin-engine turboprop that had been on a scheduled domestic service from Gondar to Addis Ababa. He was instead overpowered by the co-pilot and another passenger and then tied to a seat, after which the aircraft reached its intended destination safely.

7 AUGUST 1994

A lone assailant falsely claiming to be carrying an explosive device commandeered Compañia Panameña de Aviación SA (COPA) Flight 317, a Boeing 737 jet airliner on an international service from Guatemala to Panama with 78 persons aboard. Reportedly seeking political asylum, the hijacker was captured after the aircraft had landed at Managua, Nicaragua.

21 AUGUST 1994

IN the first suspected case of its kind occurring on a regular service, the captain of a Royal Air Maroc ATR-42-300 (CN-CDT) apparently committed suicide by crashing the twin-engine turboprop airliner near Tzuonine, Morocco, some 20 miles (35km) north of Agadir, from where it had taken off about ten minutes earlier. Designated as Flight 630, and on a domestic service to Casablanca, the aircraft entered a steep dive from a height of about 15,000ft (4,500m) and plunged to earth. All 44 persons aboard (40 passengers and a crew of four) perished in the disaster, which occurred around 18:50 local time. The actions of the captain may have been motivated by a failed romance, but the Moroccan Pilot's Union found it 'difficult to accept' the conclusions of the crash investigation.

29 AUGUST 1994

THREE assailants commandeered an aircraft operated by the Paraguayan carrier Líneas Aéreas de Transporte Nacional (LATN) on a scheduled domestic service from Pedro Juan Caballero to Asunción. After they forced the crew to land at an airstrip near the Brazilian border, where a getaway vehicle was waiting, they escaped with approximately $2 million in cash that was being carried aboard the flight.

6 SEPTEMBER 1994

AN Orbi-Georgian Airlines Tu-154 jetliner nearly became a victim of aerial sabotage when a bomb was placed aboard the aircraft before its scheduled departure as Flight 936 from Tbilisi, Georgia, bound for Moscow. The bomb, which consisted of some 10lb (4.5kg) of plastic explosive, was hidden in a suitcase that another passenger had been asked to check in 'to avoid an excess baggage fee'. When the passenger could not locate the owner of the suitcase he alerted the authorities. Those responsible for the attempted bombing and their motive remained a mystery.

A high-wing, twin-turboprop ATR of the type that crashed in Morocco, apparently through the intent of the pilot. (ATR)

22 OCTOBER 1994

A scheduled intrastate flight of the Brazilian regional carrier Transportes Aéreos da Bacia Amazónica SA (TABA) was targeted for hijack by five armed men, whose interest was in the cargo being carried aboard the twin-engine turboprop DHC-8-300 Dash 8 – a shipment of gold valued at about $1 million.

The Belém-bound airliner, with 33 persons aboard, was commandeered shortly after taking off from Itaituba, Pará, and forced to return to its point of departure; the hijackers told the pilot to report that he was experiencing mechanical trouble. After it landed at Itaituba airport, the assailants removed the gold from the cargo compartment and disappeared with it into dense forest under the cover of darkness.

27 OCTOBER 1994

A passenger claiming to have an explosive device seized control of an Aeroflot Tu-154 jetliner on the ground at Vnukovo Airport, serving Moscow, prior to its departure on a scheduled Russian domestic service to Mineralnyye Vody, with 164 persons aboard. While negotiating with the authorities the assailant was struck over the head by the pilot and taken into custody. No explosive was found.

3 NOVEMBER 1994

FLIGHT 347, a Scandinavian Airlines System (SAS) MD-82 jetliner with 128 persons aboard, was hijacked during a Norwegian domestic service from Bardufoss to Oslo by a Bosnian refugee, apparently trying to draw attention to the conflict within his country. After a four-hour siege at the airport serving Gardermoen, some 20 miles (30km) north of the capital city, the lone assailant surrendered.

8 NOVEMBER 1994

AN Olympic Airways twin-jet Boeing 737 carrying 77 persons was hijacked during a scheduled service from Germany to Greece, landing at the Greek city of Salonika, where the lone assailant surrendered.

13 NOVEMBER 1994

AN Air Algérie Fokker F.27 Friendship turboprop with 38 persons aboard was hijacked during an Algerian scheduled domestic service from Algiers to Ouargla, and diverted to Majorca, Spain, where the three assailants eventually surrendered and asked for political asylum.

24 NOVEMBER 1994

A Tu-134 jetliner operated by the Russian carrier Komiavia on a scheduled service from Syktyvkar, Russia, to Minsk, Belarus, with 70 persons aboard, was hijacked by a lone assailant who demanded to be taken to Western Europe after the aircraft had landed at Tallinn, Estonia. After several hours on the ground, however, he released the other occupants and surrendered.

5 DECEMBER 1994

A husband and wife hijacking 'team' demanding to be taken to Saudi Arabia commandeered a Let L-410 twin-engine turboprop of the carrier Puntavia de Djibouti, operating as Flight 811 on a service to Djibouti from Berbera, Somalia, with six persons

aboard. The aircraft stopped to refuel at Aden, Yemen, where the couple were arrested after a period of negotiations.

15 DECEMBER 1994

A Transportes Aéreos da Bacia Amazónica SA (TABA) EMB-110 Bandeirante turboprop with nine persons aboard was hijacked by two of its passengers during a scheduled domestic service within the Brazilian state of Amazonas, from Carauari to Manaus. After setting down at an airstrip near Tabatinga, where the five other passengers were released, the aircraft proceeded to an unknown location, carrying the hijackers and the two pilots. One of the suspects was subsequently arrested by the Brazilian authorities.

23 DECEMBER 1994

A lone assailant carrying a bottle of gasoline tried to hijack to Taiwan a Tongyang Airlines Yak-42 jetliner that had been on a Chinese scheduled domestic flight from Xiamen, Fujian, to Nanjing, Jiangsu, with 64 persons aboard. He was, however, knocked down and overpowered by crew members and other passengers, and arrested after the aircraft returned to its point of departure.

4 JANUARY 1995

A couple identified as newlyweds who reportedly could not afford a trip to Egypt apparently decided to go there for free by hijacking a Sudan Airways Fokker F.27 turboprop that had been on a scheduled domestic service from Khartoum to Merowe with 38 persons aboard. The aircraft landed for refuelling at Port Sudan, and after a period of negotiations with the Sudanese authorities the couple ended their honeymoon abruptly, by being taken into custody.

10 JANUARY 1995

A Merpati Nusantara Airlines de Havilland Twin Otter Series 300 (PK-NUK), designated as Flight 6715, took off shortly before 09:00 local time on an Indonesian domestic service from Bima, on Sumbawa, to Ruteng, on Flores. Approximately half an hour later the twin-engine turboprop crashed in the Molo Strait, between the two islands. The bodies of five victims were recovered, but none of the 14 persons who had been aboard the aircraft (ten passengers and a crew of four) survived.

The investigative committee concluded that the Twin Otter had been brought down by a 'suspected explosion' in its cargo compartment, but no determination was made as to whether this was a criminal act.

17 MARCH 1995

FIVE men who were fleeing their country commandeered an Ethiopian Airlines Boeing 737 jetliner that had been on a scheduled domestic service from Addis Ababa to Bahir Dar with 92 persons aboard. The aircraft landed at El Obeid, Sudan, and after several hours of negotiations there the hijackers surrendered.

21–22 JUNE 1995

AN All Nippon Airways Boeing 747SR wide-bodied jetliner, operating as Flight 857 and carrying 365 persons, was commandeered during a Japanese domestic service from Tokyo to Hakodate, landing at its intended destination. The lone hijacker was demanding the release of the religious leader held in connection with a gas attack on a Tokyo subway that had taken 12 lives. At dawn on the second day of the hijacking police rushed the aircraft and arrested the assailant, who was injured along with a flight attendant and several other passengers. A 'nervous' disorder was believed to be the underlying factor in the behaviour of the hijacker, rather than some political motive.

1 JULY 1995

HIJACKING for ransom was the motive in the commandeering of a Domodedovo Airlines Il-62 jetliner, designated as Flight 96 and on a Russian domestic service from Yakutsk to Moscow with 184 persons aboard. After the aircraft had landed at the northern city of Noril'sk and a demand for 1.5 million roubles had been made, the authorities captured the hijacker quickly and peacefully.

30 JULY 1995

A single-engine turboprop Cessna Caravan operated by the Nicaraguan carrier La Costeña on a domestic commuter flight from Managua to Bluefields was hijacked by suspected drug traffickers. Two days later, the body of the pilot was found at Zipaquirá, Cundinamarca, Colombia, having been shot to death.

The aeroplane had been chartered and then stolen, with the admitted assistance of the co-pilot, for use in drug-running operations.

3 AUGUST 1995

A lone assailant who claimed to have a bomb tried to hijack a China Eastern Airlines A300 wide-bodied jetliner that was on a scheduled domestic service from Shanghai to Canton. Ignoring his demand to fly him to Taiwan, the pilot landed at Hangzhou, in the province of Zhejiang, where the hijacker was captured by security personnel.

24 AUGUST 1995

IN a brazen in-flight attack, three assailants seriously wounded a member of the ruling Pakistan People's Party aboard a Pakistan International Airlines Fokker F.27 turboprop that had been on a scheduled domestic service from Islamabad to Faisalabad. Security personnel quickly intervened, killing two of the attackers and wounding the third. There were no other casualties, and the aircraft returned safely to its point of departure.

31 AUGUST 1995

A BN-2A Islander operated by a Papua New Guinea carrier was commandeered by three armed men during an intra-island commuter service from Port Moresby to Asimba. After the twin-engine aircraft was forced to land at an airstrip, the assailants, who were believed to have been gang members, robbed the pilot and the other three passengers and escaped into the bush.

3 SEPTEMBER 1995

OPERATING as Flight 4617 on an international service to Paris from Palma de Mallorca, in the (Spanish) Balearic Islands, an Air Inter Airbus A300 wide-bodied jet with 298 persons aboard was commandeered by a man protesting against France's resumption of nuclear tests in the South Pacific. The French aircraft landed at Geneva, Switzerland, where the hijacker, who claimed to have a remote-controlled bomb that was actually a mobile telephone with batteries strapped to it, was apprehended.

9 NOVEMBER 1995

AN Olympic Airways Boeing 747 was seized by an Ethiopian man who, saying he did not want to return to his country, held a knife to the throat of a stewardess about 30 minutes before the Greek-registered wide-bodied jetliner, designated as Flight 472 and carrying 114 persons, was to have landed at Athens during an international service from Sydney, Australia. After landing at the flight's intended destination, the hijacker was arrested by police.

6 JANUARY 1996

BELYING the rash of hijackings from mainland China, this attempt to take an aircraft in the opposite direction involved Transavia Airways Flight 529, an Airbus A321 jetliner on a domestic Taiwanese service from T'aipei to T'ainan with 203 persons aboard. The lone assailant, who had demanded to be flown to the mainland, allowed the aircraft to land at T'ainan for refuelling. It was there that he was arrested.

8–9 MARCH 1996

AFTER it had taken off from Ercan, Cyprus, operating on an international service to Istanbul as Flight 007, a Kibris Turk Hava Yollari (Cyprus Turkish Airlines) Boeing 727 jet with 109 persons aboard was commandeered by a lone assailant using a fake pistol. The aircraft was diverted to Munich, Germany, where the following day the hijacker was arrested after releasing all his hostages. He would later be sentenced to nearly seven years of youth custody.

10 MARCH 1996

TWO couples accompanied by two children and armed with knives and dynamite attempted to divert to Taiwan a Hainan Airlines Boeing 737 jetliner that was carrying 149 persons on a Chinese scheduled domestic service to the island of Hainan from Yiwu, Zhejiang. The hijacking was thwarted by security personnel and the aircraft landed at Zhuhai, on the mainland.

24 MARCH 1996

A Sudan Airways twin-jet Airbus A320 jetliner, on a scheduled flight from Khartoum to Port Sudan with 47 persons aboard, was hijacked by two assailants. The aircraft landed at Asmara, the capital of Eritrea, where the hijackers surrendered. They would later be granted asylum by the Eritrean government.

4 APRIL 1996

A Biman Bangladesh Airlines British Aerospace ATP twin-engine turboprop on a scheduled domestic service from Dhaka to Barisal was hijacked by a passenger who claimed to have a revolver and explosives in a bag (which actually contained bananas), and who demanded to be flown to India. He was

A version of the British Aerospace ATP, the type involved in the unsuccessful hijacking in Bangladesh. (Douglas Green)

overpowered, however, and the aircraft landed safely at its intended destination.

14 APRIL 1996

THREE assailants commandeered a twin-engine Cessna 402 on a domestic commuter service within Papua New Guinea, from Port Moresby to Wau, forcing it to land at an abandoned airstrip in the country's Eastern Highlands province. After stealing approximately $25,000 from the aeroplane and its other three occupants, they fled into the bush. Although they were subsequently captured, the hijackers managed to break out of jail and again escaped, this time for good.

7 JULY 1996

AN antique single-engine An-2 flown by the Cuban carrier Cubanacan and carrying eight persons on a scheduled domestic service originating at Bayamo, with an ultimate destination of Moa, was hijacked by an armed assailant, landing at the US Naval base at Guantanamo Bay. The hijacker, who was identified as a Cuban Interior Ministry official, asked for political asylum from the American authorities; instead, he was arraigned in a US district court on the charge of air piracy.

25 JULY 1996

A lone assailant who claimed to have a bomb that was not real commandeered an Air Algérie Boeing 767 wide-bodied jet airliner prior to its departure from Oran, Algeria, on a scheduled domestic service to Algiers with 232 persons aboard, demanding to be taken to the US. After more than four hours of negotiations the would-be hijacker was taken into custody.

9 AUGUST 1996

AN attempt to hijack to Morocco an Air Mauritanie F.28 jetliner was made by an armed assailant during a scheduled flight from Las Palmas, in the (Spanish) Canary Islands, to the Mauritanian capital of Nouakchott, but he was overpowered by the pilot, after which the aircraft landed safely at its intended destination.

13 AUGUST 1996

AN Airbus A320 jetliner of the French domestic carrier Air Inter was robbed on the ground after it had landed at Llabanere Airport, serving Perpignan, Languedoc-Roussillon, following a scheduled domestic service from Paris. After stopping the taxiing aircraft, the armed assailants opened its baggage compartment and stole nearly $1 million before they escaped.

17 OCTOBER 1996

A passenger who claimed to have a knife attempted to take over an Aeroflot Tu-154 jetliner, operating as Flight 417 and carrying 180 persons, after the Russian jet airliner had taken off from Valletta, Malta, an en-route stop during an international service originating at Moscow, with an ultimate destination of Lagos, Nigeria. He was overpowered and captured by two Austrian police officers who happened to be on the flight on an unrelated assignment.

2 NOVEMBER 1996

AN attempt by drug traffickers to commandeer and steal a Cessna Caravan operated by the carrier Brasil Central Linha Aérea Regional, on a Brazilian domestic service from Brasilia to Cuiabá, Mato Grosso, was thwarted after federal police were tipped off about the plan. The four would-be hijackers were captured on the ground during an en-route stop at Barra do Garças, Mato Grosso, and two other conspirators were arrested at a small airfield where the single-engine turboprop was to have landed for refuelling.

15 NOVEMBER 1996

A passenger reportedly facing domestic problems tried to hijack a Xiamen Airlines Boeing 757 jetliner that had been on a Chinese scheduled domestic service from Canton to Xiamen, Fujian, with 171 persons aboard. Although he demanded to be taken to Taiwan, the pilot instead continued on towards the intended destination of the flight, reaching it safely after members of the crew and other passengers had overpowered the assailant.

27 NOVEMBER 1996

A Roraima Air Charter BN-2A Islander that had been leased the previous day was commandeered during a domestic service to Georgetown, Guyana, then forced to return to Kwebanna, from where it had taken off shortly before. After the two pilots and one other passenger were removed from the Islander, the twin-engine aircraft and its remaining four occupants took off again and proceeded in a westerly direction. But it may not have reached wherever it was going, as an emergency signal emanating from it was identified several days later, possibly indicating that it had crashed some 50 miles (80km) east of the capital city.

30 NOVEMBER 1996

IN an apparent sabotage attempt, an incendiary device was found in a suitcase that had been removed from an All Nippon Airways jetliner at Matsuyama, Ehime, Japan, after the passenger to which it belonged failed to board the aircraft, which had been on a scheduled domestic service to the city of Osaka. Neither the assailant nor the motive were identified.

6 DECEMBER 1996

DEMANDING to be flown to The Netherlands, a lone assailant burst into the cockpit of a Krasnoyarskie Avialinni Yak-40 as the Russian jet airliner was on a scheduled domestic service from Krasnoyarsk to Boguchany. He was overpowered and restrained, then turned over to the authorities after the aircraft landed.

7 JANUARY 1997

A Bosnian refugee who had been facing deportation, and who was intoxicated and armed with a wooden baton and a small knife, seized Austrian Airlines Flight 104, a twin-jet MD-87 with 33 persons aboard, en route to Vienna from Berlin. The aircraft returned to its point of departure, landing at Tegel Airport, where, jumped by police commandos, the hijacker was overpowered and detained after tumbling out of an open door on to the tarmac. He was subsequently sentenced to seven years' imprisonment.

20 JANUARY 1997

DEMANDING to be flown to the US, a knife-wielding assailant commandeered an All Nippon Airways Boeing 777 wide-bodied jetliner that was on a Japanese scheduled domestic service from Osaka to Fukuoka with 192 persons aboard. After being convinced that the aircraft had to land at its intended destination for refuelling, the hijacker tried to escape with other passengers who he had agreed to release, but was captured by members of the crew and turned over to the police.

22 JANUARY 1997

A knife-wielding assailant commandeered an Air Nelson Saab 340 twin-engine turboprop at the airport serving Nelson, on New Zealand's South Island, where the airliner had just landed at the end of a scheduled domestic service from Auckland. Initially taking hostage the aircraft's three crew members, he later complied with a request to put down his weapon, and was taken into custody.

10 FEBRUARY 1997

A China Northwest Airlines jetliner, probably an Airbus, which was carrying 173 persons and on a scheduled domestic service from Chungking, Sichuan, to Zhuhai, Kwangtung, was targeted for hijack by a lone assailant who claimed he had explosives and demanded to be flown to Taiwan. The pilot reportedly manoeuvred the aircraft violently and threw the hijacker off balance, allowing for his capture, then made an emergency landing at Baiyan Airport, serving Canton.

10 MARCH 1997

AMID a string of hijackings from China to Taiwan, this was the first successful case in more than a decade that had an aircraft going in the opposite direction. A lone assailant who said he was a victim of political repression doused himself with gasoline and commandeered a Far Eastern Air Transport Boeing 757 jetliner, designated as Flight 128 and on a domestic service from Kaohsiung to T'aipei with 156 persons aboard. The aircraft landed at Xiamen, in the Chinese province of Fujian, where the hijacker was taken into custody.

15 APRIL 1997

A vintage DC-3 twin-engine transport was commandeered at a small village in south-central Congo and then forced to fly to Kinshasa by approximately half-a-dozen Congolese military personnel, who were arrested by Presidential Guard troops upon its landing at the capital city.

2 JUNE 1997

AN attempt was made by a Chinese woman to hijack to Taiwan an Air China wide-bodied jet airliner, apparently a Boeing 747, which was on a domestic service from Beijing to Canton as Flight 1301. Although no details are available as to exactly what transpired aboard the aircraft, it subsequently landed at Wuhan,

A BN-2A Islander, one of which was hijacked, stolen and apparently destroyed in Guyana (Douglas Green)

A Fokker 100, the type targeted in bombing during a Brazilian domestic flight. (Fokker Aircraft)

in the province of Hubei, where the assailant was taken into custody, apparently without further incident.

9 JUNE 1997

AN Air Malta Boeing 737 jet airliner, designated as Flight 830 and carrying 80 persons, was commandeered during a service from Valletta, Malta, to Istanbul, Turkey, and diverted to Cologne, Germany. There the two hijackers, who had initially expressed a desire to show their support for the man serving a life prison term in Italy for the attempted assassination of the Pope 16 years earlier, freed their hostages and surrendered.

The explosives reportedly being carried by the assailants turned out to be fake, as might have been the motive of the two men, who, it was suspected, having been denied refugee status in Malta simply did not want to return to Turkey.

11 JUNE 1997

IN an apparent act of vandalism, wires were cut in the front belly section, underneath the cockpit, of a Pan American World Airways Airbus A300 at John F. Kennedy International Airport, serving New York City. The damage was discovered by a maintenance worker at around 05:30 local time, three hours before the wide-bodied jetliner had been scheduled to depart, as Flight 21, on a domestic service to Miami, Florida.

9 JULY 1997

AN explosion occurred in the fuselage of a Transportes Aéreos Regionais SA (TAM) Fokker 100 jetliner, designated as Flight 283, on a Brazilian domestic intra-state service from São José dos Campos to São Paulo with 60 persons aboard, including a crew of five. One passenger was ejected from the aircraft and killed; his body was found in a field some 30 miles (50km) from the flight's destination. Six others suffered injuries in the blast, which occurred at around 08:50 local time. Despite considerable damage, with a hole measuring about 6ft by 6ft (1.8m by 1.8m) having been punched in its fuselage, the Fokker landed safely at Congonhas Airport, serving São Paulo.

The explosion was later determined to have been caused by a bomb that had detonated under a seat in the rear cabin area as the jetliner was at an approximate height of 7,500ft (2,300m). Reportedly the device had been planted by a passenger, though not the one killed, in a failed suicide attempt. He would later be charged with murder and other crimes. Within two days of the bombing, plans were announced to improve security at major airports throughout Brazil.

9 AUGUST 1997

AN Air Gabon Boeing 727 jet airliner on an international charter service from Franceville, Gabon, to Kigali, Rwanda, was commandeered by its passengers, who consisted of more than 100 Rwandan refugees being repatriated to their country. The aircraft returned to its point of departure and was surrounded by Gabonese soldiers, who ended the seizure.

12 AUGUST 1997

IN what may have been a case of a hijacking being successfully averted, a passenger carrying a knife, a flare gun and 21 flares, who had boarded a US Airways flight at the international airport serving Philadelphia, Pennsylvania, was removed from the aircraft after a cabin attendant reportedly heard him use the word 'hijack' prior to take-off.

10 DECEMBER 1997

COMMANDOS overpowered the hijacker of a Rossiya Airlines Il-62. The assailant, claiming to be wired with explosives, had demanded $10 million and safe passage to Switzerland after the Russian jetliner, with 155 persons aboard, landed at Sheremet'yevo Airport, serving Moscow. When commandeered the aircraft had been on a scheduled domestic service to the capital from Magadan.

19 DECEMBER 1997

AS described in other chapters, commercial aviation had already had to deal with suicidal passengers who intentionally brought down aircraft. But the prospect of a suicidal pilot may be too frightening for air travellers to consider. A crash occurring in Morocco in 1994 (see page 177) was believed to have resulted from pilot suicide, and a similar act of personal destruction was considered a strong possibility in the disaster that befell SilkAir Pte Ltd Flight 185.

The Singaporean-registered Boeing 737-36N (9V-TRF) had taken off from Jakarta, Indonesia, bound for Singapore. About half an hour later, at around 16:15 local time, the jet airliner entered a rapid descent from its cruising height of 35,000ft (10,700m) and then plunged into the River Musi near Sungsang, on the Indonesian island of Sumatra, and some 30 miles (50km) north-north-east of the city of Palembang. All 104 persons aboard the aircraft (97 passengers and a crew of seven) perished.

The force of the high-speed impact was such that the 737 actually penetrated the riverbed, beneath about 30ft (9m) of water. The human side of the disaster was reflected by the fact that only six of the victims could be identified. Based on weight, nearly three-quarters of the aircraft's wreckage was ultimately recovered. Although sections of both horizontal stabilisers and the corresponding elevators were found some distance from the main crash site, their in-flight separation must have resulted from the supersonic speed attained by 9V-TRF during the descent rather than from some prior defect. Nor was there evidence of in-flight fire or explosion, or any other major technical failure in the 737.

Hampering the investigation, though perhaps significant to the disaster, was the stoppage of both the aircraft's cockpit voice (CVR) and flight data (FDR) recorders. Occurring less than ten minutes before the crash, the stoppage of the CVR could have resulted from a technical failure or from the intentional pulling of the circuit breaker on the panel located directly behind the captain's seat, while the FDR could have stopped recording due to a loss of its power supply or a malfunction in the unit itself. The reason they did not stop simultaneously could not be established. Among the last sounds transcribed by the CVR were the captain voicing his intention to exit the flight deck, and a metallic snap, which could have been caused by a seat belt hitting against something. However, there was no indication of him actually leaving the cockpit. (Presumably the intentional crashing of the aircraft would have involved the incapacitation of the first officer in some manner.)

Officially, the cause of the disaster was considered unexplained, and in its report the Indonesian National Transportation Safety Committee (NTSC) emphasised that there was no evidence to establish positively that the final descent of the 737 had been intentional. In defence of one of its operators, the Singaporean authorities actually raised the issue of a possible weather factor by noting that another flight had reported thunderstorm activity some ten miles (16km) east of the track of 9V-TRF. However, the meteorological conditions in the immediate area were good, with scattered clouds and no reported turbulence. Representing the nation of manufacture, the US National Transportation Safety Board (NTSB) expressed the belief that the aircraft had been responding to the flight controls being manipulated by one or both of the pilots. The NTSC did note that simulations using radar data pointed to the combination of control inputs together with the horizontal stabiliser being moved to its forward manual and electrical nose-down limit as one possible reason for the dive.

Along with the technical aspects of the crash, the investigation carefully examined the background of the 41-year-old pilot of Flight 185, Captain Tsu Way Minh. At the time of his death, a securities-trading account he was operating had accrued increasing losses over a period going back four years. Additionally, Captain Tsu had experienced several operational-related events, including an overweight landing that led to his removal as a line instructor pilot. And although his superiors, colleagues, friends and family had not reported any changes in his personal behaviour, a separate report disclosed that he had been quieter in the days preceding his death.

The nation of registry received a certain measure of support when, in October 2001, a Singaporean court dismissed a lawsuit against the airline brought by families of some of the victims, ruling that there was no evidence that Captain Tsu had intentionally crashed the aircraft.

19 DECEMBER 1997

HIJACKED during a scheduled Peruvian domestic service from Lima to Chimbote, a twin-engine turboprop Beechcraft Super King Air 200 flown by the carrier Aero Cóndor SA was damaged in a take-off crash near Huarmey, Ancash, Peru. The aircraft had been commandeered by four of its 11 passengers and forced to land in a field, and as it was taking off its left main undercarriage leg struck a hole and collapsed. There were no injuries in the morning accident, although the co-pilot had been wounded in an earlier altercation. The hijackers escaped with some $1 million in goods stolen from the aircraft.

22 DECEMBER 1997

THIS attempted diversion to Taiwan ended in the death of the would-be hijacker of a China Eastern Airlines A300 wide-bodied jetliner, operating as Flight 5915 on a domestic service from Shanghai to Xiamen, Fujian. When the crew prepared to land at the intended destination, a struggle erupted between security personnel and the assailant, and the latter was shot and killed. There were no other casualties, and the aircraft got down safely.

A Beechcraft Super King Air 200, identical to the aircraft hijacked and damaged in Peru. (Beech Aircraft Corporation)

22–23 DECEMBER 1997

IN what may have been a hijacking and aerial theft, a twin-jet Antonov An-72 (ER-ACF) operated by the Moldovan carrier Renan vanished with 11 persons aboard during a non-scheduled service from Abidjan, Côte-d'Ivoire, to Runtu, Namibia. The aircraft was reported to have landed at the 'Alpha' base in Angola, from where it departed around 11:30 local time on the second day. It may have been subsequently abandoned somewhere in Angola.

According to one source, ER-ACF had been carrying a large amount in US dollars, and may have been commandeered or otherwise diverted with the intention of stealing the cargo. It was further reported that the aircraft's occupants may have been murdered.

31 JANUARY 1998

AN Atlantic Airlines Let L-410 twin-engine turboprop carrying 21 persons on a scheduled domestic service from Bluefields to the Nicaraguan island of Little Corn was commandeered by a reportedly mentally unstable drug addict. As it did not have sufficient fuel to reach the Colombian island of San Andrés, where the hijacker wanted to go, the aircraft landed at Limón, Costa Rica, where he was arrested.

23 MARCH 1998

IN an attempted act of suicide, a passenger poured gasoline in the cabin of a Great China Airlines Dash 8 twin-engine turboprop that was on a scheduled domestic Taiwanese service from T'aipei to Chiayi with 20 persons aboard. Fortunately, however, he was stopped by others, including a security guard, before he could start a fire. The aircraft landed safely and there were no injuries.

30 MARCH 1998

A lone assailant who wanted to be flown to Germany commandeered a Kibris Turk Hava Yollari (Cyprus Turkish Airlines) Boeing 727 jetliner carrying 105 persons on an international service from Cyprus to Ankara, Turkey. Persuaded by the pilot that the aircraft had to land for refuelling, the hijacker was overpowered by security forces at its intended destination.

10 MAY 1998

A Lockheed L-1011 TriStar wide-bodied jet airliner operated by the Portuguese airline Air Luxor was commandeered by a lone assailant while preparing for departure from Lester B. Pearson International Airport, serving Toronto, Ontario, Canada, on a transatlantic service to Lisbon, Portugal. Locking himself in the cockpit and demanding to be taken to Chicago, in the US, he was subsequently captured by police. Due to his psychiatric record, charges against him would later be dropped.

25 MAY 1998

THREE men protesting Pakistan's plans to test nuclear devices, and demanding $20 million for development in their native province of Baluchistan, seized a Pakistan International Airlines Fokker F.27 Friendship, designated as Flight 554 and on a domestic service from Karachi to Turbat with 29 persons aboard. The turboprop transport landed at Hyderabad, Pakistan, where the hijackers, apparently believing they were in India, were overpowered by commandos. One soldier was reportedly shot and wounded.

23 JUNE 1998

CLAIMING to have an explosive device that turned out to be a television remote control unit, a passenger who was identified as a psychiatric patient commandeered an Iberia Boeing 727 jetliner carrying 131 persons, operating as Flight 1121 and en route from Sevilla to Barcelona, Spain, the domestic segment of an international service with an ultimate destination of Amsterdam, The Netherlands. The Spanish aircraft landed at the city of Valencia in Spain, where the hijacker surrendered after speaking to his psychiatrist.

25 JULY 1998

FOUR armed assailants seized an Aviones de Oriente (AVIOR) Beechcraft 1900D twin-engine turboprop that was on a scheduled domestic service from Caracas to the Venezuelan state of Barinas with 22 persons aboard. The aircraft landed at a cattle ranch, where the other occupants were released, and was then flown by the hijackers to Colombia, where it was located the following month. Two suspects were arrested in connection with the hijacking.

2 AUGUST 1998

DURING fighting between rebel and government forces, a commercial jet and its crew was commandeered at Goma, in the Congo, with the purpose of transporting troops and supplies. The Boeing 727, operated by Blue Airlines, a Congolese carrier, successfully completed its flights.

4 AUGUST 1998

TWO more Congolese commercial jets were hijacked, in a sense, by government forces, with the intention of transporting troops and their supplies. Both aircraft, a Congo Air Cargo Boeing 707 and what was believed to have been another 707 flown by Lignes Aériennes Congolaises (Congo Airlines), were seized at Goma and forced to fly to Kitona, also in the western part of the country.

14 SEPTEMBER 1998

REPORTEDLY protesting the Turkish government's ban on women wearing traditional Islamic head covering at the nation's universities, a lone assailant armed with what turned out to be a toy gun commandeered Turkish Airlines (THY) Flight 145, an A310 wide-bodied jetliner on a domestic service from Ankara to Istanbul with 84 persons aboard. He surrendered after the aircraft landed at Trabzon, Turkey.

28 OCTOBER 1998

OPERATING as Flight 905 and en route from Beijing to K'unming, in the Chinese province of Yunnan, with an ultimate destination of Yangon, Myanmar, an Air China twin-jet Boeing 737 carrying 103 persons was diverted to Taiwan by the pilot, who was accompanied by his wife and child. The aircraft safely reached T'aipei, and the pilot would later be indicted on the charge of hijacking.

29–30 OCTOBER 1998

ANOTHER protest against the government of Turkey, this time concerning its conflict with the country's ethnic Kurds, was the motivating factor in the hijacking of a Turkish Airlines (THY) Boeing 737 jetliner, designated as Flight 487 and on a domestic service from Adana to Ankara with 40 persons aboard.

Armed with a pistol and a hand grenade, the lone assailant demanded to be taken to Switzerland, but agreed to allow the aircraft to land for refuelling at Sofia, Bulgaria. In the darkness, the pilot actually landed at the flight's intended destination, unbeknown to the hijacker, who was killed in the aircraft's cockpit by a special police team early on the morning of the second day of the seizure, after a stand-off lasting some seven hours. A review of security measures at Turkish airports was subsequently announced by the country's transport minister.

5 DECEMBER 1998

A passenger who had been harassing others aboard a MALEV Hungarian Airlines jetliner, believed to have been a wide-bodied Boeing 767, during a scheduled flight to Budapest from Bangkok carrying 190 persons, was injected with a tranquiliser by a doctor in order to bring him under control. However, the passenger died before the aircraft landed at Istanbul, Turkey, where the doctor, six other passengers and six crew members were detained for questioning.

4 JANUARY 1999

A Kenya Airways Boeing 737 jetliner was targeted in a brazen act of robbery at Murtala Mohammed Airport, serving Lagos, Nigeria. Having just landed following an international service from Nairobi, Kenya, as Flight 432, the aircraft was taxiing to the terminal shortly before midnight when it came across several large pieces of wood blocking its path. While the pilot was communicating with the control tower about the situation, the 737 was robbed by approximately a dozen assailants, who forced open the aircraft's cargo hold and removed as much luggage as possible. The thieves then escaped into the darkness. None of the 104 persons aboard the jetliner were harmed.

12 JANUARY 1999

DESIGNATED as Flight 923, a Southwest Airlines Boeing 737 jetliner carrying 79 persons on a domestic intra-state service within California, from San Diego to San José, was disrupted by a passenger who reportedly threatened members of the crew and asked to be taken 'to Hollywood'. The 737 diverted safely to Burbank, where the suspect was taken into custody. Later in the year, he pleaded guilty to a felony charge of interfering with an aircraft crew and was sentenced to two years in prison.

9 FEBRUARY 1999

FOUR Chinese nationals who had previously hijacked aircraft to Taiwan and were being returned to the mainland tried to commandeer the Taiwanese Dash 8 twin-engine turboprop that was taking them back. As the aircraft was landing at the airport serving Chinmen, Fujian, one of the four men stabbed a Taiwanese official with a sharpened piece of metal, although the victim was not seriously injured. He was overpowered, and similar crude weapons were found on the other three prisoners.

17 FEBRUARY 1999

THIEVES disguised as airline employees stole approximately $1.6 million in cash that was being transferred from an armoured car to a Virgin Express twin-jet Boeing 737 at Brussels National Airport, Belgium. The robbery occurred prior to the departure of the Belgian aircraft on a scheduled service to London, and before the passengers had boarded. The crew members were aboard but were unaware of the heist.

2 MARCH 1999

A lone assailant who claimed to have a bomb commandeered Air France Flight 5029, an A320 jetliner carrying some 80 persons on a domestic service from Marseilles to Orly Airport, serving Paris. The aircraft was diverted to Charles de Gaulle Airport, near the French capital, where the hijacker surrendered after several hours of negotiations. He was determined to be mentally ill.

5 MARCH 1999

THE kidnapping of a Russian high-ranking officer was the motive behind this seizure of an Askhab Airlines Tu-134 jetliner at Severnyy Airport, serving Groznyy, in the breakaway Russian republic of Chechnya. As it taxied to take-off on a scheduled domestic service to Moscow, the aircraft was forced to stop by a number of assailants, who were believed to have been anti-Russian radical Islamic fundamentalists, who then took with them one of the passengers on the flight, Major-General Gennadiy Shpigun.

12 APRIL 1999

AN Aerovías Nacionales de Colombia (AVIANCA) Fokker 50, operating as Flight 9463 on a domestic Colombian service from Bucaramanga to Bogotá, was hijacked by five members of the National Liberation Army (ELN). The twin-engine turboprop airliner, with 46 persons aboard, was forced to land at an airstrip near the town of Simití, Bolívar, some 80 miles (130km) north-west of Bucaramanga, where its occupants were placed on rafts and kidnapped by at least 50 armed guerrillas who must have been waiting on the ground. One of the passengers died, apparently due to some medical reason, on 9 June. The remaining hostages were eventually released, though some were held for as long as 18 months.

In November 1999 the Colombian authorities, who had previously refused to negotiate with the ELN, arrested 13 suspects believed to have been involved in the hijacking of Flight 9463. One rebel jailed in Venezuela also faced extradition to Colombia for his suspected involvement.

12 JUNE 1999

A knife-wielding assailant attempted to hijack to Taiwan a Xiamen Airlines Boeing 737 jetliner, designated as Flight 8502 and on a Chinese domestic service from Shanghai to Xiamen, Fujian, with 75 persons aboard. He was subdued by security personnel after a scuffle in which he was slightly injured.

12 JUNE 1999

AS they were fleeing advancing rebel forces, approximately 100 Congolese soldiers, who had taken hostage women gathered from surrounding villages, seized a Lignes Aériennes

Congolaises (Congo Airlines) jetliner at the airport serving Gemena, Congo. After the passengers already aboard it were forced to disembark, the aircraft was flown to the capital city of Kinshasa, where the unruly soldiers were 'subdued'.

23 JULY 1999

ALTHOUGH Japan had experienced relatively few hijackings in its domestic airline operations, it came frighteningly close to suffering one of the worst acts of aerial terrorism in history as a result of this bizarre incident involving an All Nippon Airways Boeing 747-481D wide-bodied jetliner. Operating as Flight 61 and carrying 517 persons, including 14 crew members, the aircraft had taken off from Tokyo, bound for Sapporo, on the northern Japanese island of Hokkaido.

Approximately two minutes after departure, a lone assailant produced a kitchen knife with a blade 8in (200mm) long and demanded to be taken to the flight deck. He then ordered the first officer out of the cockpit, and asked the captain to fly to three different locations. After refusing the hijacker's request to take control of the aircraft himself, the captain was stabbed to death, whereupon the 747 went into a descent. The co-pilot and others returned to the cockpit just in time, reportedly regaining control of the jetliner at a height of only about 600ft (180m). The aircraft returned safely to Tokyo's international airport, landing less than an hour after the hijacking had begun, around midday.

In a final twist of irony, the assailant said he was protesting lax security at Japanese airports. Considered guilty of aerial piracy and murder while being of 'unsound' mind, he was subsequently sentenced to life imprisonment.

30 JULY 1999

THE Colombian guerrilla organisation FARC was believed responsible for the hijacking of an Aviones de Oriente (AVIOR) Beechcraft 1900D twin-engine turboprop carrying 14 persons on a scheduled Venezuelan domestic service originating at Caracas and ultimately bound for Guasdualito, in the state of Apure. Forced to land in the Colombian state of Arauca, the two pilots were allowed to fly the commuter airliner to its intended destination about a week later. The eight passengers were also released on the same day.

25 AUGUST 1999

Royal Air Maroc Flight 572, a Boeing 737 jetliner carrying 88 persons on an international service from Casablanca, Morocco, to Tunis, Tunisia, was hijacked by a lone assailant who wanted to be taken to Germany. The aircraft landed at Barcelona, Spain, where, after five hours of negotiations, he surrendered.

28 AUGUST 1999

FIVE men armed with pistols and knives commandeered a Missionary Aviation Fellowship (MAF) Twin Otter turboprop at a remote airstrip at Lake Kopiago, a town in the mountains of central Papua New Guinea. The assailants then forced the Australian-registered aircraft, carrying them and 14 others, to fly to an airstrip at Fugwa, about 25 miles (40km) south of the lake, robbing some of the passengers in the process. After the Twin Otter had landed the hijackers fled, having wounded the steward.

11 OCTOBER 1999

ALTHOUGH pilot suicide had been suspected in at least three previous airline crashes, an airman's own admission of his wish to kill himself came before he wreaked havoc at Sir Seretse Khama Airport, serving Gaborone, Botswana, using a stolen airliner. Having been grounded earlier for medical reasons, the Air Botswana captain took off from the airport in a twin-engine turboprop ATR 42-312 (A2-ABB) that was part of his company's fleet.

For a period of two hours he circled the city, announcing his intention to commit suicide and demanding to speak with the nation's vice president. He then threatened to crash into the building housing the airline's office located near the airport. Finally, he set down the ATR on the airport ramp, in the process slamming into two other Air Botswana aircraft of the same type. The pilot was killed in the fiery crash, which occurred shortly before 08:00 local time. Despite the destruction of three of the carrier's aircraft, which was nearly its entire fleet at the time, there were no other human casualties.

23 NOVEMBER 1999

A lone assailant attempted to hijack to Taiwan a Zhejiang Airlines Dash 8 twin-engine turboprop that had been on a Chinese scheduled domestic flight from Yiwu, Zhejiang, to Xiamen, Fujian, but he was overpowered by crew members. Several passengers were reportedly injured when they tried to exit the aircraft while it was still taxiing after it had landed at its intended destination.

28 DECEMBER 1999

DESIGNATED as Flight 5293 and on an international service from Prague, Czech Republic, to Düsseldorf, Germany, a Lufthansa CityLine Regional Jet with 23 persons aboard was targeted for hijack by a lone assailant who wanted to be taken to the United Kingdom. Due to insufficient fuel, the German-registered and Canadian-built twin-jet airliner landed at its intended destination, where the would-be hijacker, who had lied about being armed, surrendered to police.

19 FEBRUARY 2000

A prisoner being escorted by two police guards but who was not handcuffed produced a knife and commandeered an Aerotransportes Casanare SA (Aerotaca) Beechcraft 1900D twin-engine turboprop that was on a scheduled domestic Colombian service from Bucaramanga to Cúcuta with 19 persons aboard. The aircraft was forced to land at an airstrip near El Tornillo, located some 100 miles (160km) north of Bogotá, after which the hijacker fled into the jungle. However, he was killed by a paramilitary group, which also freed the guard whom he had taken hostage.

29 FEBRUARY 2000

A lone assailant who reportedly had a history of psychological problems, and who was carrying a bottle of gasoline, a cigarette lighter and a knife, tried to hijack to Taiwan a China Southwest Airlines Boeing 737 jetliner during a scheduled domestic service from Nanchang, Jiangxi, to Fuzhou, Fujian, but was overpowered, possibly by security personnel, after which the aircraft landed at its intended destination.

A Beechcraft 1900 of the type involved in two terrorist hijackings in Colombia during a seven-month period.
(Beech Aircraft Corporation)

16 MARCH 2000

A passenger who had been disruptive aboard Alaska Airlines Flight 259 became potentially dangerous when he forced his way into the cockpit of the McDonnell Douglas MD-80 jetliner, which was carrying 48 persons on an international service from Puerto Vallarta, Jalisco, Mexico, to San Francisco, California. The first officer struck him with a fire axe before being injured himself, after which the assailant was subdued with the help of other passengers. The aircraft, which at the time of the incident had been some 100 miles (160km) south of its destination, diverted to San José, also in California, and the assailant was taken to a hospital for observation.

In view of his mental condition, which had been influenced by encephalitis, an agreement was made for him not to be prosecuted, depending upon his future behaviour.

27 MARCH 2000

AN apparently drunk and possibly suicidal passenger forced his way into the cockpit of a Boeing 737 jetliner, operating as Flight 1407 of the German carrier LTU International Airways and en route to Berlin from the (Spanish) Canary Islands with 148 persons aboard, attacking and injuring the captain. The aircraft briefly lost altitude before passengers and other crew members were able to subdue the assailant, after which the co-pilot completed the flight to its intended destination. As the passenger was diagnosed with a psychotic disorder, a German court declined to prosecute him, instead recommending psychiatric treatment.

22 MAY 2000

A Missionary Aviation Fellowship (MAF) BN-2A Islander was commandeered during an internal service within Papua New Guinea, from Erave to Batiri, by three assailants who damaged the aircraft's communications equipment and robbed the passengers. After forcing the Australian-registered aircraft to return to its point of departure, the hijackers escaped. Subsequently, the operator suspended service on certain routes within the country.

30 MAY 2000

AFTER a Tu-154 jetliner had landed at Yekaterinburg, Russia, at the end of a scheduled international service from Tashkent, Uzbekistan, a home-made explosive device was discovered in the aircraft's rear lavatory. Comprising about 1lb (0.45kg) of TNT, a detonator and a clock mechanism, the bomb was rendered harmless by a water cannon. No suspects or motive were identified.

6 JULY 2000

A Viação Aérea São Paulo SA (VASP) Boeing 737 jetliner with 70 persons aboard and also transporting gold was targeted for robbery by 15 heavily-armed assailants at Brasilia International Airport, serving the capital, prior to its departure on a scheduled domestic flight to Porto Alegre, Rio Grande do Sul. Approximately half a million dollars in gold was taken from the aircraft's cargo hold, and after a shoot-out with airport security personnel the robbers escaped. Although the 737 was struck by gunfire, there were no injuries among its passengers and crew.

17 JULY 2000

A passenger who was apparently distraught over having failed to obtain political asylum in the United Kingdom threatened a cabin attendant aboard British Airways Flight 8106 with a large pair of scissors, shortly before the CityFlyer Express RJ100 jetliner, carrying 101 persons and en route from Geneva, Switzerland, was scheduled to land at London's Gatwick Airport. He also threatened to detonate a bomb if not granted asylum. Before the landing, he was convinced by the pilot to release his hostage, and was taken into custody without further incident.

27–28 JULY 2000

AN armed assailant who managed to run past a security checkpoint at John F. Kennedy International Airport, serving

New York City, boarded a National Airlines Boeing 757 jetliner that was preparing for departure on a US domestic service to Las Vegas, Nevada, as Flight 19. Entering the aircraft's flight deck, the gun-armed assailant initially ordered the pilot to fly to Miami, Florida, then to Antarctica. During this time the 142 passengers on the 757 were evacuated, some via emergency chutes. Early on the morning of the second day of the seizure, some five hours after it began, the incident ended with the peaceful surrender of the gunman. He would later be charged with air piracy, while being ordered to undergo a psychiatric evaluation.

31 JULY–1 AUGUST 2000

TAKING hostage a female member of the cleaning staff of the Hong Kong-based carrier, a lone gunman boarded a Cathay Pacific Airways Boeing 747-400 wide-bodied jetliner that was parked on the ground at Hong Kong International (Chek Lap Kok) Airport, and was to have departed on a service to Paris and London as Flight 261. Among the demands he made was a trip to Myanmar. Early on the morning of the second day, after a stand-off lasting 2½ hours, the woman was released unharmed and the assailant surrendered to police; his weapon turned out to be an air pistol. The only other person aboard the aircraft at the time was an engineer, who remained locked in the cockpit throughout the incident. Himself a worker in the cargo area at the airport, the assailant was charged with false imprisonment.

11 AUGUST 2000

THIS case of a berserk passenger endangering the lives of others involved Southwest Airlines Flight 1763, a Boeing 737 jetliner on a US domestic service from Las Vegas, Nevada, to Salt Lake City, Utah. The 19-year-old assailant was overwhelmed after breaking into the cockpit and trying to open an emergency door. He was pronounced dead after the aircraft landed at its intended destination, the fatality being ruled as a homicide occurring during an act of self-defence. As a result, no charges were filed against anyone.

16 AUGUST 2000

AS with the theft of gold the previous month, robbery was the motive in this hijacking, which also involved the Brazilian carrier Viação Aérea São Paulo (VASP). The twin-jet Boeing 737, with 60 persons aboard, was commandeered by eight assailants during a scheduled domestic service from Foz de Iguaçu to Curitiba, Paraná, and forced to land at a remote airstrip that was also in the state of Paraná. Stealing nearly $3 million in cash from the aircraft's cargo hold, the robbers fled in a waiting getaway vehicle. Later in the month a key Brazilian drug dealer alleged to have been the leader of the hijackers was arrested.

18 AUGUST 2000

IN what was described as a 'politically motivated' act of aerial piracy, a lone assailant identified as the chairman of the Nakhichevan branch of the opposition Musavat Party and carrying a bottle of kerosene commandeered Azerbaijan Airlines Flight 254, a Tu-154 jetliner carrying 164 persons on a domestic service from Nakhichevan (Naxcivan) to Baku. Demanding to be taken to Turkey with the intention of

visiting a hospitalised Azeri leader, he was overpowered by security personnel, after which the aircraft landed at its intended destination.

8 SEPTEMBER 2000

A prisoner who was reportedly a member of the guerrilla organisation FARC and who was on his way to stand trial commandeered an AIRES Colombia Dash 8 turboprop airliner that was on a Colombian domestic service from Neiva to Florencia as Flight 8092. Reportedly obtaining a pistol that had been hidden in its lavatory, he forced the aircraft to land at San Vicente del Caguán, in the state of Caquetá, where his escape was reportedly facilitated by other members of FARC. There were no injuries, and the flight was able to continue on to its intended destination.

16 SEPTEMBER–6 OCTOBER 2000

IN an apparent dispute with the government of the Solomon Islands, members of a militia group commandeered a Solomon Airlines BN-2A Islander after it had landed at an isolated airstrip on the island of Guadalcanal. They at first demanded two million Solomon dollars for release of the pilot, but the lone hostage was released three weeks later without any ransom having been paid. The twin-engine aircraft was not recovered.

27 SEPTEMBER 2000

A China Xinhua Airlines Boeing 737 jetliner, designated as Flight 126 and on an international service to Beijing, China, from Baotou, Inner Mongolia, was hijacked by a knife-wielding assailant who demanded to be taken 'south' and stabbed both pilots after apparently learning that the aircraft was low on fuel. The would-be hijacker was then killed by an air marshal, and the wounded crew managed to land the transport safely at Jinan, in the Chinese province of Shandong.

12 OCTOBER 2000

A Super Puma turbine-engine helicopter operated by the Ecuadorean firm Aeromaster Airways was commandeered as part of the kidnapping of 11 oil workers carried out by Colombian terrorists.

The workers were initially captured on the ground in a predawn raid near Pompeya, in the Ecuadorean province of Napo. They were then flown out of the area using the Super Puma, which was later found undamaged near La Bermeja, in the province of Putumayo, Ecuador. One of the hostages, an Ecuadorean, was released soon afterwards, but an American hostage was murdered and his body was found the following January. The rest were released in return for a ransom of $13 million. Five of the assailants were later apprehended, with plans to extradite them to the US for prosecution.

13 OCTOBER 2000

A Nigerian man who was being deported got away from his police escorts and entered the cockpit of an A330 wide-bodied jetliner, operating as Flight 689 of the Belgian carrier SABENA en route from Brussels to Abidjan, Côte-d'Ivoire, with 158 persons aboard. Though he demanded that the crew land immediately, the aircraft was instead diverted to Málaga, Spain, where the assailant was arrested.

1 DECEMBER 2000

THREATENING to detonate a hand grenade in its cabin, two assailants believed to have been former soldiers commandeered a Congolese An-24 twin-engine turboprop that was on an internal flight from Goma to Kindu with 17 persons aboard. They demanded to be taken to an airport in the western part of the country, but one of them was killed and the other was captured and taken into custody for questioning.

12 DECEMBER 2000

A passenger brandishing a pocket knife reportedly made 'threatening gestures' to others aboard an American Airlines Boeing 767 wide-bodied jetliner, designated as Flight 8 and on a US domestic service from Honolulu, Hawaii, to Dallas, Texas. The aircraft landed at Los Angeles, where the passenger was taken into custody for psychiatric observation.

29 DECEMBER 2000

FOR the fourth time during the year, a passenger apparently not intending to carry out a hijacking caused terror aboard a commercial flight, with potentially disastrous consequences. In this case, a Kenyan passenger stormed into the unsecured flight deck of a British Airways Boeing 747-436 wide-bodied jetliner, operating as Flight 2069 on an international service from London to Nairobi, Kenya. Before he was subdued the assailant grabbed the controls and disengaged the autopilot, which momentarily sent the aircraft out of control over Sudan, the incident occurring at around dawn local time. Five of the 398 persons aboard the aircraft were slightly injured, including the captain, who suffered bite wounds, but the 747 reached its intended destination safely.

The assailant was diagnosed by a psychiatrist as being 'paranoid', and due to his illness no plans were made for his prosecution.

30 JANUARY 2001

AN armed assailant who was identified as a 'disenchanted' member of the guerrilla organisation FARC commandeered a twin-engine turboprop Dornier 328 operated by the Colombian airline SATENA at the airport serving San Vicente del Caguán, Caquetá, Colombia. He then forced the aircraft, with 30 persons aboard, to take off. It subsequently landed at a military airbase near Bogotá, where, more than five hours after the hijacking began, the assailant was overpowered and taken into custody.

15 APRIL 2001

ARSONISTS set two fires in or near the lavatories of a KLM Royal Dutch Airlines Boeing 767 wide-bodied jetliner prior to its departure from Schiphol Airport, serving Amsterdam, on a scheduled international service to Tel Aviv. There were no injuries, and although two passengers were initially charged for setting the fires, neither was prosecuted due to insufficient evidence.

28 APRIL 2001

AN assailant wielding a machete, who was identified as a Vietnamese national who had entered the US nearly two decades earlier, forced his way through a security checkpoint and on to an American Airlines jetliner that was in the process of boarding passengers at La Aurora Airport, serving Guatemala City, preparatory to its departure on a scheduled service to Miami, Florida. He demanded to be flown to either Mexico or 'home'. A ramp agent was injured before the would-be hijacker was overpowered by others and taken into custody.

6 AUGUST 2001

AN unruly passenger who made references to a hijacking disrupted Delta Air Lines Flight 909, a Boeing 767 wide-bodied jetliner, as it was preparing to depart from Hartsfield International Airport, serving Atlanta, Georgia, on a US domestic service to Orlando, Florida. After the aircraft had returned to the gate the passenger was arrested, and was subsequently charged with interference of an airline crew.

1 SEPTEMBER 2001

WHAT was first reported as a possible hijacking, but would later be described by an airline spokesman as a 'mentally disturbed' passenger experiencing a 'panic attack', led to the diversion of an Airbus A321 jetliner operated by the German carrier Air Lloyd on an international charter service to Berlin from Catania, Sicily. The aircraft landed at Naples, Italy, where the passenger was arrested. He was later hospitalised.

27 SEPTEMBER 2001

THIS incident involving an Air Canada Boeing 767 would normally have been considered only a minor disturbance, but was magnified many times in consequence of the terrorist attacks in the US just two weeks earlier (see Chapter 5).

Designated as Flight 792 and bound for Toronto, Canada, the wide-bodied jet airliner, carrying 145 persons, was only minutes out of Los Angeles, California, when a passenger was discovered to have lit a cigarette in a rear lavatory, against regulations. After being confronted by crew members and refusing to tell them where he had discarded the cigarette, the passenger, who was of Iranian descent, became agitated, reportedly yelling out that he wanted to 'kill all the Americans' on the flight.

The aircraft returned safely to its point of departure, escorted by two US Air Force F-16 jet fighters, and the passenger was taken into custody without further incident. He would later be convicted of interfering with an airline crew, and sentenced to prison.

8 OCTOBER 2001

AN American Airlines Boeing 767 wide-bodied jetliner also got caught up in the paranoia gripping the US aviation industry since 11 September, but this 'attack' proved to be no more than a random act carried out by a mentally-disturbed passenger.

Operating as Flight 1238, the wide-bodied jetliner had been on a domestic service from Los Angeles to Chicago with 162 persons aboard when the assailant tried to break into the cockpit after openly expressing fears that the aircraft was going to be crashed into a skyscraper. Overpowered by other occupants, he was taken into custody after the 767 reached its intended destination, escorted by two US Air Force F-16 jets.

14 NOVEMBER 2001

FOUR gunmen commandeered a Trans Guyana Airways Cessna 208B Grand Caravan single-engine turboprop that had been on a scheduled domestic flight from Lethem to Georgetown with 13 persons aboard, forcing the pilot to land at a remote airstrip in Brazil, near the Venezuelan border. Though bound and herded into a barn, the other occupants were otherwise unharmed, and the hijackers escaped on horseback. The assailants may have been drug traffickers, and at least one of them was later arrested.

6 FEBRUARY 2002

ANOTHER case of passenger rage was at the centre of this incident involving United Airlines Flight 855, a Boeing 777 wide-bodied jetliner carrying 154 persons on an international service from Miami, Florida, to Buenos Aires, Argentina. After trying to force his way into the aircraft's cockpit, the assailant was struck over the head by the first officer, using a fire axe. Slightly injured, the passenger was tied up, then taken into custody when the 777 landed at its intended destination.

20 FEBRUARY 2002

AN AIRES Colombia DHC-8-300 Dash 8 twin-engine turboprop, designated as Flight 8091 and on a domestic service from Bogotá to Neiva with 34 persons aboard, was commandeered by four armed rebels and forced to land on a highway near Hobo, in the province of Huila and some 25 miles (40km) south-south-west of its destination. During the landing the airliner struck trees and was damaged. The crew and all but two of the other passengers were released, but a Colombian senator and his son were taken hostage. The following month, two of the rebels believed responsible for the hijacking were captured by the Colombian military, but the two captives remained missing.

17 APRIL 2002

A lone assailant attempted to hijack to the US a China Northern Airlines MD-82 jetliner, operating as Flight 6621 on a domestic service within the province of Liaoning, from Dalian to Shenyang, with 71 persons aboard. However, he was overpowered by security personnel, and the aircraft landed at its intended destination.

7 MAY 2002

PLAGUED by a series of occasionally violent hijackings taking place over a period of two decades, China's aviation industry was this time believed to have been the victim of a Western-style act of sabotage, apparently motivated by monetary gain, resulting in a disaster that claimed the lives of 112 persons.

China Northern Airlines Flight 6163 had nearly completed a domestic service from Beijing before the Shanghai Aircraft Manufacturing/McDonnell Douglas MD-82 jetliner (B-2138) jetliner crashed in the Bohai Haixa (channel) some ten miles (16km) south-west of Zhoushuizi Airport, serving Dalian, Liaoning, where it was to have landed. By the following day more than 60 bodies had been recovered from the water, but there were no survivors; the victims included the aircraft's nine crew members.

The MD-82 had plummeted into the sea in darkness, at around 21:30 local time, after the pilot had reported a fire in its cabin. As further confirmation of the report, traces of an in-flight blaze were found on recovered wreckage. A passenger who had purchased seven insurance policies before boarding the flight was seated in the area where the fire apparently started, ie in row 27, and there was also evidence of the use of an accelerant, possibly petrol. Based on the tape of the cockpit voice recorder (CVR), which was retrieved along with the aircraft's flight data recorder (FDR), there had been no indication of smoke or of anything burning prior to the eruption of the fire, which must then have spread rapidly. These findings led Chinese authorities to suspect sabotage as the cause of the crash.

10 MAY 2002

A knife-wielding suspect tried to hijack to Taiwan a Xiamen Airlines Boeing 737 jetliner, designated as Flight 8336 and on a Chinese domestic service from Shenzhen, Kwangtung, to Xiamen, Fujian, but he was captured by security personnel. During his subsequent trial he was found to be mentally incompetent, and received a relatively short prison sentence of four years.

9 JUNE 2002

HAVING suffered a disastrous crash during a hijacking six years earlier (see page 47), Ethiopian Airlines was ready this time when two assailants tried to commandeer its Flight 113, a twin-engine turboprop Fokker 50 on a domestic service from Bahir Dar to Addis Ababa with 46 persons aboard. Both of the would-be hijackers were shot and killed by security personnel. One crew member was also injured, but the aircraft landed safely at its intended destination.

9 SEPTEMBER 2002

FLIGHT 17, an Air Seychelles Boeing 737 jetliner carrying 72 persons en route from Mumbai, India, to Male, in the Maldives, was targeted for hijack by a lone assailant armed with a knife who wanted to be taken to Eastern Europe. He was overpowered by crew members and turned over to the authorities when the aircraft landed at its intended destination.

28 OCTOBER 2002

AN assailant armed with a penknife who demanded to be taken to Taiwan took hostage a cabin attendant aboard a Shanghai Airlines jetliner, either a Boeing 737 or 757, which was on a scheduled Chinese domestic service from Shanghai to Fuzhou, Fujian. However, he was overpowered by other members of the crew.

12 NOVEMBER 2002

A passenger using as his weapon a container of gasoline and a lighter attempted to commandeer a Gol Transportes Aéreos Boeing 737 jetliner, carrying 73 persons on a domestic Brazilian service to Brasilia from Cuiabá, Mato Grosso, as Flight 1701. The assailant was stopped after spilling some of the volatile fluid on other passengers. Reportedly he was motivated by 'psychosocial' pressures to bring the attention of his plight to others by having the aircraft fly over the capital city.

27 NOVEMBER 2002

A former Italian policeman with a history of mental illness commandeered an Alitalia MD-82 jetliner, operating as Flight 363 on an international service from Bologna to Paris with 76 persons aboard. He threatened to blow up the Italian aircraft and ordered it to land at Lyon, Rhône-Alps, France, where he was captured. His weapon turned out to be a television remote control unit. However, his threat of self-destruction turned out to be real, as about a week after the incident he hanged himself in his prison cell.

19 JANUARY 2003

DESIGNATED as Flight 6025, an Air Algérie Boeing 737 jet airliner on a domestic service from Constantine to Algiers with 31 persons aboard was targeted for hijack by a lone assailant, who wanted to be taken to North Korea. Noting that the aircraft did not have sufficient fuel to fly that distance, the pilot landed it at its intended destination, where the would-be hijacker was captured by police.

24 JANUARY 2003

IN attempting to hijack the aircraft, a passenger set off home-made explosives aboard a Sichuan Airlines ERJ-145LR twin-engine jet, operating as Flight 434, carrying 16 persons on a Chinese domestic service to the city of Chungking from Chengdu, Sichuan. He and another passenger were injured in the detonation, and the former was captured by a security guard.

2 FEBRUARY 2003

A passenger attempted to seize an Air China Boeing 767 wide-bodied jet airliner, operating as Flight 1505 on a domestic service from Beijing with 160 persons aboard, just after the aircraft had landed at its intended destination, Fuzhou, Fujian. However, he was overpowered after trying to light gasoline he had sprinkled from a can.

7 FEBRUARY 2003

AN assailant who wanted to be taken to Russia commandeered a Turkish Airlines (THY) A310 wide-bodied jetliner after the aircraft, designated as Flight 143 and carrying 229 persons, had landed at Ataturk International Airport, serving Istanbul, at the end of a domestic service from Ankara. After initially taking two cabin attendants hostage, he was overpowered and arrested.

19 MARCH 2003

APPARENTLY seeking freedom in the US, six knife-wielding assailants commandeered a twin-engine DC-3C of the Cuban carrier Aerotaxi, operating as Flight 887 on a domestic service to Havana from Nueva Gerona, on the Isla de la Juventud, with 37 persons aboard.

The vintage transport landed around 20:00 local time at Key West, Florida. Eleven of the other occupants elected to remain in the US, although the rest returned to Cuba, but not in the same aircraft, which remained in the possession of the American authorities. (It would later be sold at auction.) As for the six hijackers, freedom came at a price, for all were later convicted of air piracy in an American court, four of them receiving prison sentences of 20 years, the other two 24 years.

28 MARCH 2003

A lone assailant apparently hoping to join his father in Germany commandeered Turkish Airlines (THY) Flight 160, an A310 wide-bodied jetliner carrying 204 persons on a domestic service from Istanbul to Ankara. The aircraft landed for refuelling at Athens, and after releasing its passengers the hijacker surrendered.

31 MARCH–1 APRIL 2003

FOR the second time in a month, a Cuban airliner on a scheduled domestic service to Havana from Nueva Gerona, on the Isla de la Juventud, was hijacked, and although this incident took considerably longer to reach its conclusion the end result was the same.

The Cubana de Aviación An-24RV twin-engine turboprop, with 46 persons aboard, was initially allowed to land at the Cuban capital, where some two dozen passengers were

The Cuban An-24 and, in the background, the DC-3, auctioned off after being hijacked to the US. (AP/Press Association Images)

released. After being refuelled and after a stand-off lasting 14 hours, it proceeded on to Key West, Florida, where it landed late in the morning on the second day of the seizure. As in the previous hijacking, the lone assailant was not greeted as a freedom-seeker by the US, and was instead convicted of air piracy and sentenced to 20 years in prison.

Also as with the DC-3 commandeered two weeks earlier, the American authorities did not return the An-24 involved in the hijacking but auctioned it off. The Russian-built turboprop was sold for $6,500, only about half as much as the vintage American-built transport.

29 MAY 2003

A lone assailant armed with wooden stakes tried to break into the cockpit of QantasLink Flight 1737, an Impulse Airlines twin-jet Boeing 717 on an Australian domestic service from Melbourne, Victoria, to Launceston, Tasmania, with 53 persons aboard. Two cabin attendants and another passenger suffered minor injuries, but the assailant was successfully restrained, then taken into custody after the aircraft returned to its point of departure. Later he would be found not guilty by reason of mental impairment. Additionally, Qantas undertook a full security review as a result of this incident.

19 AUGUST 2003

AN Air Algérie Boeing 737 jet airliner on a scheduled domestic flight from Algiers to Oran was commandeered by a 'mentally ill' passenger who demanded to be taken to Geneva. After being convinced that the aircraft had to land for refuelling at Oran, he surrendered to the authorities.

29 JUNE 2004

THREE workers were injured, one seriously, when an explosive device that reportedly resembled a wallet detonated aboard a Turkish Airlines (THY) Boeing 737-800 jetliner on the ground at Ataturk International Airport, serving Istanbul, the incident occurring after the aircraft had completed a domestic service from Izmir as Flight 317.

26 JULY 2004

OPERATING as Flight 1343 on a domestic service from Beijing to Changsha, Hunan, an Air China Boeing 737 jetliner with 108 persons aboard was targeted to be hijacked by a passenger who said he had companions and wanted to be taken to South Korea. The aircraft instead landed at Zhengzhou, in the province of Henan, where the assailant, who in fact had no accomplices but reportedly did have a history of mental illness, was taken into custody.

24 AUGUST 2004

TERROR struck the Russian aviation industry twice on this day, with both attacks apparently related to the country's ongoing struggle with the region of Chechnya.

The first aircraft targeted was a Volga-Aviaexpress Company Tupolev Tu-134A3 jet airliner (RA-65080), designated as Flight 1303 and on a domestic service to Volgograd, which crashed near Buchalki, Russia, some 100 miles (150km) south of Moscow, from where it had taken off earlier. All 44 persons aboard were killed, including eight crew members. The aircraft

had been cruising in darkness at approximately 30,000ft (9,000m) when it was apparently blown up with an explosive device shortly before 23:00 local time.

Less than five minutes after the first crash, a Sibir Airlines Tupolev Tu-154B2 jetliner (RA-85556), operating as Flight 1047 on a domestic service from Moscow to Sochi, crashed near Millerovo, some 600 miles (960km) south of the Russian capital, killing all 46 persons aboard, including a crew of eight. As with the Tu-134, this aircraft had taken off from Moscow's Domodedovo Airport and had apparently been sabotaged.

Traces of the explosive hexogen were found in the wreckage of both transports, and in both cases the residue appeared to be towards the rear of the cabin, near the lavatories. Two women who were apparently from Chechnya and who reportedly shared an apartment in Groznyy had separately purchased tickets for the respective flights shortly before boarding the aircraft. One or both may have strapped the explosives to their bodies and then detonated them in the cabin. An airline employee who reportedly accepted a bribe from one of the women and a ticket tout were later charged for actions that aided the two terrorists.

29 SEPTEMBER 2004

A lone assailant who had been rejected for asylum in Norway apparently took out his wrath on the crew of a Kato Airline A/S Dornier 228 twin-engine turboprop, designated as Flight 605 and on a domestic Norwegian service from Narvik to Bodo with nine persons aboard. As the commuter airliner was approaching to land at Bodo airport, he attacked and seriously injured both pilots and another passenger before he was restrained. The crew managed to land the aircraft at its intended destination, after which the assailant, who had reportedly planned to commit suicide, was taken into custody. He would later be deported from the country.

12 SEPTEMBER 2005

AN AIRES Colombia Dash 8 twin-engine turboprop, carrying 24 persons on a scheduled domestic service to Bogotá from Neiva, Huila, was commandeered by an unlikely hijacker, a passenger in a wheelchair who was accompanied by his son. Armed with two hand grenades, he held the airliner on the ground at Eldorado International Airport, serving the capital, apparently protesting the failure of the Colombian government to honour a $230,000 cheque awarded as compensation for his being paralysed in a police shooting 14 years earlier.

His protest apparently completed, the assailant released the other occupants and surrendered after the five-hour stand-off. He would later be sentenced to eight years of house arrest for the hijacking. His son was not believed to have been aware of the elder's plan, and was not charged.

7 DECEMBER 2005

AN apparently mentally disturbed individual who had been a passenger on American Airlines Flight 924 was killed in a freak incident at Miami International Airport in Florida.

After uttering 'threatening words' indicating he had a bomb, he ran from the Boeing 757 jetliner that was still parked at the terminal building preparatory to its scheduled departure on the final segment of an international service originating at

*A de Havilland Dash 8, similar to the aircraft hijacked during a Colombian domestic flight. (*de Havilland Aircraft Photographic Dept)

Medellín, Colombia, with an ultimate destination of Orlando, Florida. He then ran back towards the aircraft, and when he reached into his backpack, he was shot to death by two air marshals who had been on the flight, the incident occurring around 14:00 local time. No bomb was found.

17 JUNE 2006

A 21-year-old Zimbabwean student armed with a hypodermic needle and wanting to be taken to Maputo, Mozambique, was overpowered by other passengers after trying to commandeer a South African Airways Boeing 737 jetliner, designated as Flight 322 and on a domestic service from Cape Town to Johannesburg, after which the aircraft returned to its point of departure.

16 AUGUST 2006

A passenger who may have been suffering from claustrophobia became disruptive aboard United Airlines Flight 923, a Boeing 767 wide-bodied jetliner carrying 194 persons on a transatlantic service from London to Washington DC. The aircraft diverted to Boston, Massachusetts, where the 59-year-old woman was taken into custody.

3 OCTOBER 2006

OPERATING as Flight 1476 on an international service from Tirana, Albania, to Istanbul, a Turkish Airlines (THY) Boeing 737 jet with 113 persons aboard was commandeered by a lone assailant who asked for asylum after the aircraft had landed at Brindisi, Italy. The Turk initially stated that he was protesting the planned visit to Turkey of the Pope, although his apparent motive was to avoid military service in his country. He would be charged by the Italian authorities with hijacking and possibly other crimes.

28 DECEMBER 2006

AFTER starting a fight with other passengers, a lone assailant claimed to have a bomb and threatened to hijack an Aeroflot Russian International Airlines Airbus A321 jetliner, designated as Flight 271 and en route from Moscow to Geneva with 271 persons aboard. He was overpowered and arrested after the aircraft diverted to and landed at Prague, Czech Republic.

22 JANUARY 2007

A passenger who claimed to be a member of al-Qaeda threatened to set off an explosion aboard an Air Botswana ATR 42 twin-engine turboprop, which was carrying 27 persons on an international service from Gaborone, Botswana, to Johannesburg, South Africa, as Flight 201. The airliner landed at its intended destination, where the assailant was arrested by police. No link with the international terrorist organisation was found.

24 JANUARY 2007

AN armed passenger who demanded to be taken to Chad hijacked Air West Flight 612, a Boeing 737 jetliner on a Sudanese domestic service from Khartoum to El Fasher with 103 persons aboard. He surrendered after the aircraft landed at the N'Djamena international airport, requesting asylum from the French embassy. However, Chad announced its intention to prosecute the hijacker.

15 FEBRUARY 2007

AN Air Mauritanie Boeing 737 jetliner carrying 79 persons on a scheduled domestic service within Mauritania, from Nouakchott to Nouadhibou, was commandeered by a lone gunman who demanded to be taken to France. After the aircraft had landed at Las Palmas Airport, on Gran Canaria in the (Spanish) Canary Islands, the assailant was captured by other occupants and subsequently taken into custody.

30 MARCH 2007

A lone assailant who wanted to be taken to South Africa commandeered a Sudan Airways A300 wide-bodied jetliner, designated as Flight 111 and on an international service from Tripoli, Libya, to Khartoum, Sudan, with 284 persons aboard. He surrendered following three hours of negotiations after the aircraft landed at its intended destination. His actions may have been related to his recent deportation from Libya, although it was also reported that he had been suffering from psychological problems.

10 APRIL 2007

DESIGNATED as Pegasus Airlines Flight 157, a Boeing 737-800 jetliner carrying 184 persons on a domestic service within Turkey, from Diyarbakir to Ankara, was commandeered by a lone assailant who announced that he had a bomb and wanted to be taken to Tehran, Iran. He first asked that the aircraft land at its intended destination, where he surrendered.

3 MAY 2007

TWO Cuban army sergeants who had previously, with another suspect, killed a fellow soldier and hijacked a bus, were captured after boarding and attempting to commandeer a Boeing 737 jetliner, which had been leased by Cubana de Aviación from the Spanish carrier Hola Airlines, at Rancho Boyeros/José Martí International Airport, serving Havana, Cuba. An army officer was slashed to death before the assailants were apprehended. The third suspect had already been caught.

The two principal assailants involved in this crime were sentenced to life imprisonment, while another deserter who was captured separately (but not involved in the hijack) received a prison term of 30 years. A captain and a civilian involved in some unspecified manner in the conspiracy were sentenced to 25 and 15 years, respectively.

8 FEBRUARY 2008

A knife-wielding assailant entered the cockpit of an Eagle Airways Jetstream 32 twin-engine turboprop, operating as Air New Zealand Link Flight 2279 on a domestic commuter service between Blenheim and Christchurch within New Zealand's South Island. She initially demanded to be taken to Australia, and when the aircraft prepared to land at its intended destination began manipulating its flight controls, but was thrown off balance when the pilot initiated a turn.

After the Jetstream had landed she was wrestled to the floor by the captain, and was subsequently arrested by police. Although both pilots suffered wounds, the other six passengers on the flight escaped unscathed. The assailant faced numerous charges, including aircraft hijacking.

7 MARCH 2008

OPERATING as Flight 6901, a China Southern Airlines Boeing 757 jetliner was targeted for either hijack or sabotage when a passenger carrying soft drink cans containing petrol tried to start a fire in a one of its lavatories during a domestic service to Beijing from Urumqi, Xinjiang. She was taken down by security personnel, after which the aircraft landed safely at Lanzhou, in the province of Gansu.

23 APRIL 2008

A passenger who had been drinking became unruly aboard a United Airlines Boeing 747 wide-bodied jetliner, designated as Flight 862 and on a transpacific service to Los Angeles, California, US, from Hong Kong, with 348 persons aboard. An off-duty pilot and a cabin attendant were assaulted before the assailant was restrained by crew members, first using duct tape and then handcuffs. Taken into custody after the 747 had landed at its intended destination, he was subsequently convicted of interfering with an aircraft flight crew, the maximum sentence for which in the US is 20 years' imprisonment.

15 OCTOBER 2008

A passenger who was reportedly intoxicated tried to divert to France a Turkish Airlines (THY) Airbus A320 jetliner that had been on an international charter service from Antalya, Turkey, to St Petersburg, Russia, with 171 persons aboard. He was overpowered by other passengers and detained by police after the aircraft landed safely at its intended destination.

1 FEBRUARY 2009

A seating conflict between three passengers and cabin attendants escalated into a potential threat aboard IndiGo Air Flight 664, which was on an Indian domestic service to Delhi from Vasco-da-Gama, in Goa, and became particularly serious after one of the former made reference to an infamous Indian Airlines hijacking occurring nearly a decade earlier. The A320 jet airliner, carrying 169 persons, landed safely at Indira Ghandi International Airport, serving the nation's capital, after which one assailant was taken into custody and subsequently faced criminal prosecution for his actions.

19–20 APRIL 2009

An armed man described as 'mentally challenged' breached security and boarded a Canadian jetliner that had landed at Sangster International Airport, serving Montego Bay, Jamaica. The CanJet Boeing 737-800 had been on a non-scheduled international service to Cuba from Halifax, Nova Scotia, when commandeered. Some of the passengers were robbed before they and two of the aircraft's crew members were released; the other six were held hostage until the assailant was captured by Jamaican troops early on the second day of the incident.

9 SEPTEMBER 2009

Aeromexico Flight 576, a Boeing 737-800 jet airliner with 112 persons aboard and on a domestic service to Mexico City from Cancun, was commandeered by a 'preacher', reportedly on a 'divine' mission. Armed with a bible and bombs that turned out to be juice cans, he allowed the aircraft to land at its intended destination. After releasing his hostages, he was captured by security forces and taken into custody.

Picture sources

Accidents Investigation Branch (AIB)
Airbus Industrie
Air Canada
Aircraft Photographic
AP/Press Association Images
ATR
Aviation Photo News
Beech Aircraft Corporation
Boeing
British Aerospace/BAe Systems
British Airways
Civil Aeronautics Board (CAB)
de Havilland Canada Photographic Department
Delta Air Lines
Denver Post
Douglas Green
Eastern Airlines
EMBRAER
Fairchild Aircraft
Fokker Aircraft
Getty Images
Haynes Publishing
International Civil Aviation Organisation (ICAO)
Irma Carranza
McDonnell Douglas
Pan American World Airways
Paris-Match
Philip Jarrett
Popperfoto
Short Brothers Aircraft
Swissair
Swiss Federal Aircraft Accident Investigation Branch
Trans World Airlines (TWA)
UPI/Corbis-Bettmann
US Coast Guard

Index

US Air/Airways: 5 Oct 81, 151; 10 Jan 87, 160;
   12 Aug 97, 182
Viacao Aerea Sao Paulo SA (VASP) (Brazil):
   29 Sept 88, 164; 16 Aug 00, 188
Western Air Lines (US): 20 Aug 77, 142
Wien Consolidated Airlines (US): 18 Oct 71, 37
Xiamen Airlines (China): 12 May 88, 164;
   24 Jun 93, 174; 6 Nov 93, 175; 28 Dec 93, 176;
   15 Nov 96, 180; 12 Jun 99, 185; 10 May 02, 190
Zhejiang Airlines (China): 8 Nov 93, 175;
   23 Nov 99, 186
Unknown: 17 Mar 62, 13; 6 Dec 90, 29; 25 Nov 91,
   171; 31 Aug 95, 179; 14 Apr 96, 180; 15 Apr 97,
   181; 9 Feb 99, 185; 1 Dec 00, 189

HIJACKINGS/ATTEMPTED HIJACKINGS TO CUBA

Aerolineas Argentinas: 8 Oct 69, 27; 24-25 Mar 70, 29;
   28 Jul 70, 30; 4 Jul 73, 35; 20-22 Oct 73, 35
Aerolineas Argo (Uruguay): 12 Nov 80, 38
Aerolineas Peruanas SA (APSA) (Peru):
   11 Jan 69, 22
Aerolineas TAO (Colombia): 25 Aug 72, 34
Aeromaya SA (Mexico): 6 Oct 68, 21
Aeronaves de Mexico SA/Aeromexico: 25 Jul 70, 30;
   24 Jun 83, 41
Aeropesca Colombia: 21 Jan 74, 35
Aerotal Colombia: 27-29 Jan 82, 39
Aerotaxi SA (Colombia): 28 Oct 69, 27
Aerovias Condor de Colombia Ltda (Aerocondor): 6
   Aug 67, 20; 15 Mar 69, 24
Aerovias Nacionales de Colombia SA (AVIANCA):
   9 Sept 67, 20; 5 Mar 68, 20; 22 Sept 68 (2), 21;
   7 Jan 69, 22; 20 May 69, 25; 10 Jul 69, 26;
   4 Aug 69, 26; 23 Aug 69, 26; 13 Nov 69, 27;
   11 Mar 70, 29; 21 May 70, 29; 31 May 70, 30;
   26 Jun 70, 30; 25 Apr 71, 32; 29 Apr 71, 32;
   21 Jun 71, 32; 10-11 May 74, 35; 15 Dec 80, 39;
   23 May 88, 43
Aerovias Nacionales de Honduras SA (ANHSA):
   28 Apr-1 May 82, 39
Aerovias Quisqueyanas C por A (Dominican
   Republic): 26 Jan 71, 31
Aerovias Venezolanas SA (AVENSA) (Venezuela):
   21 Mar 68, 20; 12 Oct 71, 32; 18 May 73, 35;
   31 Oct 73, 35; 6 Nov 80, 38; 7 Dec 81, 39
Air Canada: 11 Sept 68, 21; 26 Dec 71, 33
Air Florida (US): 10 Aug 80, 37; 13 Aug 80, 37;
   2 Feb 82, 39; 7 Jul 83, 41
Alaska Airlines (US): 7 Mar 87, 43
Allegheny Airlines (US): 19 Sept 70, 31
ALM (Dutch) Antillean Airlines (Netherlands
   Antilles): 24 Jan 70, 28; 12 May 70, 29
American Airlines (US): 25 May 70, 29;
   25 Oct 71, 32; 9 Apr 80, 37; 22 Sept 83, 42;
   31 Dec 84, 43; 27 May 89, 43
American Air Taxi Inc (US): 5 Apr 71, 32
America West Airlines (US): 16 Jan 90, 43
Arawak Airlines (Trinidad and Tobago):
   17 Nov 71, 33
Austral Lineas Aereas SA (Argentina): 8 Nov 69, 27;
   15 Aug 72, 34
British West Indian Airways (Trinidad):
   1 May 70, 29
Capitol Air (US): 1 May 83, 40; 12 May 83, 40; 4 Aug
   83, 42
Chalk's International Airline (US): 7 Mar 72, 38;
Compania de Aviacion Faucett SA (Peru):
   17 Mar 69, 25; 8 Apr 72, 33
Compania Mexicana de Aviacion SA: 18 Nov 68, 21;
   8 Feb 69, 23; 26 Jul 69, 26; 24 May 70, 29;
   8 Nov 72, 34
Compania Ecuatoriana de Aviacion SA (Ecuador):
   19 Jan 69, 23; 11 Apr 69, 25
Continental Air Lines (US): 3 Aug 61, 20;
   26 Jul 69, 26; 19 Dec 70, 31; 16 Mar 79, 36;
   25 Oct 80, 38
Delta Air Lines (US): 21 Feb 68, 20; 12 Jul 68, 21; 13
   Jan 69, 23; 17 Mar 69, 24; 19 Mar 69, 25; 25 Mar

69, 25; 25 May 70, 29; 20 Aug 70, 31; 4 Feb 71, 31;
   31 Mar 71, 32; 11 Jun 79, 36; 25 Jan 80, 37;
   22 Jul 80, 37; 16 Aug 80, 37; 13 Sept 80, 38;
   17 Sept 80, 38; 5 Apr 82, 39; 17 Jul 83, 41;
   18 Aug 83, 42;
   28 Mar 84, 43
Dolphin Airways (US): 16 Aug 82, 40; 28 Mar 84, 45
Eastern Airlines (US): 24 Jul 61, 20; 20 Sept 68, 21;
   23 Nov 68, 21; 30 Nov 68, 22; 19 Dec 68, 22;
   2 Jan 69, 22; 9 Jan 69, 22; 19 Jan 69, 23;
   28 Jan 69, 23; 3 Feb 69, 23; 10 Feb 69, 23;
   25 Feb 69, 23; 22 Jun 69, 25; 28 Jun 69, 25;
   5 Aug 69, 26; 7 Sept 69, 26; 10 Sept 69, 26;
   16 Feb 70, 28; 22 Sept 70, 31; 13 Nov 70, 31;
   31 Mar 71, 32; 3 Sept 71, 32; 9 Oct 71, 32;
   29 Oct 72, 34; 25 Dec 77, 36; 30 Jun 79, 36;
   16 Aug 79, 37; 16 Aug 80, 37; 18 Aug 80, 37;
   26 Aug 80, 37; 8 Sept 80, 38; 12 Sept 80, 38;
   14 Sept 80, 38; 5 Feb 81, 39; 10 Apr 81, 39;
   10 Jul 81, 39; 19 May 83, 41; 14 Jun 83, 41;
   19 Jul 83, 41; 18 Jan 85, 43
Haiti Air Inter: 9 Sept 75, 36
Japan Air Lines: 6 Nov 72, 34
Linea Aerea Nacional de Chile (LAN-Chile):
   12 Nov 69, 27; 19 Dec 69, 27; 6 Feb 70, 28
Linea Aeropostal Venezolana (Venezuela):
   11 Feb 69, 23; 7 Dec 81 (2)
Lineas Aereas Costaricenses SA (LASCA) (Costa
   Rica): 23 Dec 69, 28; 21 Oct 70, 31
Lineas Aereas del Caribe (LAC Colombia):
   2 Oct 84, 43
Lineas Aereas de Nicaragua (LANICA): 29 Jul 69, 26;
   4 Nov 69, 27; 12 Dec 71, 33
Lineas Aereas La Urraca (Colombia): 20 Jun 69, 25
Marco Island Airways (US): 22 Jul 82, 40
National Airlines (US): 1 May 61, 20; 26 Oct 65, 20;
   17 Nov 65, 20; 12 Mar 68, 20; 17 Jul 68, 21; 4 Nov
   68, 21; 3 Dec 68, 22; 24 Jan 69, 23; 28 Jan 69, 23;
   31 Jan 69, 23; 3 Feb 69, 23; 5 Mar 69, 23; 5 May
   69, 25; 29 Aug 69, 26; 24 Sept 69, 27; 1 Nov 69,
   27; 1 Jul 70, 30; 30 Oct 70, 31; 3 Jan 71, 31; 24 Jul
   71, 32; 14 Dec 78, 36; 14 Aug 80, 37
Northeast Airlines (US): 26 May 69, 25; 14 Aug 69, 26
Northwest Airlines (US): 1 Jul 68, 21; 22 Jan 71, 31;
   21 Jul 83, 41
Pacific Southwest Airlines (PSA) (US): 7 Jan 72, 33
Pan American World Airways (US): 9 Aug 61, 20;
   24 Nov 68, 22; 13 Apr 69, 25; 21 Oct 69, 27;
   2 Aug 70, 30; 29 May 71, 32; 2 Jul 83, 41;
   2 Aug 83, 41
Phoenix Airways (South Africa): 15 Aug 95, 43
Piedmont Airlines (US): 18 Jun 71, 32; 28 Jan 78, 36;
   27 Mar 84, 42
Republic Airlines (US): 16 Aug 80, 37
Rio Airways (US): 15 Feb 83, 40
Rutas Aereas Panamenas SA (RAPSA) (Panama):
   9 Jan 70, 28
SA Empresa Empresa de Viacao Aerea Rio
   Grandense (VARIG) (Brazil): 4 Nov 69, 27;
   28-29 Nov 69, 27; 12 Mar 70, 29
San Francisco & Oakland Helicopter Airlines (US):
   26 Jan 72, 33
Servicos Aereos Cruzeiro do Sul SA (Brazil): 8 Oct
   69, 27; 12 Nov 69, 27; 1-3 Jan 70, 28; 1 Jul 70, 30;
   4 Jul 70, 30; 3 Feb 84, 42
Sociedad Aeronautica de Medellin Consolidada SA
   (SAM) (Colombia): 5 Feb 69, 23; 11 Mar 69, 24;
   14 Apr 69, 25; 10 Jul 69, 26
Sociedad Anonima Ecuatoriana de Transportes
   Aereos (SAETA) (Ecuador): 3 Jul 69, 25;
   20 Oct 71, 32; 18 Jan 78, 36
Southeast Airlines (US): 29 Jun 68, 21
Southern Airways (US): 10-12 Nov 72, 34
Southwest Airlines (US): 10 Feb 91, 43
Taxi Aereo del Guaviare (Colombia): 18 May 82, 40
Texas International Airlines (US): 30 May 69, 25
Trans-Caribbean Airways (US): 19 Aug 70, 31
Transportes Aereos Militares Ecuatorianos (TAME)
   (Ecuador): 6 Sept 69 (2), 26;
Trans World Airlines (TWA) (US): 11 Dec 68, 22;
   17 Jun 69, 25; 31 Jul 69, 26; 2 Dec 69, 27;

24 Aug 70, 31; 27 Nov 71, 33; 11 Dec 88, 43
United Air Lines (US): 11 Jan 69, 22; 25 Jun 69, 25;
   26 Dec 69, 28; 11 Mar 70, 28; 1 Nov 70, 31; 25 Apr
   75, 36; 13 Mar 78, 36; 20 Jul 79, 36;
   20 Jul 79, 36; 1 Mar 82, 39
Venezolana Internacional de Aviacion SA (VIASA)
   (Venezuela): 19 Jun 68, 21
Viacao Aerea Sao Paulo SA (VASP) (Brazil):
   25 Apr 70, 29; 14 May 70, 29
Virgin Islands Seaplane Shuttle (US): 5-6 June 1987, 43
Western Air Lines (US): 25 Feb 71, 32; 5 May 72, 34
Wien Consolidated Airlines (US): 18 Oct 71, 32

HIKACKINGS RESULTING IN A CRASH AND/ OR DESTRUCTION OF THE AIRCRAFT AND FATALITIES

Aeroflot (USSR): 24 Apr 73, 45; 18 May 73, 45;
   18 Nov 83, 46; 8 Mar 88, 47
Air France: 28-29 August 1976, 46
Air Vietnam (South Vietnam): 15 Sept 74, 45
American Airlines (US): 11 Sept 01 (2), 79
Cathay Pacific Airways (Hong Kong): 16 Jul 48, 45
China Southern Airlines: 2 Oct 90, 47
China Southwest Airlines: 2 Oct 90, 47
Compania Cubana de Aviacion SA (Cuba):
   1 Nov 58, 45
Donavia (Russia): 25-27 Oct 94, 47
EgyptAir: 23-24 Nov 85, 66
Ethiopian Airlines: 23 Nov 96, 47
Iraqi Airways: 25 Dec 86, 68
Korean Air Lines (South Korea): 23 Jan 71, 45
Linea Aeropostal Venezolana (Venezuela):
   28 Apr 60, 45
Malaysian Airline System: 4 Dec 77, 46
Philippine Airlines: 21-23 May 76, 46
Roraima Air Charter (Guyana): 27 Nov 96, 180
Tajik Air: 28 Aug 93, 47
United Airlines (US): 11 Sept 11, 01 (2), 79
Xiamen Airlines (China): 2 Oct 90, 47

HIJACKINGS AND ATTEMPTS IN OR RELATED TO THE MIDDLE EAST
(except those resulting in disaster)

Air Afrique (African consortium):
Air France: 27 Jun-3 Jul 76, 59; 12 Aug 77, 60;
   27-31 Aug 83, 63; 31 Jul-2 Aug 84, 63;
   23 Aug 89, 71; 24-26 Dec 94, 73
(Alia) Royal Jordanian Airlines: 8 Sept 71, 55;
   16 Sept 71, 55; 4 Oct 71, 55; 19 Feb 72, 55;
   6 Nov 74, 59; 11-12 Jun 85, 65; 5 Jul 00, 76;
   28 Sept 00, 76; 13 Sept 03, 78
Alitalia (Italy): 7 Sept 79, 61; 14 Jan 80, 61
Alyemda (Democratic) Yemen Airlines:
   22 Aug 72, 56; 25 Aug 73, 57; 20 Jan 83, 62;
   27 Aug 93, 72; 14 Sept 94, 72
Ariana Afghan Airlines: 6-10 Feb 00, 76
Ariatour (Iran): 13 Nov 00, 77
Atlasjet Airlines (Turkey): 18 Aug 07, 78
British Overseas Airways Corporation (BOAC)/
   British Airways: 9 Sept 70, 53; 3 Mar 74, 58;
   22-28 Nov 74, 59
Cyprus Airways: 18-19 Feb 78, 61; 7 Feb 85, 65
El Al Israel Airlines: 23 Jul 68, 50; 6 Sept 70, 53
Ethiopian Airlines: 25 Apr 94, 72
Gulf Air Ltd: (Bahrain, Oman, Qatar, United Arab
   Emirates): 29 Jun 77, 60; 27 Jan 01, 77
Hemus Air (Bulgaria): 3 Sept 96, 74
Iberia (Spain): 26 Jul 96, 73
Indian Airlines: 24-31 Dec 99, 75
Iran Aseman Airlines: 5 Jan 85, 65; 25 Nov 85, 66
Iran National Airlines/Iran Air: 21 Jun 70, 53;
   10 Oct 70, 54; 9 Nov 70, 54; 6 Jul 83, 62;
   26-27 Jun 84, 63; 7 Aug 84, 63; 28 Aug 84, 63;
   8 Sept 84, 64; 12 Sept 84, 64; 5 Oct 84, 64;
   11 Jan 85, 65; 5 Aug 85, 66; 2 Nov 85, 66;
   23 Dec 85, 67; 10 Nov 86, 68; 5 May 87, 68;
   28 Dec 87, 68; 25 Jan 90, 72; 29 Nov 93, 72;